BLOOD BROTHER

Blood Brother

By Elliott Arnold

UNIVERSITY OF NEBRASKA PRESS
Lincoln and London

ı

First Bison Book printing: 1979
Most recent printing indicated by the first digit below:
5   6   7   8   9   10

Library of Congress Cataloging in Publication Data

Arnold, Elliott, 1912–
  Blood brother.

  Reprint of the ed. published by Duell, Sloan and Pearce, New York.
  1. Apache Indians—Wars—Fiction.   I.   Title.
PZ3.A7535B1   1979 [PS3501.R5933] 813'.5'4   78-26788
ISBN 0-8032-1003-5
ISBN 0-8032-5901-8 pbk.

♾

Bison Book edition published by arrangement with the author
from the Bantam edition of August 1956.

Manufactured in the United States of America

For
GUY AND ANNA EMMONS
whose Arizona this is

CONTENTS

Author's Note

One of the things that has always annoyed me when reading historical fiction has been my inability to determine where in the book the history left off and the fiction began, which characters were real and which invented. For the reader with a similar resentment, I would like to say that the main events in this book are entirely true. Specifically, Cochise broke with Mangas Coloradas and made peace for the Chiricahua tribe, lived it honorably, was arrested treacherously as related in this book, and then started his war. Thomas Jeffords ran the mail, went up alone to see Cochise, became his friend and later his blood brother, and then led General Howard to Cochise's camp to make the final peace.

A number of the smaller details in the book also are true, but they have been woven into the fictitious episodes of the story. I can state that nowhere in this book, to the best of my knowledge, supported by history, autobiography, reminiscences, and personal interviews, is there anything that is in any way contrary to the large historical truth, and that includes the Camp Grant Massacre, one of the blackest pages in the history of the Southwest, described in brief in this book as it actually occurred.

It may further interest lovers of historic detail to know that many of the conversations in the book are the actual conversations as reported by participants in later years. For instance, the speech between Jeffords and Howard at their first meeting contains many sentences actually spoken by the two men, later narrated by both Howard in his writings and by Jeffords in conversation with Arizona historians. Jeffords left some accounts of his own talks with Cochise, including the first meeting. Finally, the final words of the last conversation between the two men, when Cochise speaks of meeting Jeffords sometime after death, is almost exactly reported in this book, and constitutes, to my mind, one of the remarkable death colloquies of all time.

As for the characters, almost all of the male characters in this book were living persons, and in most instances I used their true names. Of course, the bulk of their speech and minor actions are pure fiction, but never in contradiction to known history.

The women characters were invented. Jeffords, a man of many parts, confided to a number of close American friends that he was intimate with a lovely Indian girl. There is no record of their ever marrying, but knowing the intolerant attitude of the Apaches toward looseness in their women—they actually hacked off the noses of the unchaste—and knowing the basically simple process of an Apache wedding, I have taken a writer's liberty and imagined that such a wedding took place. The entire story of Jeffords and Sonseeahray is pure fiction and every detail in it was invented, against a known historical background. The character of Terry Weaver, the American girl, is also wholly invented, although it was reported that in Jeffords' later years he was, in the euphemy of the time, "cared for" by an American woman. He never married, in an American way.

I want to thank a number of persons who helped make this book possible. First of all, my deepest gratitude is given to Dr. Frank C. Lockwood, a brilliant and tireless scholar of Apache Indian history, who has, in his own words, "lived with the spirit of Cochise for twenty-five years." Dr. Lockwood, who has written a number of fascinating books on Apache and early Arizona history, notably *The Apache Indians,* was a constant guide and mentor in the preparation of *Blood Brother* and read the manuscript, making many suggestions.

The following persons also were of great assistance: John A. Rockfellow, who has a home in the Cochise Stronghold and who knew Jeffords intimately for many years, and his son, Philip. The elder Mr. Rockfellow told me personally of the first meeting between Cochise and Jeffords, and of the Cochise-Jeffords-Howard meeting, and the result of these events were told to him by Jeffords himself.

Dr. Robert H. Forbes, who also knew Jeffords before he died and who interviewed him exhaustively, was kind enough to give me his material to use. Mrs. George F. Kitt and Carl F. Miller, of the Arizona Pioneers' Historical Society (of which Jeffords was one-time vice-president) provided an endless supply of unpublished manuscripts, diaries, and books. Louise M. Milligan and Patricia Paylore, of the University of Arizona Library, brought forth from the vast resources of that institution a mighty array of documents, and no question I ever asked, no matter how obscure, was left unanswered by these indefatigable ladies.

William Donner, for nineteen years an Apache Agent, gave me much interesting information. So did "Apache Bill" Russell, an Indian genius of sorts, who says he is a cousin to Geronimo, and who very probably is. Apache Bill has a theory that the Apaches are descendants of ancient Egyptians, and has traced, to his own satisfaction, the wandering of the tribe up through Asia, across the Bering Straits, and down through Canada. But that is another story.

Finally, I want to thank Dr. Morris E. Opler, one of the great scientific investigators of Chiricahua Apache ethnology, whose *An Apache Life-Way* is the standard work in its field, and whose collection of stories titled *Myths and Tales of the Chiricahua Indians* is a wondrous and beautiful book which opens up a new world of folklore. Dr. Opler graciously gave me permission to paraphrase some of these myths, which I did in the Coyote stories. If *Blood Brother* arouses any interest in this great and fast-disappearing Indian people, I recommend strongly the interested reader start out with Dr. Opler's two books.

In describing some of the Apache rituals and some of the minutiae of Chiricahua daily life, I have drawn from Dr. Opler, as well as from a great many contemporary accounts of the Chiricahua people during the time of Cochise. It was necessary, from time to time, to alter and condense some of the complicated rites to fit a work of fiction; the puberty rite, for instance, takes four days and is composed of an endless number of details which would take thousands of words to describe in full. I believe sincerely, however, that I have nowhere violated the basic meanings of either the religious ceremonies or ordinary daily mores.

E. A.

Tucson, Arizona

COCHISE

———◆———

Chapter One

The victory fires were ready to be lighted. The women and
the old men and the children had been waiting for many days
and in the early afternoon the scout arrived, pushing his pony
hard up the long corridor that ended in the narrow entrance to
the East Stronghold in the Dragoon Mountains. The paint on
the face and body of the scout was almost washed away by
sweat and there was a long red slash on his side that was caked
with dried blood. His arrow quiver was empty and his water
bag, made of the entrails of a deer, was flattened and flapped
against his right hip. The pony held his head low and the foam
that gathered on his lips broke off and splattered on his wet
sides.

It was late fall, the time that is called Earth is Reddish
Brown; the sun was still high and poured heat, like water, into
the great cup of the Stronghold with its rocky walls rising fifteen hundred feet to their rim.

With the approach of the rider all talk ended and tension
gathered in the watching people. The scout drew rein in the
cleared ceremonial ground in the center of the Stronghold and
said, "They are coming." His woman walked up to him and
gave him a gourd filled with cold spring water. When he finished drinking, he wiped his lips with the back of his hand
and said, "He rides at the head." Then he waited and said,
"There are many horses and mules and there is cloth and there
is food and there are many guns and there are Mexican children and women."

The old men nodded silently. The women began to shriek
in the special high, piercing voice that showed their applause.
They hurried to their wickiups, sitting like gigantic mushrooms

1

throughout the rancheria, to prepare to greet the warriors returning from the raid in Mexico. The married women, whose husbands had participated in the raid, put on their finest and newest clothing, deerskin tanned and rubbed and pounded until it was as soft as velvet, covered in traditional and ancient designs in paint and silver, with many tiny bells, all with sacred meaning: zigzag lines for Lightning who fertilized White Painted Lady and produced Child of the Water, stars for the lanterns of the night, sun symbols for the great fire that marked the passage of their days. They put on earrings and pendants and amulets, made of buckskin and fitted with turquoise and abalone shell, and they hung around their necks strings of white shell beads and seeds of the mountain laurel.

Their hair was freshly washed with pounded yucca root and newly greased with the marrow from the shinbones of deer and the younger women drew their hair tightly behind their necks and the unmarried ones fixed their hair on their napes with the stiff buckskin frames in the figure of eight.

They applied red ochre to their cheeks and some painted circles over the ochre and others streaked their cheeks with mescal juice. They were freshly colored on the soft inner parts of their arms; the colors were red, obtained from the red ochre or the juice of ripe prickly pears, and black, obtained from charcoal. The young women put sachets of freshly pressed mint between their breasts and rubbed mint juice on their necks and on their thighs.

By now the music-makers with their drums of taut buckskin and their single-stringed fiddles were beginning the welcoming music and the women took rattles, made of elk bones, and joined the music-makers and began to chant a welcome to their men.

The divorced women and the widows disrobed in their wickiups until they wore nothing but breechclouts and they powdered their bodies white and rubbed mint leaves on the nipples of their breasts and thus, almost naked, joined the other women and made ready for their dance of welcome. These women, who had no men to bring them back the fruits of the raid, had only their own bodies for dancing, to show their thanks.

2

The vidette who stood at the entrance to the Stronghold and who could see for many miles into the valley raised his carbine and fired a shot. Then there were sounds of guns firing from the corridor. The women began to sing loudly and the music-makers pounded their drums and drew the bows made of horse-tail hair across their fiddles. The holy shamans began to sing their sacred verses and the naked women began to dance. The sounds of the gunfire echoed through the cup of the Stronghold and then the returning warriors suddenly filed through the slender cleft in the rock and when they passed into the Stronghold they kicked their weary ponies into action and began to shout.

The women screamed, "Here they come and he rides before them!"

The old men shouted, "Here they come and he rides before them!"

The children danced and clapped their hands then they dashed ahead of the women and old men to the returning men, and some of the men scooped up the children and set them on the necks of the ponies.

It was the last great raid of the year, before Ghost Face would come upon them and lock the high mountains in snow and cold. There were more than two hundred Chiricahua warriors, all mounted. Half of the men rode in single line and, behind them, the other half had formed parallel lines of some fifty in each, and between the lines herded the captured horses and mules. Walking among the mules were the Mexican women and children taken in the raid.

The eyes of the waiting women and old men centered upon the warrior riding at the head of the column. As he approached them on a great bay horse they began to chant his name.

"Cochise, Cochise, Cochise, Cochise."

He was a very tall man and on his horse, larger than any other, his stature was almost heroic. He rode erect and easily, guiding the bay with his knees. In one hand he held a long lance, fluttering with eagle feathers. In the other he held a long double-barreled shotgun, the receiver a shining silver, covered with intricate engraving.

His face was long and narrow and austere and was composed of planes and angles. Nothing of it yielded to a curve. His cheekbones were high and flat and his cheeks sank in ascetically to his rigid jaw. His mouth was large and wide and argued innate generosity; that generosity was held in suppression by the tight compress of his lips. His eyes were large and intelligent and set widely apart and now they glittered, the only sign on his face that he heard the cries of his people. His nose was sharp and jutted arrogantly, curved and proud as the beak of an eagle. Now, riding at the head of his men, his deadly, tireless Chiricahuas, the fiercest and most feared of all the Apache fighting men, he held his face taut and without expression, his eyes unwavering. His features were icy and he did not acknowledge the singing and shouting.

The sun lay full upon him, showing the remains of the red and black streaks of paint, showing the dull, thick, black hair, now grayed with a layer of desert dust, parted in the center,

3

braided and caught at the nape. The sun highlighted the rocky chin and the thin line of his lips held in glacial restraint. The sun showed his head sitting firmly on his broad muscular neck and showed his shoulders with their rolling muscles and showed the dried white salt of his sweat. The sun showed nothing of the pride that sang in him as he brought to his people the food and clothing and weapons and animals they needed before the lean days of Ghost Face arrived.

This was the year 1855 and Cochise was forty years old and in the prime of his vigor.

As the men approached, the women, without altering a note of their song, began to search among the warriors to see which of them was missing. As each woman recognized her own man her voice lifted with redoubled strength. When all of the warriors were gathered in the clearing the eyes of several of the women were still searching nervously, though their voices still held to the song.

The warriors remained on their animals. Then there moved to the forefront of them Nahilzay, the chief war lieutenant to Cochise. Nahilzay was almost as tall as his leader. His face was rigid and he had the eyes of a fanatic. The pupils of his eyes dilated as he looked upon Cochise whom he worshiped beyond all men. He sat nervously on his pony, his even, square white teeth biting his lip, and then, upon the smallest nod from Cochise, he lifted his head and announced the names of the men who had been killed.

Upon hearing the names, which numbered fourteen, the women of these men gave out a low animal wail and they took their children to them and returned to their wickiups. There they took off their gay clothing, removed everything of red that was on them, the red head-bands, the red kerchiefs, the red paint, and they cut off their hair and the hair of their children. They killed the horses and dogs the dead men had left behind them and with their children they carried the belongings of their husbands—knives, bows and arrows, clothing, moccasins, amulets, pendants, feathers, everything—and they buried these things immediately. And then they put black shawls on their heads and took their children to a far side of the Stronghold and sat together in a small circle and began to sing a bitter requiem.

Now the warriors were off their horses. The captured animals were herded into the community corral. The captured booty was dumped onto the ground in the center of the circle of unlighted fires into an increasingly large pile. The young warriors, particularly those who had been on their first raid, walked around like proud bantam cocks, their chests puffed out, their heads high, stiff-legged, preening among the young

4

unmarried women and divorcees. The older warriors, to whom a raid was a familiar story, greeted their wives and children un-excitedly and accepted their compliments with quiet indulgence.

No one looked twice upon the captive Mexican women and children who huddled, ashen, in a little group.

Cochise alone remained on his horse. He watched the pile of booty rise. His face continued without expression. When the last piece of loot was thrown upon the pile and the last animal secured in the corral, he dismounted and handed the reins of his bay to Tesalbestinay, his older wife. He walked to the pile of booty. The women ceased their chanting. The shamans became quiet. The music-makers were stilled. The warriors gathered around him, holding their lances upright, the feathers fluttering slightly in the breeze that passed through the Stronghold.

Cochise looked upon his people. The remains of his war-paint contributed to the mask-like appearance of his countenance. He raised his right hand. "Nochalo will make a ceremony," he said. His voice was low and flat and still there was none who did not hear him. "There are many horses. Many mules. Many guns. Pinole and maize. Blankets, good blankets of the Mexican soldiers. Cloths of many colors. Children of the Mexicans to the number of seven. Mexican women for who need them. White Painted Lady rode with her sons of the woods. Nochalo will make a ceremony."

He spoke the slow, unwordy speech used by the Apaches when they simply conveyed information. There was another speech, longer, with sentences filled with imagery and emotion, used for the great orations. It was part of Cochise's restraint that he chose the casual unsentenced language of every day to give news of the success of the raid to the people.

He stood straight as his lance. He was taller than his tallest warrior. His stature was said to have come from some ancient admixture of Comanche blood, for the Chiricahuas were a wiry people and seldom above middle height. The mixture, if it were there, came long ago, for as long as there was memory in the tribe one of Cochise's forefathers had been its leader. It was said that for three hundred years men of his blood had governed the Chiricahua people and the quality of that leadership was attested to by the fact that while an Apache chief usually named his eldest son to follow him, that son was quickly ousted and another chief chosen if he were not considered wise enough and brave enough to be the people's head. There was no unquestioned royalty among the Apaches.

Cochise said nothing of the men who had been slain and who, where it was possible, had already been buried. Once their names were called off, that was the end; their women mourned them, some for as long as five years, but they were not spoken of again since it was sinful to speak of the dead.

As the sun rested for a moment on the western rim of the great cup, looking for the last time that day upon the success of the People of the Woods, Cochise began to distribute the booty. He called out the name of Nahilzay and when that warrior, his eyes filled with devotion, stepped before him, he rested his hand for a moment upon his shoulder, and then he gave him something from the pile. When Nahilzay stepped back, Cochise called the name of Skinyea, and then Pionsenay; one after another, he gave them a share of the captured loot. If a man said he lacked a horse or a mule, Cochise bade him select one. Those who needed blankets received them. Those who asked for calico or flannel cloth got what they required.

As Cochise distributed the spoils the women again began to dance around the men and to sing and as the name of each warrior was called out by Cochise, that name was incorporated into the song and the prowess of that man raised to the heavens. When each brave received his share Cochise then gave out things to women who had no men, to the old men who were too feeble to fight; and to those who were the poorest, he gave the most. He put aside a great pile of goods for the women who were away mourning the dead, until, when he was finished, everyone in the tribe had shared in the spoils according to his need.

The women sang and the naked widows and divorced women danced and the shamans rattled their bones and pounded their drums. The children capered and shouted and the young men laughed with divorced women and made plans for the night. The horses neighed and the mules brayed loudly and the dogs which filled the camp barked in excitement. Of all living things there the Mexican captives alone held their silence.

Now the sun left the west to chase the moon around and there was a gray light on the Stronghold and the high walls were turning blue and the wind had risen and it was felt that Ghost Face was not far away. But now there was nothing to fear of winter because the warriors of the Chiricahuas had raided and plundered again successfully under Cochise, their leader, and of two hundred braves only fourteen had been killed.

When the last of the plunder was allocated, Cochise motioned with his hand and the seven Mexican children were brought before him. He looked at them, shivering and quaking, clinging to each other for support. They were frightened now. They were skinny and puny alongside the Apache children, who, at their ages, were already being instructed in the severe science of the hunt and kill. They were frightened now, he thought, but they had potentialities and before many harvests were passed they would be as deep-chested and muscled as the Chiricahua boys and by then they would have forgotten where they came from and they would know only of Apache ways and they would make warriors for his tribe. Fourteen braves were left dead in the hot sand of Mexico and seven Mexican boys were here to replace them. Seven Mexican boys and a half dozen Mexican women, who might, if they chose, take husbands from among the Apache men and bring still more warriors into the tribe.

Cochise gave away the children. His choice was made carefully. The awarding of a child was an act of great solemnity and carried grave responsibilities for the recipient. He gave them to families whose number of children was few or none.

The women were not assigned. For the time being they would serve as general servants to the entire tribe. They might continue in this capacity for the rest of their lives and no Apache would force himself upon them; rape was not an Apache habit; that was left to their hereditary enemies, the Mexicans. Later the captives might choose husbands and take their places among the other women of the tribe and become like them, no better and no worse. They might be traded off to other Apache tribes, or, but this happened seldom, they might be ransomed by their own people.

There were still several horses and mules remaining in the corral. The bulk of these was ordered slain, the flesh to be dried and cached for the long days of Ghost Face. A few Cochise ordered slaughtered for the victory feast to begin that evening.

When the distribution was ended and the final orders given, there was little left for Cochise and his own family. This was customary. The Apaches felt the poorest among them needed the most supplies and a chief was regarded as great only when he could keep the helpless ones in his tribe contented.

3

The people left the meeting place and went to their wickiups to get ready for the evening's festivities. Presently in the cleared space there were only Cochise, Nahilzay, and the two younger brothers of Cochise, Juan and Naretena. Cochise nodded almost imperceptibly to Nahilzay; the small gesture expressed his satisfaction with Nahilzay's conduct on the raid. Nahilzay's eyes sparkled and he walked away. Juan, the elder of Cochise's two younger brothers, a big, burly warrior with a chest like a bull and a head almost as empty of sense, lifted his huge share of the loot easily in one hand and with the other waved a farewell. The crude, rough warrior was a mighty strength on a raid; away from it he was nothing. He looked at Naretena with a faint grimace on his lips and shouted, "You should have been there!" Then, shaking his head and grinning, living again the danger and excitement of the raid, he strode off, his shoulder covered with his share.

Naretena did not answer him. As Juan was one extreme, so Naretena was the other. He was thin and slight. He was wifeless and he was no warrior. He was sick; he suffered from trouble in his lungs. It was said he had worms in his lungs which caused him to cough and spit, and occasionally his spittle was touched with blood. He tired easily and he had a kind of constant breathlessness which made speech difficult. His face was delicate and sensitive and there were already red flowers on his cheeks.

"Talk," Cochise said.

The two men walked to Naretena's wickiup and entered.

The wickiup, the home of the Apache, was not a permanent dwelling, since the roving habits of the people and the need for mobility in their marauding life precluded the establishment of permanent villages. It was necessary for the Apaches to be able to erect their homes in a few hours and to be able to dismantle them and get away on even shorter notice. Although the two Strongholds of the Chiricahuas, the East and the West, were the favorite resting places of the tribe, the tribe also moved constantly in the great mountains and valleys of their country, and although no enemy had ever been able to penetrate the impregnable natural forts of the Strongholds while the people were there, the habits of temporary dwellings stayed with them.

The wickiup was made by the women and that of Naretena had been constructed by the two wives of Cochise. It was a round, dome-shaped hut, about seven feet high and eight in diameter. Others in the rancheria were larger to accommodate families. The construction was simple. A round framework of long oak or willow poles was driven into the ground, the supports about a foot apart. These poles were laced together at the top with strands made of yucca leaf. Then bundles of grass were fixed shingle-fashion, with yucca strings, over the poles, and on top of the grass animal hides were placed. The door was a stiffened hide, hung on a crossbeam so that it could be swung open or closed.

Inside the wickiup of Naretena was a grass pallet covered with deerhide. In the wickiups of large families the beds were arranged like the spokes of a wheel, coming together in the center of the wickiup, where a fire was maintained in a small hole scooped out of the earth.

Everything the Apache owned was kept in his wickiup, his weapons, saddles, bridles, his shields, lances, knives, clubs, bows and arrows, his religious amulets and sacred pieces of

8

stone and wood and shell. There might be a few clay pots and water gourds, crude metates for grinding flour, leather bags to store dried food.

The interior of Naretena's wickiup was barer than most others. He lived by himself and his wants were taken care of by Cochise.

Although he did none of the things that were regarded as manly by the other Apaches, he was a man of intellect and understanding and Cochise respected him and counseled with him frequently and listened to him when he gave advice. As is the case with many superior leaders, Cochise tended to minimize and diminish the stature of leaders under him, and, of all the men in the tribe, Naretena alone held his mind.

The two men seated themselves. For a little while they sat silently, looking at each other courteously. Then, briefly, Cochise gave the details of the mission into Mexico. Naretena listened and said nothing until Cochise had finished and then he said, *"Enju,"* the Apache word for good, it is well, amen.

"Fourteen dead are not small numbers," Naretena said. "Not large either."

Cochise nodded.

"Mexicans followed?"

A faint, frosty smile appeared on Cochise's lips. "No hurry. When they started they did not try to come close."

"Americans?"

"No."

"I have seen Americans."

The smile vanished. Cochise's eyes flickered. He leaned forward alertly.

"Americans and Mexicans. Not the same," Naretena said.

Cochise looked at him fixedly.

"Tucson," Naretena said. "While you were gone. I listened. Much talk. There are new people. Ownership is changed."

"What ownership?" Cochise asked arrogantly.

"It is said thus: Americans now own the country south of the Gila River. Border is changed. No longer Mexico. We are now in the country of the Americans. There will be American soldiers. Military forts. Many soldiers. Many Americans will come to raise cattle and dig in the ground like moles for yellow and white iron."

The flow of words brought on a coughing spell. Cochise sat silently, making no comment on the information. When Naretena finished coughing he wiped his lips and continued.

"I listened. When the war between the Americans and Mexicans ended it was not settled which land belonged to Americans, which land to Mexicans. Line between countries was not drawn. These people pretend to write on the earth, on one side is Mexico and the other the United States. Many Americans came from direction of rising sun. Much talk. Americans gave Mexicans yellow iron. Now the land from the Gila down is American. We live in the country of Americans."

"Indians?" Cochise asked.

"No Indians," Naretena said. "Americans. Mexicans. No Indians."

"Settled between Americans and Mexicans," Cochise said. "No Indians. Well settled between Americans and Mexicans. Yellow iron was given and the line on the earth was changed and the Mexicans and Americans are satisfied. But no Indians." His voice became bitter and harsh and his speech turned from the broken, disconnected everyday speech to the more careful speech of the great orations. "We have lived here for many, many harvests. This is the country of our people, and of the people from whom our people came, and from their people before them. We have been here before the Americans and before the Mexicans. Still it was something to settle between them, first by war and then by the change of yellow iron. No one thought to settle with us. First the Spaniards and then the Mexicans and now the Americans. First with warriors whom we defeated and then with their men of God, but only their own God, and now with the men who are nursemaids to animals and who dig in the ground like moles. They come with their guns and their noise and they have driven away the animals we need for our food and they come into our homeland and build places to dig in the ground and they say that we must change our old way of living and live as they do and stop doing the things that do not please them. And they grow greater in numbers all the time, like sand, they are endless, and we grow smaller and soon there will not be enough room for both of us."

He stopped his speech until the emotion quieted in him.

"We are not conquered people," he said. "No warriors have defeated us." He lifted his eyes proudly. "No one has ever defeated us."

"No one of the earth," Naretena said pointedly. "Yet our numbers do not increase. Now we number no more than twelve hundred. Three hundred fighting men. The white men are without number. They are as blades of grass. Like pine needles. Like drops of rain. No end to them."

"It is closing time for us, maybe," Cochise said.

The cool evening wind scratched on the outer skins of the wickiup. The two brothers sat facing each other silently.

"Walk the path of the white man," Cochise said.

"*Enju.*"

"We must. They are warriors. Brave. We must become as they are. Learn their ways. They fought the Mexicans. Sun has set for Mexicans. It is afternoon for the Indians. We must walk

10

the white path. In my mind for a long time. The white men know something and we must learn from them what it is. The sun will set for us if we do not. We cannot fight them. We cannot destroy them. They are weeds. Ten grow where one is removed. To live we must learn and change. Other people before us have disappeared because they could not learn change. We must change or the sun will set for us and there will be nothing but darkness."

"What of Mangas Coloradas?" Naretena asked softly.

"Big talk with Mangas Coloradas. The Mimbres Apaches are his people. They are his business. We will talk. We will tell him how we shall move." Cochise stood up. "At the feast." As he strode from the wickiup Naretena began to cough again.

4

As the last of the day's light scurried out of the Stronghold and the darkness of the peace hours slipped in to take its place, the women worked hard and the men refreshed themselves and made ready for the feast of celebration. The mules and horses were slaughtered and cleaned and the meat intended for immediate consumption was brought to the fires. The fires were lighted and the meat was set to roast over them. There was roasted mescal, cakes made of mesquite bean and acorn, fruit of the giant cactus, pitahaya. Tiswin, the weak beer which was the favorite drink of the Apaches, was drawn from skin vats and poured into great gourds.

In the dark the fires glared in the Stronghold and made long shadowed speech on the ground and the wind rose and whipped the flames, and early, before the people gathered, the music-makers sat before the crackling stacks and chanted and pounded their drums and drew distant, thin music from their fiddles and guitars.

Then the warriors arrived, rested, bathed and wearing their ceremonial costumes, adorned with many of the things they had taken in the raid. They gathered in a great circle around the fires. In one part of the circle, before the greatest fire, several blankets had been folded and placed on the ground for Cochise.

Then the women arrived and formed another circle outside the men's circle. The men and the women swayed back and forth to the rhythm of the music and then the word was passed around, "Here he comes, here he comes." The music-makers stepped up the volume of their music and now the people around the fire, first the men and then the women, took up the chant.

Cochise walked slowly to his place in the circle. He wore his robes of soft buckskin, painted and stenciled with cabalistic markings to indicate the elements, hail, rain, snow, and sun. Lightning blazed across his chest. Halfway up each of his arms were leather and silver bands, set with silver and colored stones and shining seeds, all glittering in the firelight. Hanging from his right side was a leather pouch, containing two tiny pieces of wood from a tree struck by lightning. On his head was a red sash and in the sash were two eagle feathers, one bright red, the other in its natural colors. His face was newly painted with white and red.

As he stepped to his place in the circle of men and sat on the folded blankets the sound of the chanting rose until it filled the great amphitheater, until it struck the rocky walls and came back again, until there was nothing in the air, almost not enough to breathe, for the repeated crying.

> *"His name is called!*
> *His name is called!*
> *Cochise! His name is called!*
> *Cochise! Cochise! Cochise!"*

Women dancers, some in eleborate buckskin robes, others almost naked, burst into the cleared area in the center of arrangement of fires and flung themselves in reverent ecstasy. There were many among the Chiricahuas who already believed that Cochise was greater than a man. The dancers twisted and quivered and postured convulsively and the lights were reflected in the colored stones of their costumes, on the white powdered bodies of the women.

A man leaped into the arena and the women vanished. The drums left off their rapid tempo and took on a slower, more deliberate rhythm. The man was small and wiry and every move he made proclaimed the incredible control he had over his muscles. He remained twisted in one position, on one foot, leaning over to a degree that made it seem almost impossible for him to remain erect. His face was narrow with a protruding underlip. His eyes were hard and flat and seemed pasted to his face. His nose was big and curved slightly at the tip. This was Nochalo, chief shaman to Cochise, who was learned beyond all other religious men in the ceremony of the successful raid. He was wearing his holy shirt, the potent medicine garment that marked his mystic supremacy. In addition to the symbols of all the elements there were painted on his shirt the mark of the snake, the centipede, and the tarantula. In his hand was his medicine cord of four strands with painted gourds at the end of each strand, and this cord he now swung in a great circle over his head as he started his ritual of gratitude for the triumphal victory over the enemies of the People of the Woods.

12

Slowly he lessened the swing of the cord and when the four gourds fell upon his shoulders and the sacred number touched him he walked to the east, toward the direction of the rising sun. This was a special symbol for the Chiricahuas. They called all Indians People of the Woods, but they had another special name for themselves. Apache meant Enemy and was merely a Pima Indian appellation for them; Chiricahua Apache meant only Enemies from the Chiricahua or Distant Mountains. To themselves they were *Hiuhah,* which meant Men of the Rising Sun.

When he walked ten paces to the east, Nochalo paid his respect to the direction and then returned to the place whence he started; he walked ten paces north, returned, and then west and south. While he walked and gave homage to the directions he said nothing and there was no sound in the Stronghold save the sound of the fire and the low accompaniment of the wind. Nochalo held his hands across his breast and the medicine cord dangled in front of him.

When he finished with the initial obeisance he walked to Cochise. From a small leather pouch he took out a handful of tule pollen. He sprinkled a little of the pollen on the right foot of Cochise; he put some pollen on Cochise's forehead in the shape of a cross; then he sprinkled his left shoulder and his left knee and finally his left foot.

He returned to his place in the center of the arena and chanted his thanks, reminding his Power that Cochise was again anointed with the symbol of Life and he directed his Power to permit the Chiricahua leader to remain long with his people and to continue his record of unbroken success against the enemy.

As he finished the men began to drink the tiswin. Since they had prepared themselves by fasting for twenty-four hours, the weak brew soon began to affect them. They poured huge quantities of the liquid into their throats. When the gourds were emptied, their women refilled them. The tiswin soon took hold of the men and then the women brought the food.

The dancers and singers divided themselves into two groups, each alternating in their entertainment. The men ate and drank and sang accounts of the experiences of the tribe under Cochise. The feasting lasted for many hours. The Mexican captives, no longer bound, found their fear overcome by their hunger, and they too ate.

It was long after midnight and the moon was directly overhead when Nochalo again leaped into the arena. The entertainers moved away. Nochalo gave a brief demonstration of his muscular control, posturing in a way that caused the women to shriek their approval. When he finished he turned suddenly toward Cochise. His lower lip pushed itself out until it passed even the extremity of his great nose.

> *"Cochise! They say to you,*
> *You! You!*
> *They call you again and again!"*

Cochise rose and stepped before the fire. He stood erect, his head lifted, his lean face taut with pride. The firelight made shadows in the hollows of his cheeks and the planes of the shadows made patterns on the streaks of paint.

The people took up the cry.

> *"Cochise! They say to you,*
> *You! You!*
> *They call you again and again!"*

The tiswin had not been without effect on Cochise but as he faced his people all traces of it fled from him and the face that he turned slowly had in it all his austerity and restraint. Only his eyes showed the tingling that was in his veins.

Suddenly his body tensed. His eyes narrowed. His head jerked forward and he stared into the darkness. He placed his right hand to his forehead to shield his eyes from the morning sun and the people leaned forward tensely as he started the pantomime of the raid. Since he used sign symbols that were traditional all could understand him and his meaning was so plain that even the Mexican captives understood and shuddered as they relived the attack.

As the people watched they could see him flat on the ground, and they could make out the Mexican village in the distance, and through his eyes they could see the people in the village streets, and they could see the corrals filled with the sleek mules and the horses. They could see him giving final instructions to his men, and then they could see the men breaking up into a score of small groups, each under the command of a lieutenant, and they could see the smaller groups quietly taking their places at the many prearranged attacking points. They could see each man inspecting his weapons and examining his steed, and their throats were dry in the night waiting for him to give the call for attack. Then the signal was given and the people sighed and they could see the warriors begin their lightning attack from a score of places, on corrals, homes, cutting loose horses and mules, striking first here and then there, confusing the Mexican defenders who never knew from what direction the next attack would come. Again and again, from one place and then another, then from a dozen places at the same time, the Apaches charged until the Mexicans were reduced to hysteria and they

14

ran and turned and did not know where to go because wherever they went there were more Apaches. Now the men were gathering their stolen horses and mules and were starting off with them; other men gathered weapons and clothing from the village and still others did nothing but race around, screaming, firing their guns and loosing their arrows. The captives were taken. Then, as suddenly as they attacked, the Apaches rode away, broken into smaller parties still, and in different directions, as Cochise ordered, so that avengers would not know where to head, where to go, whom to follow. They took their dead with them, those they could find, and soon after they left the village they buried them, and then they continued homeward.

Throughout the pantomime the people listened with a kind of quiet frenzy. Their eyes flashed and their fists clenched as the warriors lived the battle again and those who had not been there lived it for the first time. Throughout the recital Cochise indicated very little of his own personal part in the attack. When he finished he walked abruptly from the circle and resumed his seat, his face again frozen into immobility.

Then the call was made for Nahilzay. The white teeth of the chief war lieutenant flashed as he leaped gracefully into the arena. His muscles rippled as he moved nervously around, his eyes fixed on Cochise. He began his account. He told how he had led a party of warriors and how they had attacked a corral and how his horse had been shot in the leg by a Mexican bullet and how he had been thrown from the animal and had fallen in the direct line of fire. With his eyes never leaving the face of his chief, he told how he was in so great danger that he did not call anyone by name for help, because of the Apache belief that a man thus called was bound to come to his aid, and he did not want to cause the death of another man. Then he told how Cochise had galloped across the clear field and had come to his side and had bent down and with one arm had scooped the fallen Nahilzay from the ground, and then, holding him to the side of his bay had raced out of gun range to safety.

The women screamed, "Yieeeeeah! Yieeeeeah!"

Cochise remained unmoved.

Then the small Skinyea, whose name meant canyon, took on the story, and related how the men regathered and how, soon afterwards, they heard the sound of horses. These were the Mexican *rurales* and the Chiricahuas divided themselves. The bulk of the Apaches continued with their loot, and the remaining men, led by Cochise himself, assisted personally by Skinyea, who strutted around cockily as he came to this part of the story, held back in the forest. The Mexicans were permitted to pass through them and then the Apaches attacked them from the rear and other Apaches in the van turned and attacked from the front. The *rurales,* caught between the two grinding forces, broke up and fled, leaving dead and wounded behind them, and, more important, horses. The wounded Mexicans were killed and then all the dead were stripped of their uniforms, weapons, and blankets.

Then came the turn of Pionsenay, whose name meant horse, the big, round-shaped brother of Skinyea. Then Juan, who was not too coherent to start with and who now was too muddled with tiswin to do more than demonstrate how he had released arrow after arrow, each taking their mark. So the stories were told through the night and the men listened and the women shrieked their bird-like piercing call of applause and the dancers worked themselves to sweaty lathers and the singers sang until they were hoarse. The drinking continued too and later the widowed and divorced women went into the brush with the young unmarried warriors who had specially distinguished themselves during the raid, and since these women were already known of men, it was accepted and not considered unchaste.

Finally the sun lifted his red eye over the east rim of the Stronghold. The men rose from the circle and went to their wickiups to sleep. Cochise again was the last to leave. He stood straight and untired and lifted his long arms to the new sun. He remained there motionlessly until all of *Holos* crawled over the rim and started his walk across the sky. Then he dropped his arms and turned and walked alone to his dwelling.

Chapter Two

The war between the United States and Mexico ended with the Treaty of Guadalupe Hidalgo in 1848 and in Article 11 of this treaty the Government of the United States undertook a very ambitious responsibility. In this article, the United States promised to keep Indians from raiding into Mexico, and, when this proved impossible, to give full satisfaction to the Mexican government for any losses so sustained. This same article also pledged the United States to prevent its own citizens from buying any property or captives from Indians who had stolen them in Mexico and to relieve any Indians indiscreet enough to violate this treaty of any such captives found on the American side of the line and return the captives to their own people.

With conditions in the Southwest as they were at that time, when there were not a hundred white men in all of what later became Arizona, such an undertaking on the part of a government thousands of miles away in Washington was optimistic to the point of foolishness. The reasons behind Article 11, how-

16

ever, were not entirely either humanitarian or unconsidered. Mexico refused to sign a treaty without guaranty that her border provinces should be protected and the desire seemed reasonable enough to the type of diplomatic mind that always makes treaties.

The article, of course, was doomed to failure from the start. First of all, the Americans had no control at all over the tribes of Indians who were doing the raiding and had all they could do, both settlers and military, to protect themselves much less lay down lofty rules for the Indians to obey. Secondly, while the treaty was entered into with reasonable sincerity and high purpose by the Government of the United States, which wanted peace so the rich lands of the Southwest could be developed, and to a somewhat lesser degree of sincerity and purpose by the bankrupt and corrupt dictatorship of Santa Ana in Mexico, both governments were far from the scene of action. Neither the individual American settlers nor the individual Mexicans, who swarmed on both sides of the border, were prepared or even desired to uphold it. While there were a few Americans and Mexicans who wanted to live at peace with each other and the Indians, there was a far larger number of citizens of both countries who made a comfortable living buying stolen goods from the Indians, and there were also many Americans, far more solid citizens these, who made their living supplying goods to the military at an exorbitant profit. These last gentlemen wanted no peace because permanent peace might cut down the numbers of soldiers stationed in the territory to the point where supplying them would no longer be the business it was. This group of men, known as the "Ring," for many years virtually ran Tucson. As a final fly in Article 11, there was a large class of Mexicans in Sonora and other border states who supported the old and traditional Mexican custom of getting Indians together in one place, getting them drunk, and then murdering them. Since the Mexican government always had a bounty on Indian scalps ranging in size from twenty-five to one hundred dollars, depending upon the state of the Mexican treasury, peaceful Indians would cause many Mexicans and their American companions in the Indian hunts to go broke.

The Treaty of Guadalupe Hidalgo underwrote the inefficiency of its makers in still another way. In establishing the boundary between the two countries, the diplomats used a map which was inaccurately drawn. When the vagueness of the boundary became apparent, the Government of the United States sent out a number of surveying parties to establish it.

The loose and flabby interpretation of where the border should be continued to give patriots in Washington and Mexico City a great deal about which to be annoyed with each other, and relations between the two countries were steadily worsening when, finally, to settle things, James Gadsden was appointed United States Minister to Mexico, and was authorized to buy the disputed territory for his government. On December 30, 1853, while President Pierce sat in the White House, Gadsden bought for the United States, for the sum of $10,000,000, a strip of land south of the Gila River, from the Rio Grande on the east to a point twenty miles below the mouth of the Gila on the Colorado. This land was estimated to contain 45,535 square miles, 14,000 square miles of which later became part of the Territory, then State, of New Mexico, and the rest, part of Arizona. At the time of the purchase there was no Territory of Arizona and all the new land became part of the Territory of New Mexico, from which Arizona was taken on February 20, 1863.

The only persons who were not consulted during these historic negotiations were the Indians, who had lived in the country involved for some length of time, and who, despite their cultural differences from either Americans or Mexicans, had simple but definite ideas of ownership. It was estimated at the time that in all that vast Territory of New Mexico there were but some five thousand Americans, inhabiting a country larger than several Eastern states combined. There were at that time an estimated fifty thousand Indians, of one tribe or another, and the Apaches alone claimed title to a territory three times as large as California, larger than all of New England, with New York and New Jersey added. These Indians regarded the land as theirs.

2

Toward the close of the winter in the beginning of 1856, just before the time Ghost Face departed and made way for early spring, called Little Eagles, there gathered in the Stronghold of Cochise, at the request of the Chiricahua leader, the leading warriors of Mimbres Apaches, or Warm Springs Apaches as they also were called, led by their great chief Mangas Coloradas.

These two tribes, the Chiricahuas and the Mimbres, were the kernel, the nucleus of the vast, sprawling Apache nation, which numbered half a dozen or more tribes. Of all the Indians in the Southwest the Apaches were the most warlike, and of all the tribes within the Apache cultural sphere the Chiricahuas and the Mimbres were the most ruthless, the most fanatic in their war against their ancient enemies, the Mexicans. Together the Chiricahuas and the Mimbres composed the soul of the Apache people. The balance of the Apache tribes and offshoots of tribes acknowledged their leadership, supplied them with warriors when communal war was practiced, even paid them tribute

18

when demanded. The Mimbres Apaches were great in numbers. The Chiricahuas were the smallest of all the Apache tribes, but as held together by Cochise, were the dominating, the sharp, hard head of the Apache arrow.

Mangas Coloradas was some twenty years older than Cochise and was regarded as the elder statesman in the Apache nation, although he already was far outstripped in warfare by Cochise. He was an imposing man. He was a larger man physically than even Cochise, and his largeness was everywhere on him, on his huge body, his bulky arms, his broad legs, and, mostly, on his enormous head. He had wide, penetrating eyes, and in the center of his gigantic head he wore a slender, almost delicate nose, narrow at the bridge and broadening only slightly at the nostrils.

Mangas Coloradas never was a great military leader. His strength lay in the wisdom of his advice at councils and in his diplomacy in dealing with other tribes. He had come to power many years before, following the treacherous slaying of Juan Jose, the last Apache who was regarded as chief by all the Apache tribes. At the death of Juan Jose there was a question whether he would be succeeded by the wily Mangas Coloradas or by the young Chiricahua chief Cochise, then only a youth but already renowned for his leadership. Cochise decided he preferred to remain chief only of his own Chiricahua tribe and by ritual exchange of blood became blood brother to Mangas Coloradas who took over leadership of an augmented Mimbres tribe. The other tribes then chose their own individual chiefs and the Apache nation, as it was ruled by Juan Jose, existed no longer. Whereupon Mangas Coloradas grew in stature and soon was famous for his skill in diplomatic maneuvering.

He demonstrated his brilliant powers early.

Years before he had brought back from Mexico a beautiful Mexican girl and had married her. In the course of time the Mexican woman bore to Mangas Coloradas three beautiful daughters, each more lovely than the other. When these daughters reached marriageable age Mangas Coloradas showed the quality of the gray matter in his head by marrying each of them off, one to Pedro, chief of the Coyoteros, or White Mountain Apaches; a second to the war chief of the Mescalero Apaches; and the third to Manulito, chief of the Navajos. During this time Mangas Coloradas also arranged the marriage of his own sister, Tesalbestinay, to Cochise.

No one remembered his original Apache name; he was known to all as Mangas Coloradas, which, in Spanish, meant Red Sleeves, and which was the name given to him long before by the Mexicans. It was said he was called Red Sleeves because his hatred of Mexicans was so great that when he killed a Mexican and the situation permitted the luxury, he dipped his great arms in the blood of his victim until the blood covered him from his fingertips to his shoulders.

He came to the West, or inner, Stronghold of Cochise, whom he respected above all other men on earth, in this freezing weather in the early part of 1856, from his own warm country, on a matter he surmised must be of vast importance.

The shamans from both tribes finished their rituals. The warriors were gathered before the fires, huddled in blankets, their breaths wisping thinly above them. When the last of the reverences were made, Nochalo stood before the men. This is what he said.

> *"Keep closed the cloud,*
> *Keep the black cloud closed.*
> *Cochise is outside the black cloud,*
> *Do not open its door."*

The conference was well favored. Though the winter wind raced through the Stronghold, no branch had fallen from a single tree. As Nochalo adjured his Power to refrain from confusing Cochise, the gathered men muttered, *"Enju,"* and then took a final look around them. If anywhere a tree limb had fallen to the ground during the ceremony, the conference would be called off until another day. Even more intently the men listened to hear the sound of an owl hooting, which would indicate even in a more drastic degree the displeasure of the Power.

Cochise and Mangas Coloradas sat side by side, each on folded blankets. The men made a contrast.

Cochise was locked in his normal glacial reserve. His eyes were distant and somewhat dilated, as though he were listening to an inner voice. His conviction that the destiny of his people rested with him gave him a spiritual intensity, held in check only by the tightness of demeanor.

Mangas Coloradas was far more relaxed. He was not bothered by thoughts of destiny. He was a politician. He had faith in the skill with which he handled words and ideas. He was used to dealing with all kinds of men and on his massive face there was the professional politician's expression of lambent humor. He felt a little superior to, and a little uncomfortable with, the iron-visaged Cochise.

The men sat quietly and waited for the stern Chiricahua leader to speak. For a long while he remained silent and the measure of his potent personality spread around the circle. The intensity came to each man and in the mood that was created Mangas Coloradas suddenly seemed to have the qualities of a buffoon. Then the moon rose above the mountain rim and its pale light rested lightly on the snow and Cochise began to speak. He spoke at first with a poetic cadence, speaking each sentence as though it were a line of verse.

He said:

"Are we not natives to this earth about us?

"Are we not of the rocks, the mountains, the air, the forest?

"Are not the deer and the mountain sheep part of our lives?

"Do not the birds sing for the Apache?

"Do not the eagles cross the sky for the Apache?

"Are not the deer grazing in our country?

"Are not the mountain sheep treading lightly on our rocks?

"Do not the shadows of the great eagles move on our earth?

"Do not the cattle feed upon the grass that grows upon the soil of the Apache?

"Do not the bodies of our fathers and their fathers lie beneath the earth that belongs to the Apache?

"Is not the stream that runs on our earth for the slaking of our thirst?

"Why then do the white men come here?

"Why do they kill our food?

"Why do they change our earth so the Apache cannot live upon it as before?

"Our ways of doing things have been different.

"Our beliefs have been different."

His voice was hushed and yet it penetrated to the ears of the farthest man. He was using the formal language and of all the Indian tongues of the Southwest the Apache was the most eloquent. To the words, Cochise added the Apache touches which gave the verbal language its nuances and shades of meaning: lifting his hands, spreading his fingers, pursing his lips, raising his head. Like many of the dialects of China, the words of the Apache language depended on an exact tone to give them their meaning, and Cochise used the language as an artist.

He paused and held his silence and then he reviewed the history of the war between the Mexicans and the Indians, going back to the old days when the Spanish *conquistadores* were on the land. He spoke with the Indian's indifference to time.

As he progressed in his development of his story, Mangas Coloradas was working his mind, trying to foresee what the lengthy narration was leading to. He knew that Cochise had not called the conference to discuss Apache relations with Mexico, which were too standard and too well understood to need recounting. The clue, he felt, was in the initial reference to the white men, and Mangas Coloradas wondered where that would bring them and he tried to predict the direction Cochise might take so that he would be prepared to take whatever stand he would have to.

"Now there are new white men who come to our country," Cochise was saying. "These are different men. They are different from the Mexicans. They were at war with the Mexicans. They welcomed us when we joined them in this war. Then they made their peace with the Mexicans and now they are no longer enemies of our enemies. This land where we live, these mountains, these valleys, these animals, these birds, the wind and the rain and the snow and the hail, all of these things have always belonged to the Apache. Yet for a long while the Mexicans said it belonged to them. Then the Americans bought it and now say it belongs to them."

He lifted his austere face and looked around at the natural majesty of the Stronghold. "As though this earth can be traded back and forth like a horse," he said bitterly.

"Apaches fight Mexicans. Americans get killed in the fighting because when an Apache has blood in his heart he does not pause to reflect but he kills and it is afterward that he discovers that the man he has killed is not a Mexican but an American. And the slaying of Americans has become a crime against their government, because this is now their country, so they say.

"And the Americans kill Apaches and there is no peace between them. Our people and the Americans are no longer brothers. The Americans hunt Apaches as though they were animals and there is no rest for Apaches. There are many times the numbers of Apaches and other Indians in this country than there are Americans and yet the Americans who say they own our earth because they traded yellow iron make all the laws.

"They are brave men. There are many more where they come from. More than all the Apaches, it is said. Their soldiers soon will come to Tucson. Their numbers increase. Our numbers grow less. Each day more Apaches die."

There was no sound from his listeners, who, huddled in their blankets, might have been the rocks themselves in the wavering light from the fires.

As they sat and listened, Mangas Coloradas scrutinized their faces, watched their reactions, to see how the words of Cochise affected them. They were as men in a trance, he thought. No one, he reflected, could put men in a spell with his words as Cochise could. His mind continued to work as he listened to the Chiricahua leader.

"When the great wind strikes a tree with enough force the tree must bend, maybe, or else be lifted by its roots from the earth," Cochise said, speaking now more slowly than ever. "So, I think now that it is time for the Chiricahuas to make peace with the white men, to go among them and live among them as brothers, to learn their ways and to make into our ways those things that will bring strength and wisdom to the Apaches."

There was a long, quiet sigh from the warriors.

"I have spoken," Cochise said.

Mangas Coloradas waited a long time to answer. The proposal came as a shock to him, although with his elastic imagination he was not entirely surprised. He had known for a long time that the inexorable advance of the Americans into the Southwest troubled the Chiricahua chief. He knew too that in many ways Cochise was different from other Apaches. Cochise, he thought to himself, was a terrible warrior. There was none braver, none more destructive, none more brilliant. But Cochise, he thought, wryly, was cursed with a propensity for too much thinking. While Mangas Coloradas was a great thinker himself, he never succumbed to his thoughts. Cochise, he knew, often felt pangs of an alien emotion, remorse, for some of the things he did in rage.

"My brother speaks with wisdom," he said in his deep, throaty voice, booming his words to his listeners. "My brother speaks words that have long been in my thoughts."

In the same leisurely manner he proceeded to list the acts of white man's treachery, starting with the story of Juan Jose, killed by the trader James Johnson whom he had befriended, and of the inability of the Indian to trust the word of the American.

"I have lived closely with these Americans. I have studied their ways. Many of them speak with a forked tongue. First they warred with the Mexicans. Now they are at peace with the Mexicans, although the Mexicans cheat and rob them and despise them and think them fools. Still they are at peace. This is all right. Sometimes one is at war and sometimes one makes peace, maybe. But the Americans say the Indians also must make peace, with the Mexicans, although the Mexicans still collect money from their government for Apache scalps. Peace with the Mexicans is an impossible thing. One should act for one's own people and not make laws for another unconquered people to obey."

The listeners grunted applause.

"A man does not always do the things he wants to. That is why he is a man and not an animal," Cochise replied quietly. "I do not explain Americans. I am not thinking about them. I am not thinking of Mexicans. I am thinking of Apaches. I am thinking about the children of Apaches and the children who will come from these children. The Americans are here. They will stay. They are different from the others. They will not be driven away, as were the Spaniards. I have led my people in war for many harvests, but now I say that the Americans are stronger than we are and that they grow stronger while we grow weaker.

"They have firearms which are better than our arrows and spears and when we capture these guns they get better guns.

23

They know how to use these guns. They are strange to our country and they now fight the country as well as us but soon they will learn to make friends with the country and use it as we do. They are brave men. They are so brave they are foolish often."

Cochise's voice was filled with deep respect. There were two things he respected more than anything else in men; one was truth, the other bravery.

"These Americans make homes for themselves and they are warm within their homes no matter how heavily Ghost Face treads on the land. Their clothing is strong and they have plenty to eat at all times. I have heard Apache children ask for food and there is no food to give them. Even the Mexicans who tie themselves to the white men always have food."

He stared into the fire.

"I have thought about these things. This is what I have decided. The Americans know things I do not know." He used the Apache pronoun for "I" which, in the Apache language, indicated he included all the Apache people. "I think maybe it would be a good thing for the Apaches to find out what these things are."

Mangas Coloradas nodded. The argument was forceful. He was not, however, prepared to surrender his position. While Cochise was talking he was assembling his thoughts and he now prepared to assault the Chiricahua leader at his most vulnerable place.

"The Americans do not have faith in the word of the Apaches," he said. "They will not believe that my brother is speaking the truth when he comes to them."

For the first time since he started talking Cochise turned and looked at Mangas Coloradas. His eyes were in a sudden blaze. "No man has ever accused me of speaking with a crooked tongue," he said in a deadly voice. "There have been many bad things I have done, some of them so bad Ghosts come to me in the night and swim in my head until it rocks. But I have never spoken a lie."

"It is true," Mangas Coloradas said solemnly. "Truth has a value among all our people but in none of us has it so great a value as in my brother." He felt these words to be true and he spoke them sincerely. "With my brother words mean what words mean. But do the Americans know this?"

Cochise did not answer. The idea of lying was so abhorrent to him he felt an almost physical nausea. He was a deeply religious man, as Mangas Coloradas in his cleverness knew, and he believed in the literal teaching of his religion. Being truthful, he believed his Spirits were truthful and would honor any obligation he made. To speak a lie was the same as committing these Spirits to a lie.

"I have never spoken with a forked tongue," he said when he mastered himself. "Every man knows this."

The discussion now was given over to the other warriors, who, under Apache rules of government, had the right to express themselves freely. Delgadito, a leading warrior of the Mimbres tribe, attacked the Americans for their treacherous ways. Victorio, chief lieutenant to Mangas Coloradas, said that he thought Cochise spoke wisely. Nahilzay spoke and said he did not see things exactly as Cochise had depicted them but that he would follow whatever path his leader walked. Then another Chiricahua warrior, one not yet recognized as a prominent lieutenant, whose name was Gokliya, spoke.

"One does not question the wisdom of Cochise," he said, in a sly and conciliatory voice. "Still there are things right for some men, wrong for others. For as long as the memory of our people carries we have lived by our bravery and our wits. It is not the Apache way to live like women, to grow things from the ground, to be grandmothers to cattle. Our people would become soft and womanly in such a life. Their enemies would soon rise and kill them."

"The Americans are not soft and womanly," Cochise said. "To learn their ways does not mean to become blind and deaf."

The discussion continued through the night. Of all the Indians present, only Naretena did not speak. Later the wind died and the women and old men went to sleep. It was necessary to add wood to the fire again and again. In the end, Cochise said:

"Listen to me now. I speak to the Chiricahuas. I speak openly so that Mangas Coloradas and his warriors will know what I do. For those who will stay with me it will be as I have decided. There are other leaders here if the Chiricahuas do not wish to stay with me. I know what is right for the Chiricahuas. I want all of my people to follow me. Those who follow me must walk with me with their hearts as well as their words. I shall go to the Americans and tell what I have decided. When I say the Chiricahuas want peace I shall be responsible for all the people who walk with me. It is my word that I shall give. I will guarantee my word. I want no one to walk with me who has a double mind. Leave me now if my path displeases you. There is no harm. It is your right. But those who stay with me will do exactly as I pledge. If any man who stays with me does a bad thing I shall join with the Americans and hunt him down and if this bad thing violates my word I shall myself kill him."

He used the Apache "I" which indicated he would do with his own hands what he promised.

"I speak to Mangas Coloradas. This is Chiricahua country. When I make peace it means that the land of the Chiricahuas is a peaceful land. Who violates this peace is my enemy." He turned again to Mangas Coloradas. His voice became less harsh. "We have walked together. Now I take this path. I do not want to be your enemy. I love you and your people almost as I love the Chiricahua people. But I say to you that any man who calls you chief who violates my peace becomes my enemy and the enemy of the Chiricahuas and if you protect such a man within your tribe your tribe becomes our enemy."

He looked around the encircled group. The faces were grave in the light of the fresh morning.

"Who wishes to leave me, do so now. Who remains binds himself to my word."

The men who agreed with Cochise had no problem. The ones who disagreed now had, by Apache laws, the choice of submerging their disagreement and following their leader, or of leaving the tribe. If enough of the warriors joined in opposing the Cochise proposal, they might remove him as chief and choose another.

For several minutes no one made a move and then suddenly Gokliya rose. "I walk away," he said. Several other Chiricahua braves joined him. The rest of the warriors remained seated and by their silence bound themselves to Cochise.

Cochise looked intently at the face of each of the men who were walking away. It was not good to see them go, but the number was less than it might have been. Under his steady gaze two of the men abruptly left the group and returned to their places around the circle.

"You will see Chiricahua country from the outside," Cochise said to the others. "As soon as you leave your earth you are enemies to the Chiricahuas. If they see you first on this land they will kill you. If you see them first you will kill them."

The men left the conference and went to their wickiups to gather their families and their belongings. Now Cochise spoke to Mangas Coloradas.

"It is as you see."

"We return to our own country. Mimbres men will not join with you, nor will they interfere."

"It is understood how things are between us?"

"It is understood."

The two men rose and embraced each other.

"May I never ride against my brother," Cochise said.

"May I never ride against my brother," Mangas Coloradas repeated heavily. This course taken by Cochise would make for many changes. But Mangas Coloradas was old enough and experienced enough never to accept anything as final. He had found, in his many years, that things often happened that converted the most determined men. "May we ride together again," he said.

"It will be as it will be," Cochise replied.

The Mimbres warriors left the rancheria with their chief.

26

Gokliya and the men who elected to follow him as leader collected their possessions and departed from the Stronghold.

Cochise and Naretena watched the Chiricahuas ride away.

"It is as though they died in battle," Cochise said.

"It might be better if they had," his brother replied cryptically.

Not long afterward the man Gokliya ceased to be called by his Apache name. He came to be known by the name given to him by the Mexicans. That name was Geronimo.

Chapter Three

The thin winter rains ended early and the new spring welled hot into the ancient walled mud settlement of Tucson. It was the time of the year the Indians called Many Leaves and now the hard bare desert which seemed in the winter to be too flinty, too metallic, too naked and dead to sustain life within itself, burst forth in soft pastels of green and gray. The desert which is masculine in the winter and in the summer now had its time of girlishness, when the grizzled desert vegetation, the thorny cactus, the Spanish dagger, the mescal, the mesquite, the ocotillo began to turn an almost embarrassing softness, began to open their brassy hardness to the incredible miracles of buds, which in turn opened to glorious flower. From nowhere, from the tawny unbroken hardness, they came, in purples and reds and blues and yellows and for its brief annual moment the desert denied its name and spread itself into an endless garden. It was the time of the year when the pioneers, who often remembered the land from which they came, who often mourned in the heat and aridity and dust for their green land of home, for Kentucky or Virginia or Pennsylvania, for their New England with its springs that were new births and its blinding falls, now gazed around them and breathed deeply and knew that they never again would be content save on the desert. It was not something that came to them right off; sometimes it took years: but when the desert fire entered into them it was there to stay and everything else became just pallid memory.

The sun, which had rested itself for its summer efforts behind the light, filmy curtain of February rain, now emerged and lay heavily on the yellow adobe buildings and glared on the broad plaza of the Mexican town. The mud in the streets gave way to dust, fine and gray as talcum, that filtered gauzily in each vagrant breeze. The women no longer had to hold up their skirts, giving pleasure to the indolent men who had

27

sighed at the sight of their dark shapely calves. Mexicans, civilians and soldiers, women, young girls, endless numbers of children, wandered in the narrow streets of the Old Pueblo and everywhere the talk was of the same thing, the coming of the Americans. The people were confused and frightened. Their country had been snatched from under their feet, like a rug yanked away, through an exchange of gold in Mexico City. Everything was the same, the town, the people, the weather, the desert, and yet it was now the United States and no longer Mexico, although not a single part of a single building was changed. The people had been offered their choice: to move on southward across the new border and retain their Mexican citizenship, or to remain in Tucson and become Americans. Many had moved. The people had seen something of the Americans in Tucson and they did not like what they had seen.

Some communities remain always just a collection of buildings and a collection of people living in them; other places where men elect to live come to have a color, a smell, a personality that is as strong as that of a man. Tucson had this life of its own, this life that lay within itself, that was shapely, to be seen, to be grasped. It lay in its buildings, its streets, its air, was compounded of its inhabitants, and still was apart from them, remote and secure in its own pact with history. This change, in March, 1856, was just another change in a line of changes, which perhaps were not really changes at all.

For more than a thousand years there were records that men of one color or another, one religion or another, one race or another, had made the mud city on the Santa Cruz their home. They had come and had lived and had fought and had died or were driven away by other men who held on for a while to their tenancy in the sun. For a long time to each of these peoples it was a private world, belonging only to them, in their own time, for the mountains on all sides kept it apart just as the adobe walls kept out the enemies.

There were traces of ancient Indian rancherias and there were signs of Spaniards and Mexicans. Eighty years earlier in 1776 while a great excitement was going on several thousand miles to the east the Mexicans established a *presidio* and called it San Augustin del Pueblito de Tucson and walled the city again into a sturdy fortress.

The valley of the Santa Cruz was a rich one and the bed of the river was not then ugly to the eye. The water was higher and flowed with abundance. The river provided water for small canals through fields cultivated by civilians and soldiers and from the rich earth thus relieved of thirst there came grain, beans, peas, chili, squash, watermelon, quince, pears, pomegranates. For meat there was deer and elk, wild turkey, quail and pheasant.

28

With the establishment of the *presidio* and the appointment of an *alcalde,* Tucson became a military headquarters. The population remained small, never exceeding seven or eight hundred, and the garrison was never larger than fifty.

The community was an oasis in the desert, an island in a vast sea of sand and emptiness. It was an isolated outpost, far from the world of its own people. Now and then a traveler arrived, or a rancher or farmer would come within its protecting walls, which formed the rear parts of the adobe houses built on the inside of them, when the Indians were violent, but for the most part the life of the community extended no farther than these walls and within them was a microcosm of Mexico.

In this tiny area, which later became only a remote corner of the modern city, men and women lived and loved and their children were born and a strict, unchanging, all-powerful religion controlled them. The customs of their land continued in all things, supported more strongly perhaps because of the remoteness of the source. The food and the clothing and the manner of living never changed. There in that distant outpost social manners remained almost archaic. There were *bailes,* held in ancient manner, stately dances, and when a man arrived an eggshell filled with cologne or silver and gold paper was broken over his head, as it was the custom in Spain and Portugal in the Shrove Tuesday fêtes. And in the evenings the young men would take guitars and stand in front of the windows of the ladies unfortunate enough to have been unable to attend the *bailes,* and there sing to them and tell them how the dance was a gloomy failure because of their absence.

In the late forties and early fifties there was the first indication that a change was in store for this medieval society. Americans began to drift in and they were a different breed from the dulcet-voiced Mexicans. These Americans were not pleasant men. For the most part they were scum who had been driven from California and Texas, lawbreakers who fled as peace moved into the developing West, absconders, killers, thieves, and gamblers, bad men from everywhere in the United States, who found Tucson to be an oasis of their own definition. There were other Americans, a few, quiet ones, who tried to live decently with the people into whose community they intruded, but these men were lost in the noisy venom of the others.

The Gadsden Purchase changed Tucson overnight from Mexico to the United States. When the last official Mexican census was taken in 1848 there had been seven hundred and sixty natives in Tucson, but this number had been swelled somewhat by refugees from Tubac and Tumacacori Mission, who fled from Indian outrage. On March 10, 1856, four companies of the 1st United States Dragoons arrived in Tucson to

29

take formal possession for their government and to implement the purchase.

Late on the afternoon of March 9 the Mexican garrison formed for the last time in La Plaza de las Armas with their backs to the sinking sun and then marched in formation across the Calle de la Guardia into La Plaza Militar. Their uniforms were clean and for the first time in a long time every rifle was polished and every bayonet shone. The bugler sounded retreat and then the tiny garrison marched down the Calle Real to the main gate and, as the people stood and wept and watched, they evacuated the town and started for Mexico. The natives stared as their country marched away from them.

Among the decent Americans there at the time were two men named William H. Kirkland and Pete Kitchen. These men gathered several of their friends and made ready to welcome the American troops scheduled to arrive the next day. The law-abiding element of Americans found themselves with sudden, unexpected strength; some of the worst outlaws disappeared, afraid to come again under the jurisdiction of their own country.

As the little group of Americans watched the Mexican soldiery disappear toward the south, Kirkland, who had a ranch near the Santa Rita Mountains, said to Kitchen, whose lands were south, near the border, "We ought to do something to welcome the troops."

"A flag," Kitchen said.

"I have a flag," Edward Miles, another rancher, said.

Miles departed for his ranch and returned late that night with an American Flag. It was deeply creased from the months it had been folded in a trunk, but it was an American Flag, and apart from whatever banners the incoming soldiers would be carrying, probably the only flag of its kind for hundreds of miles.

At dawn the next morning fourteen Americans marched into the *presidio* carrying the flag and a rude staff made of mesquite poles lashed together. A few curious and frightened Mexicans gathered along the sides of the buildings and watched as the Americans removed their hats and stood at attention. The staff was affixed to the building and, while the Americans held their hats against their breasts, Kirkland and Kitchen slowly raised the flag and in the weak breeze the Stars and Stripes fluttered over the Old Pueblo.

A few hours later the troops appeared in the distance, their horses flailing the powdery desert dust. The north gate was opened and then, with fife and drum making a strange music in the mud town, the blue-uniformed American soldiers rode into Tucson.

2

The passage of the American troops had not been unobserved by the Indians. Before the soldiers arrived at their new station, their numbers, their equipment, an opinion of their potentialities, were passed back and forth through the Indian grapevine.

The first task of the troops was to assure the Mexicans that their lives and property were safe. Accustomed to another type of military occupation, the Mexicans had feared what they owned would be confiscated by the newcomers. Some of the leading Mexican men of the community, Jesus Elias, Juan Santa Cruz, Solano Leon, and others, formally presented themselves to Major Enoch Steen, the American commandant, in his headquarters in the *presidio*.

Steen, a wiry, bearded officer with sparkling blue eyes and a broad good-humored mouth, greeted the delegation in a friendly manner.

"I know there must be many questions you have to ask of me," he said in fluent Spanish. "I am here to tell you whatever you want to know. Before you ask questions of me there are some things I want to say. My country and Mexico are at peace. We wish to live at peace with you. As long as there are American soldiers here the Mexicans who obey our laws will be considered in the same light as the Americans and will receive the same privileges and the same protection. At the same time and by the same authority Mexicans who violate laws will be punished the way American violators are punished. Your property is safe. Your homes and your businesses are safe. We are not come here to rob from you. It is difficult, doubtless, for a people to lose their country, but I am authorized to welcome you to remain at peace in the United States and to prosper here."

Elias, a thin crafty-faced Mexican, who appeared to be spokesman for the delegation, nodded in satisfaction. "The words of the American commandant fall upon happy ears," he said. "Our people have been worried. They will be as joyful as we ourselves are when I repeat the good message."

"The plan now is to leave but a small number of men in Tucson," Steen continued. "The main body of men will be moved farther south and will establish a fort somewhere in the Sonoita. Our main duty will be to afford protection from the Indians."

"Protection from the Indians will be as welcome as it will be strange," Elias said suavely.

"Which Indians live the closest?"

31

"The Papagos. But they are friendly."

"Who else?"

Elias held out his hands. "The Apaches."

"Always the Apaches. Which ones?"

"The closest are the Chiricahuas."

"That's Cochise," Steen said in English.

Elias nodded. "Yes, as the commandant has said, the leader is Cochise."

"What manner of man is he?"

Elias shrugged. "What manner of men are Apaches?"

"The same as anybody else," Steen said. "Some good and some bad."

Elias smiled politely and exchanged glances with the other Mexicans. "With Apaches, Señor Commandant, all are bad. There are no others, except the dead ones."

"I do not believe that," Steen said shortly.

"The Señor Commandant is new here," Elias said. "He has as yet not acquainted himself with the Apache Indian."

"I have no experience with Apaches," Steen admitted. "But I have fought with other Indians and I have become friendly with still others."

"There is no Indian like the Apache, as the Señor will doubtless soon discover for himself," Elias said. "You will find what you will find."

Juan Santa Cruz spoke for the first time. "Apaches kill and steal. They live in this manner. In my country there are entire villages that are laid waste by Apaches. My wife's brother and his son were killed by Apaches as they worked on their farm. A cousin of mine was taken by them one day as he tended his sheep. He has never been heard from again. There is none among us who can say with truth that he knows of a good Apache."

Steen began to answer that he had heard of the manner in which the Mexicans customarily treated the Apaches, but he decided, out of courtesy, to say nothing. Instead, he rose and held out his hand to Elias. "Perhaps something can be done to effect an understanding," he said.

"One does not come to an understanding with wild animals," Elias said, his voice losing its velvet quality and turning harsh. "When one sees an Apache one kills him. It is as simple as that. Just as one would shoot a wild bear or a mountain lion." Then he took the proffered hand. He again smiled. His teeth were very white. "But the Señor says that it is his duty to afford protection for peaceful people. That suffices. I will carry his words to my compatriots."

3

In the summer of 1856 Steen brought his troops to a temporary camp where the headwaters of the Sonoita River joined the Santa Cruz, in a section called by the Mexicans Calabasas. There they established themselves while engineers prospected and finally settled on a permanent campsite on the Sonoita River in the beautiful and fertile Sonoita Valley, a point twenty miles north of the Mexican boundary and twenty-five miles east of the ancient Mexican village of Tubac. The Sonoita Valley was the earliest country settled by Americans in Arizona and even at this time there were many ranches scattered through the rich land. Soldiers made frequent scouts back and forth across the valley and occasionally continued as far east as the Sulphur Spring Valley, more than seventy miles away, the flat tableland that led to the entrance of the East Stronghold in the forbidding Dragoon Mountains.

Although the soldiers sought them out they could never find any Apaches. There were frequent reports of Apache raids into Mexico, raids on a large scale, but the Indians never were seen to go, nor to return. The raids were confined to Mexico. As far as the soldiers of the 1st Dragoons were concerned there were no Apaches.

Steen issued orders that if an encounter was made with the Apaches captives were to be brought in alive so that he might in some way arrange for a meeting with Cochise. But through the weeks of the boiling weather the Apaches were as phantoms, making their regular ghostlike trips across the border and returning as silently.

Two months after the temporary camp was established at Calabasas, Steen called in his second in command, Captain Edward Fitzgerald. Steen filled a fat, curved pipe and puffed out billows of smoke. "I'm worried, Fitz," he said.

"Indians?"

"Where are they? It's too quiet."

"Maybe they decided to move back to Mexico."

"They're around. I can feel them. There's Indian in the air. They keep going forth and back from Mexico. But nothing around here. It's not natural."

"What do you make of it?"

"I don't know. Unless they're playing a cleverer game than I can savvy. Remember that Mexican, Elias, when we first arrived in Tucson. The way he talked this place was swarming with them."

"There have been no reports of Apaches from the patrols."

"You don't see Apaches. And yet I've got to see them. I

33

want to talk to their leaders. I don't give a damn what Elias and his gang of professional Indian-haters say. Apaches are human." He relit his pipe. "Everything quiet around the camp?"

"Yes."

"Come over to my tent after mess tonight. I have some Mexican liquor."

"All right, Noch."

"Go find me an Indian, Fitz," Steen said.

Fitzgerald laughed, saluted, and left.

On a rainy day in August, when the skies opened themselves and turned themselves inside out, a soldier entered Steen's tent and saluted. "Sir, there are some Indians at the sentry line."

"Papagos? Looking for work?"

"No, sir. They're Apaches."

Steen sat erect in his chair. "Apaches, Sergeant? You are certain?"

"Yes, sir. Two of them came to the guard. They came up so quietly he didn't know they were there until they were standing in front of him. Said they seemed to come up out of the ground. They said they had some chief with them back in the woods and that he wanted to see the chief of the soldiers. They said what his name was but I forget it, sir. They got crazy names."

"Would it be Cochise?" Steen asked softly.

"Yes, sir, that's the name, sir," the soldier said. "I remember it now."

"Cochise," Steen repeated. He rose and buttoned his tunic. "Have him come here immediately with his party. And my compliments to Captain Fitzgerald and tell him to come here at once, in full uniform."

"Begging your pardon, sir, but he won't come here."

"Captain Fitzgerald won't come here? Why not, sergeant?"

"I mean this Indian, sir. He won't come here. The Indian who spoke to the guard could talk a little American and he said the chief of the camp must come out to see him, alone." The sergeant saluted again. "I beg your pardon, sir, but I don't think you ought to do it." Then the sergeant reddened. "Begging your pardon, sir."

"That's all right, Sergeant," Steen said. He sat down again and began to fill his pipe. "Cochise wants me to go out and meet him alone."

"Yes, sir. I think it's a trap, sir."

"Tell Captain Fitzgerald to report here immediately and see that the Indians don't leave."

"Yes, sir."

"Who is Corporal of the Guard?"

34

"Corporal Bernard, sir."

"Tell him to give the sentry who was surprised by the two Indians extra duty. No menial punishment, but extra duty."

"It wasn't really his fault, sir," the sergeant said. "He said they just appeared out of nowhere."

"It's the duty of the sentry to see that no one appears out of nowhere. That's what he's there for."

"Yes, sir."

When Fitzgerald entered the tent Steen said, "Sit down, Fitz. I just received word Cochise is in the valley wanting to see me."

"In the valley?"

"He sent word in that I must go to see him alone."

"Giving you orders?"

"He doesn't trust Americans, Fitz," Steen said, rubbing his face.

"Well, send out word that you don't trust Indians, especially Apache Indians," Fitzgerald said. "He wants to see you," he repeated disgustedly.

"No. I'm going to see him," Steen said.

"Wait a minute," Fitzgerald protested.

"This is the chance I've been waiting for." Steen's blue eyes sparkled.

"You're not going out there, Noch. You won't be a hundred feet from camp when you'll have a dozen arrows sticking into your carcass. I have enough to do without taking command here."

"I'm going." He took his long-barreled revolver and slipped it into his holster.

"I'll go with you."

"No. He said alone. You remain here and take command if anything goes wrong. That's a direct order, Fitz."

"Yes, sir."

"I don't want any tricks. I don't want anybody following me. You're to stay here until I return, or until I'm gone an hour."

"If you return," Fitzgerald said.

"If I don't return make a report immediately and take command until further orders."

"Yes, sir." He paused. "Noch."

"Yes?"

"Watch yourself."

"Sure."

"I told your wife I'd take care of you," Fitzgerald said.

"Sure," Steen said.

He called for his horse and slipped his Wesson rifle into its scabbard. He summoned a Mexican who could speak the Apache language. "Pedro," he said. "I want you to come with me and act as interpreter with some Indians."

"Yes, sir," the Mexican grinned. "But I do not speak Papago so well. Juan speaks it much better."

"Not Papago, Pedro. Apache."

The boy turned pale. "Apache? Where?" He looked around nervously.

"We are going to leave camp to speak with Cochise, chief of the Chiricahua Apaches," Steen said.

Pedro backed away. "Please, sir Major, not Apaches. Please to pick another."

"Get a horse, Pedro," Steen said.

"Apaches do not like Mexicans. They kill Mexicans."

"Get a horse and follow me," Steen said quietly.

When he reached the outpost where the Indians waited, the soldier there saluted. "Corporal Bernard, sir. I sent the guard to detention and ordered him to send a replacement. I'm remaining on duty here until the replacement arrives."

Bernard, a native of Tennessee, a giant of a man who had been something of an object of amusement among the soldiers because of his great clumsiness when he first joined the outfit, had pummeled his way to respect with his sledgehammer fists. Next to him stood an Indian almost as large as he was.

"Very good, Corporal," Steen said. "I thought there were two Indians here."

"One went back to talk to his chief," Bernard said. "Are you going out with him, sir?"

"Yes, Corporal."

"May I accompany you, sir?"

"No."

"If there's any trouble, sir, manage to fire your gun. I'll be right out."

"Thank you, Corporal Bernard," Steen said.

"Pedro," Steen said. "Tell this Indian to take me out to Cochise."

The boy translated with a panic-stricken face. Then the Indian spoke. "He says he is Pionsenay," Pedro said. "He says to follow him."

"Good."

"Please, sir Major," Pedro pleaded. "Please not to go."

Pionsenay turned and started off in the rapid, tireless trot of the Apache warrior. Steen spurred his horse. "Follow me," he said.

After riding for a quarter of a mile with the Indian pacing him easily, Steen reined in his horse when Pionsenay lifted his hand suddenly. The Indian said, "Wait. Cochise will come."

Steen dismounted. He filled his pipe and began to smoke calmly. Pedro stood at his side shaking. Presently there was a slight sound and then a dozen Indians surrounded them. Despite himself Steen started. The Indians seemed to have emerged from the trees. He resolved, if he returned safely, to countermand his order for extra detail for the sentry.

One man stepped forward and Steen marked him instantly for Cochise. Pionsenay said something swiftly.

"He says that this is Cochise," Pedro said. His face was ashen as he looked upon the Indians. Instinctively he moved closer to Steen.

Steen held out his right hand in the sign of peace. Cochise repeated the gesture. Then he studied the face of the American officer.

"I come to talk peace for the Chiricahuas," Cochise said in his quiet, penetrating voice.

"Good. I have waited long to talk to the great chief of the Chiricahuas. I too wish peace."

"Let us talk."

"There is no need to talk in the forest like animals," Steen said quietly. "Come to my camp and there we can smoke and talk in comfort."

When the words were translated Cochise's eyes flickered with quick suspicion and the other men with him immediately began to warn him not to go. "There are many soldiers in the camp," Cochise said. "There are five parties of soldiers away from the camp but there are still many left there."

Steen understood immediately that Cochise was telling him how closely his soldiers had been under surveillance.

"I am here alone," he said. "I came to see Cochise when he stood among his warriors."

Cochise smiled faintly. "I will go to your camp," he said. Again his warriors protested. "I am no less brave than the blackbearded *nantan* of the American soldiers," he said sternly. He looked at Steen. "Your word that my people and I will be safe."

"I give you my word." Steen held out his hand.

Cochise looked puzzled. Then he put out his hand and the men touched fingers.

4

The soldiers gaped as the party rode into camp. Steen and Cochise rode side by side and the Indians followed in single file. Pedro was the last. The sentries called for the password and upon receiving it, came to attention and saluted as Steen rode by. Cochise sat erect and proud and kept his face expressionless. His eyes took in the military precision of the procedure and he approved.

When the party reached headquarters a soldier ran forward to take Steen's horse. "Take the horse of Cochise," Steen ordered instantly. The soldier, bewildered, walked to where Cochise sat stonily on his huge bay. Steen called to Pedro. "Tell Cochise that the soldier will guard his horse well while he is with me."

Upon translation, Cochise leaped lightly from his horse and handed the reins to the soldier. The soldier walked away, still confused, and muttered to himself, "He handed me the reins like a damned general."

Steen gave orders sharply and soldiers relieved the Indians of the rest of their horses. The Indians looked with some suspicion as the horses were led away. As the group walked toward the headquarters Fitzgerald stepped out. He came to rigid attention and saluted as his superior approached. After returning the salute Steen introduced the two men. Fitzgerald held out his hand and again, still puzzled, Cochise touched his fingers. The eyes of the Chiricahua leader moved everywhere. He took in everything, the appearance of the camp, the manner of the soldiers, the manner in which Steen gave orders, the appearance of Fitzgerald. Nothing escaped his attention. Each item was stored in his mind for future discussion with Naretena.

When the men were seated in Steen's office, the major sent an orderly to his tent to bring in a bottle of whiskey and glasses. Cochise, who was scrutinizing everything in the office, hardened when he saw the whiskey bottle. "The Mexicans give this firewater to Apaches," he said. "When they are asleep they kill them."

"I have already given my word," Steen said. "You are free to leave at your pleasure."

"We will not leave," Cochise said. "But the talk must take place with cool heads. It is better to save the firewater for afterwards."

"As you wish," Steen said.

Cochise walked slowly around the room, examining everything. Steen knew enough about the ways of Indians not to attempt to hasten the discussion. Time never was of importance to an Indian. If necessary they would remain and talk all night.

The Indian paused before a large wall map. "What is this picture writing?" he asked Steen.

Steen attempted to explain the use of a map. Pedro fell down from time to time trying to change the English words into a language which had no equivalent for them. When Steen showed Cochise where the Dragoon Mountains and the Chiricahua Mountains were located on the map, the Apache's face again became suspicious and he exchanged a glance with Nahilzay, who by now was at his side.

The appearance of the heartland of the Chiricahua people on the sheet of paper affected the Indians profoundly. It seemed to them that in some way Steen possessed a power over the territory because of his having it drawn on the paper. The military markings on the map were not unlike the cabalistic symbols on the sacred medicine shirts of the shamans and the Indians knew that these markings on those shirts gave the shamans power over the elements.

Steen, fearing that the whole conference might be thrown off because of this unexpected obstacle, tried valiantly to explain what the map actually was. But the Indians remained far more impressed and fearful of this mysterious document than they had been by the soldiers and other signs of purely military nature in the camp. Cochise, whose superstition was, like all his other qualities, developed to a greater degree than most men, interpreted the map as another sign of American power and reaffirmed in his mind the necessity of coming to terms with these strange new people.

Steen, in his turn, began to understand in a little while what effect the innocent markings on the wall were having on the Indians, and he shrewdly stopped explaining and permitted the Apaches to remain impressed.

After studying the map for some time, Cochise asked Steen, "Is the method of preparing these things a secret?"

"It requires instruction," Steen said.

"Could one learn?"

"With proper instruction," Steen said.

"Might the land of our enemies be placed on such a paper for us?"

"It might be," Steen said, "if the Chiricahua people and the Americans were brothers."

Cochise sat down and when the others also were seated he said, "I come for peace. The Chiricahuas never regarded the Americans as enemies, only Mexicians. Still there is bad blood and there is fighting. I come to put an end to that fighting and to say the Chiricahuas and the Americans should live as brothers."

Steen nodded gravely.

"The Americans know many things. I want the Apaches to learn of these things. A tree must change with the seasons. In return for this learning I come to offer our mountains and our valleys and our rivers and the yellow and white iron that Americans and Mexicans value. The Americans raise cattle and sheep. The Chiricahuas will protect them. The country of the Chiricahuas will be peaceful and quiet."

When Pedro translated, Steen replied, "The Americans do not wish to take from the Chiricahuas their mountains and valleys. There is enough room here for both peoples. The Americans who come for silver and gold will not intrude on the hunting lands of the Apaches. The Americans want to live at peace with the Apaches. The Americans come with many things, with clothing and food and horses and cattle, and they want to trade with the Apaches just as they trade among themselves."

"*Enju*," Cochise said.

"The Americans will come in increasing numbers. They will build homes and roads in the mountains."

Cochise rose and walked over to the map. He studied it keenly for a few moments, and then, in a grasp of its significance that startled Steen, he moved his hand over the Chiricahua country, and said, "My people live here. This is Chiricahua land. I have no control over here, where the sun rises, nor here, where the sun sets, nor here, in the north, nor in Mexico. This Chiricahua country I control and my people will not war upon their American brothers. And my people will see that bad Indians do not come into Chiricahua country and make war."

"Your words warm my heart," Steen said. "It is planned before long to establish a stage line across all of the west and part of that line will pass through the Chiricahua country, through what is called Apache Pass. It makes me happy to be able to inform my government that the great Chiricahua chief will be at peace with us. The government of the United States also desires to establish a trading post in Apache Pass. This store will have clothing and food and other things to trade with the Chiricahuas."

"The wagons and the store may come into Chiricahua country," Cochise said with great dignity. "Apache Pass lies between the Chiricahuas and the Dos Cabezas. Chiricahua warriors will guard the pass and see that the men who work there and who travel through do so in peace and safety."

"I will notify the official Indian Agent for the Chiricahua Apaches of our agreement," Steen said. "He is located many miles from here, but he will be happy to hear the good news."

"Agent for Chiricahuas?" Cochise asked. He laughed contemptuously. "I have never accepted any Agent."

"That is true," Steen said evenly. "But the *nantan* in the East regards the Chiricahuas as his children, as he does with all Indians, and although the Chief of the Chiricahuas has never talked with the Indian Agent at Fort Stanton, still he is there and wishes to be your friend."

Cochise thought for a long while. Nahilzay, who had none of Cochise's calm, and who had sat through the entire discussion in a nervous tension, starting at each sound, muttered something to Cochise and the leader nodded. "I do not know this Indian Agent," he said finally. "He may be the Agent for your government but he is not Agent for the Chiricahuas. He may be a good man or he may be a bad man. Indian Agents are not always to be trusted and many Indians who have given themselves in trust have come to sorrow. I know nothing about this Indian Agent who has been appointed for the Chiricahuas and I make no promises to him. It is to you, *Nantan* Steen, to whom I give my word and to you I will hold myself and my people responsible."

"It is as you wish," Steen said with respect.

"There is something else," Cochise continued. "I do not speak with two tongues and I keep nothing hidden in my mind. This peace that I make for myself and my people is made only with the Americans. We still are at war with Mexico."

Steen pursed his lips and looked at Fitzgerald. "I was afraid that the Chiricahua chief would feel that way," he said. "My country is at peace with Mexico."

"It is no matter to me with whom your country is at peace," Cochise retorted proudly. "That is the right of your country, to make war or to make peace. But the Apaches were at war with the Mexicans long before the Americans came to this country and will continue to be so. Your people have come to our country and have traded back and forth with the Mexicans and have exchanged land which never belonged to you. You have done this because you are strong. Apaches understand this. We have done things because we were stronger than the ones we did them to. The Chiricahuas do not say, get out of this country where you do not belong. But they do say, our old enemies remain our old enemies. I ask no treaties which include Mexicans. Mexicans still collect gold for Apache scalps from their government. Are these the people you would have me call brothers?"

As he spoke, his voice getting bitter and harsh, Nahilzay began to tremble. When he finished, Cochise raised his eyes to his lieutenant and presently Nahilzay became calmer.

Again Steen looked at Fitzgerald. The captain shrugged his shoulders imperceptibly. "You speak honestly to me," Steen said at last. "I speak the same to you. When my government made a peace treaty with Mexico it was agreed that we would try to prevent Indians from raiding below the border. My country also pledged itself to prevent Americans from buying goods taken by Indians from Mexicans. My country also pledged itself to return all captive Mexican women and children to their homes. I tell you this so that you know how my duty lies because I am bound in honor to obey the orders of my government."

"I like the sound of your words," Cochise said. "It is always possible to keep a pledge when those who make it know in advance all the parts of the pledge. My people will see that you do not have cause to quarrel with them."

"What you don't know won't hurt you," Fitzgerald said philosophically in English. "That's not to be translated, Pedro."

"Let us now have our drink to brotherhood," Steen said.

Later the men left the tent. Steen called an orderly and told him to bring food, clothing, and tobacco to give to the Indians. Then he called for his quartermaster and asked for some blankets. When all the gifts were handed out, Steen said, "Accept these things as a present from my government as a token of our friendship."

Cochise took the reins of his horse and pulled the beautiful animal close to him. He rubbed his neck tenderly and then he handed the reins to Steen. "He will carry you always in safety," he said. He said something rapidly to Nahilzay, and that brave, with somewhat less grace, gave his horse to Fitzgerald. Then Cochise gravely handed Steen his lance and his bow and quiver filled with arrows. "Whenever we meet the American *nantan* needs no more weapons than I have on me now," he said.

Chapter Four

In the fall of 1856 and through the early months of 1857 Americans poured into the Southwest. There they found endless miles of grazing land, acres of fertile soil, almost perpetual sunshine and warmth in the lowlands, mountains filled with silver and some gold. They found themselves in an untouched wonderland, a place of almost monstrous beauty. Some of the pioneers were persons who started out originally for the even more fabulous El Dorado of California and who stopped traveling when they found themselves in the Santa Cruz Valley or viewed the Sonoita. They seemed to have found a new world for themselves, where mountains were like no mountains they had ever seen, hard and rocky and bare, their boulders visible for incredible miles, where the vegetation seemed to belong to some remote earth, where the desert was a desert, and then suddenly not a desert, and then as suddenly a desert again, where there was no rain and then torrential rain and then no rain again, where their world was larger than any world they had ever lived in.

With this great influx of pioneers who were spreading their country westward, came another great class of immigrants who were not farmers or ranchers or miners. After the initial exodus of the bad men from Tucson at the time of the military occupation, swarms of renegades descended into the country, finding there the last refuge from law and order, the final frontier. From California and from Texas and from the East and from Mexico they came, Americans and Mexicans who were outlaws wherever civilization was in control. The great

42

Vigilance Committee of San Francisco, it was said, did more to populate the territory than did the silver mines. Tucson became their headquarters and soon quartered more vice, more crime, than any other place on the continent. The sleepy mud city of the Mexicans became a haven for the murderers, bandits, and gamblers who could find no rest elsewhere. Saloons and gambling halls and brothels were more numerous than any other kind of enterprise. Men walked around bristling with guns, and shootings took place daily in the narrow sun-baked streets. An early historian wrote that "Arizona was perhaps the only part of the world under the protecting aegis of civilized government in which every man administered justice to suit himself, and where all assumed the right to gratify the basest passions of their nature without restraint. It was literally a paradise of devils."

The pioneers came in hordes from the East and Middle West in those months, fifty thousand and more strong, an endless, slow-moving ant-train of hopefuls, looking toward the won-derland of the West, the gold in California, the miracle land on the Pacific, the dreamy end of the rainbow, to most of whom the sprawling empty New Mexico territory was only something to cross, to hurry through, to get into and out of as quickly as possible, the last final obstacle and challenge and toll of nature before the spill into the Promised Land beyond.

They crossed the Rio Grande on their southern route and from the river, which was to them the precipice for the plunge, stretched the endless grassy Mesilla Valley, where many of them tarried and then settled, a mesa that lay between the Mogollons and the towering distant peaks of the Sierra Madres, the Mother Mountains, in northern Mexico. There were the valleys of the Mimbres and the Animas and the Antelope. They crossed a high, blinding plateau where their eyes made out distant mountains that took days to reach, and they came to the Peloncillos, where later the boundary line between New Mexico and Arizona was drawn, and through passes in the Peloncillos they descended into the San Simon Valley, moving from cold to hot, from winter to summer, from thin altitude to almost oppressive depths, always the extremes, crossing the beetling hills at both ends of the Chiricahuas, dressed in pine, until they entered the sweeping, endless Sulphur Spring Valley.

To reach the valley they traveled through Apache Pass, be-tween the northern part of the Chiricahuas and the southern part of the Dos Cabezas, the ten-mile channel, with its narrow, resentful walls, its scattered canyons, its gigantic rocks and falling stones, the whole pass so high as almost to be a peak. Then the descent and the forty-mile journey over level plains fringed with distant hills to Dragoon Springs at the northern slope of Dragoon Summit in the heart of Chiricahua country, with the blade-like peaks of the Chiricahuas to their south and the rugged Galiuros on the north.

Their path then led through deep gullies and dried-out water runs, through miles of mesquite, until they finally came to the San Pedro. The trail wandered through the valley, and everywhere there was the giant cactus, the sahuaro, looking like strange creatures immobilized forever in tortured positions. By now the travelers were in constant torments of fear; all throughout their route they had seen the bleached bones, faded crosses, marking the violent finish to the hopes of pioneers who had come before them. Their path was marked with bones, as though the whitened skeletons were their guides. Fear was their permanent mood. In the twilight the country might have been a section of the moon, with the unearthly, convulsive cactus scattered like sentries. The Spanish dagger spiked the horizon and it was only when they came close, and when the season was right, that the bewildered travelers saw the unexpected blossoms bursting from their metallic stems. Above all this, their sharp untreed outlines giving them personality and distinction in the thin air, the rocky edges of the hills looked down, and in every strange outline the pioneer was certain he saw a waiting Indian.

Beyond the San Pedro the trail crossed the low divide that severed the San Pedro and the valley of the Santa Cruz. There was the Cienega Creek, its bed covered with salt grass, and then the steady climb to the rolling hills of the Rincons, through the foothills of these mountains, and then the final emergence into the Santa Cruz, where lay the ancient mud city, Tucson. And though the sight of the pueblo was a welcome one, and it meant the end of travel and fear and danger, of horror at the Indian smoke signals; although it meant a temporary rest, a time for nights of sleep without fear, yet the scrawny mud city was always an anticlimax, a pitiful upthrust of human endeavor, the most that man could show for hundreds of years of trying, completely minimized by the extravagance of nature all around it.

The trail through the unknown country was more than a physical journey. It was a spiritual adventure. The conclusion of it, if the Indian permitted a successful conclusion, was like a rebirth. Men never were the same when they ended that journey. Whatever they had within them had been strained and drawn to its uttermost. Some things had been killed and others born within them, and they were different men. They spoke differently and there was a different look in their eyes and whatever they did or said henceforth was colored and shaped by their experience.

In the early part of 1857 the first American military establishment was completed in the Sonoita and the Ist Dragoons under Major Steen took possession of their new headquarters, which was called Camp Buchanan after the newly elected President of the United States. And to this remote, almost foreign outpost of the military there almost immediately reached the planning hand of politics. From the very start, an inordinate amount of supplies and equipment was sent by orders from Washington to this minuscule fortress. In later years it was said that this inundation of equipment, far in excess of anything the military garrison there needed, was part of the planning for the Civil War seen to be inevitable by many persons from the South who were in important positions in Congress. Buchanan had a number of violent Secessionists in his Cabinet, and it was they who organized the flow of materiel to the post, it was said, planning for the camp to be a depot for a Confederate Column which was to march from Texas and take possession of the silver mines of Arizona and the gold fields of California.

This Camp Buchanan was the sole fort in the area, apart from a small detachment stationed in Tucson. Its location in the Sonoita was an added attraction to the settlers who feared Indian depredation, and the Sonoita became the favorite settlement for ranchers and farmers. There was warfare to the east where Mangas Coloradas ruled, and fighting to the west, near the Colorado River. The Pinal Apaches, and the Tontos and Coyoteros, were unfriendly and made sporadic attacks on the Americans, but in the land of Cochise there was peace.

2

Cochise removed his tribe from their most permanent rancherias in the Dragoon Mountains across the broad Sulphur Spring Valley to the slopes of the Chiricahua Mountains and settled them close to the vitally important springs which made Apache Pass so strategic a place. In the desert country trails were cut from water hole to water hole and from the moment a traveler started out on his day's journey his one thought and hope was that he could reach water before nightfall, or before his supply gave out. The ugly, frightening stretch of Apache Pass was granted, by some whimsical freak of nature, a supply of constant water, and as much as travelers loathed to surrender themselves to the terror of the pass itself, the water made that a necessity.

The Chiricahua Mountains were the traditional home of the Chiricahua Apaches. There Cochise was born, and his father before him. The Strongholds, forty miles to the west across the valley, were the fortresses of the tribe, the impregnable, natural rocky havens where the Chiricahuas could repair after battle, where a few warriors, placed at the narrow entrances, could hold off any number of their enemy indefinitely, where videttes, placed at high posts, could command views of a day's march away and have ample time to warn the people of danger. The Strongholds made perfect places for the Chiricahuas to leave their women and children under the care of a few warriors while the bulk of the men went off on raids, secure in the knowledge that their families would be safe in their absence.

Cochise, planning ahead, hoped never again to have to use the Strongholds for defensive purposes. There were religious ceremonies which had, by tradition, to take place there, since the Chiricahuas felt closer to the Great Spirit, and to White Painted Lady, and to her son, conceived immaculately, Child of the Water, in the contained isolation of the Strongholds. But for these ceremonies, he reasoned, the tribe could journey across the valley, and for their normal life could prosper on the warm, lovely slopes of the Chiricahuas.

The progress of the new peaceful life of the tribe was received in various ways by the Apaches. The older people, and most of the women, took to the new life gratefully. The women built their new wickiups with care and effort hitherto unexpended on what had always been regarded as temporary dwellings, since now, according to the plans, they would not have to pack and move on sudden notice. The women, who did all the domestic work among the Apaches, now applied themselves with greater industry than ever before. Hides were tanned and made into soft buckskin; moccasins were sewn, as were leather bags for storing supplies. A few of the women, who had the knowledge from their parents, wove intricate baskets, made simple clay pottery and water gourds.

The warriors, however, did not take gracefully to their new unemployment. From childhood the Apache male was trained in nothing but the hunt and the raid; his entire education was concentrated on those two pursuits. Now many of them grew indolent; they fretted and drank and spent their sober hours manufacturing bows and arrows and lances, the only handiwork of which they were capable. They gambled more than ever, spending hours at the hoop and pole game, and, at night, during the winter which is the only time it may be played, at the moccasin game. There were still organized raids into Mexico, but since these were so skillfully planned by Cochise that there was no need to repeat them too often, there was much leisure time, and this time, by order of Cochise, could not be spent wandering in the hills and on the plains in search of a victim here or there.

Reports of the discontent of the young braves were brought

46

to Cochise by Nahilzay. Cochise, when he listened, replied, "It does not worry me. These men are young and filled with fire. An eagle does not change his nature overnight. These men still are too close to the old days. They will soon forget.

"They hear stories all around them about the great success the men of Mangas Coloradas are having. Even the Tontos, the fools, make successful attacks.

"On the sides of some of these mountains there are the marks of picture writing," Cochise said. "There are caves in the hills which show that an ancient people lived in them. That ancient people has vanished. Why? Because they could not adapt themselves to changing times. They continued to live in their traditional way, although all around them there was change. The Chiricahua people will not die off that way."

Nahilzay nodded. "These are deep thoughts. They are beyond my understanding and beyond the understanding of the men out there. It goes as you wish, now, only because you have ordered it so. No one pretends to understand why. But food is not increasing. The animals are fleeing from the Americans. The herds no longer come to their old places."

"Then we will seek them out in new places," Cochise said. "Gather the warriors. They grow fat from laziness. Organize a hunt. A big hunt. See that the hunt is long and difficult. Let the men rid themselves of their energy. Only one thing: be sure it is to the north."

"Why north?"

"Mexico is south."

"I do not understand."

"Then listen to me. I have made peace with the Americans. One day perhaps there will be peace with the Mexicans."

"Peace with the Mexicans?" Nahilzay asked, aghast.

"Yes. We have the friendship of the Americans now, even though they know we continue to raid in Mexico. The American *nantan* has to accept that because he is not strong enough to do otherwise. But that will not last forever. The Americans come in great numbers. Soon there will be enough of them to insist that we obey all—all—the American laws. When that time comes the Chiricahua people will be out of the habit of going to Mexico, maybe."

"We might find food enough if we go north," Nahilzay said slyly. "But there is no clothing to the north. There are no weapons. There are no horses or mules or sheep."

"We will get those things from the Americans, maybe."

"How?"

"As the Americans get them from each other, by buying them."

"With what?"

47

"There are different ways. We can find the white iron the Americans value. We can work. We can raise cattle as the Americans do."

"Raise cattle," Nahilzay said with disgust.

"The Americans do not look upon the raising of cattle with disrespect. There is another way, more to your liking, maybe. Wagons will soon come through our country. We have promised to protect these wagons from bad Indians. The Americans will give presents for that."

Nahilzay snorted. "It is nowhere thought among Apaches that they will be grandmothers to cattle and Americans. The warriors will refuse."

"The warriors will not refuse to do anything I order them to do," Cochise said very quietly.

Nahilzay pondered over this and then he outstretched his arm and placed his hand upon the shoulder of his leader. He said gravely, "No matter what path you lead, I follow. If it is my life that is needed, it is yours too. But among us no man is forever leader unless the people wish it so. Apaches have rights as they have always had them. If it is decided by them that some devil is twisting your mind so that you are no longer fit to lead them they will choose another leader."

"Listen to me," Cochise said, fixing his eyes upon Nahilzay. "I speak to you because you are the closest to me of my warriors. I have two sons, but you are the son who has fought by my side. I do not do these things because I have come to think of them suddenly. It is as though these decisions have been made for me and that I but follow them." His voice burned. "I receive advice. Can you understand me? It is put into my heart by one who knows of these things. My people will listen to me. If we do not alter our ways it may be close to the end of our time. Do not ask me how I know this. Believe that I know. It is written on my heart until it is as plain to me as a tree or a mountain or this hand that I hold out. It is my mission to do this and I shall live long enough to accomplish this mission and no longer."

Nahilzay turned pale at this voluntary mention of death. "It is better not to speak so before the others," he said at last.

"I speak to you."

"Keep it between us."

There was a hidden tone in his voice and Cochise focused his eyes on him and asked, "What are you saying?"

"Gokliya spreads word that you have been bewitched."

Cochise recoiled as though he had been struck in the face. "Bewitched," he repeated.

Nahilzay spat. "May a coyote eat him!"

Cochise began to tremble with rage. Apache belief held that there were condemned men who were corrupted by dark forces and who lost control of their senses to these forces; they spoke and appeared to be the same as other men, but they were doomed. To accuse another man of being bewitched was to charge his subjugation by these forces.

"Bring Gokliya here," Cochise said.

"He is in Mexico. He has twenty warriors who call him leader."

"Bring him here," Cochise repeated. He now was in control of himself and his voice was again quiet.

"If he refuses to come?"

"There are men here who seek a warpath," Cochise said.

"If he still refuses?"

"Give him safety. I will do him no harm."

When Nahilzay departed, Cochise sought Nochalo and ordered a ceremony performed to exorcise the evil spirits convoked by Gokliya's accusation.

Cochise had two wives. Tesalbestinay, the elder, the sister of Mangas Coloradas, was the mother of his elder son, Tahzay, who was then just past ten years. Tesalbestinay had given Cochise, originally, three children. The eldest was killed in the Sonora Mountains in Mexico many years before by a party of Mexicans who called some of the Chiricahuas into their camp, pretended to offer goods in exchange, and then, after getting the Apaches drunk, had murdered them. The second child was Tahzay, who had grown to be a quiet, thoughtful youth, on whom Cochise's great hope for succession rested. The third child, a daughter, died soon after she was born, of children's illness. Her birth was a difficult one, and after that Tesalbestinay was unable to carry a child again.

She was a year or two younger than Cochise, but because of the hard life of the Apache women, she looked older than he. Her beauty was long gone. Her face was now almost haggard. Her eyes alone, big and luminous, were still beautiful, and Cochise had for her a deep affection and a profound respect. Her years had given her wisdom and she was not unlike her brother in the value of her counsel. She had long ceased to be a wife to Cochise and now had assumed the stature almost of an older sister. Next to Naretena there was no person in the tribe with whom Cochise would rather discuss his thoughts; he accorded her a respect in that field that was alien to all Apache philosophy. All Apache wives harangued their husbands, and many of them were far wiser than their husbands, but, while the Apache warriors often unconsciously were guided by their wives, they made it a point of male honor never to let themselves believe so.

The name, Tesalbestinay, meant She Sticks to her Cradle, and it was a childhood name, which, contrary to Apache custom, had lasted through her mature years. It was given to her in affection by her mother because from earliest girlhood she had shown a great love of dolls and as she grew older she showed deep affection for children and it was foretold that she would make a good mother.

The younger wife of Cochise, a girl not much beyond her twentieth year, was called Nalikadeya, which meant Maiden who Walks along a Ridge, from her habit, after her puberty rites, to take long walks by herself and from her dreamy love of nature and the living things around her. She was the daughter of an old battle-companion of Cochise's father. Her mother was dead and her father was regarded as an elder statesman in the tribe.

She was the mother of Cochise's younger son, Nachise, who was then just two years old.

Among the Apaches names were given to persons a long time after they were born, when they started to demonstrate characteristics which would make their name appropriate. There was no difference between male and female names, except that there was a slight tendency to name girls after flowers. Generally, however, one would not know, from a name, whether the person referred to was man or woman. As children grew older the first name, given to them when they were ten or twelve, usually was replaced by another name, indicating either their adult character, or commemorating some striking event in their lives.

The name Cochise was pure Apache. Chise, in Apache, meant wood, and was the name given to the future Chiricahua leader when he was a boy. Later when the boy began to demonstrate the qualities of firmness and strength that characterized him throughout his life, the prefix Co was added to the name, changing the meaning from wood to hickory wood. Nachise in similar manner meant oak wood. Tahzay meant raccoon and originally was given to the boy by his mother as an affection-name.

Tesalbestinay and the two boys shared one of the wickiups. Cochise lived in the other domed hut with Nalikadeya. The cooking and other household work were done jointly by the two women and since each of them occupied her own unchallenged position in the family life there was no hard feeling between them. Of the two Tesalbestinay was, perhaps, the less disturbed. She no longer had anything to be jealous of. She knew her position in Cochise's life would never alter again. The younger woman still had bursts of wild jealousy and sometimes had violent quarrels with her husband, already accusing him of casting about his eyes for a third wife. On these occasions Cochise might, if he were too filled with tiswin, beat her

50

into silence; more usually he merely moved into the other wickiup until Nalikadeya quieted down.

The women were at work as Cochise approached. Tesalbestinay was busy scraping flesh from deer hide to prepare it for tanning. Nalikadeya, a comely, well-shaped young woman, was stirring the fire under the mutton being roasted for the family. There were no regular eating hours in Apache families. Food of one kind or another was always kept in readiness for whenever any member of the family became hungry.

As he approached his dwellings he paused for a moment to look upon Nachise, grubbing in the ground at his mother's feet. As he stood there, gazing fondly at the child, Tahzay burst into view. The boy was sturdy and well-formed. His body was straight and strong and his chest already was barreling out from his constant training. Within a few years Tahzay would enter upon his novitiate and start the four raids as an apprentice, after which he could take his place as a warrior among the Chiricahuas. Already he was an expert with his small child's bow and arrow. With the other children in the tribe he worked endlessly to develop his body and to perfect himself in the use of weapons for the hunt and the raid. It would not be too long, Cochise thought, before Tahzay would take his place with the braves who could run seventy-five miles a day through the hard, cactus- and mesquite-laden country, up and down mountains and canyons, with a tirelessness that was the despair of the Mexicans and Americans who tried to follow them.

"Today?" Cochise asked.

"A race."

"Win it."

Tahzay looked at his father adoringly. "After that contests."

"I will be there," Cochise replied.

The boy's face sparkled with pleasure. "I will try to win the race," he said.

Cochise put his arm around him. "You must be strong, my son," he said. "You have only yourself to look to in this world. You may have many friends but when the important time comes only your legs and your brain and your eyes and your ears and your muscles are your friends. When you get into trouble do not look around and do not call upon anyone to help you. Look to yourself and if you have prepared yourself properly you need look no further."

Tahzay nodded gravely.

"Someday you will be the leader of the Chiricahuas," Cochise continued. "There will be many changes. Keep your eyes open and watch the changes and understand them and if you do not understand them come to me and ask me. You will

51

find enemies everywhere and you will thank the enemies who are honest enough to say they are enemies. The worst enemies are those who say they are friends. Trust no friend until your eye is clear enough to recognize friendship and your ear is keen enough to know when a man speaks with a forked tongue. When you have found a true friend, value him. He is worth more than your horse and your arrow. A true friend comes sometimes just once in a man's life. He is like a right arm. If he is lost he cannot be replaced. Remember all this and think about it.

"When you are a man, it may be that your people will live in peace," Cochise went on. "I am working for this. But maybe it will not be that way. No matter how it is you must be prepared and you must be a leader and make everyone listen to you. Remember you are fit to lead your people only as long as you remember that everything you do must be for their good. No matter what you think, it is the good of the people who call you leader that is most important." Cochise smiled affectionately. "Go to your race," he said.

The boy scurried off.

Tesalbestinay listened quietly as Cochise spoke to their child. Nalikadeya held her face averted. Cochise then picked up the baby, Nachise, and held him out straight in one hand and laughed at him. "This one soon will be in contests," he said. "His legs feel now as strong as oak branches." Nalikadeya flushed at the compliment. "His brother will need him as a strong right arm," Cochise said. He looked at the two women. "I have been lucky," he said quietly.

Polygamy seldom caused friction in an Apache household. It was normal for several reasons. The chief reason was that the warlike activities of the men always kept the male population substantially smaller than the female. Also for religious reasons Apache men never cohabited with their wives from the time they first became pregnant until they weaned their children, and since Apache women nursed their babies until they were at least two years old, the period lasted almost three years. The lengthy nursing was the result of a belief that this was necessary to give a child security.

"Food?" Nalikadeya asked.

"After the contests."

Cochise squatted next to Tesalbestinay and watched her working. After a while he asked, "Is it well with you?"

"Yes."

"What do the other women say?"

"They say their men will live longer, maybe."

"And they approve of that?" Cochise asked with a straight face.

52

Tesalbestinay broke into a faint smile that seemed to give beauty to her face. "There are too few men now," she said.

"There may be more when children grow up."

He got up. He looked steadily at her.

"It goes well," she said.

3

The contests were held in a small canyon. When Cochise arrived eight boys were standing in a line. Pionsenay was talking to them in his slow, drawling voice. In his hand he held a small gourd of water.

"Each of you take a mouthful," he said. "But do not swallow it. Hold it in your mouths. You are going to run four miles with this water in your mouths."

The eight boys, dwarfed by his bulk, nodded eagerly. They took the water in their mouths, and then at a signal from Pionsenay they started out trotting. Tahzay, his head erect, did not look at his father as he ran past, graceful as a young deer. Pionsenay ran behind the boys to see that they did not rest on the way. His brother, Skinyea, called out derisively, "Try to keep up with them, old cow."

Pionsenay grunted. "Come along, little one," he said. "I'll carry you on my shoulder."

When the boys returned they again lined up, and then, as Pionsenay walked from one to the other, they spat the water on the ground. All the boys but one had held the water in their mouths without swallowing it.

"What happened to you?" Pionsenay demanded sternly of the unfortunate one.

"I stumbled and swallowed the water," he said miserably.

"Your wickiup."

The boy turned away without a word. His father, sitting among the other men, rose and followed him silently. He was much ashamed.

A warrior named Machogee glanced at Cochise. He moved his finger idly on the ground. "I have a fine son," he said casually. "He is hard to beat."

"I have a good boy," Cochise said indifferently. "Bring your boy in."

"He is here."

"Good. My boy is here."

The challenge made and accepted, the son of Machogee and Tahzay faced each other and began to wrestle. They wrapped their wiry arms around each other and struggled for a hold. The other men and boys squatted and watched them silently.

"I have a paint horse," Machogee said.

53

"My black one," Cochise said.

Other bets were made quickly as the boys labored. The son of Machogee suddenly grabbed Tahzay's wrist and twisted his arm around his back and began to exert a pressure upward. Tahzay fought to get away but the other boy continued to force the arm upward. Tahzay bit his lips. The other boy raised the arm another degree and Tahzay's face contorted in pain as he strove to keep himself from crying "Enough." The men watched stolidly. The boy kept up the leverage until Tahzay felt that his arm would break. Then, quickly, he managed to twist around and caught the other boy under his leg with his free arm and threw him down, causing him to release his grip. Before the son of Machogee could recover Tahzay was on top of him, his knee digging into his groin, his arms pinning the other boy's shoulders to the ground. Then Tahzay moved swiftly and got a headlock on the other boy and wrapped his legs around his waist and began to squeeze. The boy's face filled with blood and his eyes began to bulge.

The men watching made no move.

Tahzay continued to apply pressure. The other boy suddenly relaxed but he still did not cry quits. Tahzay squeezed still harder and then the boy fainted and his head rolled loosely on his shoulders. Tahzay rose and Poinsenay threw some water on the other boy's face.

"It was brave," Cochise said. "He did not give up."

"Yes," Machogee said. "I will bring the horse."

"No," Cochise said. "He did not give up." The bets were all canceled.

Now Pionsenay gave slings to the boys. Machogee's son, recovered, took his place again. Pionsenay led the boys to a flat place where there were many small round stones on the ground. "All right," Pionsenay said. "Four boys on one side, four on the other. This is going to make you quick."

The boys separated to a distance of about twenty-five feet and then, at a signal, picked up the stones, fitted them into the slings, and hurled the stones at each other. The boys had to hurl the stones and try to dodge the stones thrown at them. The stones were not light and were expertly thrown. One of the stones struck a boy in the eye. Blood streamed down his face. The boy did not stop, but, with one eye blinded, continued to hurl and dodge stones. The son of Machogee, still a little confused from his wrestling, was not as quick as he might have been and a stone struck him on the wrist, breaking it. He tried to continue to pick up stones and throw them but the pain was too great and he dropped out of the contest without a word and walked away. Machogee followed him.

The contests continued all afternoon. After the sling practice the boys took small bows and arrows and shot at each other.

Then there was a foot race to a point four hundred yards away and back.

Tahzay, who had come in third in the water-carrying race, won the foot race. He and the boy who came in second then were given a privilege. They picked up two switches. The race was held again and this time Tahzay and the other boy ran behind the runners and whipped the slow boys across their ankles.

4

Eight times the sun rose and set before Nahilzay returned to the rancheria with Gokliya and his warriors. Most of the followers of Gokliya were strangers to the Chiricahuas. They were for the most part men discontented with the leadership in their own tribes who had abandoned their own people and formed a new unit under Gokliya.

Gokliya entered the rancheria with a great show of boldness that he did not altogether feel. He was in full war paint, which was in bad taste because he had come to the camp by invitation and with a guarantee of safe conduct. He rode in on a beautiful gray, stolen in Mexico a few days earlier. He carried a Mexican military carbine slung across his shoulders and his quiver was filled with arrows.

He dismounted and walked haughtily to Cochise.

"This man walks well armed," Cochise said dryly.

"This country is said to be unkind to strangers," Gokliya retorted.

"There is no need for you to be stranger here," Cochise said with some mildness. "You grew to manhood here and every rock knows you."

"This place is strange to me," Gokliya replied. "I recognize nothing here, neither the rocks nor the people living here."

"Eyes may become clouded."

"My eyes are clear," Gokliya said angrily. "A cloud has descended and now covers the vision of some people."

"I have given you safe conduct," Cochise said softly. "Speak freely."

"Safe conduct," Gokliya sneered.

Cochise retained control of himself and when he spoke it was still in a quiet, mild voice. "There does not live on this earth today any man who has insulted me." He lifted his head and let his eyes fall full upon the face of Gokliya and although the eyes of the Chiricahua chief were calm and unangry soon Gokliya dropped his own eyes and shifted uneasily.

"There was no intent to insult," Gokliya said, hating himself for speaking so before his own followers.

"It is said that there is a new name by which men call you," Cochise continued.

"Yes," Gokliya said, smiling proudly.

"It is Geronimo?"

"Yes."

"It is a name bestowed upon you by the Mexicans in whose country you now make your home?" Cochise asked. His words were not emphasized but for some reason Gokliya flushed.

"There are many whose names are given by Mexicans," Gokliya said.

"That is true. And since the Mexicans are a wise and brave people the names they award are wise and brave and are given to warriors who prefer them to their own Apache names."

Gokliya looked around him in discomfort. He felt he was losing face before his own men and he didn't know how to stop it. "You did not summon me here to discuss my name," he said.

"No," Cochise said. "You are right. There are other things to say." He looked calmly at Gokliya and continued, "I have heard that there are certain words you have applied to me. I do not like those words."

"Man speaks many words," Gokliya said.

"You know the words I mean," Cochise said, without raising his voice. "While you have cut yourself off from your people you have not so quickly forgotten the ways of your people. Among us words have meaning. Among us there is no jesting about things not of this earth and only to be dealt with by the holy shamans. I do not repeat the words you have cast against me because it might be that some men here might not accept them."

Gokliya looked nervously at the Chiricahua warriors who were listening. He moved back slightly until he was closer to his own men.

Cochise stood up and seemed to fill out until he was larger than himself. He threw back his shoulders and his face, up to now pleasant and relaxed, grew stern. "Do you have any of those words left within you to repeat here and now?" he asked.

"I am in your camp," Gokliya said, shifting uneasily, "among your warriors."

"My warriors keep silent. I speak to you just as one person to another, with just the two of us standing here. Do you have any of those words left?"

"No," Gokliya said.

"Then listen. You grew up here among us. Then you walked away. This is my country. All around here is my country, these mountains and these valleys and the stones and grass and the air. All these are mine. Keep out of this country. You have

56

come here tonight in war paint. Do you want to war with me?"

"No."

"Then we are not enemies. If you wish to alter your ways and come back among us you may do so. But until then you will stay out of my country. From now on your presence in my country will say that you want war, unless it is that you are decided to return to your people. From now on I order the death of you and of your men if you appear in my country."

"It is well," Gokliya said, fighting his rage. He felt as though he was being lectured to as a small boy.

"Go now in peace," Cochise said. "Do as you will elsewhere. Except for one thing: you will never again speak the words you have already spoken about me. It is understood?"

"Yes."

"It will come back to me. Do not think that words can be spoken and forgotten. Words have wings and they will fly to me. And the day that they come to me I will swear an oath for your death no matter where you hide yourself."

"They will not be spoken," Gokliya said.

"Go then and take your braves with you."

Gokliya hesitated. The words had been as lashes. He felt he had to say something to reinstate himself with his men.

"Is there anything else you wish to say?" Cochise asked politely.

Gokliya remained silent.

"Is there any challenge you wish to make to me, personally and alone?" Cochise asked.

Gokliya remained silent and then suddenly he raised his head and gave a terrible, agonized scream. He held his clenched hands against his sides and tears of rage fell upon his cheeks. He ran quickly to his horse and mounted and then hysterically kicked the sides of his horse and galloped out of the camp. His warriors watched him and half of them followed him slowly. The remainder came to Cochise and one of them said, "We walk with you."

Chapter Five

A tall, spare, red-bearded man stood leaning against the bar in a saloon in Mesilla, the New Mexican gateway to the new lands to the west. He held his arm around a girl. His other arm rested lightly on the bar, his fingers caressing a small glass of whiskey. He leaned his slim waist against the bar so that the hand fondling the whiskey glass was close to the revolver that hung on his hip.

The bartender, a short, pale man, watched him anxiously. The bartender looked at him and then at the girl and then at another man standing at the bar a few feet away. "Let's have no trouble," the bartender said. "How about it, fellows? Let's have no trouble. Let's all have a drink. The drinks are on the house."

The red-bearded man pushed the girl behind him and started to light a long cheroot. He kept his eyes on the other man. His eyes were a deep sapphire and they looked even bluer against the red beard. They were deeply set on either side of a strong straight nose that ended over lips that were too thick for meanness and too narrow for sensuality. The lips looked pale surrounded by the beard.

He held a match in front of the cigar until it had a fine cherry point and then he flicked the match away. "You heard the man," he said mildly. "Have a free drink."

"Let's have no trouble, Cap," the bartender said to the man with the red beard. He moved down the counter to the other man. "Let's have no trouble, Will," he repeated.

"There isn't going to be any trouble," the red-bearded man said easily. Although he spoke to the bartender his eyes never left the other man.

"I told you to keep away from my girl," Will said. He was light-haired and slender and his eyes were dangerous.

"I like her," the red-bearded man said. He put his arms around the girl, keeping himself between her and Will. "She says she likes me."

"Watch out for him, Tom," the girl said. "He moves fast."

"She was saying to me last night that she is disgusted with you," the red-bearded man went on. "She says since you been skinning mules you got to be smelling of mules." He spoke with the cheroot in his mouth, his head cocked slightly to keep the smoke from his eyes.

"Jeffords, you god-damned Indian-loving son of a bitch, you ain't fit to be around white people," Will said in a deadly voice.

The bartender paled. "Oh, Holy Mother of God," he groaned.

Jeffords shook his head. "Now you said it to *me*, Will," he mused. "Seems to me someone told me that you been talking like that when I wasn't present but I couldn't believe it. Now you came right out and said it to me." He shook his head. "You shouldn't have said that, Will. That comes under the heading of a man's own business and out here a man is supposed to mind his own business."

"Watch him, Tom," the girl said.

"Maybe you better get some air, Lucy," he said. "Will is a

bad boy and he uses bad language." He shifted slightly so that his right hand now touched the butt of his revolver.

"Please don't make trouble, boys," the bartender pleaded.

Will started to move and Jeffords shot him in the right hand without drawing his gun from his holster. His body hadn't moved. His fingers moved to the butt and lifted the gun horizontal and then pulled the trigger. Will's hand dropped to his side.

"Maybe you better go somewhere else," Jeffords said softly. "This town is crowding us a little. There are lots of mules all over and a bright boy like you ought to find work wherever you go."

"Jeffords," Will said. His hand was covering with blood.

"Don't say anything else, Will," Jeffords cut in. "You'll remember it and I'll remember it and then we'll stay mad at each other. Maybe you got a little sick from smelling mules and that was why you've been talking the way you have. If you keep on talking I may have to kill you next time. So don't say anything. Have the free drink and get Doc Brainard to fix up your hand and move on a little."

Will started to say something and then he jammed his hat on his head with his left hand and started for the door. On the way he paused for a moment where the girl was still standing and then he walked out without a word. The girl rushed over to Jeffords and put her arms around him.

"Lucy," he said. "You're a bitch."

"Tom Jeffords!" she said.

"That Will Harden was a nice boy."

"He's been telling stories about you all over town," she flared. "He's been saying you think more of Indians than you do of your own kind."

"I know," Jeffords said. "I could have stopped that. You got him worked up about me because you wanted to get rid of him."

She put her arm around him. He pushed her away and drank his whiskey.

"I don't like to shoot men over women," Jeffords said. "There'd have been a reason if it was over Indians. Especially bitches."

"You didn't talk that way last night, Tom Jeffords," Lucy said angrily.

"That was last night."

The girl's lips curled. "Maybe Will was right."

"Take Lucy," Jeffords said to the bartender. "She came out here and she was a nice girl. Came from the best house in Memphis. I remember the place from when I was shipping up and down the river. Look at her. Is it the sun?"

Lucy moved toward Jeffords and he caught her hand. "I hate your face," she said.

"I do too," he said cheerfully. "That's why I keep it hidden. Have a drink."

"I wouldn't drink with you if you were the last man in the country." Then she softened suddenly. "Tom, don't treat me this way."

"All right," he said.

"Please, Tom," she said.

"All right. Have a drink."

She slipped her arm through his. "Don't be hard with me."

"All right."

"Don't talk that way about Memphis," she said. "It ain't that way with us."

"No."

"Besides it was the best house on the river. Not like this place."

"Yes."

"I don't know why I came here," she said miserably.

"Sure you do. You heard there was a lot of money out here in the silver mines. Anyway Memphis is getting too quiet."

The girl's eyes flashed for a moment and then she put her head against his arm. "Nobody else talks to me that way," she said. "Nobody ever talks to me that way."

"Better get some sleep," he said.

"Tom, take me away from here."

"Get some sleep."

"Will I see you tonight?"

"Yes."

"What time? What time will I see you?"

He touched her lightly on the cheek. "I'll be here, Lucy," he said.

She looked at him and smiled. She pushed her cheek against his hand and closed her eyes. "All right, Tom," she said. She walked toward the door leading to the back of the saloon. She turned and smiled at him and then disappeared through the door.

Two men were seated at a table in the far corner of the saloon. They rose and walked to the bar. One of the men nodded to Jeffords. "I beg your pardon," he said. "Are you Captain Thomas Jeffords?"

"Yes?" Jeffords looked at the two men. "From the East?"

"We're out here for the new Butterfield stage line," the man said. "My name is Buckley, William Buckley. This is Mr. Silas St. John."

"Glad to meet you," Jeffords murmured. He turned to the bartender. "Set them up, Pete." Then he said, "What can I do for you gentlemen?"

"We're just down from the Indian Agency at Fort Stanton," Buckley said. He was a thick, heavy-set man with a black mustache. "The agent, Dr. Michael Steck, told us to look you up."

"Steck? How is he?"

"He was all right."

"Told you to look me up? What for?"

"As I said before, we're out for the Butterfield people," Buckley said. "We're putting a stage and mail line through to California. St. John and I and some other people are prospecting through the country picking the route and establishing station points."

Jeffords nodded. "I heard about the Butterfield business. Pretty ambitious, going through the Indian country."

St. John, a tall, slender man with a thin, sensitive face, spoke for the first time. His voice was low and musical. "Steck told us you might want to do some work with us," he said.

Jeffords looked surprised. "Me? I don't know anything about stage lines."

"Steck seems to think you could be of great value to us, Captain Jeffords," St. John said. "He spoke at great length about you, about your having been a riverboat captain on the Mississippi and the Great Lakes and working as a surveyor up in Colorado and a prospector down here. He said you know the country west of here as few men do."

"I've been mining," Jeffords agreed.

"Perhaps you will be good enough to listen to us then," St. John said.

"Let's sit down."

When the three men were seated at a small table, Pete, the bartender, at a signal from St. John, brought a bottle of whiskey and three glasses to the table. After pouring drinks all around, Buckley said, "Butterfield, that's John Butterfield, has a contract with the government to build this line and run it. St. John here used to be connected with the old San Antonio and San Diego Line and when we took them over he agreed to come on in with us."

"The San Antone outfit only started last year," Jeffords said.

"I know," Buckley nodded. "But we took the mover. We're intending to run stages from St. Louis and Memphis in the East all the way to San Francisco. We're going to put up stations all along the route. We're complete up to this point and now we're going to push through the Chiricahua and Dragoon Mountains to Tucson."

"Apache country," Jeffords said.

"Yes," St. John said. "Apache country. That's why we've come to you. Steck says that you know the country 'and that, more importantly, you know Indians and understand them.

61

He says that you speak some of the Apache dialect. You would be invaluable to us, Captain Jeffords."

"I'm not a stage-line man," Jeffords said.

"You've tried your hand at many things, Captain Jeffords, why not this?" Buckley asked.

"Where are you from?" Jeffords asked unexpectedly.

"Watertown, New York," Buckley said in some surprise.

"I thought I had the accent close to home," Jeffords said. "I'm from Chautauqua originally."

"Your speech sounded familiar to me too," Buckley said, seizing on a point of contact with Jeffords. "You don't talk like a riverboat man."

Jeffords poured a drink and drank it off. "I've been a lot of things," he said. "Started out as a lawyer. Practiced a little back East and then got bored. Headed West. Last time I practiced law was in Denver. Then I found I liked it better in the open. Felt cramped in a courtroom. I started working as a surveyor. Then I became interested in mining."

"It's time for another change," Buckley said heartily. "How about coming to work for Butterfield? There's good money in it and enough excitement, even for you, Captain Jeffords."

Jeffords shook his head. "I don't think so," he said.

Buckley's face fell. "Why not?"

"Oh, I like it here," Jeffords said.

"Like Mesilla? What is there to like in Mesilla? The place is full of Mexicans. There is nothing to like here that I can see. Before the year is out Tucson will be a bigger town than this."

"I like it here," Jeffords said. His blue eyes were very pleasant.

"We'd make it well worth your while, Captain Jeffords," Buckley said.

"I don't think so. I don't particularly like to work for anybody. I have a little place up the mountains I want to dig around in."

"Is there any offer we can make to you?" St. John asked. "We don't know anything about the Apache country. We need a guide and someone with your experience with the Indians."

"Let me think about it for a while," Jeffords said.

"Will you?" St. John asked. "The big depot for this section of the line will be in Tucson. If ever you see your way to joining us will you just come over and see us there?"

"Who do you have to run your station agency in Tucson?"

"A man named William Oury," Buckley said.

Jeffords stiffened slightly. "Oury?"

"Do you know him?" Buckley asked.

Jeffords poured another drink. "A little. In Texas."

"Well, maybe having an old friend of yours in Tucson will

62

help persuade you to join us," Buckley said. St. John, whose eyes were much keener, said nothing.

Jeffords emptied the glass. "He's no friend of mine," he said shortly.

"You wouldn't have to have too much to do with him," Buckley said quickly. He finished his drink and got up. "I'm sorry you feel as you do, Captain Jeffords. But I'll be traveling back and forth between here and Tucson for some little while to come. We'll be seeing each other and if you ever change your mind, well, there will always be a place for you."

"Thanks," Jeffords said.

Buckley held out his hand. "Think it over, Captain Jeffords. We sure could use you."

Jeffords shook his hand. "Maybe later on," he said.

"Coming, Silas?" Buckley asked.

"I'd like to talk to Captain Jeffords for a few more moments if he is not too busy," St. John said.

"Not at all," Jeffords said.

"I'll see you," Buckley said. He walked out.

St. John smiled. "I don't want to take too much of your time, Captain Jeffords, and I'm not trying to add my suasion to Buckley's." St. John slowly filled his glass and drank a little of the whiskey. "Dr. Steck spoke at some length about your interest in the Indians," he said. "I'm rather interested in them myself." He looked up at Jeffords and his fine face broke into an apologetic smile. "I don't want to seem rude but I do think we have something in common there. Dr. Steck said that you know more about Indians than most men around here."

Jeffords looked keenly at the other man. He felt himself attracted by St. John's quiet breeding and intelligence. "Most white men don't try to find out anything about Indians," he said. "It's not a very popular subject in this part of the country."

"We heard your discussion with your friend before," St. John smiled.

"Don't think it was the girl," Jeffords said. "He was just using the girl. Men don't get into shooting talk about that kind of girl." He lit another cigar. "Harden trades in mules. Couple of weeks ago he talked a Navajo out of a couple of sweet critters. Promised the Navajo some clothing for his family and himself. Harden said he would fix up the whole Indian family. He gave the Navajo half a dozen yards of cheap calico and when the Indian raised a fuss he told him to shut up or he'd have him strung up for mule-stealing."

"Yes?"

"That's all."

"What did you do?"

"Harden sold the mules by then. Got a good price for them. I told him to turn half the money over to the Indian."

"Did he?"

"Yes."

"He apparently wasn't very happy about it," St. John chuckled.

"No."

"I thought there must have been something more than appeared on the surface."

"Lucy isn't a bad girl."

"Men talk about the Indians out here the way they speak about Negroes in the South," St. John said.

"Just about."

"I'm not as conversant with the subject as you are, Captain Jeffords, but I have tried to find out a little about it. From what I've seen the average American out here refuses to acknowledge the fact that an Indian is a human being."

Jeffords studied St. John for a few moments. "They're not too bad. Some good and some bad. If somebody ever tried to understand what makes them operate maybe we'd all get along better."

"I've heard a few stories about Mr. Oury," St. John said. "I think I understand the basis of your feelings toward him."

"Oury's typical, only more so," Jeffords said.

"His attitude toward the Indians has become rather celebrated," St. John said. He picked up his half-emptied glass of whiskey. Jeffords noticed his fingers, long and slender and as sensitive as his face.

"I'll drop in and see you if I'm ever in Tucson," Jeffords said suddenly.

"Good," St. John said. "I'd like to continue this discussion with you some time again."

The men stood up. "What's the damage, Pete?" Jeffords called out.

"Please, Captain Jeffords. You were drinking with us," St. John said immediately.

Jeffords nodded. "All right. I'll buy you a drink in Tucson."

"I hope I won't have to wait too long," St. John said.

Jeffords walked out of the place and St. John went to the bar to pay for the drinks. "He seems to be quite a man," he said to the bartender.

"Cap?" the bartender shook his head. "Funny about him. Hard to figure out. He's a bad one, all right, and yet he ain't."

"How do you mean?"

"I don't rightly know. He don't make friends. Yet he could have killed that kid easy as not. Shooting him in the hand just left that fool Harden live to plug him some other time."

"You refer to Harden as a kid. Jeffords doesn't seem much

64

older," St. John said. "I wouldn't put him much past twenty."

"He ain't," Pete agreed. "Maybe twenty-five. No more. But he don't act like no twenty-five."

"The beard fools you, perhaps."

"Well, it's that, and it ain't only that. Sometimes I think he ain't got sense and other times I think he's got too much sense." The bartender shook his head. "He ain't a very popular man around here. Good thing he knows what to do with that shooting iron of his. There's lots of hombres who would like to see him out of the way, one way or another."

"He seems very quiet to me," St. John said.

"Oh, it ain't that he looks for trouble. Ain't no one quieter than Cap'n Jeffords. Only he's got funny ideas that Indians got the same rights as white men, maybe more. That ain't exactly a healthy way to think out here."

"I guess not."

The bartender began to polish some glasses. "Can't figure him out. That Lucy. You know what she is. Last week Cap'n Jeffords came down out of the mountains with pay dust. Not much. Just a nice little pile. He don't never seem interested in making a big strike. He says he likes moving around looking and if he found too much he'd have to quit. Anyway, he had this little pile. He gave Lucy a fistful to go back home. She comes from somewhere in Georgia. Lucy took the dust and lost it on the wheel the same night. Cap, he didn't say nothing, didn't bawl her out nor nothing. Just sort of smiled in that way of his and didn't say nothing." The bartender rubbed a glass to diamond shine. "Funny hombre, he is, all right."

"Isn't he?" St. John said. "Keep the change." He walked out of the saloon.

"Thanks, mister," Pete called out.

2

Early in August, 1858, Buckley, St. John, and a number of American and Mexican helpers started out in an eight-wagon mule train from Mesilla and headed westward to locate and construct stations which would link Mesilla and Tucson in the newly acquired territory. The contract made by Butterfield with the government called for operation of the line to start within a few months.

It was in the full summer heat. The sun catapulted into a cloudless sky each day and rolled boilingly in a blazing arc across its unbroken turquoise sea. The rich Mesilla Valley was heavy-laden with crops, rising thickly from earth quenched by irrigation ditches. The land was quiet and wore a mood of peace and it was difficult to understand that this

65

land was a frontier, edging on a vast, unexplored unknown.

The mule train crossed the Rio Grande and paused for a little while north of Mesilla opposite Doña Ana at a place called Picacho and then started on a long fifty-mile leg to a place indicated on the crude maps possessed by Buckley and St. John as Cook's Spring, where St. John from his earlier experience with the San Antonio line decided a station would be erected. From the summit of Picacho Pass the men could see Cook's Peak in the distance, rising boldly from the plains.

The train kept itself as compact as possible. Men were assigned as guards and rode with the drivers with rifles across their knees. The travelers were now in the country of Mangas Coloradas and his Mimbres Apaches.

Buckley and St. John rode on horseback a little ahead of the train.

"The more we head into this Indian country the more I wish Jeffords had seen fit to come along with us," Buckley said, straining his eyes in all directions.

"What did you think of him?" St. John asked.

"Tough. Steck says he knows his Indians." Buckley looked around nervously. "I thought he was going to kill that fellow in the saloon. I was watching his hand. I never saw it move down to that gun."

"It was fast. They tell me shooting from the holster is getting popular out here. Only a few bad men down in Texas learned how to handle a revolver that way."

"Do you see anything up there?" Buckley asked suddenly.

St. John pulled his rifle out of the saddle scabbard. "Where?"

"Straight ahead."

St. John peered into the distance. "I can't see anything."

"I guess I'm imagining things," Buckley said. "The stories about these damned Indians have got under my skin."

The train proceeded without incident to Cook's Spring and several men, with one of the wagons, were left there to build a station. Then the train continued on and twenty miles farther crossed the Mimbres River. Buckley and St. John rested in one of the wagons, and two other men, James Hughes, a friend of Buckley, from Watertown, and James Laing, who came from Kentucky, took their places as scouts.

Seventeen miles from the Mimbres River at Cow Springs another wagon was left with its complement of men to build a depot there, and thirty-one miles farther on, at Soldier's Farewell Springs, still another wagon left the train and the men set to work. Availability of water was the guiding reason in the establishment of the stations.

From Soldier's Farewell the train crossed rolling, metal-hard country up to Stein's Peak, located just a few miles east of what later became the state boundary between New Mexico and Arizona. There, in a little hollow which had been scooped by nature out of the side of a steep incline, another station was located, and since this particular section was said to be the favorite hunting grounds of Mangas Coloradas, the station ordered was a substantial one, with a stone corral and fortified buildings.

Throughout the journey Buckley had never lost his nervousness. Shadows, rolling stones, rocks in the distance, all made him start and reach for his rifle. St. John tried to lighten his mood, lest it communicate itself to the other men, particularly the Mexicans, who were within a shade of bolting the job as it was.

"So far, so good," Buckley said as the train made camp at Stein's Peak.

"Indians are said to seldom attack any party as strong as we are," St. John said reassuringly. "We're almost like a small troop. We ought to hit Apache Pass pretty soon."

"How long is that?"

"About ten miles. We'll be in Chiricahua country soon."

"That's Cochise, isn't it?" Buckley said heavily.

"Yes. I think we've gone through the worst of it. Cochise is not at war. I think we might have had more trouble from the Mimbres Indians than the Chiricahuas."

"I'll believe an Apache is peaceful when I see him dead and buried," Buckley said. "They're all treacherous."

"Don't tell that to Jeffords," St. John said with a smile.

Buckley looked around the country jerkily. "The hell with Jeffords," he said.

"Take it easy, Bill," St. John said. "We're not in trouble yet."

In the morning the diminished train started out for Apache Pass. Buckley and St. John who had stood guard during the early morning hours went to sleep in one of the wagons. There were now four wagons left. The Mexicans rode together in the second and third wagons and the Americans divided themselves between the first and last, with Buckley and St. John riding in the fourth wagon. Two hours out of Stein's Peak Buckley and St. John were awakened by a violent jolt.

"Axle's broken," Buckley said. He jumped out of the wagon, followed by St. John. Buckley looked ahead. "Where's the rest?"

"Over the hill. They got a little ahead of us," Laing, who was driving, said.

"Over the hill? I told you to keep close to the wagon in front of you," Buckley said angrily.

"I have been having trouble with these mules," Laing said in his soft drawl.

"How far ahead do you figure the others are?"

"Not too far."

"Run up that hill and fire your rifle. I want them brought back until we can change this axle."

Laing nodded. He started up the hill.

"Hurry," Buckley shouted. "These wagons make so much noise they won't hear you if they get too far off."

He bent down to look at the broken axle and as he did so an arrow entered the wooden frame of the wagon just above his head. He heard the dull sound as it struck the wagon and when he lifted his head slowly the feathered tail of the arrow was still vibrating. Buckley turned his head and saw Laing running back and then, from out of the ground, from out of the rocks and the trees, the Indians surrounded them.

"Oh, God!" Buckley said.

"Get inside the wagon, quickly," St. John said. "Get inside, everyone, and keep your heads down."

Buckley clambered into the wagon and lay flat on the floor. "Are they Apaches?" he asked.

"I think so," St. John said coolly. "We're not finished yet," he said. "There are five of us here and five men with rifles can hold off this gang for quite a while. The noise may bring the others back."

"They've got too far away by now," Buckley groaned. "God damn it, Laing, I told you to keep within sight of the wagon in front of you."

"Better pay attention to our friends, Bill," St. John said quietly.

The Indians were circling the wagon. Their course was out of gun range up to a point and then at that one point, one of the Indians would cut in close and lay over the far side of his horse and fire his gun or his arrow under the neck of the animal and then get away. The point at which the attackers broke away from their circle kept changing so that the men in the wagon never knew from what side the shots would come.

"You can't hit them," Buckley said through his teeth. "When they get close enough you can't hit them for their damned horses."

"Shoot the horses and then pick out the Indian when he gets thrown," St. John said.

One of the men in the wagon groaned. He tore at his throat. The arrow pierced his neck completely and the point came out under one of his ears. Then the man stopped clawing and died.

"That leaves four," Buckley said. He fired his rifle. "Got him," he said. "I wonder what Jeffords would do now," he said. "Maybe he would be able to step out and have a nice talk with them."

The Indians now were shrieking as they raced around the wagon.

68

"They're really painted up," Laing said.

"Apache war paint," St. John said.

"Everybody save one bullet," Buckley said suddenly.

The men in the wagon had picked off four of the Indians when Buckley suddenly shouted, "My God, look." He pointed to the crest of the hill. "More of them."

The newcomers came down the hillside swiftly. Then they began to fire.

"What in hell's going on here?" Buckley said. "They're shooting at the other Indians." He wet his lips nervously. "Maybe it's another tribe."

"I think they're Apaches, too," St. John said. "Hold your fire, men. Our friends have stopped bothering with us and they're trying to fight off the newcomers."

"What do you make of it?" Buckley asked.

"I don't know. Let's just sit tight."

Lying in the wagon the Americans watched as the newcomers closed in on the attacking Indians; there was a quick struggle and then the attacking Indians broke ground and raced away.

"What do we do now?" Buckley asked.

"Wait and see. Look at that big Indian in the front. He's holding out his hand. That's the peace sign."

"It's a trick," Buckley said. "They just want to get us out of this wagon." He lifted his rifle. "He's not fooling me," he said.

"Put down that gun," St. John said.

"I'm no fool, St. John," Buckley said.

St. John pushed the muzzle of the gun down. "Keep that gun down." He jumped lightly from the wagon. He laid his gun ostentatiously against the side and walked toward the tall Indian, holding his hands out to show he was unarmed. The big Indian leaped from his horse and walked up to meet him, his hand still upraised in friendly greeting. "Cochise," he said.

St. John's eyes widened. He pointed to the big Indian and asked, "Cochise?"

The Indian shook his head. He pointed toward the west with his hand and then repeated, "Cochise."

"Chiricahua?" St. John said.

The Indian nodded violently and repeated, "Cochise, Chiricahua," and again pointed west.

"Bill," St. John called out.

Buckley lifted his head slightly. "Yes?"

"I think these Indians want to be friendly."

"Or else they're smarter than the other ones."

"No. I think I trust them."

Buckley stepped down from the wagon and slowly approached them. The big Indian held out his hand and Buckley, holding tightly to his rifle with his left hand, raised his own right arm.

"These Indians are not painted up," St. John said. "I think this one is trying to tell me that he wants to take us to Cochise."

"Cochise," Buckley said.

"And I think we better agree to go," St. John said.

"It's a trick."

"They haven't tried to take our guns away," St. John pointed out. "If we attempt to fight them we'll end up in just one way. We can always start shooting. I think meanwhile we ought to go along with them."

The other two Americans, Laing and Hughes, now stepped down from their places in the wagon. The Americans and Indians looked at each other curiously and then Laing suddenly grinned. The big Indian nodded and grinned back.

The body of the dead American was removed from the wagon and a grave was quickly dug. The Indians, dismounted, watched silently. Then the Americans set to work to replace the axle. The big Indian watched them intently for a few moments and then he grunted something to his men. Several of them went to the wagon and lifted the rear end clear from the ground and held it while the new axle was slipped into place. Then the wheels were fitted on.

"Well, let's go," Buckley said gloomily. "God knows where we'll end up."

Laing and Hughes climbed to the driver's seat. Buckley and St. John got horses. "Let's not try anything funny," St. John warned. "We can't outrun them and we can't outshoot them."

The Indians rode on either side and in the front of the wagon and the big Indian again pointed the direction. They rode for several hours and then they entered a narrow, rising pass.

"I think this is Apache Pass," St. John said cheerfully. "This is where we wanted to go, isn't it?"

"This is a hell of a time for jokes," Buckley said.

"Take it easy. Three hours ago I didn't think we'd be alive at this time."

"I wonder where the rest of the wagons are."

"They had time to get a good start."

"You'd think they would have noticed we weren't behind them."

It was now late afternoon and the sun had passed over the far side of the long cut. The rocks in the pass rose almost perpendicularly on either side of the narrow trail; several of the boulders seemed to be far off balance, past the point where they should fall off and roll down into the pass.

Presently the Indians turned into a canyon that cut off to one side of the pass. They rode for another hour. The quick twilight ended and it was dark. The wagon jolted over rough country, through gullies and up and down hills. Then suddenly they were in an Indian camp. Buckley looked around. Scores of fires lighted the encampment. Buckley sighed heavily. "Indians," he said. "Hundreds of them."

The wagon was led into the center of the camp. The Indians clustered around the wagon and looked inside curiously. Then a tall, lean man approached. The big Indian who had led the party in began to speak rapidly to him. The tall man nodded and his face tightened with anger. He began to address the big Indian, and the questions were whipped out in a furious series of guttural sounds, like the pattering of small stones in a moving river.

"Maybe he's raising hell because they didn't kill us instead of hauling us all the way here," Buckley said.

St. John shook his head. His brow was knitted. "No," he said thoughtfully. "There's something going on here. I think that man must be Cochise."

"Here he comes."

The tall Indian walked up to him. The anger was gone from his face. He started to talk in his own language, and then turned from face to face. The men shook their heads. Then he started, more slowly, to speak in Spanish.

"I understand a little Spanish," St. John said to him.

The tall man spoke slowly for several moments. His speech was halting but expressive. When he finished, St. John said, "He says that he is Cochise and that these are his people. He says the Chiricahua people are at peace with Americans and that tomorrow he will bring us to some white soldiers. He says that he saw those other wagons going through the pass earlier. He says that he is sorry for what happened to us, that we were attacked by some renegade Apaches led by a man named Geronimo, and he says that he is happy that his own warriors came in time to save our lives and bring us safely to him."

"Tell him to bring us to the troops tonight," Buckley said. "I don't want to spend a night in an Apache camp."

"I think not," St. John said. "We'll have to accept his hospitality the way it is offered."

"I'm running this job," Buckley said angrily. "Tell him we want to get out of here tonight."

"These men have been able to kill at any time," St. John said. "We've been in their hands for quite a while. This man does not mean trouble—unless we force it on him. I'm afraid you'll have to trust me in this."

As they spoke, Cochise watched them keenly, his eyes falling upon the face of each man as he spoke in turn. There was a faint trace of a smile on his face as he cut in and spoke

71

again to St. John. When he finished, St. John said, "He understands what we're arguing about. He says that we are safe here."

Buckley breathed heavily and he seemed to slump. "All right," he said.

St. John walked to the wagon and tossed his rifle inside. Laing and Hughes followed his example, and then Buckley walked slowly to the wagon and put his in with the rest.

"Eat," Cochise said. He pointed to the fires.

"Let's eat," St. John said.

"Might as well," Buckley said glumly.

St. John nodded to Cochise and walked with him to the fire. St. John felt he trusted the Apache completely and he began to enjoy the experience. He looked around him with great interest, smiling at the women and scratching the heads of some of the children who came up to him. The children examined him closely, and St. John goodnaturedly held out his arms and let the children cluster around him.

The campfires were built larger and the men gathered around them. St. John went to the wagon and took out some of the store of food. He carried some dried beef, bacon, and hard biscuits, and gave them to Cochise. Then the men began to eat of the roast meat and corn cakes handed to them by the Indian women.

When Buckley finished he wiped his lips and lighted a cigar. "That wasn't too bad," he said contentedly. "At least I'll die with a full stomach."

"What do you think you ate?" St. John asked.

"Beef, wasn't it? Or venison. I guess it was venison, all right. These Indians do all right."

"It was mule meat," St. John said.

Buckley gagged. "Mule meat?"

"The Indians love it," St. John said. "So did you."

Buckley puffed on his cigar and then he got up and walked away. "I think I'm going to be sick," he said.

The other two Americans rose after a while and crawled into the wagon and went to sleep. Using their imperfect Spanish, St. John and Cochise spoke with each other long into the night.

3

When the four Americans awoke in the morning they found the camp already astir. Buckley drank coffee and ate some biscuits but would touch nothing else. They started out immediately. Cochise took some thirty of his warriors and led the trail himself. They rode for about four hours and then Cochise lifted his hand and the party stopped.

He rode ahead alone for a short distance and then returned and signaled for the others to follow. They went up a slight rise and then, on the further slope, they saw the camp of an American military patrol.

The sentry sounded an alarm. Cochise again rode forth alone. When he came to the camp he dismounted and stood silently by his horse. In a few moments Major Steen was at his side. The two men embraced.

"Cochise," Steen said warmly.

"I have a wagon with four of your countrymen. They are part of many wagons. They were attacked by bad Apaches led by Gokliya."

"Gokliya?"

"He was a warrior of mine. He is now called Geronimo. He has gathered renegades from several tribes."

"I heard about the attack," Steen said. "The other wagons got through the pass last night. They said one of the wagons had been surrounded by a hundred Indians and that all the Americans had been killed. We were going to try to pick up the trail today. We have been marching since early morning and the men were given a rest. How did you know where to find us?"

Cochise smiled: "The birds told me," he said.

"I wish the birds would speak to me some time," Steen said. "It seems you can always put your hand on us anytime you want to no matter where we are in this country of yours."

"There are many birds," Cochise said.

"I wish you would teach the American Army to send signals so expertly," Steen said. "But never mind that. Where are the survivors?"

"Behind the hill," Cochise said. "And, *Nantan* Steen, Gokliya had no hundred warriors. Twenty was all he had."

"I thought as much," Steen said. He sent a soldier up to bring the men in. In a few minutes the wagon came rumbling down the hill accompanied by Cochise's men. As soon as the wagon reached the camp Buckley jumped out of it and ran up to Steen. He grabbed his hand and began to shake it heartily. "I'm damned glad to see you, Major," he said.

"Steen, 1st Dragoons, at your service, sir."

"I'm Bill Buckley, out here for the Butterfield people. You don't know how glad I am to see you and your men."

"Thank you," Steen said.

"We've had quite an experience, Major, quite an experience. But it's all over now, thanks to you."

"Thanks to Cochise," Steen said.

"This white man has not been happy in our company," Cochise said dryly.

When Pedro translated this Buckley opened his mouth to

make a retort. Steen touched him on the arm. "I think·you owe Cochise your life, Mr. Buckley," he said quietly. "He has pledged himself to protect the stage route through Chiricahua country and I think he has given evidence of efficiency. If you are representative of the Butterfield people you will be committing the greatest mistake of your life if you provoke the enmity of this man. Believe me, Mr. Buckley, the success or failure of your venture lies with this Indian." Buckley pulled savagely on his mustache and walked away abruptly. A darkness passed over the face of Cochise, as though a cloud crossed by. Steen placed his arm on Cochise's shoulder.

"I have been looking for you," he said. "I am leaving Fort Buchanan."

"The news is bad," Cochise said. "Where do you go?"

"Many days' journey from here," Steen said. "Far in the direction of the rising sun."

"It is not good that you leave," Cochise said. "You are the friend of the Chiricahuas and they are your friends."

"The Army is that way," Steen said. "I asked to remain here because I think I can be of most service to the Army right here. But I have been ordered East for more learning."

"More learning?"

"We have schools in the Army to teach us our profession." Cochise waved his arm. "This is your school. It is here that you can learn."

"I think so too," Steen said. "But unfortunately I have to obey orders."

"Who will be the new boss at the fort?" Cochise asked.

"I do not know. But he will want to continue the peace with the Chiricahuas."

"I have a warning that it will not be as good," Cochise said.

"From one of your little birds?" Steen asked.

"From another kind of bird," Cochise said. "A bird of bad luck."

"You must not think so," Steen said. "There must be good will. Whoever the new *nantan* is he will want to continue right where I have left off."

"Maybe," Cochise said.

"I know it to be so," Steen smiled. "I have something for you. A farewell present." He took a metal tube from his saddlebag and unscrewed one end of it. From the tube he extracted a rolled-up sheet of paper. He unrolled it and held it before the Indian.

"The picture writing," Cochise said.

"You will remember me by it," Steen said. He rolled the map up and slipped it back into the tube. "This will protect it from the rain," he said. He handed the tube to Cochise.

74

"I wait for the day when your learning is complete and you return," Cochise said.

"I await that day," Steen replied. He looked up suddenly. "You've been a good friend, Cochise." Then he called Buckley. "Are you people aiming to build your stations around here?"

"We want to put one up in Apache Pass and another at Dragoon Springs," Buckley said.

"Do you want to speak to Cochise about them?"

"What does an Apache know about a stage line?" Buckley asked.

St. John said, "You're quite right, Major. Let me speak with him."

"Use my interpreter," Steen said, turning his back on Buckley.

"We get along quite well in Spanish," St. John said. "I know a word or two of Apache by now as well." St. John walked over to Cochise. "We wish to use Chiricahua country for our wagon line," he said. "If the Chiricahua chief does not object we wish to build a station in Apache Pass and another at Dragoon Springs."

"If he doesn't object," Buckley snorted.

"I have given my word," Cochise said, his eyes on Buckley. "The Chiricahuas will cause no trouble."

"It is my hope that when the station is completed at Apache Pass the Chiricahua people will come there often and be friends with the Americans. There will be a trading store there with many things the Chiricahuas love. When the store is opened it would be an honor if the Chiricahua people come to us and receive gifts showing our thanks."

"I will tell my people."

"I don't thank the Chiricahua chief for saving our lives," St. John said quietly. "Some things are greater than any thanks. I hope that the Chiricahua chief is always apart from danger, but if he should find himself in danger I hope that I may in some way do for him what he has done for us."

"You speak like a brave man," Cochise said. "We are friends."

St. John went to his wagon and took a new Wesson carbine from within it. "May this bring plenty of meat to Cochise," he said.

"This is a good thing," Cochise said. He looked at Steen and then at Buckley and then at Steen again. "This is a good thing." He embraced Steen warmly and then embraced St. John. He leaped lightly upon his horse and held the gun in the air. *"Hasta luego,"* he said, waving to St. John. Then he rode up to Steen. *"Adios, amigo,"* he said.

"Hasta luego," St. John said.

"Adios, amigo," Steen whispered.

The Indians rode swiftly up the hillside.

"That was pretty decent of you, mister," Steen said.

"A rifle for four lives? Decent?"

At the crest of the hill the Indians paused and Cochise lifted himself in his saddle and waved his hand. Steen and St. John waved back.

"Yes," Steen repeated softly. "Quite decent."

4

Steen sent a small patrol to bring back the rest of the train, which, by then, had passed Dragoon Springs and was on its frightened way to Tucson. The train arrived the next day, the men in the three wagons shamefaced and apologetic. Buckley, brusque and active again, brushed aside their explanations and began work immediately on the station in Apache Pass. To show before all his lack of trust in Cochise and his promise, Buckley ordered the Apache Pass station built stronger and more solid than any station he had ordered up to now. A location several hundred yards from the nearest spring was picked and there Buckley specified a large stone corral, fifty feet long and fifty feet wide. St. John thought that the construction of this fortress-like station might be illy interpreted by Cochise, but Buckley was in such bad humor he said nothing.

When the work was well under way, Buckley ordered one wagon and its crew to remain there and finish, and then the three remaining wagons started out for Dragoon Springs some forty miles away. Steen had informed Buckley that Dragoon Springs was a passing point for the Apaches from the north on their way to Sonora and Buckley again specified that the depot there must be strong as a small fortress. This time St. John demurred mildly. "This is Cochise country," he said.

"All Indians are alike to me," Buckley said shortly. "They're all waiting for their chance to get white men and in my opinion Cochise is like the rest, maybe a little slicker."

Upon Buckley's orders a stone corral forty-five feet long and fifty-five feet wide was built. Within the corral a large stone building was constructed. Buckley remained on hand until the corral was finished and the walls of the building were standing. When he prepared to move on, St. John said that he thought˙ he would remain until the depot was finished before he continued on to Tucson.

"Why do you want to stay here?" Buckley asked.

"The country interests me," St. John replied.

"Country, hell! This Cochise seems to have hypnotized you." St. John didn't reply.

"Better come along with me, Silas," Buckley said.

76

"I'd rather stay on for a little while."

"All right. You may as well stay and fix this place up."

"I'll keep Laing, Cunningham, and Jimmy Hughes," St. John said. "Better leave some Mexicans, too."

"Who do you want?"

"I don't care. Three of them will be enough."

"I'll leave you the Ramirez brothers and Bonifacio Mirando. They work well together."

"They'll do."

"When you finish, leave Laing and Hughes here and come on in to Tucson."

On the morning of September 8, 1858, Buckley took the last two wagons and left the partially completed station at Dragoon Springs.

The men worked on the construction of the building all that day and in the evening had a quiet meal around the campfire. St. John stretched out comfortably in front of the fire and listened to its cheerful crackling and stared at the stars. From time to time he heard the distant barking of coyotes and once or twice, the dismal hooting of an owl.

"This is big country," Laing said, puffing on a pipe. "A lot different from Kentucky. That's small country, beautiful as all hell, but small country."

"I come from quite a big country myself," said Cunningham, a native of Iowa. "But it's a different kind of bigness. You can get close to Iowa. This place always seems to be away from you. Like as if it didn't like people." He sighed. "It's a lot warmer here than where I come from."

"Don't talk about cold," Hughes said. "Upstate New York really gets it. By this time of year the nights begin to get frosty and the trees all turn brown and yellow and a man really gets to feeling good. I don't think I could ever get used to this place. I like to know when it's summer and when it's winter."

"Long way away," Laing drawled softly. "It gets cold in Kentucky, too, except you don't ever think of it as cold. When I think of home I never think about the cold times. I just naturally think of everything being green, and how it's soft and warm in the summer and the air gets smelling so good."

"People say there's talk of war back East between the North and the South."

"Ah, won't be no war," Laing said. "No use fighting among ourselves. Now take Jimmy Hughes. He's what you might call a Yankee. Sometimes he figures things one way and I figure them another. But we don't naturally kill each other about it. We talk it over." He lit his pipe again. "People who want to do any fighting ought to come out here. Plenty of Indians who'd just naturally like to accommodate them."

"A million people can't just sit down and talk things over

77

with another million people," St. John said. "They usually let their talking be done for them by men who don't want to talk things out."

"Think there might be a war, St. John?" Cunningham asked.

"I don't know. I've been away from the East so long I feel out of touch. It seems a far way from here." St. John looked at the three Mexicans who were sitting silently, listening. The Ramirez brothers from Sonora were big, dark-skinned Mexicans who looked as though they had more than a small share of Indian blood in them. Mirando, from Chihuahua, a smaller man, seemed a different type altogether.

"People who want to fight ought to come out here," Cunningham agreed. "Maybe they'd see there were some more important things to do than go around shooting at each other. Indians would like nothing better than to have the white men kill each other off."

"What do you men think?" St. John asked the Mexicans in his courteous manner. "Do you think there will be a war between the states?"

The Ramirez brothers didn't answer. Mirando said, "Americans always fight. Fight Mexicans. Make peace with Mexicans. Fight Indians. Make peace with Indians. Fight with themselves. Then make peace with themselves. I think Americans like to fight."

"Seems like you might have something there," Hughes said.

"We always win our fights," Laing said. "Whether we start them or not we always finish them. We licked the damned British twice and then we licked . . ." He caught himself as he was about to say, "damned Mexicans."

"You also won the war with the Mexicans," Pablo Ramirez, known as Chino, finished softly.

"That's all forgotten," St. John said quickly. "That war is ended."

"Yes," Pablo said, his eyes glowing in the firelight. "The war is ended and now part of Mexico is part of the United States."

"You got paid for it," Cunningham said.

"Mother Mexico is not for sale," Guadalupe Ramirez murmured in Spanish. What he said was caught only by St. John.

"Ten million dollars," Pablo said. "That much silver can be mined in a year, in less than a year."

"Go tell that to Santa Ana," Laing said lazily. "He's the hombre who engineered the deal."

Pablo's dark eyes flashed for a moment and then he wrapped his blanket more tightly around himself and lay down on his side. The men spoke for a while longer and then prepared for sleep.

"Laing, you stand guard the first half," St. John said. "Guadalupe, you stand from midnight to daylight." He got up and stretched. "Better put the mules inside the building," he said.

"Mules inside?" Hughes asked. "I sleep outside."

The Mexicans said they would remain outdoors. Cunningham went to a room in the south part of the building where the stores were kept. He spread a blanket on the floor and stretched himself out. St. John went to a room in the northeast corner of the building, near the gateway. Laing sat outside under the walls of the corral, and the Mexicans and Hughes made themselves comfortable around the fire.

St. John lay on his back and looked at the sky through the roofless building. The stars were bright and low and unblinking. There was no moon. He lay there and he smoked and he found himself thinking about Cochise and about Jeffords. He was somewhat surprised at first to think of the two together, at the same time, as though they were in some way connected. As far as he knew they had never met. And yet, he thought, there was something similar about Cochise and Jeffords. Just what, he didn't quite know. A certain strength? No, not quite that. A certain quality of self-containment, perhaps, a certain security within themselves. It was odd, he thought. He had been West for a long time and he had met a great number of men. Americans, Mexicans, Indians. Most of them were strong characters, in one way or another, some of them strikingly bad characters. Yet none of them had affected him as had Jeffords, and then, almost immediately afterward, Cochise. He tried to think what it was that some men possessed that caused them to affect other persons so powerfully. Cochise had it. You couldn't be around him for five minutes without feeling it, he thought. And Jeffords had it. Buckley thought he had it, but he hadn't it at all. Oury didn't have it either, although he was a strong man, physically and mentally. It didn't go with noise because Buckley was louder than either Jeffords or Cochise and he didn't have any of it, except perhaps for Mexicans who were intimidated by loudness. But Cochise had it and Jeffords had it, and it went beyond their color and their blood. It was a horizontal thing, a high horizontal thing, and it touched men who were big enough to reach it. He thought a meeting between Jeffords and Cochise would be an interesting thing to witness.

He lay there and smoked and thought and listened to the sound of wolves in the distance. It was a strange country, he thought, and the strangeness was a horizontal thing too. The moon came over the open roof of the building. After a while he looked at his watch. It was bright enough for him to see the dial. It was midnight. He felt wide-awake. He got up and stretched again and then he went outside. Laing was still sitting against the wall of the corral, quietly smoking his pipe. He looked up in some surprise as St. John walked up to him and asked, "Can't you sleep?"

"I guess not. Where's Guadalupe? Time to change the watch."

"By the fire. He's up, I think. He just added some wood."

St. John went over to the fire. The Mexicans were rolled in their serapes. St. John peered at their faces, and then leaned down and touched Guadalupe on the shoulder. "Time to stand watch," he whispered.

The Mexican rose without a word.

"Did you get some sleep?" St. John asked.

The Mexican nodded silently.

Laing got up and tapped his pipe against the corral. He walked into the house. He threw a blanket on the floor in the large middle room of the house and lay on it and in a moment he was asleep. St. John looked around the building. He glanced at the mules. He peered into the room where Cunningham was sleeping. Then he returned to his own pallet and lay down again. He dozed lightly.

He woke to the sound of the mules stirring. He rose on one elbow and listened. He looked at his watch. It was after one o'clock. Then he heard a faint whistle and then he heard the sound of heavy blows and then a feeble moan. He jumped up and at that moment the door to the room was pushed open and in the bright light of the stars and the moon he saw three men. They came closer and he saw it was the three Mexicans. Guadalupe was holding a broad axe. Pablo held a stone sledge and Mirando grasped a chopping axe.

"Is there trouble?" St. John asked.

The three Mexicans closed in on him and then he made out the expressions on their faces and he understood. He was a slender man, but his slenderness was one of wiry muscularity, and he moved swiftly. He kicked out hard with his heavy boot and he felt the boot connect with Pablo's groin and he heard Pablo scream and double up. Then St. John saw a glint of light and it was the axe, swung by Bonifacio, and he warded off the blow with his right hand, diverting the axe blade downward, feeling it strike and enter into his hip, and then he threw a short straight jab from the shoulder and his fist struck Bonifacio in the face and the Mexican went down with a breathless grunt. Guadalupe was on his left now, striking short vicious blows with the short-handled broad axe. The first swing caught St. John on his right hand and he succeeded in turning it; the second swing caught him on the forearm below the elbow and there was a tingling, as though his arm went suddenly to sleep, and then a dull burning hurt. St. John reached for his Spark's rifle leaning against the wall and Guadalupe got in another swing which cut through St. John's left arm, reaching the bone between the elbow and the shoulder. Feeling faint with pain, St. John got hold of his rifle by the barrel with his right hand and swung the heavy stock. He knocked the axe from Guadalupe's hand and then he tried to turn the rifle around to fire it as a pistol, with one hand. The Mexicans, all on their feet now, turned and fled through the door and out the gateway.

St. John was bathed in sweat. The room seemed to sway around him. He struggled to lift the heavy, long-barreled rifle to his shoulder with one hand and fire it after the fleeing Mexicans. The rifle was too heavy. He dropped it and then he bent and reached under his saddle, which he had been using for a pillow, for his revolver.

The Mexicans heard the sound of the rifle falling to the floor and thought St. John had fainted. They reentered the building. St. John fired at them with his revolver. Again they turned and fled into the night. Then St. John felt his senses leaving him. He slipped into a coma and collapsed on the floor.

A few minutes later he recovered slightly and tried to move. His left arm was bleeding badly and hung useless. His right hip was split open. He rested for a moment to gather his strength and then he struggled out of his shirt and with his teeth and his good arm he tore it into strips. He bound his two wounds. He pulled himself to his feet and dragged himself outside the building. He fell against some sacks of barley. He called out to the other men but there was no answer. He tried to move again but his eyes seemed to fill with blood. He lay on top of the barley sacks in a position where he could see and he held tightly to his pistol and he waited for daylight.

The night hours were long. He heard the moans of the other men. He was unable to see where the sounds were coming from. He was unable to move without danger of again going unconscious. It grew colder toward morning and he shivered and his throat was parched. He wet his lips. It seemed an endless time until the first gray light appeared in the east. He felt a little stronger and he had stopped losing blood. He slid down carefully from the sacks of barley. The movement reopened the wounds. The strippings from his shirt were covered with blood, some of it caked, with new wet blood flooding over the dried part. Slowly he dragged himself along the ground, pausing to rest when he felt himself getting weak. He came to Cunningham. Cunningham was still alive. His head was opened in three places from three separate axe blows. He lay with his eyes shut, unmoving. His lips were laced with dried saliva. Now and then they opened and he moaned slightly.

St. John pulled himself into the building to where Laing was lying. The Kentuckian's skull was split open. Part of his brain was bulging out. He was still conscious and when St. John drew near him he tried to rise. His eyes remained shut.

"Don't move, Jimmy," St. John said.

Laing opened his mouth slightly and his lips were covered immediately with a bloody saliva.

"Don't move," St. John said hoarsely. "Don't move."

Then St. John found Hughes. His head was completely crushed from a blow of what appeared to have been the stone sledge. He had died instantly. St. John grew faint again. He fell flat on his face and tried to remain conscious. He pulled air into his lungs. The wounds on his arms and hip were opened again and he was losing blood. He made a tourniquet from a handkerchief. He put a small stone on the wound in his left arm and then put a stick under the handkerchief and turned it until the flow of blood stopped. I mustn't keep it on too long, he thought almost automatically, it gets poisoned if you keep it on too long. Then his mind seemed to go away from him and he lay back. When he was in control of himself again he looked at his hip. The gash there was the width of the axe blade. There was little he could do about it. He took out the wad of shirting, dried now into a hard, stiff ball, and put in a fresh wad. Then he went away again and when he came back he found the blood had coagulated. He tried to move. When he moved his hip began to hemorrhage and soon he was too weak to move any more and he fell back and stared at the sky and he thought how hot the sun was and he felt the sweat rolling under his clothes and he listened to Cunningham and Laing moaning softly.

Through the day, Thursday, he lay there and listened to the men groan and when he tried to move to them the blood belched from his hip and left him so weak he fainted and then he was helpless to move any more and he lay quietly and listened to his friends die. It became very hot during the day and he felt he was getting feverish and his throat ached with his thirst. The water was too far away. He thought of the cool spring outside the corral, thought of the water, feeling the sun beating on him and dying through his throat and thinking of the water.

Then in the evening the outside was filled suddenly with coyotes brought to the corral by the smell of blood. The mules were braying with their thirst and hunger, jumping and stamping in the building and he lay there and listened to the howling of the coyotes and the braying of the mules and his throat seemed aflame. He felt better after the sun set. It became cooler. He found some pebbles and put them in his mouth to make the saliva flow. In the middle of the night he heard Cunningham shift a little and then groan again and then sigh, long and soft, and he knew Cunningham had died. He tried to call out but his throat was too dry and the words wouldn't come out.

When it got light Friday he heard a violent flapping of many wings. He opened his burning eyes and looked around. The air was thick with birds, buzzards, magpies, and crows. They swooped above him and lighted on the walls of the corral and on the rafters above the unfinished building. They stared at him and he waved his arm feebly and they flew off. Then he saw them dive on Hughes and begin to tear at his face. He fired his revolver at them and they flapped away noisily. In a few moments they returned and hacked again at the dead man's face.

He lay there through the day again and through the night and in the night he heard the sounds of wolves at the corral walls. He heard the wolves fighting among themselves and when they tried to get into the corral he fired at them. He was a little crazy now. He was in no pain. He lay in a semi-stupor, his mind drifting, and each time that he had a moment of sanity it was with surprise that he still was not dead.

When the sun rose Saturday the wolves disappeared but the birds returned. He felt that he could not last much longer. He thought of killing himself to end his torment. Then he heard Laing moaning feebly. He tried to move toward him but he could not get very far.

Saturday night the wolves returned and began to devour Hughes not a dozen feet from where St. John lay. When they turned to him, their eyes burning like distant fires in the dark, he fired at them. When he thought they were getting near Laing he fired in the air above them and in that way managed to keep them away from Laing.

On Sunday morning when the birds returned he seemed to suddenly regain full sanity and he realized it was the sanity that preceded death.

Three wagons approached the station. They were led by Colonel James B. Leach, on a mission to survey the country for military roads. Leach, who had come from Tucson, had been asked by Buckley to look in at the station. As he approached the building he saw no sign of life. Leach suspected an Indian ambush and turned off the road, detoured a mile, and then climbed out of the wagons and cautiously approached the station on foot.

The men entered the gate of the corral. They walked up to St. John.

"Thank God," St. John said. "Water."

Leach held his canteen to St. John's lips. He looked around with a practiced eye. "Indians?" he asked.

St. John moistened his throat. The water seemed to burn in his mouth. He swallowed a little and then took another sip.

"Damned Apaches," Leach said.

St. John wet his lips. "Not Apaches," he said in a hoarse whisper. "Not Apaches. Mexicans." Then he fainted.

Leach and the other men buried Hughes and Cunningham in a single grave. Laing was still alive, although his heart beat faint and unsteady. Leach dispatched two soldiers to Fort Buchanan for a doctor. He told them to go by way of Tucson, which was longer, but safer for two men. He made St. John and Laing as comfortable as he could.

On Monday morning Laing died without regaining consciousness. The two soldiers reached Fort Buchanan on Wednesday morning and Assistant Surgeon Bernard John Dowling Irwin started out instantly with an escort. Irwin cut across country and arrived at Dragoon Springs Friday morning, the ninth day after the attack by the Mexicans. As he jumped from his horse he said, "Those damned Indians again."

St. John looked up tiredly. He shook his head. "Mexicans," he said. "The three Mexicans who were helping us build the station. Not Indians."

"Mexicans, hey?" Irwin shook his head. He was a large, black-haired, black-bearded man. He seemed disappointed. "Let's look at you." He knelt and examined St. John's left arm. It was filled with maggots, "Have to amputate," he said briefly. "The arm is infected. It might kill you if I leave it on."

St. John closed his eyes and nodded.

In the bright sunlight Irwin went swiftly and efficiently to work. He amputated the arm at the socket. He cut surely and without mistake. St. John went unconscious.

Six days later St. John was strong enough to be placed in a wagon and taken to Fort Buchanan where he received further treatment. Five days later he was able to walk and ten days after that, just twenty-one days from the day his arm was amputated, he mounted a horse and rode north to Tucson.

5

The first stage coach on the Butterfield line left St. Louis on the morning of September 16, 1858, at eight o'clock. Its route was through the northwestern tip of Arkansas, diagonally across Texas to the Pecos, and up the Pecos into the Territory of New Mexico. The coach reached Soldier's Farewell on October 1. At Stein's Peak it was discovered that a few days before Mangas Coloradas and two hundred and fifty of his men had ridden up to the station and had demanded as a "gift" twenty sacks of corn, which were duly presented to them. The coach, traveling day and night, with remounts at each station, arrived in Tucson on Saturday, October 2, and a half an hour later continued on its way. It arrived in San Francisco on the morning of October 10, less than twenty-four days from the time it departed from St. Louis. Its mail had been carried by train from St. Louis to Tipton, Missouri, the end of the line for the Pacific Railroad and there was placed in the coach. The distance from Tipton to San Francisco was two thousand five hundred and thirty-five miles.

Chapter Six

In December, 1858, Cochise received an invitation from the station agent at the Apache Pass depot to bring his entire tribe to the station, with its newly completed store, to receive presents as a gesture of good will from the Butterfield people, who had by then on numerous occasions felt the power of the friendly hand of the Chiricahua chief.

The line had been operating less than three months and on four different occasions men from the Chiricahua tribe had intercepted raids on the coaches by enemy Indians. The smoke signals of the Chiricahuas and their uncanny accuracy in communicating with each other had caused travelers to marvel. Each time before the fascinated and frightened eyes of the passengers the Chiricahua warriors had appeared soon after the attack and had routed the attackers, and on one occasion the passengers had had an opportunity of witnessing summary justice as administered by Cochise himself.

On this occasion Cochise found that the raiders were men who followed Geronimo and who were therefore guilty not only of the general crime of poaching in the Chiricahua country but of the specific crime of having violated Cochise's explicit orders to them. Four of the attackers were captured alive by the Chiricahua warriors and after their identity was established Cochise ordered them executed.

The raid and interception occurred not far from the San Pedro River. The four renegade captives stood quietly as judgment was pronounced upon them and made no attempt to escape although they were not bound. The flat black eyes of the doomed men were expressionless, asking nothing, giving nothing. In ordering their death, Cochise stated briefly the four men were present when he gave his original orders for the followers of Geronimo to remain outside Chiricahua country. The men had no excuse and sought to find none.

Two of the four men were Chiricahua Indians. They formerly had been warriors under Cochise and were known to him personally. They did not attempt to presume on this old relationship. They knew that when they walked away from the Chiricahua tribe and pledged their fealty to Geronimo they severed themselves entirely from their old leader and they knew they were guilty of trespassing and that the judgment was just. They knew that if the situation were reversed and they had remained loyal to Cochise and had caught renegades in their present position they would have imposed the same punishment they now were to receive.

"There is nothing else to do," Cochise said from across an abyss of Indian fatality that no American could ever understand. "The decision was made before. There are men and women and small children in my tribe whose lives would not be safe if I did not maintain the peace here that I have pledged."

He gave his orders shortly and quietly while the passengers in the stage coach watched with horror. Although none of the Chiricahuas paid any attention to the four captives, they did not move. They stood quietly, in their own passive acceptance, with a calm they might have shown as mere spectators.

As the four men watched stoically, four poles were erected and forced down to the hard desert earth. The prisoners were bound to the poles and twigs were thrown at their feet and four Chiricahua men knelt without word and twirled the fire sticks in their containers. There were four wispy trails of smoke and then four small flames and then the twigs caught fire. The warriors threw heavier pieces of wood on the flames and soon the flames rose higher and reached halfway up the four men.

The men did not move nor did they open their mouths. They stood silent and their eyes were on Cochise and there was no resentment in them. The Chiricahua chief looked from face to face; his own face showed nothing of the thoughts that filled his mind.

The American passengers in the coach could watch no longer. A few of them turned their heads and were sick. The silence of the four men on the pyres was the most horrible thing of all.

When the four men were dead they were taken down from the poles and were buried and their single grave was marked by a huge boulder rolled into place by six of the stoutest braves. Then without further word Cochise led the coach for a short distance and, seeing them safely on their way, turned on his horse and led his men away.

And that evening Cochise spoke long with Naretena, telling him alone of the misery that curdled his heart. "Who makes the decisions that cause little people to do things?" he asked. "Who makes these situations? Is he the same as the one who puts the answers in the heads of men who have to meet them?" he asked his brother.

"Two are more than one," Naretena said. "Three are more than two and four are more than three. And the Chiricahua people are more than any four men."

"We have decided that in order to live as a people, the Chiricahuas must win the trust and friendship of the Americans," Cochise said slowly. "This must be done."

"Keep saying it to yourself, my brother," Naretena said. "At the most difficult times keep saying it to yourself. The four men who were put to death today gave their lives as an investment. Others will live longer because of it."

Cochise nodded. "Your words bring rest, as they always do."

The invitation from the Butterfield people was welcomed by the tribe. The Chiricahuas were in that period of change when they were abandoning some of their old ways and were not yet comfortable in new ones. During the period of adjustment there was considerable discontent, particularly among the younger warriors who felt they were in some way being cheated of their birthright by the restrictions imposed by Cochise.

The Americans were passing through the country steadily and in greater and greater numbers, from the East and from the North. While most continued on their way to California, many were settling in the great valleys. Whether they remained or moved on, their passage was a noisy one. Their transit was emptying the countryside of game far more rapidly than Cochise had thought possible. Ranchers and farmers appropriated water holes and caused the game animals who used to come to those holes to move elsewhere.

Within the space of months the numbers of deer and elk diminished speedily; the animals moved to distant and almost inaccessible places. The mountain sheep found new summits to roam. There had been wild turkey, not in great amounts, but enough to fill the larder of the Indians who hunted silently and did not cause entire flocks of birds to fly away over noisy gunfire. There had been coveys of quail; but now the birds were decimated by Americans who shot them on the ground, killing enough in a day to feed an Indian tribe for a week.

The Apaches would not eat fish, since in their belief the fish was linked with the snake and the snake was cursed. The Chiricahua Apaches did not plant corn or grain nor had they ever in their history. Working the soil was something unknown and alien to them and this they could not adapt themselves to overnight. Their country, in the hills, was not suitable for farming; additionally the work was held in contempt by them and not even Cochise would command his tribespeople to become farmers..

Cochise found by now that it was not the spirit and emotions of his people he had to control as much as the simple economics of their living. He organized hunts, held athletic contests, used the power of his shamans to help soothe the headstrong warriors. And yet it was none of these devices, but instead the mystic hold Cochise himself held over the people that kept them in line. No leader of any Apache tribe anywhere held his people bound to him as he did and at this time he needed all his influence.

Everywhere in that bloodstained land Americans were considered fair prey. Some of the reasons were legitimate, according to Indian standards, which were all the Indians had to go by. The Americans, in many cases, were more cruel and ruthless than the Indians and some of the things they did were worse than the worst outrages of the Indians, since the white men were theoretically civilized and were supposed to have known better. Some of the reasons were not legitimate, and many Indian attacks were just the furious excesses visited upon newcomers by barbaric men who had always fought with strangers, who lived and died by violence, and who accepted death with an indifference that denied even curiosity.

Everywhere, that is, except in the vast wilds which were regarded as the domain of the Chiricahuas.

2

On a bright December day Cochise brought his people to the small oasis that had been created in Apache Pass by the Butterfield Stage Line.

The Indians were dressed in their best. Their deerskin blouses were stained in bright colors. Their thigh-high moccasins, now folded down over the knees, so that the pliable leather made a sort of circular pocket around the calf of the leg, were newly sewn. The toes of the moccasins curled up like oriental boots; this curl was devised by the Apaches to protect their feet from the many sharp stones. The horses were curried and many braves rode their favorite steeds, the little paint ponies so loved by the Apaches. On the slender legs of the ponies were deerskin boots, rising as high as the fetlocks, to protect the horses in the wild, thorny country.

The depot itself contained several rooms. One of the rooms served as the living quarters for the agent, Hank Culver, a big, red-faced good-natured man, and for his hostler, Fred Walsh, a short, stocky Californian. The second room was used as a storeroom and contained feed for the mules, kept in the corral as replacements for the tired animals which brought in the coaches, and contained as well food for the equally tired travelers who were always exhausted and frequently in a state of great fear when they arrived at the station. The third room was a kind of public lounge, containing rude beds on which the travelers could catch a little sleep during the change of animals or when the stages were delayed for one reason or another.

A fourth room in the building was the office of Captain James H. Tevis, the official Government Trading Agent at Apache Pass. Tevis was a dour-faced, bearded newcomer to the territory.

Around the outside of the building cottonwood trees had been planted, and the small, tender growths had taken root and were thriving in the shallow soil.

The tribe came down from the mountains early in the day. Cochise, knowing that the Americans had a great fondness for the yellow iron which occasionally was washed down in the mountain streams, had had the women of the tribe collect a few of the nuggets.

As the Indians approached Culver went to the main gate to meet them.

Cochise rode at the head of his people. His black eyes were bright and his face was peaceful and happy. To him the meeting symbolized the friendly relations he had established. Behind him rode Nahilzay, Juan, Pionsenay, Skinyea, and Naretena. Behind the warriors walked the women and children, laughing and excited.

Culver walked out the corral gate and met Cochise a hundred yards from the station. Cochise raised his hand and the Indians stopped. Culver smiled in a friendly way and then said, carefully, since it was the only word in Apache that he knew and he had learned it specially for this occasion and it was uneasy as yet on his tongue, "Welcome."

Cochise sought for some word in English with which he could repay the compliment, but he knew nothing of the language of the Americans, and he abandoned the quest and did the next best thing he could think of. He answered in Spanish, which, while it was not the language of the Americans, was also not the language of the Apaches, and indicated consideration. *"Gracias,"* he said.

"Welcome," Culver repeated and he waved his arm and gestured toward the corral.

Nahilzay watched Culver keenly and without trust. There were too many memories of similar invitations extended by both Americans and Mexicans, invitations to feasts and parties which ended in the planned mass slaughter of the Indians. Nahilzay had previously voiced his suspicions to Cochise. "We have done many things for these people," Cochise had replied. "We have rescued their coaches. We have proven we are useful. They will not plan treachery against ones who are doing good for them. They know if they destroy us other Indians will take our places here and may not be so useful." Nevertheless, Nahilzay was not entirely reassured, and resolved to remain alert.

Inside the walls of the station, Walsh and Tevis stood waiting. With them was an Apache who had worked for a priest in Tucson and who was called, as were all Apaches who made peace with white men, a "tame" Apache, as though he were an animal who had become a pet. His name was Tali and he served as an interpreter.

The warriors seated themselves in a great circle, with Cochise on a raised seat made of folded blankets. To his right sat his warriors in the order of the military stature, and to his left sat Culver, Tevis, and Walsh. The women made their usual larger circle around the inner circle.

"This is a happy day," Culver said. "Nowhere is there a greater chief than Cochise. And nowhere greater warriors than the Chiricahuas. It might have been that the Chiricahuas and the white men would have fought as enemies. Instead, through the wisdom of Cochise, the Chiricahua Indians and the white men sit down and meet in peace with each other and the men and women of the tribe may walk freely among the Americans and when the Americans travel in the country of the Chiricahuas they know no fear for the wise and powerful Cochise is their friend and watches over them."

The speech was exactly as St. John had written it and caused Culver to commit to memory. St. John had put it together with great care and sincerity.

Cochise listened with quiet serenity to the words. When Culver finished he reassured the white men that they were considered as friends by his people. There were speeches by Tevis and Walsh, and then the three Americans bade the Indians to remain where they were, and they rose and went into the building.

There they gathered large bundles of red flannel cloth, blankets, calico, sacks of corn, maize, and barley, and carried them out.

"These are for you and your people," Culver said, when the presents were piled high. "There is more inside. They are the thanks of the white men for the good things you have done for us."

The presents were distributed to the excited people. Then Cochise said, "The Chiricahuas do not come with empty hands." He said something rapidly to the women and those with the gold nuggets dropped them in a blanket in front of the white men.

"My God," Culver said. "Gold."

90

The three Americans fell to their knees and began to examine the nuggets, babbling like children. Cochise smiled. Nahilzay looked on with contempt. Naretena glanced at Cochise and shook his head slightly.

It was the same with all Americans and all Mexicans, Cochise thought. The little pieces of yellow iron, which a person could not eat, which he could not use to warm himself or clothe himself, which could not be used on weapons because they were too soft, affected all white men the same way. They became childish and their eyes glittered and they would kill more easily because of the yellow iron than anything else.

Tevis, his hands juggling the nuggets, got up from his knees. His beard trembled in his excitement. "The things in my store will always belong to the Chiricahuas in exchange for this gold," he said eagerly. Then he realized Cochise could not understand him. "Tali," he yelled. "Tali. Come here and translate for me." Then he repeated what he had said. "There will be food and blankets and sweets for our Indian brothers in exchange."

Cochise replied with a thin smile. "There is not much of the yellow iron but whatever is found will be brought to you."

"Any time," Tevis said. "Any time. The store will be filled with anything you need. Your people will be welcome here at all times."

Cochise called his people together and, after more pleasantries were exchanged, the Indians gathered their presents and started back for the hills.

Riding at the head of his people, Cochise thought how simple it was sometimes to make the Americans happy. They were wise in many things, he thought, but in some things they were as children. It was just as though he gave a small Indian child a bow and arrow, or as though his wife made a doll for a little girl. The Americans lost the dignity of their manhood when they saw the yellow iron. They gushed and became effusive and uncovered their emotions as no Indian ever would under any circumstances. They had no restraint. No Apache woman, no oldster in his senility, would make the sounds Americans made when they saw the yellow iron. For some reason they valued the yellow iron more than the white iron, although there was no difference except for color. It was more than he could understand. The Americans who could make such fine guns and build strong homes and who fought bravely and who knew how to die like men were people he could respect. He preferred not to see them when they were under the spell of the yellow iron.

He filled his lungs with the clear, cold afternoon air and looked at the sun low in the west. The hills were a soft purple.

He thought how much he loved his country and he thought that the Chiricahua people must be much loved by their Spirits to have been given such a place to live.

3

The cold hand of Ghost Face squeezed the Chiricahua Mountains and the icy fingers touched everything. Below, on the desert, it was still hot in the day but in the mountains there was a heavier fall of snow than had come in many winters. The wind was like sharp arrows and as it swirled the snow and dug into the flesh of the people, the old men said that the wind would bring sickness. They said that the wind was being blown at them by their enemies far away and that the measure of the hatred of their enemies was in the strength of the wind. The cottonwood trees were bare of leaves and the thick hedge of juniper was barely visible above the snow and in the distance on the mountainsides the pines were white and now and then a gust of wind tore the snow from the pine branches and blew it wildly in the air.

The Chiricahua Apaches were in strange circumstances and they were confused. Here was the bottom of their year's living and in some ways they were richer and in other ways poorer than they had ever been. They had blankets to keep them warm and their wickiups were strong and well built. On the other hand, there was a lack of warm clothing. The Apache could endure violent extremes of temperature, from freezing to intense heat, with nothing on except his gee-string, but it did not make him happy, and his women and children were not as hardened as he was. The deer and the elk were gone, and without them there was nothing to provide the shirts and trousers, the hip-moccasins. There was grain from the government store, but there was no fresh meat.

A few of the Apaches had looked around and had found some more of the yellow nuggets and had got white man's clothing in exchange. But the clothing was designed for the cattlemen and farmers in the lowlands and offered little protection against the cold. Besides, no Chiricahua Apache, no matter how much he tried, could accustom himself to white man's shoes. A few had got prospector's boots, but feet that had never worn stiff shoes before blistered rapidly and the boots were discarded. The Indian women tried to repair the old moccasins, sewing new soles on the frayed bases, cutting a little more from the base each time so that soon the moccasins which originally were long enough to reach the hips, now barely covered the calves.

The Apaches had been cold and hungry before, but hitherto they had accepted their plight as the natural way of things, to be improved when the season improved. Now they forgot the other bad times, and began to wonder whether their condition wasn't solely the result of the policies of Cochise. No one thought of deposing him, his hold on them was too great; and yet, in their wickiups, the people grumbled and complained and shivered and were hungry.

There was news, too, which caused disquiet. The Americans, with the help of Mexicans and Indians who served them, were striking everywhere against other Apache tribes. There was a steady stream of reports of the merciless hunting down of the Indians. The Americans seemed to have one goal: to exterminate those Indians they could not capture and put in their reservations.

Since there always was enmity among the Apaches themselves, the first reports of the action of the Americans against other tribes pleased them, until suddenly, from deep within themselves, there developed a tribal loyalty, a loyalty to their own kind, and they began to view the white man's warfare against the Apache with hatred that was not unmixed with fear.

In the early part of 1859 Cochise received couriers almost every week, and learned from them how the other Apache tribes were faring. After a particularly depressing message was given to him he ordered a sweat bath constructed so that he and his brother might hold counsel.

As with virtually every action which filled the life of the Apache Indian, the sweat bath had a religious significance. It was more than a physical cleansing. While it made the men feel good physically—no women were ever permitted to indulge in this ceremony—its spiritual therapy was more efficacious. The sweat bath was a vital part of Apache life and as the body relaxed in the thick steam and the vapors cleared the head, the ideas and decisions that were made in that atmosphere were regarded as particularly sound.

The bath house had to be reconstructed for each occasion. It was made in a specific way by men who were versed in this art. These men were not regarded in the same exalted light as were shamans, but their status was a religious one nevertheless, and no ordinary person would dare to construct a bath.

The structure itself was not unlike a wickiup from the outside, although it usually was somewhat smaller. The entrance always faced east, to the direction of the rising sun. Just inside the door was the pit for the hot stones.

When Cochise and his brother arrived the boss of the sweat bath had everything ready. Although it was bitterly cold Cochise and Naretena wore only loincloths. The body of Naretena was thin and beginning to waste. Cochise, in perfect physical condition, bore on his muscular frame the scars of many bullets and arrows.

At the entrance to the bath they were rubbed down briskly with pounded juniper, and then the required piece of sage was affixed to their heads. They took a drink from a container into which mesquite beans, in the sacred number of four, had been soaked. They were handed small sticks with which to scratch themselves inside the bath, since it was forbidden to scratch with the hands lest a bad infection, leaving permanent scars, result.

When the preliminaries were completed, four large rocks were brought to the bath house by means of forked sticks by the boss of the bath and these rocks were thrown into pits. The boss spilled water on them and then Cochise and Naretena hastened inside, through the rising steam, and the boss shut the door, made of stiffened buckskin, after them.

When the brothers were inside, the boss, seated outside, started to sing the necessary songs, and Cochise and Naretena joined him. The songs extolled the value of the baths, and spoke of the beauty of the earth and the splendor of the sky, and of the wisdom of the People of the Mountains.

The ceremony finally ended, Cochise and Naretena sat in long silence and let the steam penetrate them. Because of his sickness, Naretena did not often take the baths, since they left him weak.

After a while, Naretena said, "The mind is heavy."

"Bad news," Cochise said.

The two men could not see each other in the opaque wall of steam which had risen between them. They sat on their haunches, their arms folded across their chests.

"Word from Mangas Coloradas," Cochise said. "News from the Pinal and Tontos. Word before that from the Mescaleros. Word is the same. Killing, killing, more killing. Americans hunt them like animals. Word is the same. They say to me: Apaches must join together and fight the Americans as one people, as the Americans fight them. They say to me that Apaches can defeat Americans, if they fight together, but that this way all will die. They say to me Americans want to kill them or put them inside fences. Mangas Coloradas wants all the Apaches to fight together, in one war, each tribe helping the other. He says to me that is the only way the Apaches can survive."

"You say?" Naretena asked.

"I am trying to know. Where does loyalty lie, to the Chiricahua people or to all Apache people? We have fought often among ourselves, but still we are the same, and the American is different. Am I being unfair to other tribes? We have our Strongholds. No white man can ever find us there. We are safer than the others. The Americans hunt them down day and night. We can escape. Am I failing in my responsibilities? Will the Chiricahua people one day find themselves alone against an enemy?"

Naretena pondered his answer. Then he said, "I do not believe so. Americans act as they do because of earlier actions of the Apaches, caused by still earlier actions of Americans and Mexicans, and it is that way far back. No one remembers where it started. The hatred between Apaches and Mexicans is ancient. While the hatred between the Apaches and the Americans is not so ancient, still fixed feelings are developed, and the Apaches and the Americans are controlled by these feelings."

Cochise listened in silence. Talk with his brother always clarified problems as nothing else could.

"The other war chiefs say that by joining together we can defeat the white men," Naretena continued. "They are wrong. It is natural for them to think so because the Apaches have never been conquered. But they are wrong. More and more I am coming to know that now the white man is mighty, soon he will be invincible. Together or apart the Apaches will be defeated if they continue to be at war with the Americans. There is only one path for survival, one way to change the feelings that now are the cause of this bloodshed. That way is for a great Apache leader and for his people to show the Americans that the Apaches can live as brothers with them. It may seem at the beginning that this leader is being a traitor to his own people because he does not put on the war paint to fight the common enemy. But at the end it will be this leader who will be a savior to his people. Some will die now so that others may live in peace and dignity later."

"You speak words that are in my heart, Oh my brother," Cochise said. "The voice inside me tells me I am doing right. But how good to hear it from you!"

"I speak from my own heart," Naretena said. "It was not given to me by the Great Spirit to remain long among our people and I think sometimes I have been given to understand things as though this understanding were in place of slowly gained knowledge."

It was seldom that Naretena spoke of his inevitable early death, which was understood and accepted with Indian fatality. Cochise was deeply moved. After a silence, he said, "I am trying to save the Chiricahua people from a reservation." He used the Apache phrase "earth made into a cage." "A reservation would be worse than if all the people died. I have heard stories about these reservations. It is better to kill an eagle than to put him in a cage. The deer and the antelope cannot live tethered like a mule, or confined to a corral. If the Chiricahua people were confined to a reservation they would die as a people. They might live in numbers, even grow larger in numbers, and they might become fat and live many years, but they would die as a people. The thing that lives in our breasts cannot be confined to a corral for live people. What we are we are because we are free and have always been free. We are as the wind."

He remained silent again, and then continued. "There are some Indian peoples to whom a reservation means nothing. They have lived in villages and they have learned to grow things from the land and make things with their hands to exchange for what they need to live. A reservation fence could be built around such people and they would not know it until their grandchildren are men." His voice was scornful. "But we are a free people. Our lives are on our feet and in our horses and in our weapons. That is why we must make our peace with the Americans, before they make it for us, and in their own way. I am trying to shape our people from within ourselves, instead of having the shaping done from outside, at the point of guns."

The bath boss opened the door and placed freshly heated stones inside and then poured more water on them.

"I do not understand Americans," Cochise continued. "I think I understand them, maybe, sometimes, and they seem to me to be separate from their people, men with whom I can speak with nothing else in the air between us, not the fact that I am an Indian and they are Americans. One can never do that with Mexicans. When one speaks to a Mexican he speaks to his people first and to the man second. For a little while, talking to a good American, I can think there is something important that is going back and forth between us. And then suddenly there seems to be a wall, and the American is behind that wall, in company with all other Americans, and all the Indians are on the other side, and speech and thought is no longer between one man and another man, but between an Indian and an American. There are many kinds of Americans as there are many kinds of Indians, but always there is this wall, and no matter how different an American may seem for a little while to be, still he is found behind this wall, with other Americans, never on the same side as the Indians. What is inside of them as Americans is stronger than what is inside of them as one man or another man. It is the same with us, exactly the same. Will this wall ever come down? Will things appear to be going peacefully and then suddenly the wall will appear and we shall be on opposite sides?"

"You have chosen a new path for your people," Naretena said. "No one knows the markings on this path. There is nothing on it to guide because no one has walked it before. Such a path is a strange one, filled with doubts and questions and fears. It is important only that you know that the path

96

leads to the goal you wish in the end to reach and then the loneliness and strangeness of the path means nothing."

"Some of the Americans treat us with respect and dignity," Cochise said. "Steen was such a man. He believed us to be men who could reason and think. And yet most Americans believe us to be animals, strong wild animals, to be handled carefully because we have sharp claws. Steen was different, I think. An American can be different, maybe. But some Americans only pretend they are different and somewhere or other their inner thoughts betray them. Their true thoughts lie waiting and one way or another they come out. Americans speak of Apaches who live at peace with them as 'tame' Apaches." Cochise spat out the words again. " 'Tame' Apaches! I will have respect for our people before anything else. I will have it known that we are men and women and not animals, that our word is good, better than the word of most white men. Our ways are different from theirs but they are no worse. We will not be regarded as animals or as small children nor yet as peons."

The system of peonage, Spanish in origin, had long before spread up into the Territory of New Mexico and the system had absorbed not only Mexicans but Indians. The Apaches, independent and strong, had never been taken as peons and always held in contempt the less warlike Indians who had succumbed.

"There will be no Chiricahua, man or woman, who becomes peon to the white man," Cochise said slowly. "Not if we have to die, all of us, our men and our women and our children."

4

By February the tribe was out of meat. Hunters roamed over the snow-covered hills but there was no trail anywhere. The animals were gone. A rabbit might be shot, a squirrel might be picked off in the lowlands. But that was all. The big game animals were gone. And this was the time of the year when the people needed meat more than at any other time. The weather continued cold. Although the adult Apaches, inured by generations of exposure to both intense heat and cold, could survive almost naked in the coldest weather, still they suffered greatly and their undernourished babies craved meat for warmth and strength. In that winter, when the branches of trees snapped and fell to the ground, there was a sudden epidemic of death among the smaller children of the Chiricahua tribe. The sound of mourning from bereaved mothers hung over the camp like a cloud.

Cochise sent a party of men over to the West Stronghold to get some of the jerked beef stored there. This dried meat was not to have been touched. It was the insurance Cochise had provided for some future time when the tribe might be besieged in the Stronghold by an enemy. Now it was brought to the tribe and Cochise told himself that perhaps the tribe would never have to hide in the Strongholds again.

The food lasted through the worst days of the winter and then when the cold weather started to break and the season of Little Eagles looked in upon the land and decided to remain a little while, Cochise called for a large-scale raid into Mexico to cheer his dispirited people after their bad time and to encourage them to continue amenable to his long-range policy with the Americans.

The announcement was received with joy and excitement. While there had been a few, sporadic raids by small isolated parties, this would be the first large-scale raid, led by Cochise himself, in many months. The men divested themselves of the winter lethargy, and set to work actively preparing their weapons and gathering their equipment. They boasted to their women that they would bring great booty from Mexico.

In the space of hours the tone of the camp changed. The empty stomachs were forgotten. The gaming places were deserted. The hoops and poles, the playing cards, made of dried pony skins cut into oblongs, were put away. Men lay frequently with their wives to try to leave behind another child in the event that the Great Spirit summoned them for the final journey during the raid.

In the household of Cochise there was another kind of excitement. This was to be the first raid in which Tahzay would accompany the men as a novice, the first of his four raids before becoming a full-fledged fighting man.

The tall, quiet, thoughtful elder son of Cochise tried to hide his excitement with a suitable show of indifference. As a novice he would not participate actively in the raid, save in an emergency. His duties would be chiefly to serve the other warriors, to act as a sort of general lackey. The fact that he was the son of the tribal chief made no difference, except perhaps to require him to show even more servility and diligence. While he was serving as novice the meanest brave in the tribe had the authority to give him any order, and he had to obey without question.

As the boy worked, Tesalbestinay looked knowingly at Cochise and her eyes crinkled. "Is this a journey for children?" she asked innocently.

"We are only going on a friendly visit," Cochise replied.

Tahzay reddened and kept his eyes fixed upon his work.

"Oh," Tesalbestinay said, as though understanding for the first time. "I see. I wondered why you were taking the small boys with you."

"Perhaps you would like to come, wife. There will be no danger."

"No," she said. "I think I will stay here and defend our camp, maybe. It may be more dangerous to remain at home."

Sweat started to creep down the neck of the boy but he said nothing. He gritted his teeth and went on with his work.

Nalikadeya showed her beautiful teeth in a sympathetic smile and said, "Pay no attention. They are proud of you."

"Proud?" Cochise asked. "At his age a man had a wife and was full warrior when I was young."

"Young people do not develop so quickly these days. It is a wonder girls look at them," Tesalbestinay said.

"Maybe I can find a Mexican woman to make into a wife for Tahzay," Cochise said.

"Maybe," Tesalbestinay agreed. "Mexican women do not need much in the way of a husband."

"They are satisfied with anything. Even Mexicans."

The chafing was the traditional prelude for a boy embarking upon his novitiate. Tahzay would have been disappointed if his mother and father had omitted it from the ceremony; but still it was embarrassing.

"I hear that Oraya soon will be given her puberty ceremony," Tesalbestinay said. "Her father thinks one of the great warriors of the tribe will ask for her, maybe."

Tahzay thought he would sink through the floor. Oraya was a pretty young Indian girl to whom he had completely lost his heart.

"She is a likely girl," Cochise said. "One of the leaders will want her, maybe. Nahilzay. Or Pionsenay."

"Nahilzay has been long in choosing a wife," Nalikadeya said. "Maybe he will be longer. Pionsenay has had three, two of them still living."

"They are rich men and brave," Cochise retorted. "They can afford as many wives as they want."

Cochise walked to his son and placed his arm on his shoulder. The boy looked up, his face burning. When Cochise spoke his voice was serious and empty of laughter. "You are a good son," he said. "I am proud of you. Our people are proud of you. They say good things about you. They say you will be a good leader later on, maybe. You have good legs and good arms and good eyes and best of all you have a heart that belongs inside of a man and I am proud of you."

The boy's eyes were shining and he fought manfully to keep from showing the pleasure he felt.

"It is necessary for a man to tell his son many things before he goes on his first raid, sometimes," Cochise continued. "I have to tell you nothing. I am satisfied you have learned your lessons well. There is nothing I need say. I have no fear for your conduct."

Tahzay returned to his work without permitting himself to thank his father or tell him how his words stirred his blood. He looked around the wickiup, filled with evidence of his father's greatness in the field: saddles, bridles, bits, quirts, saddlebags, bows, arrows, quivers, bow covers, shields, wristguards, spears, slings, flint knives, and war clubs. Standing by itself was the pride of Cochise's armory, his double-barreled shotgun, its silver receiver kept shining at all times.

Cochise nodded to Tesalbestinay and she left the wickiup; she returned presently and handed a deerskin-covered bundle to Cochise.

"My son," Cochise said.

"Yes, father."

"Rise from your work and come to me."

The boy stood up and walked to his father.

"You work well on arrows," Cochise said. "What I have here is not needed, maybe." He opened the bundle and took from it a long bow, almost full size, almost the length of two arrows, the first approximation of an adult bow that Tahzay had ever had. For weeks Cochise had worked secretly making it, cutting it from an oak branch, in a distant part of the camp. He had split the branch, shaped and smoothed the wood, and, after it was dried, greased and bent it back and forth until it was pliable. Then he had curved it and had tied it with a thong and had placed it on hot ashes, watching carefully to see that it was not burned. After it was cooled he had buried it for ten days to get its shape fully into it.

When the bow was ready for decoration, Cochise had boiled animal hooves and horns, and from the glue he obtained he sealed onto the shaft pieces of sinew, in the middle and near the ends. Then he had painted the outside a bright red and on the inside he had painted stars and crosses. Finally he had fastened the sinew from the loin of deer for the string.

Tahzay took the bow. His jaw muscles worked as he held his face impassive. He did not thank his father. Apaches never gave thanks when they appreciated a gift, the presentation implied knowledge that it would be appreciated and expressions of gratitude indicated a certain lack of closeness between the donor and the receiver.

Then Cochise took four arrows made of mulberry. Eagle feathers were affixed to the butts of the shafts. "It is not intended that you loose arrows this day," Cochise said. "If it is necessary to do so, however, you will use these four arrows before all others."

Tahzay took the arrows silently. Then Cochise gave him a wristguard made of buckskin, an arrow quiver, and a long spear made of young spruce. The final gift was a sharp steel knife in a buckskin sheath, obtained by Cochise from Tevis' store.

"I will use these so that you will not be ashamed of me," Tahzay said. Then, because he could no longer contain his emotions, he asked for permission to leave the wickiup, and then hurried out.

When he was gone, Tesalbestinay said in a low voice, "He is a good son."

"He is good," Cochise repeated.

To change the subject, Tesalbestinay turned her humor on Cochise. "There has been plenty of talk about how your son is going to fare on this raid. How about you? Are we going to have food again or are you getting too old?"

"There will be food, wife, and in plenty."

"I do not know. Sometimes I think you grow less a man."

He raised his head and laughed. "I have married a magpie," he said.

"See that you talk with your weapons," Tesalbestinay retorted sharply. "Your people are hungry and your family is hungrier than any of your people."

"What food there has been has gone to those who needed it most," Cochise said.

"Your own family needed it as much as any."

"Would you have us in plenty while others starved?"

She shook her head. "You did as you had to do. But there is still nothing to eat here."

"There will be food when we return."

"Good. It will be welcome."

"Would you like another husband, woman?" Cochise asked. "No."

"There are some blind men here who would take you from my hands."

"You are my husband," Tesalbestinay said.

"And you?" Cochise asked Nalikadeya. "Do you look for another household?"

Nalikadeya lifted her young face to him. Her love for him was ever close to expression. "I am content," she said softly, thinking of the night. She picked up a guitar and began to sing in a sweet voice. She sang:

"Man, man, you are thinking of something,
Man, man, you are thinking of something;
You are thinking of what you are going to get.
The journey on which you are going will be worthwhile."

Cochise listened gravely and then he left the wickiup. There were conferences to be held with his lieutenants. There were arrangements to make with the shamans, to insure favorable religious omens for the raid. There were preparations for the dances to be held that evening to celebrate the departure.

Nalikadeya watched him depart with eyes filled with desire. Tesalbestinay interpreted the hunger and she quietly closed her own eyes and cast her thoughts back many years.

5

The men were gone for many days. There was a sudden, unexpected resurgence of cold weather. The women in the camp made their fires in front of their wickiups and then brought the live embers into the firepit in the center of the dwelling and huddled over the warming flames.

More than two weeks went by and still the men did not return. The food in the rancheria all but vanished. Then the snow came again, out of season, and the women found their strength leaving them.

One evening when the icy cold filled the camp on the heels of the departing sun, Nalikadeya, pale and sick with the cold and hunger, said to Tesalbestinay, "There is nothing left to eat. Not even grain of any kind."

"It is good to get used to hunger," Tesalbestinay said.

"I will go down to the station where the Americans are and ask for food, maybe," Nalikadeya said.

"You will not," Tesalbestinay said sharply.

"My son is hungry," Nalikadeya said. "His father will not want him to waste away."

"His father will want less for you to beg of Americans," Tesalbestinay said.

The issue became in Nalikadeya's mind one between Tesalbestinay and herself. The actual hunger was almost forgotten. She had suggested going to the station without any real desire to do so, but the active opposition of Tesalbestinay crystallized her determination. "He has always said the white men are our friends. We hunger. What are friends for if not to provide food when one is starving?"

"I know Cochise," Tesalbestinay said quietly. "It will anger him to have you go begging for food."

The quiet superior tone of Tesalbestinay's voice infuriated Nalikadeya. "He will not want us to starve," she said shortly.

Tesalbestinay turned her back. Nalikadeya left the wickiup and started for the Butterfield station in the pass. It was bitter cold. She was barefoot. Her moccasins had worn through too often and could no longer be repaired. She shuddered in the razor wind. Her face started to freeze and her hands lost their feeling. She walked carefully but she could no longer feel anything when her feet touched the ground. She fell. When she rose her knee was skinned and the blood ran down her leg.

She struggled on, forcing her tiring body against the wind, moving by instinct. She could no longer see clearly. Her eyes were burned with the wind and there were tears in them. It was late when she finally reached the station. Once there she became frightened at what she was doing and she stood quietly outside the corral. It was warmer down in the lower country and she recovered somewhat. Then the wind came down from the hills and cut into her face like sharp stones and she fell against the wall under the impact. She staggered to the main gate and then rapped on the door leading to the trading store.

A man's voice called out, "Who's there?"

She became petrified with fear at the sound of the voice. She stood there quietly.

"Who the hell is out there?" The voice called again. Then the door was thrown open and she recognized the man called Tevis.

"It's an Apache girl," Tevis said. "She's alone."

"Tell her to come in," Walsh said. "Is she good-looking?"

"I can't tell. She's covered with snow. Come on in," Tevis said to the girl. She could not understand a word either he or Walsh had been saying. He motioned with his hand. She looked at him with frightened eyes and then she rushed past him into the warm room and ran quickly to the fire and held her hands in front of it.

Culver got up and scrutinized her. "I think she's one of Cochise's wives," he said.

"What?" Tevis said. "Look at her. She looks like a tramp. Don't tell me Cochise would let his wife walk around like that." He looked at Nalikadeya, "Speak English?"

She swayed slightly and then recovered herself.

"She's half frozen," Tevis said. "She looks as though she hasn't eaten a meal in a week. Somebody wake up Wallace. He can talk Apache." He dipped his hand into a sack and took out some corn. He brought it to the fire to roast. The girl looked at the corn and wet her lips. She reached out her hand. Tevis held the raw corn toward her. She took it hastily and put it in her mouth. "This kid's starved," he said.

Culver brought out some dried beef and hard biscuits. The girl devoured them and when Tevis parched some corn she swallowed handfuls of it. The men watched her silently and with sympathy. Another man entered the room. This was Clay Wallace, one of the stage drivers, who was at the station at the time. An old-time Westerner who had lived in Tucson before the Americans took over, he had some knowledge of the Apache language. "Who are you?" he asked. He was a red-faced, heavy man. He wiped his eyes sleepily.

"Cochise is my husband," she said. The fire felt so good, she

103

thought. She stood close to it and the heat melted the snow. The melted snow washed away some of the caked blood on her legs and made a reddish puddle on the floor.

"Look at her," Tevis said with indignation. "She's barefoot and all cut up. And she's just a kid. Cochise ought to be ashamed of himself letting his wife go around that way."

"What does the American *nantan* say?" she asked. When Wallace translated, she said, "He is away."

"Away!" Tevis bellowed when Wallace repeated the words in English. "A hell of a time for him to be away when his own wife is starving this way."

"She's pretty," Walsh said.

"She's just a kid," Tevis said.

"Apaches marry them young and break them in themselves," Walsh said coarsely.

"Quit," Wallace said. "Apache women don't do business that way."

"I'd like to find out," Walsh said.

Nalikadeya had removed her soaking skirt and held it in front of the fire. She wore nothing but a small garment around her waist. Walsh stared at her.

"Cochise would hang you by your thumbs and build a fire under your feet," Wallace said. "These Apache women don't do things like that. Navajos, yes, but not Apaches. I know."

"By God, she looks good," Walsh said.

"Wallace is right," Tevis said sharply. "We don't want any trouble with Cochise."

"What is she standing around half naked for?" Walsh demanded.

"She's paying us a sort of compliment," Wallace said. "She's treating us as though we were Apaches. They wouldn't try anything funny."

The men sat and stared at Nalikadeya, as, in complete innocence, she warmed herself and, when her skirt was dried, put it on again.

Tevis looked at her and shook his head. "Wallace," he said. "Ask her if she wants to stay here for the night." When Nalikadeya looked frightened and shook her head, he said, "Well, ask her if she wants to take any food back with her." The girl nodded happily. He went to the storeroom and returned with a sack of corn.

"Ask her if she can manage to get back to camp with that," Tevis said. "The poor kid."

"I will get back," she replied.

"You tell Cochise he ought to be damned ashamed of himself," Tevis said with heat. "American men never allow their women to starve and walk around in the snow barefooted."

As Nalikadeya struggled back up the mountains to the camp

she pondered on the different ways Americans and Apaches lived. She wished that she could have explained to them that Apache women lived as she did, and that they walked in the snow, often with bare feet, and that it was not as serious as the man with the long hair on his face seemed to think. She had to giggle a little, even in the cold and even with the dead weight of the bag on her shoulder, at the long hairs on the man's face.

6

The men returned the second day after Nalikadeya had gone down to the station. Their ponies were loaded with loot and food, but Cochise was in bad humor. On the way back from the raid, which had taken the men farther down into Mexico than they had ever gone before, when they were still on the Mexican side of the line, they were surprised by Mexican soldiery, in greater force than they had ever before encountered. The Indians had a long string of captured mules they were leading back to their camp when the soldiers intercepted them. Cochise had ordered a rear guard to hold them off and directed the rest of his warriors to go on ahead. The rear guard succeeded in delaying the Mexicans until the rest got safely away, but it had been a violent action and several Apaches had been killed. These men, added to those who had lost their lives during the actual raid, made the trip a costly one.

Cochise had a morbid fear that his race slowly was being exterminated. He would have willingly traded the whole of the loot for the lives of the men. He brought his men over the long trail to the camp deep in black thought. It was as though he was playing some kind of gigantic gambling game, in which he was pitting his people against a coordinated attempt to wipe them from the face of the earth. Everything he did, he thought grimly, was a part of this gamble. Each move advanced or set back his people. The death of his warriors was the greatest of these setbacks. Within his own lifetime, his own chieftainship, things had become different. And yet his lost warriors had died as men, he thought, and that was something. They had died violently and with dignity, as an Apache warrior should die.

His thoughts were heavy and long as he rode. He thought how there must be two living things within his single body, the one thing able to think and plan and understand, and the other able only to act quickly by instinct. Though he hated the word he knew what the Americans meant when they called an Apache "tame." They meant an Apache who buried forever the special, unique freedom from rational responsibility that made Apaches different from other Indians. That was the ultimate price to pay, he thought. If things went as he had planned for them to go, some lesser relinquishment might be made and life still be lived with the intruder. But rather than see his tribe become a nation of "tame" Apaches, rather than see them as eagles whose wings had been clipped, he would rather see them all dead, and himself the first dead among them.

As he rode there was one thing to enliven his gloomy thoughts, the courage and purpose demonstrated on the raid by Tahzay. A cool, obedient, unexcited novice who had undertaken several missions during the raid, Tahzay had, when an emergency forced the issue upon him, ridden to the forefront of a fight, and to his calm had added bravery. In the midst of the fury and excitement, Tahzay, fighting with a small party of warriors, might have been a young Cochise, totally without fear.

Tahzay was one who could be trained, he thought with satisfaction, to carry on the long-range plan he had formulated. Now, if Nachise only developed in a similar way, he could depart on the final journey with the knowledge that his work would not be undone.

As the warriors approached the station of the stage line Cochise ordered a wide detour and led the men around the lower foothills of the Chiricahua Mountains, and by a circuitous way into the rancheria. Before he got to the camp he sent a rider ahead to announce the arrival.

Fires were built and dancing and singing started. Mules were slaughtered. The women put on their new clothes. An air of great festivity animated the rancheria. Cochise quietly gave orders that only half the normal amount of food be prepared for the feast and all the rest dried and stored away for future emergency.

He handed his horse and weapons to Tesalbestinay. Tahzay started to walk away with his horse to lead it to the corral. His mother stopped him, and gravely relieved him of the reins, and then asked for his weapons. Tahzay, bursting with pride, quietly handed over his bow and quiver, still containing some arrows, and then his spear, its burned and sharpened tip red with caked blood.

Then, his head very high, the son of Cochise walked alongside his father to their wickiup.

7

The feast that night was in the great tradition. The people ate as though they had never tasted food before. The songs were loud and the dances were long and the stories that were told that night were varied, and there was something in them about the doings of Tahzay, who had won for himself a sincere respect. Cochise watched the faces of the people and he felt

106

content that they would not decline to accept Tahzay as the next Chiricahua chief.

As the night wore on the men got drunk and again Cochise was tormented by the deaths the raid had cost. He fell into a profoundly depressed mood. He kept his feelings to himself, not wishing to interfere with the pleasure of the people.

In an effort to lift himself out of the blackness into which his thoughts had plunged him, he turned to Nahilzay, sitting as usual on his right, and said, "It is good to see our people again with food."

"They were very hungry," Nahilzay agreed.

Juan, Cochise's brother, his broad good-natured face covered with sweat from the tiswin and the fire, leaned over and said, "They would have been hungrier if it was not for your woman."

"What do you mean?" Cochise asked, watching the dancers.

"Your woman, the young one, went to the stage station and got a sack of corn from the Americans," Juan shouted. "My woman told me about it."

Cochise had a gourd filled with tiswin at his lips. He ceased swallowing and slowly put the gourd down.

"What are you saying?" he asked his brother.

"How is it that you do not know?" Juan asked. "Two days ago your young woman walked down to the stage station and received a sack of corn there. She carried it back here by herself. It was not much, divided among everyone, but it helped to lift the fingers of hunger out of their bellies. My woman said it was cold and the snow was falling and it was night when she went down to the station. It was a brave thing."

Cochise was on his feet. His mouth twitched. He walked over to where the women were seated. Nalikadeya was swaying to the rhythm of the dancers. Her eyes showed that she too had been drinking generously of the tiswin. When the other women moved to make way for Cochise she looked up. She smiled at him. He moved his head almost imperceptibly and turned and strode toward his wickiup. Nalikadeya rose quickly, her body tingling with desire. She could not resist a quick look of pride at the other women. Cochise had summoned her early, earlier than any other woman had been called by her husband. She held her head high as she hurried after her husband.

Inside the wickiup he turned abruptly and faced her. "Why did you go as a beggar to the Americans?" he asked harshly.

The question was so different from what she expected it took her a few moments to understand it. Then she said, simply, "We were hungry."

"Were you so hungry it was necessary to humiliate me by going to the Americans as a beggar?"

"You have always said the Americans were friends," she said, bewildered by his anger. "We were hungry and if they are friends, as you say, it was nothing to ask them for help." That would surely end the discussion, she thought. She came closer to him and pressed herself against him so that he could smell the sweet mint on her breasts. "I was not afraid," she said proudly. "It was cold and it was snowing but I was not afraid. I walked all the way down and all the way back with a heavy bag of corn on my shoulder." She giggled. "The Americans are funny, with their long hairs on their faces. They have funny ideas about things. One of them said I should not be walking around in the snow in bare feet."

Cochise pushed her away from him. "What?"

"The government man they call Tevis. Do not Americans have funny names?" She giggled again. "He seemed very angry that I was in bare feet. He said, 'Tell Cochise he should be ashamed to have his wife walking around in the snow in bare feet.' "

"What else did he say?" Cochise asked hoarsely.

"He said Americans never let their wives walk around that way. Are American wives always sick then?"

She giggled happily again and swayed a little from the tiswin and then Cochise slapped her in the face. She looked at him startled and he slapped her again, knocking her down. She crawled to him and clung to his legs and he lifted her and slapped her a third time.

"We are not begging people," he said, his eyes aflame with rage. "We are not begging people." He struck her in the face again and knocked her onto a pallet.

She crawled from the bed toward the door and then she got up and ran out. Cochise walked out after her. He could taste bile in his mouth. He suddenly picked up a small Mexican boy, taken in a raid some time before, and, carrying him under his arm, he started for the station.

The thought of how Nalikadeya had exposed him to the ridicule of the Americans was almost too violent to be contained. He thought of how the Americans must have laughed when they saw the wife of the Chiricahua chief, barefoot, cold, hungry, coming to them like a starving animal in the night. His head ached with his fury. His feet were not entirely steady but he moved swiftly down the trail. When he came to the station he rapped hard on the door. He heard a voice and he rapped again. The door opened. Walsh stood in the threshold. Cochise pushed him aside roughly and walked into the room. Culver and Tevis were playing cards. Wallace was seated in a corner.

The men stared at Cochise, holding the child under his arm, and then the Chiricahua strode up to Tevis and thrust the child into his arms. "Here, nurse girl," he said. "Take care of your baby."

Then he walked out of the room, afraid to trust himself with Tevis. The government trader sat in his seat, the Mexican on his lap, and he looked at the other men flabbergasted. "What the hell did that savage say?" he said to Wallace.

"He called you a nursemaid and told you to take care of your baby," Wallace said.

"What for? What's this all about?"

Wallace got up. "Maybe he didn't like what you said to his wife," he said quietly.

Tevis had forgotten about the incident. "His wife?" he asked puzzled.

"The Indian girl who was in here the other night. You told her to tell him he ought to be ashamed of himself."

"I only said what I would have said to anybody," Tevis protested.

"Anybody but an Apache," Wallace said.

Tevis wiped his brow. "He was drunk," he said uneasily. "He'll probably forget all about this tomorrow." He looked at the Mexican child and then he looked at Wallace. "What in hell am I going to do with this thing?"

Outside the corral Cochise stood quivering. He struck the stone wall of the corral with his fists. He wanted to kill. He went to the door and pounded it again.

This time the Americans drew revolvers before they called out to come in. He entered the room again. His face was working under its smeared and distorted paint. He pointed to Tevis and said, "We are enemies. You try to kill me and I will try to kill you. Whichever does it first, all right." He looked at the drawn revolvers. Tevis had the feeling that he was going to throw himself upon him unarmed. He cocked his pistol. Cochise turned and walked out.

When he had slammed the door behind him, Wallace looked at Tevis. "You got trouble," he said laconically. "You got a child, too."

In the morning Cochise was somewhat cooled off and Naretena, in his quiet and thoughtful way, advised him to return to the station and reestablish friendly terms with Tevis.

"I have said we are enemies," Cochise said.

"A man can say things when he is filled with tiswin. Go back to the station. This is not an important thing."

"It will be told everywhere how the woman of Cochise begs for food," Cochise said, beginning to work himself into another rage.

"He was just trying to be kind to your woman," Naretena said soothingly. "The fault was hers, not his. Would you have had him refuse to give her food? Would you have had him shut the door in her face and leave her outside without help? He was acting as a friend. A friend does not question, he gives help."

Cochise bit his lip. " 'Tell Cochise he ought to be ashamed to have his woman walk around this way,' he said."

"He was speaking as a friend," Naretena said. "And you are ashamed, are you not?"

Cochise said nothing.

"You are angry more with yourself than with him," Naretena said sagely.

"I will not kill him," Cochise said finally.

"Tell him so."

"I will not tell him so."

"If he does not know he will kill you, maybe."

Cochise snorted.

"Their guns fire long," Naretena said quietly.

"Then I will kill him first," Cochise said shortly. "That will settle everything."

"That will settle nothing," Naretena said firmly. "You will kill him and then the Americans will regard you as having broken your word. That one killing will start a new war between the Americans and our people."

Cochise remained silent.

"I will go there and speak to him," Naretena said.

"You will not."

Cochise resolved to settle the affair in his own way. Nothing was done for some time. He avoided the station and after a while the quarrel seemed to be forgotten. Then one day Tevis acquired a beautiful horse and, having forgotten all about Cochise's threat, he mounted it and took it for a gallop in the hills to test its mettle. He rode for some distance and then dismounted and let the horse graze while he stretched out under a tree and rested. He was lying there comfortably when he heard a whining sound, a musical, twanging sound, repeated three times before he could move, and he sat up, startled, and found there were three arrows in the ground, in a neat curve, a few inches from where his head had rested.

He drew his revolver and looked around nervously. The horse was some distance away from him. He was standing in a small cleared area, surrounded by boulders. Behind any one of a hundred of these huge rocks there might be an Indian. He suddenly remembered Cochise's threat and he looked everywhere wildly. Cochise might be fitting a fourth arrow into his bow. Then he looked at the three arrows in the ground. They stood in a perfect arc. There had been no error. They had not missed him. They were not intended to have struck him.

He called, "Cochise! Cochise!" There was no response. He put the revolver back into its holster and held his empty hands above him. "Cochise! Cochise!" No one answered him. He walked deliberately and unhurriedly to his horse, mounted, and then rode back to the station.

A few weeks later Tevis was captured by two of Cochise's warriors and was taken to the Indian rancheria. He was bound to a tree. The Indians went about their business, passing in front of him, but no matter what he said no one would answer him. Cochise, refusing to listen to him, ordered a great brew of tiswin. While the Government Agent watched, a pit was dug and the bottom covered with a cowhide. Corn was put in and water poured over it. The brew was allowed to ferment.

In the night Tevis was unbound and was allowed to sleep, guarded by an Indian. The next morning women trampled the brew with their bare feet. Then Cochise walked up to Tevis. He gazed intently at him, saying nothing. Tevis, greatly frightened, looked back quietly. He had had time to think and he had resolved that if he was going to be put to death he would show the Indians that an American could die as bravely as they could.

Cochise sat down and said something sharply to Tesalbestinay. The woman built a fire over the pit. Tevis wet his lips. So it was to be that way. He had never bargained for that kind of death. He hoped he would not cry out in pain.

Cochise called for Goanola, an old shaman, with whom Tevis was on very friendly terms. Goanola had been a frequent visitor at the station and had often received gifts of tobacco from the Government Agent, and had learned to speak a passable English. The old man glanced at Tevis and then sat silently next to Cochise.

"Old man," Cochise said. "Tell this man that we now are quits. Tell him he shamed me and that I have frightened him and that now we are even and it is between us as before."

The shaman managed to convey the gist of the statement to Tevis. Cochise stood up and untied the Agent and then he handed him his revolver and cartridge belt. Then, to indicate his trust in Tevis, he turned his back to him and gave orders to his wife to prepare food.

When he turned back to Tevis, the Agent, his eyes on Cochise, said to Goanola, "Tell the Chiricahua chief that I meant no insult. There is no one I respect more than I respect him. Tell him I know that he has had it in his power two times to kill me."

Cochise grunted and handed Tevis a large gourd filled with tiswin. A roast was put on the fire and Tevis joined Cochise in eating. He had disliked the taste of the Indian beer at first, but after a few swallows he found it more to his liking. He marveled at the huge quantities of the liquid that disappeared into the Indian's throat.

Later in the evening Tevis felt a slight tug on his arm. Goanola bent down and whispered, "Go. There are many who are getting filled with tiswin. They know what happened between him and you. They may get the idea they will be favoring him by doing you harm."

Cochise was staring dully into the fire. Tevis stood up. Cochise did not look at him. Tevis walked away from the fire. Then Goanola led him out of the camp. "He will do you no harm," the old shaman said. "Have no fear. He binds himself by his word."

"I understand," Tevis said.

"Understand him and you will be doing good. He has many things on his mind. I have lived almost twice his years and I have never heard of an Apache leader trying to do what he is trying to do. Understand him. Do not think he is bad."

"I understand," Tevis said quietly. "I thank you."

"There is nothing to thank me for," Goanola said. His face was very old and in the clear moonlight the many wrinkles that rippled over it could be plainly seen. "It was not you I tried to help. It was for him and our people. One man is nothing and our people are everything. He has a plan. I do not want anything to happen to his plan. There must be no trouble between your people and ours."

"You are strange," Tevis said. He stood at the edge of the pass. "I do not understand many of the things you do. You are a strange people and in many ways you are wonderful." He thought for a moment. "And he is a great leader."

Goanola pointed down the pass. "Go. Forget this. Think of him as a friend as before."

8

The season of Many Leaves turned to the season of Large Leaves, and Large Leaves in its turn gave way to Large Fruit and through the summer of 1859 there was peace and quiet in the Chiricahua country.

The incident with Tevis brought about some changes that improved the condition of the tribe. Tevis, who had become a staunch supporter of Cochise, arranged for the donation of a small herd of cattle to the Indians, and some of the younger warriors, despite their repugnance for what they considered menial labor, were instructed in the raising of the animals. Although they hated the work, they learned the details of cattle raising with a rapidity which astonished their American instructors. They were quick and astute, and soon they were proud of their herd.

Additionally, in the fall, the season called Thick with Fruit, Cochise arranged with the Butterfield people to supply the station in Apache Pass with firewood. The Indians went into the hills and worked hard, felling trees and dragging the wood to the station.

The station operators paid the Indians fairly and with the money they were able to get food as they needed it. It was very strange to the Apaches to be working as they were, and there was some difficulty at the start, but Cochise was firm and no one would disobey him. Then the Indians came to like the arrangement. There was food and clothing and trinkets in Tevis' store, and the Indians took pleasure in going there whenever they pleased, wandering around the store like children in a fairyland. Tevis dealt honestly with them and kept a true account of the moneys due them, and no one felt he was accepting charity.

The customs of the Indians were strange and occasionally amusing. Tevis was startled at first to see a stalwart brave suddenly dash behind a counter and hide when an old Indian woman entered the store. Then he learned that the woman was the mother-in-law of the brave and that the brave could not lay eyes upon her. He became used to the intricate devices the Indians employed to uphold this tradition. He listened to an Indian woman speaking to an infant in her arms, while, with his back to her, a brave listened. He discovered that the woman was speaking only ostensibly to the child, that the words were intended for the ears of the man, but that the woman could not speak to him directly.

He also discovered the odd tastes of the Indians. He had received a supply of candy—licorice and peppermint. He had thought the Indians would enjoy the sweetmeats, but after a few tastes they refused it. Even the small children did not care for it. Then one day, quite accidentally, an Indian inquired about a bottle of castor oil on a shelf. Tevis gave the bottle to the Indian dubiously. The Indian tasted it and then emptied the bottle. He found that the Apaches considered castor oil a delicacy and liked especially to grease their stomach with it before embarking upon a tiswin orgy. He handed out the entire supply he had in the store and the Indians clamored for more as word got around. Within a week he received several gallons of it, and found that it was the most popular item in all his stock.

Tevis developed a genuine fondness for the Indians. He learned to do business their way—which meant a complete indifference to time. Indians would spend hours looking at things in the store before they would select what they wanted. If they

113

wanted some yardage of cloth, for instance, they would look at every bolt of cloth in the store before indicating their choice. A brave who wanted a pair of trousers would examine every pair of trousers, even though they were identical, before he chose the pair he wanted. At first this almost oriental conception of the value of time irritated Tevis; he was impatient with the slowness of the Indians. But after a while he relaxed and took things easy. It was a pleasant way to conduct a business. It was hot. There was nothing to hurry about.

There was only one untoward event during this year. In the late fall of 1859 a strange man appeared at the station. He gave his name as Dr. Franklin Hunt and he said he was a scientist. He was short, fat, with a bald head he protected carefully from the sun, and a goatee that made the Indian girls giggle when they first saw him. Strangely he had a fair knowledge of the Apache tongue and within a short while he managed to inform the Chiricahua people that he regarded the prices charged by Tevis for his goods as too high. He further informed the Indians that he had a large stock of goods due to arrive in a very short time, and when they arrived he would be happy to dispose of them among the Apaches at much cheaper prices than Tevis asked. Also, he added, he planned to give each Indian a present.

The only thing he asked, in return for this kindness, was for the Indians to bring him specimens of the yellow and white iron they sometimes discovered in the hills and the dried stream beds. He suggested that the Indians keep his promises secret from Tevis, because if Tevis found out he would be sure to see to it that Hunt was sent away, and if that happened the Indians would fail to get the wonderful presents which were now on their way.

The Indians passed the word around, and while they cut and hauled wood they looked around for specimens for the scientist. They also kept his secret. Tevis, suspicious of Hunt, could not put his finger on anything to cause him to order the man to leave. He satisfied himself with warning Hunt against attempting to do anything to anger the Indians. Hunt blandly assured him that he was merely conducting a scientific study.

During the next few weeks the Indians brought the nuggets of gold and some specimens of silver ore to the scientist. He collected the precious metal in a large sack, and kept assuring the Indians that the goods and presents soon would arrive.

The goods finally arrived. It consisted of cheap trash. With great ceremony, Hunt presented each Indian with some trifling present—a string of beads, a cheap knife, a piece of cheap material. He thanked them and packed and prepared to depart on the next stage.

114

The disappointed Indians showed the worthless presents to Cochise and told him what had happened. He sent a runner down to the station with orders for Hunt to come up to the camp.

"Tell Cochise I am leaving on the next stage," Hunt told the runner. "I won't be able to accept the honor of his invitation."

A short time later the runner returned. "He said to come up," the Indian said.

"You better go," Tevis said. He was enjoying this.

"I have no time. The stage is due soon," Hunt protested.

"Better go," Tevis repeated. "Or maybe you won't need a stage to travel to where Cochise will send you."

"He doesn't attack stages," Hunt said, blanching. "You told me that yourself."

"He don't make a regular practice of it," Culver drawled. "But he might make an exception in your case."

"He said to come quick," the runner said.

"Somebody come up with me," Hunt pleaded.

"No," Tevis said. "You better go alone. Maybe he has some specimens for you."

Hunt looked at the station as though he wanted to run inside. The runner took his arm and shoved him forward. Hunt looked nervously at the men in the corral. Then he sighed and walked ahead of the runner.

At the camp Cochise had assembled his people in formal array. The warriors were in one group, the women in another, and the children in a third. The people stood silent as the little man with the goatee appeared.

Hunt took off his hat and wiped his steaming head with a large handkerchief. He sought out Cochise and said to him, in Apache, "There has been a mistake. Let me explain." Cochise looked at him stonily. Hunt puffed out his chest. "You cannot do anything to me. I will report you to the government. I will have the Army sent after you."

"Look what you have given us," Cochise said in deep contempt.

Each Indian threw at Hunt the piece of trash he had given him.

"You are a thief," Cochise said. "You make trouble. My people work with the Americans and they are our friends. That is how it is. But there is no place here for a thief. If you want to keep your life in your little fat body get out of here. Go. Run. Do not stop until you are on the wagon. And do not come back here again."

Hunt did not require a second suggestion. He turned and began to waddle down the trail.

"Thief," Cochise called out. "One thing more. Leave that

bag of yellow iron at the station. If you take it with you I will send some men to catch you on the wagon and then you will not get away from here again."

Hunt fled down the hill. The stage was ready to leave as he arrived at the station.

"Never thought I'd see you moving under your own power again," Tevis said.

Hunt didn't answer. He clambered aboard the stage and huddled in a corner. His face was a sickly green. Tevis picked up the bag of silver and gold. "What about this, professor? Aren't you going to take your specimens?"

Hunt's eyes were glassy as he looked at the sack. "The devil with it," he said.

"What?" Tevis asked incredulously.

"Keep it," Hunt said, his lips twitching. "Why don't we start? Aren't we late in getting away?"

Tevis took off his hat and scratched his head. "I'll be damned," he said.

Hunt leaned out of the stage. "Driver, hurry! Hurry! Hurry!"

As the stage rolled away Tevis stood there staring after it. He looked at the bag of gold and at the stage and he scratched his head again. "I'll be damned," he repeated softly.

There was another incident that pointed up the relations between the Chiricahua Indians and the men at the stage station during that time. A young man named John Lawrence arrived one day to assist Tevis in a periodical stock-taking. Lawrence was a slim, quiet, almost studious youth, who went about his business inconspicuously. In some unknown manner he got into a quarrel with a young Indian brave. There was a brief fist-fight and Lawrence knocked the Indian down. The furious warrior, ashamed at having lost face before other Indians, demanded at a council meeting of the tribe that he be given satisfaction. He asked for a general attack on the station.

Cochise questioned the warrior and investigated further, and finally ordered that no general attack would be made, but agreed to permit a personal duel between Lawrence and the Indian if Lawrence wished to have one. The young clerk had no actual desire to fight any duel, but he felt his honor was being challenged and he agreed to meet the indian with pistols.

On the appointed day Cochise came down to the station with several hundred of his warriors in full military dress. There were only about eight or ten Americans at the station and they looked with some nervousness at the warlike manner of the Indians.

Dueling pistols were produced and carefully examined by Cochise and then given to the two men. They were placed back to back and told to walk twenty-five paces, turn and fire.

The duelists reached their turning points at the same time and turned toward each other. The Indian lifted his revolver quickly and fired. The ball went over Lawrence's left shoulder. By that time the young clerk had raised his pistol and, taking careful and unhurried aim, fired a ball into the Indian's heart. The Indian fell dead.

There was a low sigh from the other Indians. The Americans gripped their own guns, ready for anything. Cochise walked slowly to the dead Indian. He knelt and examined him. Then he rose and walked to Lawrence. The young man was pale. Cochise placed his hand upon his shoulder and said in Spanish, "You are a brave man."

Then he gave a curt order. Two Indians picked up the body of the dead Indian, and without another word the Apaches left the camp.

Chapter Seven

About ten years earlier there started the first of a chain of events that had a profound effect upon the story of Cochise and his warriors. On the 30th of September, 1849, a young and beautiful Mexican girl named Inez Gonzales was departing from her home in the Hacienda La Palma on the mesa west of the upper Rio San Pedro near the small town of Santa Cruz in Sonora. At fifteen, Inez was regarded as one of the great beauties of the community, and on that day she was starting out on a journey to visit her sister in Magdalena to attend the Fiesta de San Francisco. Included in the party were two other women, Mercedes Pacheco, an aunt to Inez, and Jesus Salvador, personal servant to the girl. A small detachment of Mexican *rurales*, led by an uncle of Inez, Lieutenant Limon, accompanied the party to protect it from hostile Apaches who frequently raided the seventy-five miles of country that lay between Santa Cruz and Magdalena.

In Cocospera Canyon, Pinal Apaches attacked. Lieutenant Limon and his soldiers were massacred. Inez, her aunt, Jesus Salvador, and a small boy, Francisco Pacheco, son of Mercedes, were taken captive. A year later Inez was sold to two Mexicans, Peter Blacklaws and Pedro Acheveque, and later was rescued by John B. Bartlett, of the United States Boundary Commission at the Santa Rita mines in New Mexico, and was returned to her parents. Her aunt and the little boy, Francisco, never were heard of again, but a great deal was heard of Jesus Salvador, the servant.

Jesus Salvador was taken as wife by one of her Apache captives and from this union came a son, who was called, later on, Mickey Free. While still carrying her boy on her back in Apache fashion, in 1855, Jesus, working along the bank of the Gila River gathering sahuaro fruit, managed to steal away and made her way down the Gila canyon. She traveled for miles with the child before she was missed and then got to the open plains that stretched away to the south of the Gila below the mouth of the San Pedro and there was taken in by a tribe of friendly Pima Indians.

Later she went to Tucson and after that to a settlement on the Sonoita River near Calabasas, and after that back to Santa Cruz, where she arrived in the spring of 1856. When the Americans moved into the Sonoita Valley following the realignment of the boundary, a number of Mexicans crossed the line, among them Jesus and her son. Presently she began to live with an Irish rancher named John Ward in the Sonoita Valley.

In October, 1860, when Mickey Free was a child of about six, he was playing on the ranch trying to catch a burro on a little point of land that jutted from the house into the valley some three hundred yards away. Ward, who also dealt in lumber, was away from the ranch on business. Mickey Free raced after the burro and found himself in the hands of a small party of Indians. They were Pinal Apaches who had from time to time kept an eye on Jesus Salvador and her son, and who considered Mickey Free one of their own.

The Indians took the child captive, broke into the corral and released a herd of work oxen and some horses, and fled. By this time Jesus Salvador was out of the house screaming. The Pinals made no attempt to molest her, but disappeared with the child and the animals.

When Ward returned home he found the woman in a state of collapse. She told him what had happened. He started to trail the Indians and followed their markings as far as the San Pedro River. There he lost trail. But he knew that the Chiricahua Indians, under Cochise, had a camp in the Dragoon Mountains to the east of the San Pedro, and Ward was convinced that the child and animals had been taken by the Chiricahuas. Ward knew that Cochise and his people were supposed to be at peace with the white men, but he had no faith in the promises of Indians.

2

At this time the commandant at Fort Buchanan, which served to protect the American settlers in the Sonoita Valley, was Colonel Pitcairn Morrison, Seventh Infantry, a depressed

118

and unhappy officer. The site picked for the establishment of Fort Buchanan had proved to be an unwise one. It was situated in an extremely unhealthy locality. Malaria was current among the soldiers and Colonel Morrison himself had suffered from an attack and was just recovering.

Buchanan was a sorry fort in other ways. It actually was no fort at all. There were no protecting walls. The buildings were dismal adobe structures, scattered around untidily. Soldiers had to be constantly on the alert or they might be attacked by hostile Indians right within the camp grounds. There was no place for any entertainment and the general atmosphere of the camp was one of discontent and unhappiness.

Colonel Morrison was bored with his job. It was far away from every place, a lonely, isolated outpost, as cut off from the world as though it were on an island in the middle of the ocean. Tubac offered some relaxation with its fine homes and cultivated residents, and Tucson offered relaxation occasionally, but apart from these two places there was little to do. Colonel Morrison thought glumly how in the East, Army officers were preparing for the talked-about war between the states, but out in this god-forsaken part of the country there was nothing but Indian trouble, and Indian trouble was nothing a man could meet in military fashion. There were sporadic attacks with their inevitable "pursue and punish" sequels. This usually involved more pursuit than punishment. It was dull and routine, and Colonel Morrison wished heartily that he was back East where war was conducted in a civilized manner and an officer might have some chance for promotion.

A fine-looking man with the lean, aristocratic head of a greyhound, Colonel Morrison was seated in his headquarters on a hot October afternoon, wondering when he might find an excuse to visit Tucson again, when he was informed by an orderly that Mr. John Ward, the rancher, wanted to see him immediately. Colonel Morrison, foreseeing the usual thing, Indian trouble, sighed and told his orderly to show Mr. Ward in.

The rancher, big, redheaded, and hot-tempered, burst into the room. Colonel Morrison looked at him with some distaste and asked courteously, "What can I do for you, Mr. Ward?"

"My kid was stolen by those god-damned Apaches," Ward said loudly. "I want a posse of soldiers right away to track them bastards down and get me my kid."

Morrison disliked noise. He lit a long black cigar carefully. "What Apaches?" he asked in the same polite voice.

"Chiricahuas," Ward said. "They grabbed the kid right off my land, and stole my oxen and horses." He pounded the desk with his fist. "This is America," he shouted. "Law-abiding citizens deserve protection from their government. I want some soldiers pronto before the trail gets cold."

"Striking my desk won't bring back your child," Morrison said quietly. "Did you say Chiricahua Apaches? We haven't had any trouble with the Chiricahuas for years."

"Who ever heard of Apaches who didn't cause no trouble when they got a chance?" Ward said scornfully. "That's the trouble with you Army men. You listen to these damned lying savages and believe what they say. Do I get some soldiers or do the settlers have to get up a vigilante committee?"

Morrison sighed inwardly. That was what the Army was there for, to help the so-called law-abiding settlers in this horrible place. "How do you know it was Cochise?" he asked.

"I been out west a long time, Colonel," Ward said sarcastically. "I know how to follow a trail. I got back to my ranch a couple of hours after they grabbed the kid and drove off with the animals and their trail was still hot. I followed it right to the San Pedro. Cochise and his bunch of bloodthirsty murderers live in the Dragoons on the other side of the river. That's how I know it was Chiricahuas, Mister Colonel."

"Your argument is irrefutable," Morrison murmured.

"Do I get some soldiers?" Ward demanded.

"It's a task for a mounted patrol, Mr. Ward," Morrison said. "I don't have any cavalrymen at the moment. As soon as some are available they will be at your disposal."

"When will that be?"

"I do not know, Mr. Ward. Assignment of personnel to Fort Buchanan is something beyond my control."

"The kid will be murdered by then."

"I am very sorry, Mr. Ward," Morrison said. "I sympathize with you, believe me." He leaned back in his chair. He was not a callous man and the worry of the rancher made him pity him, noisy and uncouth as he was. Still, what could he do? It was very hot and uncomfortable and he wished Ward would leave.

"No wonder these damned Indians think they can get away with anything they damned please," Ward said nastily. "We're supposed to have military protection here. We got an Army, only it's the wrong kind of Army. How the hell are we supposed to live in this country?"

"I'm sure I do not know, Mr. Ward," Morrison said. "Also I do not like to be addressed in the manner you are addressing me. My promise stands. The first patrol that returns will be assigned to you. If I am assigned additional mounted troops, you shall have first call on their services."

Ward glared at the officer. He jammed his hat on his head. "That better be damned soon," he said.

When Ward was gone Morrison carefully flicked the ash from his cigar. He decided to go to Tucson after all.

Dr. Michael Steck, Agent for all the Apache Indians, including many tribes he had never seen or had any relations with, looked with some interest at the second lieutenant sitting in front of him. Dr. Steck was an old-timer in the West and he had had a great deal to do with Indians before he took a government position. He was interested in the young officer, a typical specimen of the new-type Army man the government was sending from the East to deal with the troublesome Indian problems.

The second lieutenant was named George Nicholas Bascom. He was a native of Kentucky. He was a graduate of the Military Academy at West Point, class of 1858. He had done very little between the time of his graduation and the present time, October, 1860, but he now was happy and excited. He was twenty-two, a commissioned officer in the United States Army, and he was en route with a small detachment of men to Fort Buchanan in the western part of the Territory of New Mexico in the heart of the Indian country.

He had found his military duties in the East quite dull and he was eager to get into the notorious Indian country where a young officer might distinguish himself very quickly, he thought, and soon find himself promoted, or, at the very least, breveted to a higher rank.

Lieutenant Bascom was slender, fair-haired, and pink-cheeked. He had a faint, almost invisible blond mustache which gave his upper lip the appearance of not having been wiped after his last meal. Although it was hot he was in dress uniform, new and lustrous blue. His pale blue eyes were shining.

"You are looking forward to duty at Buchanan," Steck said.

"I am looking forward to field duty," Bascom said. "I've been bored to death attending tea parties back East."

"I daresay you will not find too many tea parties at Buchanan," Steck said dryly. The young man's impetuous statements in the last half hour had amused the Agent. He wondered how long it would be before the heat would slow him down.

"I have been doing considerable reading on the Indians," Bascom said. "And I've developed some theories I would like to put into practice."

"Have you?" Steck asked. "Such as what? I would enjoy hearing your theories."

"I believe these Indians respect only one thing: force," Bascom said with confidence. "They live by force and they will obey force. I think it is an error to attempt to temporize with them."

"That's an interesting theory," Steck said.

"They are savages," Bascom continued. "You can't talk sense to savages. You can't reason with them. You must crack the whip and they will obey. They interpret reasonableness as weakness."

"Do they teach you that at West Point?" Steck asked.

"We receive a general military education," Bascom replied. "But I've talked to officers who've had Indian experience." Bascom pounded his fist into the palm of his hand. "I can't wait to get out there."

"Are you going through Mesilla?"

"Why?"

"There is a man there who knows as much about the Apaches as anyone I've ever known. His name is Tom Jeffords. Captain Thomas Jeffords. Not a military title. Got it on the Mississippi. You might look him up and exchange ideas."

Bascom, who had appeared interested when Steck mentioned the word "Captain" and then lost interest when he was informed of the origin of the title, said casually, "I'll be at Buchanan. If he ever gets out there he can look me up."

"I will tell him next time I see him," Steck said gravely.

Bascom stood up and adjusted his uniform. "I'm very happy to have had the pleasure of meeting you, Dr. Steck," he said.

"Thank you, Lieutenant. I feel the same. I am always interested in the military leaders who are sent to our part of the country."

"If you ever get out to Buchanan, look me up," Bascom said.

"I shall. Please convey my compliments to Colonel Morrison."

Bascom nodded and left. Steck rubbed his chin and stared at the ceiling.

4

Bascom entered Colonel Morrison's office stiffly, in the approved military manner. He saluted smartly and said, "Sir, George N. Bascom, Second Lieutenant, reporting for duty."

Morrison returned the salute, somewhat languidly. "Sit down, Mr. Bascom. It is a pleasure to have you."

"Thank you, sir."

"Have you reported to the Adjutant?"

"Yes, sir."

"Where are you from, Lieutenant?"

"Kentucky, sir."

"Do you have everything you need? Have you been assigned quarters?"

"Yes, sir."

"Good," Morrison said wearily. He opened his cigar box and offered it to Bascom, who accepted politely. He carefully extracted a long black stogie and received a light from the young lieutenant. "You are most welcome here, Mr. Bascom. You will find your duties not too onerous, I hope. There are officers and noncommissioned personnel who will give you every assistance and answer whatever questions you may have from time to time. Please feel free to visit me at your pleasure."

Bascom rose. He removed the cigar from his mouth. "Thank you, sir," he said.

Morrison, believing the interview finished, looked down at his desk and began to go through his papers. When he looked up Bascom was still standing there. "Yes, Mr. Bascom?" he asked.

"Sir?" Bascom said, his cheeks getting pinker.

"Yes, Mr. Bascom?"

"Sir, I would like to receive as much active duty as possible."

"Yes, Mr. Bascom."

"Yes, sir," Bascom became slightly embarrassed. "I am not trying to appear impudent, sir, but I thought I would like to say that I would appreciate field duty as rapidly as possible."

Morrison studied Bascom with tired eyes. He thought he knew the kind. Where did they get that energy? He had been in this hot country so long he forgot almost that men could be that way. But he knew the type. Eager for action, expectant of promotion, sulky when it was not forthcoming as quickly as anticipated. "I think we can accommodate you, Mr. Bascom," he said.

"Thank you, sir," Bascom said, beaming. "I've done very little since graduation and I am anxious to catch up."

"I will try not to disappoint you," Morrison said.

Bascom saluted again. He executed a smart about-face, and walked out erectly. As he left the room, the orderly entered.

"Yes?" Morrison said.

"Sir, it's Mr. Ward again."

Morrison frowned and shook his head. Ward had been in to see him several times a week for the last two or three months. "Send him in," he said in an exhausted voice.

Ward appeared constantly at the post throughout December. His temper grew blacker and his language less restrained as the days progressed. Morrison ascertained that he had attempted

123

to raise a civilian posse but that he was so disliked by other Americans no one would join him. The colonel felt, after all, that the rancher, despite his unpleasant personality, had a legitimate grievance and he promised him, sincerely, that the first detachment of horsemen he had available would be given over to his request. Ward swore violently that the child was probably dead by now, but Morrison pointed out that the reason for kidnaping children was to induct them into the tribe and that it was not likely that the child had been murdered.

In the middle of January, First Sergeant Reuben Bernard returned from a furlough he had been granted to his home in Tennessee. This was the same Bernard who had been a corporal under Major Steen. Since that time he had made a name for himself in a number of encounters with the Indians and had advanced rapidly through the noncommissioned ranks. When he returned from his furlough to Fort Breckenridge, farther north, in signal recognition of his previous year's prowess, he was given command of a dozen mounted men and ordered to bring the detachment down to Buchanan.

Bernard was now a confident, assured, veteran Indian fighter. His assurance increased with his assignment as head of the only mounted detachment at an infantry post. Upon his arrival at Buchanan, Morrison informed him that he had an assignment for him immediately.

"A child has been kidnaped from the ranch of a local settler named Ward," Morrison said. "I will assign a commissioned officer to your detachment. You will attempt to locate the Indians who took the child and some animals belonging to Mr. Ward and recover them, if possible."

Bernard was disappointed, but he was too good a soldier to show it. In the last year he had led dragoons on missions without a commissioned officer being in charge and he had expected this arrangement to continue.

Morrison summoned his orderly and requested a roster of officers available for a patrol. He studied the roster and then he said to his orderly, "My compliments to Mr. Bascom and tell him to report to me immediately."

The orderly located Bascom at the sutler's store and gave him the colonel's message. He hurried to the commanding officer's office.

"Mr. Bascom," Morrison said. "This is First Sergeant Bernard."

"Sir," Bernard said, saluting.

"Sergeant," Bascom said frigidly.

The two men eyed each other, Bernard, huge, bearded, and Bascom, slight, his fair complexion reddened from the sun.

"Mr. Bascom," Morrison continued, "Sergeant Bernard has reported in with a detachment of dragoons. The sergeant and his men are experienced Indian fighters." He rapidly reviewed the story of the Ward incident. "You will take command of the detachment and attempt to recover the child and, if possible, the missing animals. Ward is around here somewhere. He usually is. I have already sent for him. Take him with you if he desires to go. He said he followed the trail of the abductors to the San Pedro and then did not attempt to cross. He says the kidnapers were Chiricahua Indians."

Bernard looked surprised. "Sir, did you say Chiricahuas?"

"Yes, Sergeant."

"Cochise is not on the warpath, sir."

Bascom was annoyed that an enlisted man, even though he was a noncommissioned officer, should show greater knowledge of Indian affairs than he himself possessed.

Morrison nodded. "I thought not either, Sergeant. But Ward is certain the Chiricahua Apaches were the culprits. Find out what you can. If it was Cochise, try to get the child back. I don't want too much trouble. You won't have enough men. But it is our duty to help recover the child, if possible." He looked at the two men. "Are there any questions?"

"No, sir," Bascom said.

"That is all then," Morrison said. "This is your first assignment, Mr. Bascom. I hope it will be successful."

"Yes, sir," Bascom said, blushing under his sunburn. He was more embarrassed than ever. There was no need to point him up as a novice in front of Bernard, he thought.

Bernard was even more annoyed. It was bad enough that he had to go out under the orders of an infantry officer, but a newcomer, a dude, and a shavetail at that, was too much.

Ward entered the office.

"Mr. Ward," Morrison said icily. "A patrol of twelve men under Lieutenant Bascom has been assigned to go out and attempt to recover your child and missing animals. If you so desire you may accompany them and render whatever assistance you can."

"It's about time," Ward said.

"We will find your child, Mr. Ward," Bascom said brightly.

"I hope so," the rancher said.

"Good luck, gentlemen," Morrison said.

Bascom moved rapidly to leave the room ahead of Bernard, as an officer should. Bernard stood back courteously and allowed him to pass. Bascom resolved to make it plain from the start that regardless of how much experience Bernard had, he, Bascom, was in command of the expedition. The presence of Ward made it additionally necessary that military discipline be enforced. When the three men were outside the headquarters, Bascom turned to Bernard and said, "Sergeant, you will get your men ready within ten minutes." It was the first order

Lieutenant Bascom had ever given as a commander of men and he hoped his voice had the quality of command that was taught at the academy.

Bernard saluted smartly and said, "Yes, sir." He went off to gather his men. Some of them groaned at having to go out on an expedition so soon after reporting into camp. Bernard lined them up and said, "We are going to have a second lieutenant in command, an infantry officer." The men expressed disgust. "Remember one thing," Bernard said. "We are dragoons. We are soldiers and we know how to obey orders."

He led his men proudly to Bascom, saluted, and said, "The troop is ready, sir."

As do all soldiers when they are confronted by a new commanding officer, the dragoons studied Bascom closely, looking for signs of weakness. They decided that while his seat on his horse was not too bad, still it was no dragoon seat either. He looked young and inexperienced and seemed to be a little too eager. They had seen that bright look in the eyes of other young officers.

Bascom, feeling their gaze upon him, sat stiffly in the saddle. "All right, Sergeant," he said. "Follow me." He started to move off when Bernard called out, "Mr. Bascom, sir."

"Yes?"

"Can you speak Apache, sir?"

"Of course not," Bascom said.

"Somebody's got to palaver with these Indians," Bernard said. "I speak a little of the lingo but not enough to serve as interpreter. Perhaps Mr. Ward can speak it."

"Me, speak that hash?" Ward asked.

Bascom felt himself growing embarrassed again. He should have thought of the interpreter and he was ashamed that Bernard had to remind him in front of the men. "Send a man to headquarters to get an interpreter," he said.

"Yes, sir," the Sergeant said. He dispatched one of his troopers and the man returned with a Mexican named Antonio. Then the soldiers left camp.

The patrol under Second Lieutenant George Bascom left Fort Buchanan on January 29 and arrived at the Apache Pass station of the Butterfield line on the third day of February. By that time Bascom had made a number of blunders, not military blunders, but blunders indicating his rawness and unfamiliarity with the country and the way of living in it. The dragoons, all of whom were old hands at this game, developed a certain contempt for the young officer, and Bascom, who was not completely a fool, was not unaware of it. He was unhappy. He had ideas about the camaraderie of the open march, and he had often thought how, when he actually commanded men, he would be a good and friendly officer, a sort of wise father to his men, the kind of officer men would cheerfully die for. He would have liked to have established this admiring and amicable relationship but he had no idea of how to start. Instead he could feel the patronizing attitude of the soldiers. It drove him in the opposite direction. Unable to feel at ease among the men he avoided all social contact with them. In the camps that had been established each evening, instead of joining the men, discussing the day's events, planning the next day's march, laughing and joking with the soldiers, he had remained aloof, spending his time only with Ward. The men decided that in addition to being an inexperienced fool, their commanding officer was also a snob.

Ward, who hated Indians as only a pioneer in the Southwest could hate them, spent his times with Bascom filling him with stories of Indian outrages, painting pictures of treachery and blood. The hard-bitten rancher found enjoyment in the wide-eyed attention Bascom gave him, and he spent hours telling him one wild tale after another. The stories, some of them undoubtedly true, others greatly distorted, and still others plain inventions, had a profound effect on Bascom, who sat silently before the campfire in the middle of the Indian country and listened to the gory stories against a background of screaming coyotes and howling wolves and the chill hooting of owls.

The stories supported Bascom's own preconceived ideas about how to handle Indians. He considered Ward an authority and believed him implicitly. By the time the patrol arrived at the stage station, Bascom was furious with all Indians and hated them as though they had wronged him personally.

5

Walsh, the hostler, was feeding the mules in the corral when the soldiers pulled up. He called to Culver and Wallace, the latter again laying over at the station, and those two men stepped out of the building. Tevis was away on business and the three men were the only ones at the station.

"I wonder who that is," Culver said curiously.

"First time there's been a mounted patrol around here in a long time," Wallace said.

"Got a civilian with them. Looks to me like Johnny Ward from Sonoita," Walsh said.

"He's a bad actor, they tell me," Wallace said.

When Bascom reached the stage depot he announced, "I am Lieutenant George Bascom, Seventh Infantry. I would like some water for my men and horses."

"Sure," Culver said. "Help yourself." He walked up to Bascom and held out his hand. "I'm Hank Culver, station agent here."

Bascom leaned down from his saddle and grasped the hand. "I'm glad to know you, Mr. Culver," he said. "This is Mr. John Ward from Sonoita."

"I know Ward," Culver said shortly. "This is Fred Walsh, who works here, and Clay Wallace, one of the drivers."

Bascom dismounted. He told Bernard to take charge of the men and see that their thirst was satisfied. Then he looked around. Culver watched him curiously and then he asked, "What brings you up here, Lieutenant?"

Bascom assumed an expression of inscrutability. He had well-taught ideas about military security. "We are taking a little trip down the Rio Grande," he said casually.

Bernard looked up in surprise. It was not customary to play secret with so routine a job as looking for Indians.

When the men and animals were ready, Bernard mounted the soldiers. Bascom and Ward climbed on their horses and Bascom thanked Culver for his courtesy. He started to ride off, and then, as though suddenly struck with the idea, he turned around and said, "By the way, we are going to make camp a short distance from here. I would like to meet this Cochise, the Chiricahua chief. If you see him, bid him to come and visit with me at my camp."

"Cochise?" Culver asked, somewhat puzzled.

"Yes, he hangs around here, does he not?"

"He has a camp up in the mountains," Culver said. "He's been working for us, supplying us with firewood."

"Does he come down here often?"

"Once in a while."

"Well, when you see him, tell him the white flag is flying over my tent and I would like to meet him," Bascom said.

"Sure," Culver said, still puzzled.

Bascom nodded to Bernard who gave the order and the troop rode off. The more the sergeant watched Bascom's manner of doing business the more he disliked it. There was a sneaky subtlety to the method which irritated his rugged open nature.

Culver watched the troop depart. "I'll bet old Cochise will be down here soon," he laughed. "He's probably been watching that schoolboy and his soldiers for a couple of days by now."

"If his signals are working as usual he probably knows the name of every mother's son in that outfit," Wallace chuckled. As Bascom led the troops away he turned to Ward with a wise smile and said, "I did not wish to arouse the old redskin's suspicions. That's why I pretended we were on another kind of

mission and I just wanted to meet him socially." He winked
and Ward nodded appreciatively.

Bernard, riding a few paces behind, compressed his lips and
tried to figure out what was happening. He had the feeling that
things were moving in the wrong direction.

The soldiers had not departed by more than an hour when
Cochise walked down to the station. With him were Naretena,
Nalikadeya, Nachise, and two grown sons of Juan. As Culver
and Wallace had foreseen, the passage of the troops had been
known to the Chiricahua leader long before they arrived at the
station.

It was a hot day. The Indians wore nothing but breechclouts,
save Nalikadeya, who wore a light cloth shirt and skirt.

Cochise greeted Culver and sat down. After a few minutes
he said, "Soldiers were here."

"From Fort Buchanan," Wallace said.

"They are riding to the Rio Grande," Culver said and Wallace translated rapidly. "The officer in command said that he
was going to make camp a short distance from here and he said
if I saw you to tell you he would like you to visit with him."
As Cochise raised his head quickly and suspiciously, like a
hunting dog on a strange scent, Culver went on swiftly, "He
said to tell you that the white flag was flying over his tent."

Cochise relaxed. He turned to his brother. "The new chief
at Buchanan," he said. "The soldiers are to tell us that the new
chief wants to be friends like *Nantan* Steen."

Naretena nodded. "That is it," he said.

Nachise, who was now about eight, laughed and said, "Soldiers give things away."

"New red flannel, maybe," Nalikadeya said.

Cochise smiled indulgently at her. "You never get enough
presents," he said. "We will go visit with the new soldier *Nantan.*"

"The camp is in that direction," Wallace said. When Cochise
looked up with an odd expression on his face he realized that
Cochise probably knew exactly where the camp was.

"Where is *Nantan* Tevis?" the Chiricahua chief asked.

"Tucson," Wallace said. "Getting more supplies."

"Do you have enough wood?" Cochise asked Culver.

"We need more," Culver said.

"Good," Cochise said. "Now we will go see the new soldier
captain."

In the camp Bascom waited. He had had a Sibley tent
erected for himself and over it he had affixed a white flag.
Bascom felt that he was handling things perfectly. He felt
that he had set a trap and that all he had to do was wait until

his victim walked into it. He was tingling. His big moment was coming. He knew he would show his enlisted men that while he might lack some knowledge of moving around in this desert country, in military matters he was a leader.

Ward suddenly pointed. "There comes Cochise," he said. Bascom looked. He saw the four men, the young woman and the small boy. The Indians seemed dirty and sweaty to him and they looked like tramps. "Which one is Cochise?" he asked.

"The one in front," Ward said.

"That's Cochise?"

"Yeah. Why?"

Bascom shook his head. He was ashamed to tell Ward he had expected an Indian chief to look like an Indian chief. He didn't know exactly what that was, but he had vague ideas about lots of eagle feathers, painted face, bows and arrows, and fancy costume. The people walking toward him looked like hobos, and Cochise looked like a dirty bum. "So that's Cochise," he said to himself with some disgust.

The Indians approached the camp confidently. The white flag was flying plainly and it had been so long since Cochise had trouble with white men that he suspected nothing. By now he was certain that this was a routine ceremonial visit, and he expected the usual presents and exchange of sentiments of friendship.

As he entered the camp Cochise saw Bernard and recognized him as one of Steen's soldiers. He nodded affably to the sergeant and Bernard waved his hand. Bascom saw the exchanged greetings and his irritation with Bernard grew.

Cochise walked directly to the tent with the white flag and entered, followed by the other Apaches. Inside the tent were Bascom, Ward, and Antonio, the Mexican interpreter. The Indians filed into the tent and sat silently on the ground and prepared for the normal interval before speech would start.

Cochise did not notice that Bascom, as soon as all the Apaches were within the tent, nodded imperceptibly to Ward, who left the tent. And he could not know that once outside Ward told Bernard that Bascom ordered the tent surrounded by soldiers.

Bernard frowned at the order. "What does he want soldiers around the tent for?" he asked uneasily. "He got Cochise in there under a white peace flag."

"I don't know, Sergeant," Ward said. "But you better obey orders."

Bernard, shaking his head, disposed his twelve soldiers around the tent, and when Ward saw that the order had been carried out, he reentered the tent and nodded slightly to Bascom. Then Bascom began to speak, and as he spoke Antonio translated his words.

"Cochise," he said, violating in his first word the custom of not using a man's name in speaking to him unless the man is very close to you or the situation one of emergency. Cochise, sitting calmly in the pleasantly cool tent, waiting for the normal friendly discussion to start, looked up sharply when he heard and recognized his name. "I am here to get back from you the small son of this man John Ward, as well as some oxen and horses stolen by your warriors from his corral," Bascom said abruptly.

When the words were translated Cochise stiffened as though he was struck and his eyes blazed, and then, looking at the childish face of the officer, he controlled himself. He sat for a while, thinking on the words Bascom had used, and when he spoke his voice was quiet, although all the friendliness was gone from his face.

"For more than five harvests my people and I have been at peace with the white man," he said. "During that time no one belonging to the Chiricahua people has taken any child or animals belonging to an American. Tell me what the boy looked like and how many and what kind of animals were taken and I will send my warriors to the other tribes of Indians near here and try to find them for you."

"Mr. Ward says it was Chiricahua warriors who took the child and animals," Bascom retorted.

Cochise made himself more comfortable. He was in no hurry. The matter had to be settled and that would take time, because he could see the baby-faced soldier captain was not a reasonable man. "My people have not been at war with the Americans for more than five harvests," he repeated patiently. He felt certain that soon the young officer would see how impossible the accusation was and he would apologize and then together they would make plans to see which tribe had taken the child.

"They were not Chiricahua men who took the child," Naretena said. "It is as he says. There has been no conflict between our two peoples for many harvests."

"I have often helped the Americans," Cochise said. "I will be glad to do so on this occasion. If the child is described to me and the kind and number of the animals I will send warriors to the Pinals and the Tontos and the Mescaleros and the Coyoteros and the other Apache tribes and if the child is with one of them he will be brought back."

Bascom looked at Ward with some indecision, but the rancher said, "The cutthroat is lying." He stopped Antonio from translating the words, but Cochise caught their sound and his eyes narrowed.

Naretena spoke again and one of Juan's grown sons spoke and then the other son. Then Cochise spoke again, and as he

131

again protested his people were innocent of the abduction, he began to feel a warning chill go through him. The talk was not going well. Conflict with the Americans was almost a forgotten thing and at first he did not read the nature of the warning. Then his hawk eyes saw the boredom in the face of the young officer. He looked more closely at Ward, to whom he had paid scant attention until then, and he sensed the baleful hatred in the beefy small-eyed man. There was a sudden instinctive mental back-tracking, and Cochise's mind began to work, as an Indian mind, as it had not worked in five years. Instantly it was as though there had never been a peace; the old suspicions came to life, the old fears rose again. Apache-like, his face remained inscrutable. He felt himself moving away, inwardly, until there was a black emptiness between him and the two Americans who sat before him. He continued to talk calmly and patiently and he knew as he watched the effect of his words that he had completely lost control of the situation. He felt a numbness in the air, as though thunder would suddenly sound, and his attitude communicated itself to the other Indians, who stirred nervously.

Bascom, listening to the naked man in front of him, was more and more assured of himself. He wearied of this endless discussion. He thought he had allowed these filthy creatures to talk too much. For more than an hour now they had done nothing more than deny all knowledge of the abduction. Bascom decided he was called upon to make a decisive move. He felt Ward and the soldiers outside, particularly the superior Sergeant Bernard, were sitting in judgment on him.

"Cochise, you are a damned liar!" he said suddenly.

When Antonio translated these words the blood fled from the face of the Chiricahua leader. His heart began to pound with violence and he felt for a moment that he could not breathe.

Bascom, misreading his silence, said again, "You are a damned liar!" Then, after a glance to make sure the soldiers were still outside the tent, he said peremptorily, "You and your people will be my prisoners until the Ward child is returned."

The words were not fully translated when Cochise was on his feet with a piercing scream of rage. Then, half in English, half in Apache, he said, "I am no prisoner of yours, you son of a bitch!" He whipped out a long knife from his breechclout and with a powerful sweep of his arm he slashed open the tent and he cried to the other Indians, "Follow me!" And before Bascom or Ward knew what he was doing he leaped through the jagged rent in the tent and shouldered his way past the bewildered soldiers.

He crouched low and ran, zigzag, in Indian fashion, away

from the tent, and the soldiers, as soon as they collected themselves, lifted their carbines and fired after him. One of the balls struck Cochise in the leg as he dodged and twisted away, behind rocks and trees. He continued to run, leaving a thin trail of blood, until he crossed a small hill and descended into a narrow canyon.

When the other Indians tried to follow him they found the soldiers prepared. Naretena was knocked down by a blow from a gun butt and one of Juan's sons was stabbed in the belly with a bayonet. The others were quickly captured.

Bernard, who was inspecting the horses in another part of the camp when the fight started, hurried back to the tent. He rushed up to Bascom, and the lieutenant, himself confused and a little frightened at what he had started, ordered imperiously, "Sergeant, turn out the detachment. Cochise escaped. Get after him and find him."

Bernard looked at the white flag still fluttering over the tent. He held his first words within him, and said, "There will be trouble, Lieutenant. We better get down to the station and warn the men there."

"I ordered you to go after Cochise, Sergeant," Bascom retorted furiously.

"He is gone now, sir," Bernard said. "We'll never get him now. Believe me, sir. It's better to get down to the stage depot and warn those men. There might be real trouble."

"All right," Bascom said. "Get going."

Once in the hills Cochise collected some of his warriors. He was still crazy with rage but he controlled himself enough to think carefully. He did not want war with the Americans. It was ridiculous to go to war with the Americans because a stupid child had called him a liar. The first thing was to recover his wife and brother, his small son and his nephews. After that the matter could be settled with a wiser representative of the American Army.

On horse, with a score of men behind him, he raced down the pass to the stage station. If he could capture the three men there he could hold them as hostages for the members of his family. Later he could make the station men understand why he had done what he did.

He appeared at the crest of the hill above the station and called out, "Culver! Culver!"

When the Agent appeared Cochise motioned for him to come to him. Knowing nothing as yet of the affair at the camp, Culver, joined by Walsh, walked over to where the Indians waited. The Americans were unarmed and in their shirtsleeves.

As they reached the Indians, Cochise signaled and the warriors surrounded the two men and then seized them. The Americans, utterly startled, fought back instinctively. They knocked over two of the Indians who had dismounted to bind them and then turned and fled back to the station. The Indians, excited and screaming now, raised their rifles and fired. A ball struck Culver as he reached the station and he collapsed into the open door.

At this moment Bernard arrived with the troops at the other side of the station. They climbed over the corral wall and crept around the building. One of the soldiers grasped Culver by the shoulders and dragged him inside. Just then Walsh, who had run in another direction, reached the corral wall. He started to clamber over it. As his head appeared over the wall a trooper fired. Walsh fell dead, hanging over the wall.

When Cochise saw that the station was occupied by the soldiers he summoned his men out of gun range. He paused for a moment on the hilltop and looked down at the station. He struggled to calm himself. He had seen Culver fall and he had seen Walsh struck and he knew that events were moving with an inevitability that was beyond his control. He thought of the five Indians held by Bascom. He had to get more Americans to trade off for his own people. He sat on his horse and then the aimless horror of the last few hours fell upon him and he lifted his head and gave the wild Apache cry of fury and then he turned his horse's head and tore away.

6

He took a secret trail to the East Stronghold, thirty-five miles away. Now that there was trouble his instincts led him to that sanctuary. On the way he encountered Nahilzay with another small group of warriors. Nahilzay read his chief's face instantly and his eyes glittered as Cochise told him briefly what had occurred.

"Near the pass," he said. "There are nine wagons."

"Take some men and capture the Americans," Cochise said. "Take them alive. I want no more Americans killed."

Nahilzay nodded. He trembled with excitement. It had been years since Chiricahua Apaches had fought in their own country.

"Remember," Cochise repeated. "No Americans killed. This thing has gone far but not too far."

"There will be no white-eyes killed," Nahilzay said, using the epithet for Americans employed by Apaches when they wanted most to show their hatred.

"Meet me near the stage station at sunrise," Cochise said.

Nahilzay galloped away, his men behind him. Another Apache rode up and told Cochise the stage coach from Tucson was en route for the station.

"There is a little wooden bridge over the ravine," Cochise said. "Knock it down. That will cut off the stage from the station. Take the passengers in the stage prisoners."

The Indian, amazed at the order, went off to obey it. He reached the bridge, a narrow span crossing a thin, steep chasm. He knocked down the guard rails on the bridge and, with other Indians, spread out in an ambush, waiting for the stage.

The coach appeared. The Indians opened fire. The first volley shattered the leg of the driver, King Lyons, and killed one of the lead mules. William Buckley, the line superintendent, who was making the trip to inspect the Apache Pass station, took the reins from Lyons and pulled the coach to a halt. Several passengers leaped out and cut away the dead mule. When they were back in the coach, Buckley began to whip the remaining mules and the coach lurched ahead. The Indians fired again. The passengers, crouching low, returned the fire from the coach.

Buckley, cursing, whipping the animals furiously, raced the coach to the bridge. The mules flew down the steep approach to the span and then they came to the ravine and they hesitated for a second and then leaped across. The axles of the coach slid along the bridge, the wheels hanging free on one side. The mules reached the other side and began to pull again, maddened by the sting of the whip. The wheels bit into the hard far side of the ravine and then regained the roadway.

Never ceasing his whipping, Buckley drove the coach to the station. In front of the corral one mule fell dead. Buckley and a passenger carried Lyons into the station. The other passengers, seven in all, fled in with them.

"What in the name of God is going on!" Buckley shouted.

Wallace said, "Cochise. Trouble."

"Cochise?" Buckley panted. He looked around. "Where's Culver?"

"Shot."

"Walsh?"

"Dead."

Bascom walked over. "I am Lieutenant George Bascom, Seventh Infantry," he said.

"Cochise," Buckley said, breathing hard. "That treacherous red son of a bitch."

Nahilzay brought his men stealthily toward the wagon train. The men of the train were gathered around a fire. The Indian's blood was burning inside of him. He gave a silent signal and the Apaches appeared out of the night and fell upon the drowsy men. Within a few seconds the Apaches had ten captives and not a shot had been fired.

Nahilzay examined his prisoners closely and then he raised

his head and gave his thanks to the Great Spirit. Cochise had ordered that no Americans be killed. There were ten men captured. Two of them were Americans. Eight of them were Mexicans.

Nahilzay gave the old orders. The Mexicans were tied to the wheels of the wagons. The horses were cut away and gathered. A flaming torch was thrown into the group of wagons and soon they were afire and soon they made a pyre that lighted the countryside and the screams of the Mexicans filled the night. Nahilzay savored the agonized cries as one who had not heard them in a long time and then they tied the two Americans to horses and rode away.

In the night Cochise came to his Stronghold. The long ride had cooled his anger and he sat down to think calmly. What was happening was of importance. Each move made was beyond recall. It was a time for contemplation. He wished with all his heart that Naretena was there to counsel with him.

He held mixed feelings. There was the basic outrage to his word and his person. There was fright for the safety of the five Indian captives. There was concern for the future relations of the tribe with the Americans. There was contempt for Bascom. He thought how he had been twice called liar by that child. He could think of nothing else then. He bit his lips and asked the Great Spirit for help.

He sat alone and sleepless through the night.

In the morning he started back for the station. He appeared again on the hilltop, out of range of the guns. With him were the two Americans captured by Nahilzay. Cochise planned for a careful discussion which might yet end the catastrophe that he saw was in the making. When Nahilzay told him about burning the Mexicans to death he scarcely listened to him, and so intent was he with his own plans, he did not notice the blood lust that filled the eyes of his chief lieutenant. Nahilzay was like a wild animal that had been caged for a long time and now was freed.

Cochise called out in the still clear air, "Agent Wallace."

Inside the station Wallace stirred. "Stay here," Buckley ordered. "It's a trap."

"Agent Wallace!" Cochise shouted again.

"Let me go out, Mr. Buckley," Wallace said. "I know Cochise and I can speak to him."

"It's a trap," Buckley repeated.

"He won't try anything while we got his family tied up," Wallace said. He got up and walked to the door. Then he suddenly entered the corral.

"Agent Wallace," Cochise called again. "Tell the white soldier boy I have two Americans to trade for my people."

Wallace called Bascom to the door. "He says he has two American prisoners. He wants to exchange them for the Indians."

"Tell him to release those white men or I'll hang the Indians," Bascom said.

Bernard shook his head warningly. "Better make the trade, sir," he said. "I think you did wrong to try to arrest Cochise in the first place when you had a white flag flying."

"I am not interested in your opinion, Sergeant," Bascom said coldly. "Tell him to release the Americans, Wallace, and then return the Ward boy, and then I'll free his damned relatives."

"I won't tell him that, Lieutenant," Wallace said. "I am going out to talk to him."

He walked to the gate and out of the corral and then up the hill to where Cochise waited with his men. Cochise recognized him. His first instinct was to greet him as a friend, but then he remembered that Wallace had been one of the three men who had sent him down to see Bascom the day before. Suddenly the whole episode appeared to him to have been a carefully planned trap to get him into the hands of the white soldiers. "What have your white brothers got to say?" he asked Wallace harshly.

"I come by my own will," Wallace said. "I come to ask you to release the prisoners you have and then maybe I can get the white lieutenant to free your people."

"Is that what you have to say, Agent Wallace?" Cochise asked evenly.

"The lieutenant says he wants the Ward child," Wallace replied.

"I do not have the child," Cochise said angrily. "No one of my people has the child. The soldier boy was the first to take prisoners. He will be the first to free them."

"He will not do it," Wallace said.

"Then I will make you a prisoner too," Cochise retorted. "The soldier boy will want to make the trade then, maybe." He gave a short order and Nahilzay threw a lariat over Wallace and jerked him toward him. He trussed him and put him with the other two Americans and then the Indians rode off.

When they disappeared with Wallace, Buckley began to make plans. He had by then judged Bascom for an inexperienced, useless officer. He asked for the service of a soldier, and then instructed the soldier to go to Tucson and bring William Oury, the Agent there, a full account of the affair, and to ask Oury to send a courier to Fort Breckenridge for troops. The soldier left that night and made a daring journey across the country. He reached Tucson safely and Oury immediately did as he was requested, and at the same time set out himself with a small party for Apache Pass.

When the courier reached Breckenridge, Lieutenant R.S.C. Lord, of Company D, 1st Dragoons, and Lieutenant Isaiah N. Moore, of Company F, were ordered to Apache Pass with their men.

By now the wheels were turning, each wheel turning another wheel. What had started in the tent in Apache Pass a few days before between two, men, now involved many men, in many places, and what had happened was beyond change.

On the eighth of February the soldiers and some civilians at the station drove their horses and mules to the springs located about six hundred yards away. Water had begun to run out at the station and the animals were suffering. Cochise, foreseeing this, had men lying in ambush around the springs, and the Indians fell upon the party, stampeding the animals, killing one of the civilians and wounding two other men. The Americans fled back to the station, leaving some of their animals behind.

On the ninth, Cochise again appeared upon the hilltop and, with Wallace speaking for him, again demanded the release of the Indians. Bascom retorted that he would free them after Cochise produced the Ward boy and turned the child, together with the three Americans, over to him.

Cochise again declared he knew nothing about the Ward boy. Bascom turned his back and walked into the building and Cochise again rode away.

Two days later Bascom was in the corral giving some orders to Sergeant Bernard concerning the disposition of sentries. Bernard glanced over his shoulder to the hilltop and he stiffened visibly. "You were disappointed in the appearance of the Indians before, sir," he said. "Look at them now."

Bascom turned around. He stared at the hilltop for a few seconds and then he slowly extracted his field glasses from their case and lifted them to his eyes.

More than a hundred Chiricahua Apaches in war paint were spread across the hill. Some distance in front of them, in full ceremonial dress, his face covered with black, red, and yellow paint, eagle feathers jutting from his headband, his arms and uniform covered with beads and war amulets, sat Cochise, on a flashing paint horse. The Indians were heavily armed with arrows, carbines, and spears.

Bascom was unable to stir. He felt the sweat break out on his forehead. As he stared in horrified fascination, Cochise lowered a long spear and shoved Wallace forward. The driver, the noose of a lariat tightened under his arms, stumbled a few

138

yards down the stony hillside, with Nahilzay paying out the line as he moved forward.

Wallace was still in his shirtsleeves. With his glasses Bascom could see the driver's shirt was torn and dirty, and his face was haggard and drawn.

"Bascom!" Wallace called out in a hoarse voice.

"Yes," the lieutenant called back.

"Can you hear me?"

"Yes."

"I can hardly talk," Wallace said, "I been freezing and I haven't had anything to eat. Listen, Bascom, this is the last chance. I been starved and I been freezing. I have had nothing to eat since Cochise captured me. I been sleeping at night with nothing else on me than this shirt and pants. Listen to me, Bascom. Cochise still says he will let all of us go. There are three of us, two other Americans and me. They are worse off than I am. Cochise says he will let us all go if you let his relatives go. He says this is the last time he will make the offer."

From Wallace, Bascom turned his glasses on Cochise. It was difficult for the young officer to believe he was the same man who spoke so quietly to him in the tent. Cochise's face was bony and rigid. The streaks of paint effectively hid whatever expression the hard features might hold. Bascom lowered the glasses. He looked around him. The soldiers and the civilians were standing around, watching him closely. He looked last upon Bernard, still standing next to him.

Bascom gritted his teeth. "Tell him to bring the Ward boy down with the three Americans and we will make the exchange," he called to Wallace. He looked at Ward; the rancher nodded his approval.

"He says he ain't got the Ward boy," Wallace pleaded.

"Tell him I still say that he is a damned liar," Bascom said arrogantly.

Now Bernard spoke up. "Lieutenant," he said. "For God's sake, take him up. You will get three Americans for five Indians. That's plenty fair. An American life is worth a dozen of theirs."

"Those three Indians include three fighting men, Sergeant," Bascom said. "Plus a woman and a child, against three Americans who are not fighting men. I want the Ward boy as well."

"Sir, Cochise doesn't lie. Believe me. He is known not to lie. If he says he hasn't got the Ward child he hasn't got him. For the love of God let those damned Indians free and save the Americans while they're still alive before there's a real war on here."

Bascom had the uncomfortable feeling that the other Americans were in support of Bernard, all, perhaps, save Ward. Instead of influencing him, this imagined opposition only strengthened his objection. "These Indians have to learn who is in command in this country," he said in a level voice. "If I give in now we will never again be able to control them."

"Lieutenant, listen to me," Bernard said. "I know these Indians. The other soldiers here will agree with me. An Apache chief is not the supreme boss in his tribe. If any other chief captured these white men he's got the right to do with them as he pleases, no matter what Cochise says. It's unusual to get this much bargaining and patience and I don't know how Cochise is holding those fighting men of his in line, but, for God's sake, take him up on it before it is too late."

"I came here to get the Ward boy and I am not going back without him," Bascom said.

Bernard lost his temper at that. "Damn it to hell, Lieutenant, there are three white men whose lives are at stake!"

"Sergeant, I will thank you not to forget yourself!" Bascom retorted dangerously. "I was ordered to get the Ward boy and I will not settle for anything else."

"The hell with orders, sir," Bernard said. "Those Indians will torture these men to death. You've never seen what's left of a man when they get through with him. I say accept the trade while there is still time."

Bascom looked at Bernard coolly. "Sergeant Bernard, you are insubordinate," he said. "Consider yourself under arrest. I will prefer charges against you at a court-martial. I am in command here. Return to the building and remain inside until you receive further orders from me."

Bernard did not move for several moments and then his huge shoulders slumped. He saluted and walked away from Bascom and entered the building. When he was inside, Bascom turned back to Wallace and said. "I'm sorry, Wallace. My offer also stands. When Cochise stops lying and brings down the Ward boy his people will be freed. Not before."

Wallace, who had been able to hear the argument between Bernard and Bascom, who had hung on to every word, twisted his face pleadingly. "Please, Lieutenant," he said.

"I'm sorry, Wallace. That's final." Bascom walked into the building.

Wallace sagged in his tracks. Then he suddenly tried to pull himself free and get to the corral, such a short distance away. Nahilzay, whose eyes had never left him, reared his horse and jerked Wallace backward. The driver fell down and then he turned and tried to hold onto a rock. Nahilzay kicked his horse and pulled Wallace along the ground up the side of the hill. The driver, lying face down, bounced and tore himself against the stones. He tried to regain his feet and was pulled down again. Then Nahilzay, with a wild scream, before the eyes of the people in the corral, raced his horse back and forth across the hilltop, dragging Wallace behind him like a sack of grain. The Indians rode away and stretched out behind Nahilzay; still at the end of the lariat Wallace was dragged along, his body making no mark on the hard earth as it was pulled at the speed of a horse in gallop.

7

Oury, the Butterfield Agent in Tucson, and his party of civilians, joined with the soldiers from Breckenridge, led by Moore and Lord, at a rock tank, two miles west of the pass. They arrived at the station together.

There arrived at the same time Assistant Surgeon Irwin, the same man who had amputated St. John's arm at the Dragoon Springs station. Irwin, who came from Buchanan with a small party of infantry soldiers in response to a request sent by Bascom by courier for medical help, had encountered a party of Coyotero Apaches returning from a raid, and in Sulphur Spring Valley had engaged the Indians, capturing three of them together with thirty stolen horses and forty head of cattle. Irwin had the captives with him when he arrived at Apache Pass.

Lieutenant Moore, a first lieutenant and an experienced Indian fighter, who now was ranking officer at the station, sent out a scout to try to locate Cochise. Moore, disgusted at the course of action Bascom had taken, thought he might still be able to patch things up. The patrol found the Chiricahua rancheria in the Chiricahua Mountains. The village was deserted and only buzzards and crows wheeled in the air. The buzzards settled at a point on the outskirts of the camp and the soldiers investigated. They found three bodies, mutilated and pierced by lance wounds. They brought the bodies to the station and one of them was identified as that of Wallace. The driver's features were burned away but he was recognized by certain fillings in his teeth. The other two men were from the train attacked by Nahilzay, although no one there knew them.

Moore, his desire for conciliation forgotten, immediately ordered the captive male Indians, with the exception of the child, Nachise, hanged in reprisal. By now Bascom was thoroughly upset. The events of the last ten days were too much for him. He protested the hanging, saying, "I am in control of the Indians. They are my captives. I'll be blamed if I dispose of them that way."

"These Indians were not responsible for the deaths of those three men, Lieutenant," one of the civilians said. "It is not just to hang them for what the other Indians did."

"I am ranking officer here," Moore said. "I will assume all responsibility."

"The three Indians I captured are my prisoners," Irwin said. "I have the right to dispose of them any way I please."

"They will all be hanged," Moore said with finality.

Wallace and the other two Americans were buried in a single grave. Then Moore ordered the captive Indians brought out. The five relatives of Cochise had been held in a small storeroom since the day of their capture, and had been permitted to leave only to relieve themselves. No one had spoken to them since their capture and they had no idea of what had occurred.

It was the morning of February 19. The Indians were brought from their prison. When they saw the faces of the Americans they understood immediately what was to transpire. Naretena and the unwounded son of Juan held the other son, whose bayonet wound had not been treated, erect between them. Naretena touched the head of Nachise and then he said to Nalikadeya, "Tell him that the many must not suffer for the mistake of the few."

The three Chiricahuas and the three Coyoteros were led to a group of oak trees on the crest of a mound that sloped down to the triple grave where the Americans lay buried. There the largest oak was selected and the six Indians were hanged.

8

Nalikadeya and Nachise were taken to Fort Buchanan and released. Bascom was commended in official orders for his conduct of the affair and the hanging of the Indians was specifically approved. One month later First Sergeant Bernard was tried by court-martial on charges preferred by Bascom. By that time there were more important troubles and he was needed. He was acquitted.

Chapter Eight

In the afternoon the sun blackened its face and the sky emptied its tears and the cloud birds threw rocks at each other. The wind spoke of its fury and then in the night the colliding of the sky rocks was noisy and brought out Lightning to show the mountain peaks against the sky, as though it were day, and with each brief visit the six bodies could be seen swinging from the branch of the oak tree.

The wolves and the coyotes were silent in the storm and the

anguish from above kept the swinging bodies free from the sharp beaks of the buzzards and when Cochise and Juan, with three chosen warriors, Nahilzay, Skinyea, and Pionsenay, cut down the bodies they found them untouched. There was nothing written on them of death, no cut, no wound, nothing except the dark rim around the necks where the rope had bitten, and the swelling and the blackness of the faces.

While the thunder gave its approval and the rain showed its sorrow, a grave was dug for the three Coyoteros and since there was none there who knew the men, only a simple ceremony was made. The bodies were laid in a single grave with their heads in the direction of the mountains behind which the sun set and the graves were left open for a short while so the rain could wash the dead faces and make them clean for the journey.

The bodies of Naretena and the two sons of Juan were placed across the horses, Naretena being taken by Cochise, and Juan taking the elder of his sons. Holding his right hand over his brother's body, Cochise led the small group away, taking the bodies through the rain and the thunder to the West Stronghold.

The wife of Juan and the wives of his sons lay flat upon the earth and beat the earth with their hands. Cochise took his gun and fired four shots in the air, and then four shots again and then four again. Then Cochise and Juan laid the bodies out and carefully washed the faces of the three dead men and then painted them with red and yellow to make them look good on their journey. They put on their choicest clothing and their most sacred amulets and charms and then each body was raised on a favorite horse and they were held erect and led through the silent people to a small canyon.

There the bodies were placed in graves, with their heads facing west, and their weapons were placed in with them and small packets of maize were placed in their hands. The graves were covered first with dirt and then leaves and then rocks, and then the horse of each man was stabbed in the throat and the blood was allowed to fall upon the grave. Then the saddles were placed in a single pile and Cochise threw a torch upon them.

Finally the wife of Juan and the wives of his two sons cut their hair so that it was above their ears and they took off their clothing and put on blackened rags, and they mourned. And although it was not required, Cochise and Tesalbestinay did likewise and joined them, and on the seventeenth day of their mourning, when Nalikadeya and Nachise returned from Fort Buchanan, having made the journey on foot, without speaking to anyone of her experience the younger wife of Cochise cut her hair and put on rags and joined the mourners.

Thus they sorrowed for twenty days. And on the twenty-first day Cochise obtained from Nochalo some ghost powder and built a small fire. He threw the powder on the fire and the powder made great clouds of black smoke. Cochise wrapped himself in a blanket, covering his head, and sat close to the fire so that the smoke came through the blanket.

For the twenty-one days no one spoke to him, and he spoke to no one.

2

On the twenty-second day Cochise summoned his warriors together in the great clearing in the Stronghold and there he ordered ceremonies for a war of vengeance.

When the warriors were gathered in a large circle he walked to the center and in slow speech told what had happened. The moon was just rising as he spoke the first words and it was far across the sky when he finished. The words came from his lips like drippings of ice, as he told the long story of his effort to make peace with the Americans. Then his voice rose as he recounted the events at the Apache Pass station and when he described what had occurred within the tent his fury was such that his words seared the ears of his listeners and they shifted and quivered and some men wept with rage. When he concluded he spoke as a lifeless body and in this monotone he related how the bodies were cut down from the oak branch where they had been hanged.

He removed his red turban and placed it upon the ground. He raised his arms stiffly above him. He lifted his face to the sky. He spoke in a voice so remote it seemed unconnected with anything human.

"There will be war to the end with the white-eyes! There will be ten white-eyes slain for every Indian slain! There will be no end to this war and there will be none spared from it! This I pledge! This I pledge! This I pledge!"

Nochalo rose and stepped into the firelight. With two holy medicine sticks he lifted the red turban without touching it with his hands and replaced it upon the head of Cochise, and Cochise repeated, "There will be ten white-eyes slain for every Indian slain! This I pledge!"

Four men came from the east to the fire. They were Juan, Nahilzay, Pionsenay, and Skinyea. They walked abreast, stiff and straight-legged. They walked around the fire four times and then two stood on the south side and two on the north. They danced toward each other and changed sides, turned, and recrossed. They did this four times as Cochise remained rigid, as though made of granite, his arms still extended above him. As they danced they softly cried, "Waah, waah."

144

From a place outside the fire a group of men began to intone, beating on taut rawhide drums. Nochalo lighted a long twist of tobacco and breathed out smoke to the four directions. The four warriors danced and the singers chanted and Nochalo prayed and Cochise remained transfixed.

For four nights the dancing continued and at the end of the fourth night Cochise dispatched a courier to Mangas Coloradas telling him that he would join forces with him, and after the courier departed fires were lighted on top of the mountain peaks, to summon Apaches to a war of extermination against the Americans.

When the courier was gone and the fires were lighted and the warriors still were dancing at the fire, Cochise went away from his people and walked alone to the grave of his brother and there he fell upon the earth and wept.

THE SECOND BOOK

JEFFORDS

————◆————

Chapter Nine

At the start of the Civil War in April of 1861 Captain Thomas Jeffords offered his services to the Union forces in New Mexico and since no man excelled the tall, red-bearded miner in his knowledge of the country and the ways of hostile Indians, he was taken on eagerly as a government scout and courier.

He served in that capacity in the Battle of Val Verde and there made the brief acquaintance of Captain George Bascom, who fought bravely and was killed in action in that engagement.

The great struggle which divided the nation far to the east sent only its backwaters to the distant Southwest, where, to pioneers fighting to maintain their precarious hold on the land, it took second place to the new outbreak of Indian warfare.

In the summer of 1862 headquarters for the Federal Army in New Mexico was located at Fort Thorn, near Las Cruces, under the command of General Edward R. S. Canby, commander of the Department of New Mexico. On a hot afternoon General Canby summoned Jeffords and when the lean, spare prospector entered his office he rose and greeted him warmly. Jeffords congratulated Canby, who only recently had been promoted from colonel, and the general, a short, black-bearded man with lively expression, laughed and replied, "War will do that, young man. I see that you are still a captain."

"Naval rank," Jeffords grinned. "Mississippi River and Great Lakes. I believe the rank is somewhat higher in the Navy."

"I would like to change that into an Army rank, Jeffords," Canby said. "Perhaps a grade or two higher."

"Thanks, General, but no."

"There is a war on."

146

"You didn't call me in to make a soldier out of me, did you, General?"

Canby shook his head. "No, Jeffords. I think I know better. But I need you again."

"I'm not doing a thing right now," Jeffords said quietly.

"Good. Have a cigar."

Jeffords selected a stogie with great care, sniffed it appreciatively, and then accepted a light. "These look suspiciously like West Virginia stogies," he said dryly. "Confiscated?"

"Perhaps."

"They find new words for everything in the Army," Jeffords said, breathing out a mouthful of smoke. "Confiscated."

"Sit down, Jeffords," Canby said. The general opened the collar of his tunic and selected a cigar for himself. Jeffords watched him intently, his clear blue eyes alert.

"Jeffords, I want you to go to Tucson for me," Canby said abruptly.

Jeffords puffed on the cigar and said nothing.

"Do you know what has been going on over there?" Canby asked.

"Not completely," Jeffords replied.

"It is necessary that you do know, completely," Canby said. He looked up at Jeffords slyly. "I am assuming that you will accept the mission to Tucson."

"Why not?"

"I'll go back a little before the war started," Canby said. "You know that the Apaches are on the war path. The Chiricahuas, led by Cochise, have gathered together several hostile tribes and it can be said with some truth that for the first time in many years the Apaches have forgotten their own differences and are fighting the white men as a nation. I don't know whether you know about the incident that started off all this trouble, but a Lieutenant Bascom dealt very indiscreetly, almost foolishly, with Cochise in a matter that was actually of very small importance."

"I knew a Captain Bascom at Val Verde," Jeffords said.

"That is the same man. He is dead now and he died a soldier's death and I do not wish to speak ill of such a man, but what he did was not wise and as a result the Apaches are embarked upon the greatest war since we have taken over the Southwest. They have reason to be very optimistic. In June Fort Buchanan was ordered abandoned and its stores destroyed and its complement of some five hundred men removed for action in our present war. This was instantly interpreted by the Indians, who of course could know no better, as a sign of surrender. They have assumed it was their action which caused the abandonment of the fort and the evacuation of the soldiers."

Canby unrolled a large map of the territory and Jeffords pulled his chair around so that he could follow him.

"Fort Breckenridge was also ordered abandoned," Canby continued, "leaving the country without any military protection whatsoever. As you may imagine the Apaches are having a field day. They consider that the Army is afraid to stand up to them. They know nothing of course of the war we ourselves are engaged in. Blood is running everywhere. Mining has been abandoned. The Butterfield line is no longer in operation and the stations are vacated. Ranchers have left their ranches, cattle, sheep, homesteaders have fled from their homes —those who were not killed by the Indians. These people who have managed to escape have congregated in Tucson and Tubac and at one or two heavily fortified ranches, such as Pete Kitchen's place in the Sonoita.

"The Indians are absolutely merciless. They are putting to shame their own records of outrage. Men, women, and children are being slain everywhere without the slightest compunction. There is no place in the desert or the mountains that isn't strewn with charred bodies, burned wagons, bleached bones. Apache Pass, right here"—Canby indicated the place on the map—"where the Bascom affair occurred, is probably the worst place of all. I am told that one is almost able to walk from one end of the pass to the other without having to set foot on the ground—so thick are the wagons and skeletons of victims."

Canby rose and began to pace up and down, leaving a long trail of black smoke behind him.

"If I seem to be dealing with this condition in a somewhat melodramatic manner, Captain Jeffords," he said, "believe me that whatever I say is less than the truth. And I feel I must acquaint you with the details before you leave."

Jeffords nodded and stretched his legs.

"The Apaches no longer attack in small numbers," Canby continued. "They no longer are content to raid for cattle and horses. This Cochise seems to have gathered together great numbers of Apache warriors and, what is worse, seems to be using his forces in a manner so skillful that my only regret is that he is not fighting on our side. From what I have been able to learn the man is something of a military genius of sorts, and he is using the peculiar talents of the Apaches and the very nature of the country in a manner that is absolutely irreproachable from a military viewpoint." Canby looked quickly at Jeffords. "The man is our deadly enemy," he said quietly. "But as a military man I must express my admiration of his leadership."

Canby sat down and mashed out his cigar and lighted a fresh one, pushing the box toward Jeffords.

148

"The Apaches now are attacking in forces as high as two and three hundred at a time. They roam the countryside, striking everywhere, unpredictably, and they leave destruction and death in their wake wherever they go. It is hard to believe but they had the audacity to attack the hacienda of the Santa Rita mines in Sonoita and force its abandonment. Then they struck at the headquarters of the mines at Tubac and caused the officials to leave there. They surrounded Tubac and for days cut the inhabitants from all supplies. Finally, in what appears to be a giant demonstration of arrogance, they laid siege to Tucson itself and quit their siege only when they were ready to do so and not before."

The general appeared lost in his thoughts. Then he continued, "Now, about Tucson. At the time of the start of this war of rebellion there seem to have been just sixty-eight native-born Americans in the town. They convened and voted to join the Confederacy. No one stopped them. They proclaimed their country a territory of the Confederacy. This might have been merely a token, pointless announcement, except that it was implemented by an action taken by Lieutenant Colonel Baylor, whom you know of, I believe, a Rebel commander of mounted rifles. Baylor, upon reaching Mesilla, issued a proclamation last August establishing the Territory of Arizona—for the Rebels, of course. He separated Arizona from New Mexico here"—pointing to the map—"and he appointed himself governor.

"Five months ago, in January, Baylor sent two hundred Rebel soldiers to Tucson to occupy it in the name of the Confederacy, which he did, without firing a shot. He might still own the town if it had not been for General James Carleton and his California Column. After a magnificent march from California this body of volunteers retook Tucson, again without shooting, the Rebels abandoning the city upon the approach of the Californians. I received this information from a captured Rebel soldier.

"General Carleton now is apparently in command of Tucson. As soon as he occupied the town he attempted to communicate with me. He sent a small party, two or three men, I believe, and these men were set upon by Apaches. All were killed except one man who seems to have made a miraculous escape and to have reached the Rio Grande at Picacho where he was taken prisoner by the Rebels. From prison he managed to get word to me." Canby smiled slightly. "It does not matter how I received this message. It suffices to say that I did. The man could tell me no more than he had dispatches from Carleton. The last word I have received from Carleton was that he had reoccupied Tucson. That was back in May. What happened between then and now I know nothing of. But I am

149

certain that the message General Carleton tried to get through to me must be of paramount importance."

Canby paused and gazed silently at Jeffords.

"That is where you come in, Captain Jeffords," he said at last. "I must know how strong the California Column is and how well it is equipped. Everything I might plan to do from this point depends upon what is happening over there and what I may expect to happen in the weeks to come. If Carleton is in strength we can plan on a campaign to drive the Rebels out of New Mexico and I will know my rear and right flank are secure. If Carleton has a token force in Tucson, it may be that he will need assistance from me. I cannot move without knowing the exact situation in Tucson."

Canby studied the map again. "Between here and Tucson lies the heart of Apacheria. You know more about Apaches than I do. But it is my duty to state the facts as I know them. I am in no position to order you to venture on this journey."

"I'll go," Jeffords said.

"You are not in the Army, Captain Jeffords, but I know your loyalty to your country."

"I don't need that," Jeffords said quietly.

"I am not waving a flag, Captain Jeffords. I am saying all this because I believe the assignment a difficult one and I want you to depart with full knowledge of its importance."

"You would not send me if it wasn't important, General," Jeffords said. "That's enough for me."

Canby nodded. "Thank you, Tom," he said. "You make it quite simple. When can you leave?"

"Now."

"Don't you have any affairs to settle?"

Jeffords smiled faintly. "No," he said.

"Do you want any men to accompany you?"

"No. I have an old buzzard I've been knocking around with. I'll take him."

"If you want an escort you are welcome to one."

"We'll travel better just the two of us."

Canby sat upright in his chair and his manner became military. "Leave as soon as you can," he said. "Get to Tucson. See Carleton. I'll prepare a paper authorizing you my official courier. Find out how Carleton is situated. How strong he is. How many men and exactly what equipment he can put into the field. If he is strong I need him here, with every man he can spare. However, he will know his own situation and if he feels he has to remain in Tucson, or leave a garrison there, I will abide by his decision."

"Yes, sir," Jeffords said.

Canby called an orderly, and dictated a brief letter accrediting Jeffords and then signed and sealed the document. "Here you are, Captain Jeffords," he said. "I have no further instructions."

"I'll try to be back in two or three weeks," Jeffords said, slipping the letter into his pocket.

"There is no need for you to return."

"You want General Carleton's answer, don't you?"

"He probably has an experienced courier."

"I'll bring the answer back myself."

"I shall wait on your return, Captain," Canby said, his eyes gleaming. "One thing more. I have spoken about the Indians. I think they will be your greatest danger. But there is another enemy."

Jeffords nodded.

"I have prepared a small map. It indicates the disposition of the Confederate forces. I think that you might get somewhat better treatment from the Rebels than from the Apaches, but it would nullify your mission."

"They might have some more of these cigars," Jeffords said.

"Are you fully equipped? Weapons? Horses? Blankets?"

"Yes, sir." Jeffords smiled. "Can you spare a few more stogies?"

"Help yourself, Tom."

"You shouldn't have spoken about the Rebs," Jeffords said mildly. "They're lost out here, too. Those poor little fellows belong back home, not here in Indian country." He lit another cigar and dragged in a mouthful of smoke. "You know, General," he said, "out here this fighting between ourselves strikes me as being plain foolish. Back East maybe it makes sense but out here, no. Hanging together we'd have all we could do to keep the Indians off our necks. Now we're scrapping among ourselves and the Indian sits back and picks off from both sides, whichever is more convenient. Even the Indians stop fighting among themselves and get together when they got a bigger scrap against us on their hands."

2

Outside the building an old man squatted on his haunches. He was short, grizzled, and gray-haired and his face resembled the side of a Western mountain seen from a distance. It was lined and seamed and the nose and bony forehead looked like a faraway peak and mesa. When Jeffords stepped from the building he looked up and said in a querulous voice, "Took you an awful long time. I been waiting for more than an hour. I thought you got throwed in jail."

"Let's move," Jeffords said, walking past the old man.

"Where we going, Tom? Tell me where we're going?"

"Where are the horses?"

"Down to the corral where you told me to leave them. Tell me where we're going."

"Tucson. Get down to the quartermaster and get some jerked beef, some biscuits, and some bacon fat."

"Tucson? We ain't joined the Army again, are we, Tom?"

"No. Remember, just bacon fat, no bacon. Dried beef and biscuits and bacon fat. Meet me at the corral."

"Now why would the quartermaster give me beef and biscuits and bacon fat?" the old man asked. "I ain't no soldier."

"He knows all about it," Jeffords said.

"Then we have joined the Army again," the old man said in disgust. "I thought you was too growed up to get us mixed up with soldiers again."

"Get enough from the quartermaster for a week's supply."

"A week?"

"I'll be at the corral. And hurry. We don't have too much time."

At the corral Jeffords inspected two horses and two pack mules. He looked at his rifle, his shotgun, and his two revolvers. He examined the extra cartridges for all the weapons. When the old man returned with the food Jeffords told him to see that all his guns were working.

He divided the food and ammunition and packed them expertly on the mules, together with blankets and canteens of water. He put the shotguns under the mule packs and the rifles in the scabbards on the saddles. He put the map and the letter of authority in a leather pouch and strapped it around his waist.

Then he turned to the old man, and said, "Hank, we got to get to Tucson. It ought to take us about five days, maybe less, maybe a little more, depending on what we run into. The stage used to do it in two days, traveling day and night. We won't have any changes and we won't be able to follow the trail. I'm not worried about that. We'll tack back and forth and we both know the country pretty well."

"Tom, you said twice we was going to Tucson, but you ain't told me yet why. Seems like I got a right to know why we're heading into Indian country."

"You're right, Hank. I have a message to bring to General Carleton in Tucson from General Canby."

"Tom, you're a mining man. How often do I have to tell you that? What for are you wasting our time with soldiers?" Hank protested.

"They tell me there's a war on, Hank," Jeffords said.

"Let them fight their danged war. We got other business." Hank spat. "I lived to be an old man to become a messenger boy." He bit off a chew of tobacco. "We ain't Northerners or yet Southerners. We're Westerners and we're mining men.

152

Why ain't we up in the hills trying to find some gold?" He sent forth a stream of tobacco juice.

"You'll have to quit chewing pretty soon," Jeffords said. "Indians can follow that juice trail like it was a highway."

The old man glared at him. "First being a messenger boy. Now no chewing."

"Want to stay here, Hank?"

"I sure do," Hank retorted. "Only you can't find your way without me."

"That's right, Hank. Now I'll tell you why we're going." He told the old man what Canby had said. "That's it. We're on a government mission. It's important, if you figure winning the war and keeping the country in one piece is important. Now you know. If anything happens to me my papers are in this pouch. You go on and see General Carleton and give him the information."

"Nothing ain't going to happen to you with me around." The old man looked up belligerently. "Why didn't the general ask to see me too?"

"He did," Jeffords said gently. "I told him he had to convince me before he could convince you."

It was late in the afternoon when they started. They rode out of the camp slowly and picked up the old stage route. It wouldn't be until the next day they would hit dangerous Indian country. They would travel from just before dawn, when Apaches generally attacked, to the hottest part of the day and then rest. Then travel again until dark and take turns sleeping until starting time before the sun rose again.

"Reckon the general picked us because we know this danged country better than the Indians?" Hank asked suddenly.

"Reckon so," Jeffords said.

Hank swelled. "Nobody knows this country like we do. How long we been prospecting together, Tom?"

"Almost five years now."

"Maybe we'll get us a medal for this, hey, Tom?"

"Maybe."

"But this ain't our business. Our business is digging. When we get finished with this we go back to our own business, don't we, Tom?"

"Yes."

They rode in silence. Jeffords' eyes seemed aimless but they missed nothing. Hank rode as though he was half asleep, his eyes almost closed in a permanent squint against the sun, the deep ridges of crinkles around them holding the pack dust of years now ingrained into his skin. From the narrow openings of his eyes he appeared almost in a doze and yet the smallest moving thing caught his attention and stiffened him instinctively, his hand moving to his rifle automatically. The scurry

153

of a rabbit brought the right hands of both men to their weapons before the sight and sound were fully translated to their brains. They were able, as were most men who had to preserve their lives by their alertness and skill, to perform ordinary tasks with only a part of themselves, while other parts functioned as though they had life of their own, watching, listening, sometimes acting violently.

"Better roost pretty soon," Jeffords said.

"I been looking for a place."

"That rise ahead looks all right."

"I been thinking about that."

From the rise they could command a view of the country in all directions. It was twilight, the bright radiant twilight that comes only upon the desert; the air was so transparent there was almost no such thing as distance; the mountains moved closer and the plains were foreshortened. Jeffords looked over the ground. It was covered with light gravel. It would be difficult for even an Indian to creep up the hill on such ground without making a noise. The men tethered the animals and fed them. Then Jeffords and Hank chewed on a few pieces of beef and ate biscuits covered with bacon grease.

"You can chew," Jeffords said.

Hank's eyes lit up; he hastily bit off a hunk of tobacco and began to chew before Jeffords could change his mind.

"Not on the road tomorrow," Jeffords said. "But any Indian who's looking for us will know we've camped here."

"Won't you have none, Tom?"

"No."

"I don't see how you can pull that black smoke into your lungs," Hank said. "Seems to me the inside of your chest must look like a chimney."

"Hold the blanket over my head while I light this," Jeffords said. When the cigar was lit he cupped the glowing end with his hand.

"Seems to me a smart educated man like you would know what that smoke was doing to you. Why don't you get a nice healthy habit like chewing?"

"Maybe I will someday." He smiled at the old man. "Roll up and get some sleep. I'll wake you later."

"I ain't tired. You sleep."

"Roll up." The last time they had camped out the old man had remained awake the whole night. "I got some thinking to do."

Hank curled up in the blanket. "You think too danged much."

"Don't go to sleep with that wad in your mouth. You might choke."

Hank didn't say anything. It was their standard joke. Hank

154

could hold a wad in his cheek and sleep all night and when he woke start chewing again almost before he opened his eyes.

Jeffords leaned back against a rock. The cheroot tasted good. He held the lighted end protected and smoked it slowly. The smell of tobacco mixed well with the smell of sage. The night was very quiet. Occasionally a coyote howled and the sound came crashing through the night and when it disappeared it left a hole in the night where the sound had been. He felt good. It was the best time for him, alone. In the night and alone with the soundless small things and not having to talk. There was too much talk and most of it unnecessary and most of it lying. Alone on the desert he felt he could reach to something, something he could never get to anywhere else, something that belonged to the beginning and made everything else that happened in between of no importance.

Tomorrow, he thought, they would be in the country of Mangas Coloradas and the Mimbres Apaches. He knew a little about him. He was a politician, an Indian politician. After passing through his country they would enter the Chiricahua country. That was Cochise and he was something different again. He had heard a great deal about Cochise, whose name now was synonymous for Indian cruelty. But even professional Indian haters had a different tone in their voice when they spoke of him. Most of them said, oddly enough, that he was a man of honor.

It was some hours later when he leaned over and shook Hank. "I'm awake," the old man said. "Feel fine." He sat up chewing. "Get some sleep."

"Wake me up just before it gets light," Jeffords said. He wrapped the blanket around him and stretched out. He looked up at the stars and he heard the soft sough of the desert wind. He thought he might be the only person alive in the world.

3

When they started in the morning Jeffords saw that something was troubling his partner. He refrained from questioning him, and finally the old man said, "Tom, I been thinking."

"About what?"

"We should have two pieces of paper with two names writ on them." Jeffords looked puzzled. "Nothing is going to happen to you, Tom," Hank continued, "but suppose it does. How can I carry the message when it's got your name writ on it?"

Jeffords mulled over this and then said, "I'll write another note with your name on it, and then you could show both pieces."

"Well, that might be all right," Hank said.

"I'll do it right now," Jeffords said. "I'll write it down on

155

the same piece of paper that has my name on it." He stopped the horse and took out his letter of identification and wrote on the back of it, "In case anything happens to me this will be brought to you by my partner, Hank Thompson." He read it to Hank.

"That's just right," Hank said.

"When are you going to learn to read?"

"When I get old enough," Hank said, winking slyly.

"You've been giving me the same answer for five years."

"Seems like you would get tired asking then."

"When we get to Tucson I'm going to start teaching you myself."

"When we get to Tucson," Hank agreed.

"You won't disappear? Like the last time?"

"No."

"What's come over you? Last time you ran away for ten days."

"I was only a desert rat then."

"Oh."

"I been thinking. I figure if the United States Government sees fit to make a messenger out of me I ought to be able to read the language." Hank shook his head. "You know, Tom, plenty of men are depending on us. All them soldier boys over to Thorn waiting to hear what we're going to find out and all those soldier boys over to Tucson waiting to move when we tell them. It's like being boss of the Army."

"You like it?"

"Well, when there's a war on a man has got to stick by his country or he ain't a man."

"What about your digging? Are you quitting that?"

"I ain't made our pile yet, have I?"

"No, you haven't made our pile."

"Then don't ask foolish questions. But now there's a war on."

A little later Jeffords said, "Better leave the trail and head for those mountains."

"There's a cut through the hills just north of here," Hank replied. "We went looking for pay dirt up there a couple of years ago."

"That's the way I mean."

"There's a ridge. Good way to keep your eye out for Indians."

They left the stage route and after cutting across country at an angle resumed an almost parallel course in the mountains. They rode slowly and for the most part silently; as is the case with two men of their temperament, after years of breaking trails together there was almost no need of speaking. They seemed able to communicate with a sort of telepathy. The sun rose red and hot on the parched country and the desert changed from early morning gray to its coat of changing colors, the pale, first, bluish colors, getting redder, the rising sun sprawled like pink blood on the mountains, the blood color deepening the warmth of the sun falling full on them, and then the warmth turning to the early day heat.

"Looks like it might be another scorcher," Hank grumbled. "I hate this damned country."

"You been out here how long? Fifty years?"

"Since I was a boy."

"I don't believe you ever were a boy. I think you were born an old man with a pick in your hand and a wad of tobacco in your jaw."

"I was born like anybody else," Hank said.

"How come you stay out here if you hate it so much?"

"I don't know. When I strike pay dirt for us I'm going to quit."

"What are you going to do?"

"I'm going to sea," Hank said, looking up defensively.

"To sea?" Jeffords asked, as though he had not heard this a hundred times before.

"Yes, sir, to sea. I'm going where there ain't no sand and no mountains and no cactus and no rocks. I want to go to somewhere where it rains all the time. I want to lay in a little boat and drag my hand in the water for the rest of my life."

"You'd be back in six months. You're not a sailor. You're a pack rat."

"Like to make a little bet?"

"Sure." It was the hundredth time they made this bet.

"All right. I'll bet."

"How much?"

"Well," Hank said, rubbing his lip. "I figure we'll make a million when I strike so we can bet, say, fifty thousand."

"It's a bet. Fifty thousand that you will be back here six months after you pull out."

"You got a bet."

"Did you hear that?" Jeffords looked around.

"Sure I heard it. Think I'm deaf? Them was shots."

Jeffords strained forward in his saddle. He listened intently, his right hand already removing his rifle from its scabbard. Then he heard the shots again, coming distantly from the west, and it seemed that in hearing them he could instantly smell the smoke and the powder. Then he heard another volley. He adjusted the telescopic sights on his rifle and then they moved forward again, slowly, warily. They listened again and then altered their direction. They saw a rise leading up to a high tableland and they went up on it; reaching the mesa, which made a high platform, they rode forward again.

157

"Indians," Hank said, his voice automatically becoming a whisper although no one was near them. "They ain't shooting at us."

They made their way carefully, moving deliberately and skillfully, with old experience, from rock to rock, pausing, listening, watching between moves. The firing came from the valley below the tableland. They dismounted and tied their horses back from the edge of the mesa, close enough to be able to get back to them quickly, and then crawled forward. When they reached the edge and looked down they saw the old story.

There were three wagons formed into a rough triangle. Around the wagons, protected by boulders, were the Indians. Jeffords and Hank watched for a few minutes, counting gun bursts. It seemed there were about a dozen Indians. They could count only two bursts from the wagons.

From where they crouched they could see four or five of the Indians stretched out flat on the ground firing from crevices between the rocks, unprotected from the rear.

"About three hundred yards?" Jeffords asked, adjusting his sights.

"A wee mite more," Hank said. "I'd say just a mite more."

Hank rested his rifle on a rock and stretched out to make himself comfortable.

"We're not supposed to get mixed up in Indian fights," Jeffords said. "We're on an official mission."

"There are white men down there."

"We don't own ourselves now," Jeffords said. "The thing for us to do is get on these horses again and detour."

"There are Indians shooting at white men down there," Hank said. "Make up your mind fast."

Jeffords compressed his lips. He knew what he should do and he knew what he would do. "You take that one with the feather in his head," he said quietly. "I'll take the big boy lying next to him."

"This'll only hold us up a couple of minutes," Hank said.

"I'm going to get around that big rock over there. Don't shoot until I'm set."

"Dang it, Tom. I wish you would stop talking to me like I was a dude. I was shooting Indians before you was born."

Jeffords crept some twenty yards away and then lay down behind a boulder. He lifted his hand and waved to Hank and then he aimed carefully, squinting through the sight, and then he heard Hank's gun fire and he pulled his own trigger; he saw one Indian roll over and then another jerk back and then collapse.

They fired again and another Indian flattened against the rock in front of him and then they saw several of the Indians turn around and look in their direction and they fired again and missed; taking steadier aim, they fired again, and an Indian dropped his rifle and clapped his hand to his side.

"Stop shooting at the same danged Indian that I am," Hank called out. "Waste of good ammunition."

Jeffords was apart from his work, thinking only that the new Wesson rifle and the new improved 'scope was everything it was supposed to be, and then he heard a brittle click on the rock in front of him and a piece of the rock chipped off and he fired again. As the Indians rose and turned toward them there were two shots from the wagons and one of the Indians fell over and the others got up and started to run, in their low, crouching animal way, zigzagging, and he didn't try to shoot any more because the field of vision in the sight was too narrow for a moving target at that distance.

"They're running," he said.

"Yeah," Hank said. "It's all over."

Jeffords grinned and then he turned suddenly. His throat went dry. "Hank," he said.

"Don't use that tone of voice to me," Hank said. "I lifted my head too high."

"Hank. You stupid bastard," Jeffords said. He got up and ran over to the old man. He saw a small hole through his neck. Jeffords took out his whiskey bottle and started to unscrew the cap.

"Don't waste it," Hank said.

"I shouldn't have got you into this," Jeffords said.

"We're working for the government, ain't we?" Hank asked.

"Yes."

"Hell, it's better dying than I deserve. It ain't just another Indian fight while we're looking for gold or even silver."

"No."

"Guys get shot in a war," Hank said.

"Don't talk so damned much."

"Hell, I'm a goner. Don't be scolding right up to the finish."

He was right, Jeffords knew. Even if there was anything that could be done, the place it could be done was too far from there.

"Don't waste no time digging a hole, Tom. Get moving on."

"Hank, you old goat."

"Take it easy. You ain't got nobody to look after you now."

"Hank."

The old man closed his eyes and then he stopped breathing. Jeffords held his head against him for a few minutes and then he laid it gently on the hard granite ground. He tried to think of something to say but he had forgotten all the right words a long time ago. He stood up. It was quiet below. He lifted the body of the old man and put it across his saddle. He was surprised to find how light he was.

He got on his own horse and leading the other animals he rode down from the mesa toward the wagons. Before he reached them he could see some of the bodies. There were seven he could make out. A figure stood up as he approached. It looked like a boy.

When he got closer he saw that one of the men on the ground was still alive. There was a white rag stuck into his side and the edges of the rag were red. The boy stood erect and Jeffords saw that it wasn't a boy, but a young girl.

"You ought to know better than to try to make this trip with three wagons," Jeffords said.

"There were eight when we started. The Indians got between us," the girl said.

"Where are the others?"

"They kept going."

"Friends of yours?"

"No. We made up a train in Mesilla."

Jeffords got off his horse.

"You might do better than ask a lot of questions," the girl said. "My father is wounded." Then she saw the body of Hank. "How is he, your friend?"

"Dead." Jeffords knelt beside the wounded man. Then he glanced up. "Keep looking around. Maybe they'll come back." He turned back to the man. The death was on his face. He uncapped his whiskey bottle and forced a few drops into the man's throat. He opened his eyes.

"Thanks."

"Don't try to talk."

"It doesn't matter. Name is Weaver. My daughter, Terry. On our way to Tucson. Take care of her."

"Sure."

"There is some gold in a little pouch in the wagon. It'll pay you."

"Talk sense. Who do you know in Tucson?"

"Nobody. Figured on homesteading."

The man's face got gray. He closed his eyes. Jeffords called to the girl. "Better come over here and say goodbye to your father," he said.

Weaver opened his eyes again. "Thanks," he said. "You came just in time."

"Don't worry about the kid."

"Thanks."

"Don't move. You're finished but don't move. Save your strength for what you want to tell your kid."

"Yes," the man said. He wet his lips. Jeffords gave him another swallow of whiskey. "I'll watch," he said to the girl. "Your father wants to talk to you. He's got about three minutes."

"You don't have to say it," the girl flared angrily.

"Get down there and talk."

He walked away and looked across the country. In a few minutes the girl came up to him. "He's dead," she said. Her eyes were dry.

"Got a shovel?" Jeffords asked.

"There's one in our wagon."

"We'll bury your father and my partner. There's no time for the others."

"You can't leave them lying like that," the girl said.

"There is no time. The Indians may come back for their own dead. Apaches bury their dead right away, where they were killed."

"It appears that they have more compassion than you have," the girl said. "I won't leave those other bodies unburied."

"How old are you?"

"Fifteen. What has that got to do with it? They're Christians and deserve a Christian burial." The girl shivered slightly. "We've seen too many bleached bones on the desert."

"We'll bury your father and my partner. People like you and your friends travel out here like fools and get yourselves killed and get other people killed trying to help you. I got work to do. We'll make a single grave and put your father and my partner in it and then get out of here. Now get the shovel."

"Don't order me around."

"Miss," Jeffords said evenly, "I haven't got time to put you across my knee and whip you. Get that shovel. And while I dig you keep your eyes open and then we'll get the hell out of here."

"You don't have to use language like that."

"Get the shovel. I don't know where it is in the wagon."

The girl stood tense, looking at him, and then she burst into tears and ran toward one of the wagons. She returned with a shovel and threw it at Jeffords' feet.

"Stop crying," he said. "You have to keep your eyes clear. You can cry when I'm finished."

The girl wiped her eyes with her fists. "You are wicked and cruel and detestable," she said.

"Keep moving around and watch for Indians."

Jeffords dug a grave and put the body of Weaver on one side. Then he went to Hank's horse and very gently lifted the light frail body and carried it to the grave. He laid it alongside the other body. He straightened out Hank's coat and fixed the head so it wasn't twisted on his neck and then he crossed the hands over his chest. He let his fingers rest lightly on the old, furrowed face. Then he stood up. The girl was at his side.

"I forgot about him, I guess," she said. "I'm sorry."

"Do you know any words?"

"Words?"

"They ought to have something out of the Bible."

"I know the Lord's Prayer."

"Say it."

Jeffords took off his hat. The girl removed her own broad sombrero. He saw her hair was flaming red and tied in a knot behind her ears. She whispered the prayer quietly and then Jeffords covered the bodies with dirt.

"We should have waited until they were covered to say the prayer," the girl said.

"Hank's hearing wasn't so good," Jeffords said. "It was better this way." He took two spokes from a broken wheel and laced a cross together with rawhide and then stuck it into the grave. "Let's go," he said.

The girl fell upon the grave. She pressed her cheek on the ground, on her father's side, and whispered something. Then she stood up.

"Get on Hank's horse," Jeffords said. "You can use his gun. Can you ride regular saddle?"

"Of course."

"Know how to use a gun?"

"Yes."

"Get the sack of gold your father spoke about."

"Stop giving me orders," the girl said, her temper rising again.

"Get the sack. We have to move right away."

"You think I'm a child."

"My name is Tom Jeffords. I know yours. We'll be together for a few days. We might as well stop fighting."

The girl went to the wagon and returned with the leather pouch and a small valise.

"What's that?" Jeffords asked.

"Things of mine."

"Leave them."

"They are all I have. I won't leave them."

Jeffords looked at her. She was quivering. "All right," he said. "I'll strap them on the mule."

"What about everything else?" the girl asked. "The wagons and the wagon-mules?"

"They must be destroyed."

"It's everything we have," she said. "Everything from where we came from."

"Terry," he said, using her name for the first time. "We cannot take these things with us, not even the mules. And it is better to destroy everything than leave anything that may be of use to the Indians."

She looked up at him. "I know," she said.

162

"That's better. You're very pretty when you smile."

Later she got on Hank's horse. "I'm ready," she said.

"Good, let's go."

The girl looked at the grave. "Ever since my mother died I've cooked for my father. I've washed for Daddy and I've mended his clothes and I've taken care of him from Maryland out to here."

"We'd better start, Terry," he said, with that odd gentleness that sometimes appeared in his voice.

"And I thank you for coming to my rescue, Mr. Jeffords. And I'm sorry your friend was killed on account of us. It was not Christian of me to have acted and spoken as I did."

Jeffords began to feel embarrassed. "There's time for that later," he said.

"I'm trying to be civil to you," the girl replied, suddenly angry again. "Is everyone out in this horrible country as uncouth as you appear to be?"

"If I had time I'd bend you over my knee," he said.

The girl sat erect in the saddle. "Would you, Mr. Jeffords?" she asked quietly.

Jeffords realized that she was quite beautiful. Her hair was the true red, not like his, which was brown on his head and turned red only in his beard. Her eyes were a strange blue, with violet overtones. Her skin was very white, the white skin of the true redhead, and from days in the sun it was splattered with freckles which oddly did not detract from her loveliness. And, he thought, she was no child.

"Listen, Terry," he said gruffly. "We're in Indian country. You know that, don't you? They may come back and if they do they will find just two of us."

The girl spurred her horse for answer. Jeffords called out, "Not that way. Follow me."

4

At sunset they made a dry camp. He had returned to the ridge and had followed it, and then had cut across country on an old trail known to Hank and himself. From where they made camp they could look down and see the mark of the old Butterfield trail. They were protected in the rear by a high, almost overhanging wall of rock, and in the front by a sheer cliff. On either side they could see the trail for some distance.

They had spoken little to each other during the day. Jeffords was filled with thoughts about Hank. The girl, too, seemed to want to be left alone. They were both grateful for the other's silence.

After they dismounted Jeffords said, "Wait here." He walked ahead until he was out of sight and a few moments later returned. "It seems all right. Go on up the trail a ways and relieve yourself."

The girl turned scarlet. "Mr. Jeffords, you are the most vulgar man I've ever met."

"Hurry back. It's getting dark."

The girl's eyes filled with tears.

"What are you crying about?" he asked.

"Mr. Jeffords, I've asked you not to treat me as a child."

He walked over to her and lifted her chin. He looked at her gravely. "Terry, you've had a very hard day. Don't try to be tough. Nobody is that tough. It's not good for you inside to keep your feelings all tied up. I'm not treating you as a child. I'm treating you the way I would treat another man. I'm trying to make you feel that way. I'll have to use you that way, to keep watch, maybe to handle a gun."

The tears made her eyes look very soft. "Now you're trying to make me feel good, Mr. Jeffords."

"Tom," he said.

"Tom."

"Sure I'm trying to make you feel good. Your Daddy just got killed. I wish someone would try to make me feel good."

She wiped her eyes. "Was he an old friend of yours?" she asked in a very womanly voice.

"Yes, Terry."

"And if it weren't for us he would still be alive."

"Yes."

"I must seem like a very poor exchange." She bit her lips and then turned hurriedly and walked up the trail.

When they were finished with their cold meal they leaned against the rock wall. He didn't light a cigar.

"Where do you come from, Tom?" she asked.

"Upper New York State. Place called Chautauqua."

"You are a long way from home, too."

"Yes."

"Are you married?"

"No."

She doubled her legs under her chin. In the clear night he could see her profile plainly. "Do you have a family out here?" she asked.

"No."

"Are you all alone then?"

"Yes, Terry."

"I am alone now, too." She stared out into the night. "Tom?"

"Yes?"

"I belong to you. In a special way."

"To me?"

"Yes. If it weren't for me your partner would be alive. He

164

is dead because of me and he is buried next to my Daddy. Don't I take his place, in a way?"

"In a way."

"Is it being like a child to be frightened?"

"Are you frightened?"

"Yes." She turned to him and he lost the shape of her face. "Not of this, Tom, not where we are now. But of everything else. When we get to Tucson and you get rid of me I'll really be alone."

He wanted to put his arm around her and reassure her, as though she were a child, but he couldn't quite make himself feel that way. "Better get some sleep."

"We'll divide the night," she said. "I'll stay awake while you sleep later. That's what you said."

"All right."

"You will wake me? Just as though I were Hank?"

"Yes, Terry."

He wrapped a blanket around her. Then he bent down and kissed her on the cheek.

"Why did you do that, Tom?" she asked clearly.

"I think you are very brave."

"No," she said. "I'm really frightened. Inside frightened."

"Try to sleep."

In a little while she lifted her head. "I don't care what you think," she said. "I belong to you in a very important way."

"I thought you were asleep."

She sat up and took his cheeks in her hands and kissed him on the lips. "I'm beholden to you, Tom," she said in a whisper. "You can't undo it."

"Good night, Terry."

"Good night, Tom. And thank you."

He tucked her in again and presently she was asleep. He peered closely at her face in the night and asleep it was a very young face.

He did not waken her throughout the night. He found a clump of rocks that afforded protection and huddled in them, he smoked several cigars and listened to her sleep and thought of Hank. Late in the night he saw distant fires of Apaches signaling to each other. He tried to line up the fires to ascertain how the Indians were dispersed, and he decided finally that his original plans to swing to the south of the Butterfield route, until Apache Pass, at least, were still sound.

He wondered if he would be able to keep up his rate of travel with the girl. He had to get unused to thinking of things in terms of Hank, and for the remainder of this journey to plan in terms of a fifteen-year-old girl. He wondered what he would do with her when they reached Tucson. What did you do with girls that age? Fifteen was not young out where they were now. Mexican and Indian girls that age were usually either married or close to it. If Tucson was like the towns he had known in New Mexico she probably would not have much to worry about along that line.

Later he got up and eased his tired muscles. He looked at the animals. He walked around slowly until he had the veteran camper's feeling that dawn was not far off and then he knelt down and touched her gently. She stirred and then she opened her eyes. He saw bewilderment on her face and then brief fright and then she smiled. She sat up and yawned and asked, "Time for me to stand watch?"

"Time to move on."

She looked around. "Did you let me sleep all night?"

"Yes."

"That wasn't part of the bargain," she said. "You were going to treat me like another man."

"I know. But I started to think during the night and I enjoyed my thoughts so much the night was out before I knew it."

She looked at him angrily. "Tom Jeffords, I told you yesterday I was not to be treated like a child."

"Don't get redheaded so early in the morning," he said.

She shook her head furiously and stood up. She was stiff from lying on the ground and she would have fallen over if he had not reached out and caught her. "The mountains and the desert make funny country. You have to get used to them. Now bend up and down and loosen yourself."

"I will not," she said through her teeth.

"You have a lot of riding ahead of you today," he said. "I might have to leave you behind somewhere."

She tried to bend down and groaned. She put her hand on her back.

"Stiff?"

"It is," she admitted ruefully.

"Not used to riding steady like we did yesterday."

"No."

"Lie down."

"What for?"

"I'll rub it loose." He dug the heels of his hands into the small of her back. She started to squirm and he held her there and worked her back. "Now try moving around."

"I feel as though I'm crippled," she said. She stood up and twisted her body. "It does feel better."

"Good. Now can you wait a little while before we eat?"

"Of course."

"Then let's get moving. Apaches usually attack at dawn."

"I know that," she said.

166

When they were on the trail again she said, "I don't know why the Army doesn't come out here and kill every one of them."

"I guess the Army has its hands full right now," he said.

"I wish this silly war would be over soon! All the soldiers ought to make up with each other and then come out here and wipe out these Indians."

"What are your sympathies in the war?"

"I haven't got any sympathies. My Daddy was against all war. He said of all wars civil wars were the cruelest. He didn't believe in slavery though and that was one of the reasons we started west. We started before the war started. When I think of all the boys back home out getting themselves killed I know Daddy was right. Killing each other while the Indians attack anybody they please. I'll never forget how my Daddy was lying there for more than three hours with a bullet in his side and still shooting at those Indians. He told me if he died before any help came to shoot myself quickly before they could capture me."

"What do you think the Indians would have done to you?"

"What do Indians usually do to women they capture?"

"Nowadays they kill them. Most of the time."

"That would be the most merciful thing. I wouldn't be as afraid of that as of some other things."

"Apaches seldom attack white women, Terry," he said. "You would either have been killed or else brought to the tribe as a servant. They would have worked you pretty hard and maybe after a while one of them would have wanted to take you as his wife. But I don't think that what you are most afraid of would have happened. And anyway it's nothing for a girl your age to be thinking of."

"I believe you are trying to defend them," she said.

"No," he said. "Perhaps to explain them a little."

"What is there to explain about them? They're wild animals."

"No, Terry, not quite."

"What do you mean?"

"It's a long argument, Terry," he said.

"We have a long ride. What do you mean?"

"They have something to be said for their side."

"For killing? For torturing travelers?"

"Well, we didn't exactly try to make friends with them."

"I don't know what you're talking about."

"It goes way back, Terry, before your time. Before my time. This was always Indian country. They considered that they belonged here."

"Belonged here? It's our country, isn't it?"

"Well, maybe as far as the rest of the world is concerned

167

it's our country, all right. But the Indians always sort of figured that it was their country. They figured that living here for hundreds of years made it theirs. There was a great deal of double-crossing on both sides. Nobody can say now who started it. But there was plenty on both sides. For instance, did you know that the Mexican government—not the people, but the government itself—will pay fifty dollars for every Apache scalp anybody brings in? Like a bounty on wild-cats?"

"I don't believe it."

"And it is hard to tell from a scalp whether it came off an Apache head or off the head of another kind of Indian, say one of the friendly Indians like the Papagos or the Maricopas. Or even if it came from a Mexican or an American. A scalp is a scalp. There are Americans and Mexicans who make a living that way. They get Indians drunk and then kill them and scalp them for the bounty."

"The Mexican government may do that but we don't," she said.

"No. We put the Indians on reservations."

"What's wrong with that?"

"It depends how you look at it. From the American viewpoint there's nothing wrong with it. The Indian thinks different. What right have we to barge out here and tell people who've roamed around this country long before any white man ever heard of America that he has to stop roaming and stay put? Maybe it wouldn't be so bad at that, except that they always pick the worst sections of any country for reservations. Places with malaria, or where things won't grow, or where the wild animals have been scared off so the Indians can't hunt. They take these Indians who have lived pretty much as they please for as long as they can remember and overnight force them to live in a sort of outdoor jail. They become charity cases. If they behave they can live on government handouts. And some of the Indian Agents are no bargains. They're fools, some of them, and some of them are plain common crooks who steal from the Indians they're supposed to watch. Not all of them, but enough to make most Indians keep away from reservations to the point of going to war."

"You sound as though you were a good friend of the Indians," she said.

"I kill hostile Indians when I see them," he replied. "My oldest friend was killed by them yesterday. That's the way it is out here now. You kill them or they kill you."

"I hate them," she said passionately. "I'll always hate them. I'll never forget how they killed my Daddy."

"No," he agreed. "You won't. And your father never harmed them. Only he and the other people in your party

168

paid for what Americans did before them and those Americans were probably avenging something the Indians did before that. And that's how it goes."

"You make it sound as though you think Indians are human like Americans and can be treated that way," she said.

He reached into his pouch and took out the map General Canby had given him. He spread it across the saddle and studied it. He looked at the country, and then at the map again.

"Why are you going to Tucson, Tom?" she asked suddenly.

"Business."

"If you know so much about Indians why don't you help the government?"

He looked at her quickly. "I'm a prospector."

"Why aren't you in the war?"

"I'm not a soldier."

"My brother wasn't a soldier. When the war started he joined up and learned."

He folded the map and returned it to the pouch. They changed their direction slightly and rode along in silence. He reined in his horse. He dismounted and began to examine the ground.

"What's the matter?" she asked.

"Been some horses here." He knelt down and looked closely. "Shod with skins."

"What does that mean?"

"The Chiricahuas shoe their horses with deerskin boots. It makes a peculiar mark." He followed the trail on foot for a few yards. Then he pointed to a large stone that had been recently turned over. The upper part of the stone was covered with a dried mold. "That's a signal," he said. He continued to look around and then he saw some horse droppings. He picked up a twig and broke the dropping apart. "About six hours ago, I'd say. It looks as though there were about a dozen of them. They went north. They left this rock overturned as a message for someone who was coming along later." He continued to walk until he came to a mesquite tree. The trunk had a rubbed-off place, about sixteen inches from the ground. "Probably establishing a rendezvous. North of here. We'll keep going south."

He got back on the horse and looked around. The girl had turned pale. "They're not around here now, are they?"

"I don't think so. That trail is pretty old. I'm just wondering whether the ones they left the message for have come through yet or are still on their way. The hoofprints are mixed up."

"I'm frightened, Tom," she said, starting to shake.

"Sure you are," he said easily. "So am I. We'll have to keep our eyes open."

"Do you think they'll find us?"

"Not if we can help it."

"Tom, this is terrible country."

"No. It's not the country."

"When will we get to Tucson?"

"Two or three days."

"I'll never leave Tucson," she said. "If we get there alive I'll never leave it again."

He pulled his rifle from its scabbard and examined it carefully.

"I don't know why we ever left home," she said. "It was so lovely there. Even if there is a war, it's nothing like this."

He pointed with his rifle. "Look." A thin column of smoke was rising in the clear air to the north of them.

"Indians?" she asked.

"Apache signals. I saw them last night while you were sleeping."

"It looks so close, Tom."

"The air is fooling you. That column is at least twenty-five miles away. Maybe farther."

"You're just telling me that."

"No."

"Honor bright?"

"What?"

"My brother and I always used to say honor bright when it was the truth. We never lied when we said honor bright."

"Honor bright," he smiled.

Her face suddenly became radiant. "We will get through to Tucson," she said. She laughed and looked around happily. "I'm getting hungry, Tom," she said.

"Well, that's a good sign. We'll eat and rest soon. Just a little more riding before it gets too hot."

When they made camp at a place that suited him they dug into the beef and biscuits. "I never thought jerky could taste so good," she said. "I'm starving."

"Stiff yet?"

"No. It's all worked out." She chewed the beef. "This is such a strange country. Things grow different than anywhere else I've ever seen. It's almost like another world."

He nodded.

"It's frightening," she said. "I feel as though I never lived anywhere else before. As though I never did anything before. I feel almost as though I was just born."

"Nobody makes a mark on this land," he said.

"What do you mean?"

"Back east the people change the look of the land. You can look around and you know that people live there. They make

170

over the land so that it is different from the way it was originally. Out here the people come and go, but they never leave any impression. I imagine things must have looked pretty much the same around here a thousand years ago, or ten thousand."

"It's not warm and close," she said.

"It provides for those who know what to look for. Look at all the cactus around. The Indians use cactus for a great many things although to look at cactus you wouldn't think it was good for anything. They get fruit and food and make soap out of the different kinds. This stuff here, with the needles. That's the worst of all. Cholla. Keep away from it. Seems that if you get closer than six inches to it you'll be full of needles. That stuff over there is almost as bad. Call that candle cactus."

"What's that?" she asked, pointing to a bush of long green spikes.

"Mescal. Indians use that a lot. If you get underneath those spikes there is a soft pulpy fruit you can roast. It's pretty good. Indians make a liquor out of it, too. There's a tribe of Apaches called the Mescaleros." He got up and broke off one of the spikes. "See those little points along the blade. That shows it's mescal. There is another plant called Spanish dagger which looks like this except there are no points." He walked over to another plant and broke off a twig. "Smell this," he said.

"That's wonderful," she breathed.

"Sage." He smelled it. "Sometimes when the wind is right that smell will come and hit you so hard in the face you get a little drunk on it."

"You do love it here."

"It's a little too complicated for that." He chewed on the sage and then said, "You get used to it after a while and then you suddenly find you can't do without it."

"Thank you, Tom," she said.

He looked up at her. Her eyes were misty. "Thank me for what?"

"I'm not frightened any more. Thank you for telling me about the cactus and sage. I'm quite all right now."

He threw the chewed twig away.

"You must be exhausted, Tom," she said. "You haven't slept at all since we started. Please lie down and rest and I'll watch out."

He looked keenly at her.

"Please, Tom, I'm all right. I enjoyed your telling me about the cactus. Please lie down and rest."

He nodded. "Keep your eyes open. You get a pretty good view from here. If you get sleepy walk around a little. If you find you can't stay awake, wake me first. And don't get away

171

from your rifle." He folded a blanket for a pillow and stretched out. He pointed to a tree. "Wake me when the sun gets behind that tree. We still have a lot of traveling to do today."

5

He woke with water dripping on his face. He sat up quickly. The sun was shining but the ground was still damp. He looked up. He was under a protruding rock, about two feet from where he had gone to sleep. "Terry," he called. She came around the rock. Her face was glowing. Her hair was still wet and hung loosely down her neck. It was the color of mahogany. "Did it rain?"

"Yes, Tom."

"Why didn't you wake me?"

"Why?"

"Water. We could have collected drinking water."

"You didn't wake when I moved you under the rock. You just changed your breathing and went back to sleep."

"You should have wakened me," he said angrily. "We could have cut our trip short by miles if we didn't have to get to a water hole." He walked out of the shelter. "I'm sorry," he said sheepishly.

"I've been traveling a little, Mr. Jeffords. Even before I met you."

There were two canteens fixed under the seams in the rocks so that water had poured into them. "I let it run off for a while before putting them there. And I took a shower."

"You what?"

"It was wonderful. It poured and way off I could see the sun still shining and the water came down so hard I just got out of my clothes and stood there and the water was so good."

"What about the animals?"

"I got them sheltered. The packs didn't get too wet. I got them some water, too." She looked at him with a shining smile. "Am I a good trail partner, Tom?" she asked.

"Yes," he said, pulling his beard.

"And I watched everywhere. There was no sign of anything. Even when I took the shower I kept the rifle where I could get to it quickly. The rain was so beautiful. It was like being on a cloud somewhere and looking down. And there was such a lovely rainbow."

"Are you tired?"

"No. I'm ready to go." She ran a comb through her hair. It hung well below her shoulders. "I feel wonderful. Maybe I wasn't really frightened before. Maybe I was just dirty."

"That sounds like a woman," he admitted.

"I keep feeling nothing ever happened to me before. I feel as though everything that happened before all happened to somebody else." She looked around. "I even feel as though nobody ever saw what I'm seeing before. I feel as though I'm the first person in the world who has ever seen that mountain."

He smiled softly. "Let's go," he said.

The next day he found Indian tracks again and they detoured again. On the third day he said he thought they might reach Tucson that night. He slept in the early afternoon. He was wakened by Terry, her eyes wide with fright. "I think there are Indians nearby," she said through dry lips.

He picked up his rifle. "Where?"

She led him to the edge of a canyon and pointed down. Far below he could make out a half dozen figures on foot. "No horses," he said. "They're not looking for anything."

"What do we do?"

"We stay right here for a little while until it's dark."

"Do you think they know we're here?"

"I don't think so."

"Tom, if they find us, promise me one thing."

"I know."

"Will you promise?" She clutched his arm. Her face was so white the freckles seemed raised from the skin.

"All right."

"Honor bright?"

"I promise."

"Say it. Say honor bright."

"They won't find us, Terry."

"You won't say it," she cried. "Tom, I won't be captured by them."

"I won't let them capture you," he said.

"Swear it, Tom," she whispered.

"I swear it."

They waited until dark. Then he said, "I'm going to cut the pack mules free. We're near enough to Tucson not to need them and we may have to move fast. I'll hide your little bag here and we'll pick it up again some other day. We may have to give these horses a run. If you have something especially precious and it doesn't weigh too much take it out of the sack."

They started to move again. The start was too late to make Tucson during the night. Three years earlier Jeffords and Hank had worked those hills and he was grateful for his knowledge now. They made camp after midnight and she fell asleep like a small child as soon as she was on the ground. He watched through the rest of the night and early in the morning he saw what he had hoped he would not see. In the distance he made out moving lights. He woke her. "We have to move," he said. He pointed to the lights. "Torches. They're signaling."

"Are they coming this way?" She spoke now truly as a small child.

"They're not too close yet, If we move fast we'll be all right."

"Tom," she said.

"I won't forget."

They got on their horses and started off. Then as it got light they heard the beating of drums. They spurred their horses. They heard shots and the whistling sound of arrows and then over a hill to their left they came. "Run for it now," Jeffords said.

They broke their horses into a gallop, coming down out of the hills to the valley outside of Tucson. In the distance Jeffords could see the high edifice of the Catholic Church. They raced on. The Indians fired occasionally but they were out of range. The horses began to sweat.

"Not much farther," he shouted. "They won't come too near the town. Give the horse everything."

They dug rowels into the horses' sides and the exhausted animals gasped and strained to move faster. The foam tore from their mouths and splattered the riders. There were several more shots and then Jeffords said, "They're dropping back. There are not enough of them to come any closer to the town."

They slowed their horses and then a patrol of six cavalrymen rode out of the town gate and galloped toward them. "We're all right now," Jeffords said, panting a little. He looked at her and smiled. She grinned back.

The soldiers came up to them. Jeffords shook his head. "You make a welcome picture," he said. "Is General Carleton in command here?"

The sergeant in command of the patrol said he was.

"I'm an official courier from General Canby at Fort Thorn. I have some dispatches for General Carleton," Jeffords said.

Terry looked up. "A prospector," she said.

"I'll take you to his headquarters, sir," the sergeant said immediately.

"This girl is the only survivor from a wagon train attacked by Indians. Can you get her to some place where she can get some rest? It's been a tough trip."

"We have a building that is being used as a station hospital," the sergeant said.

"Good. Can you see that she gets to bed? She's all right. Just needs some rest."

174

"I'll take care of that, sir," the sergeant said.

"I don't have to go to any hospital," Terry protested.

"You need some sleep. On a bed," Jeffords said.

They entered the city. "General Carleton's headquarters is in the *presidio*," the sergeant said.

They paused in front of the building. "Don't let me stay there too long," Terry said. Then she said, "Tom."

"Yes?"

"It wasn't too bad. With me, I mean, was it?"

"No, Terry," he said gravely. He got off his horse and entered the building.

Chapter Ten

The Mexican dragged himself on the ground until he reached Cochise's feet and then he lifted his head and said, "Mercy, mercy."

Cochise looked at him contemptuously.

The Mexican put his face on the moccasin of the Indian and kissed it. He rubbed his cheek on it. "Mercy, great chief," he said. He started to cry. The tears made muddy paths down his cheeks. "For the love of Christ, mercy."

Cochise slowly lifted his other foot and put the sole on the Mexican's head and pushed. The Mexican rolled back. He lay on his side and he brought his hands together in a gesture of prayer. "Mercy. For the love of the good Christ, mercy."

Cochise nodded curtly to Nahilzay. Nahilzay dragged the Mexican to his feet. He pushed him roughly until they came to a hole in the ground. When the Mexican saw the hole he fell upon his knees again and dragged himself back to Cochise and wrapped his arms around his legs and cried, "No, not that, mercy, mercy, for the love of Christ, have pity on me."

"How many times fifty dollars?" Cochise asked in Spanish. "How many times?"

"I will pay. I have money. Mercy, mercy," the Mexican pleaded.

"Plenty money," Cochise said. "Plenty Apache scalps. Plenty money." His face was like rock. Nahilzay again dragged the Mexican away and pulled him to the edge of the hole. He quickly bound the Mexican's arms to his sides and then slid him down the hole, feet first. He descended until only his head was above the ground. Then Nahilzay kicked in dirt and packed it so that the Mexican could not move, could only twist his head frantically upon his neck and roll his eyes like a

175

frightened horse. Nahilzay poured sweet syrup on his head and face and then the Indians sat and watched.

The Mexican, who had supplied his government with scalps, some of them actually Apache, for a number of years, and who had been captured and brought to the Chiricahua rancheria, began to scream. The ants came soon. They came first in single files and then in columns and then in streams. Soon the face and head of the Mexican was alive with them. Nothing could be seen of his skin and hair. He opened his mouth again to scream in his agony, a broken, torn scream like an animal in pain, and the sweet syrup ran into his mouth and the ants ran after it. He tried to push the ants out of his mouth with his tongue. He tried to bend his head to rub his cheek on the ground. The ants ate the syrup and then they started to eat the flesh and now the man's screams filled the camp. Presently all the Indians save Cochise tired of the sport, tired of watching the final writhing of the Mexican's head, now like round vegetation on the ground, and they walked away. Cochise remained and stared at the man.

It was not more than fifteen months since Cochise had begun his war of vengeance upon the white man and yet he seemed to have aged ten years. His face was locked and there were lines dug deep from the sides of his nostrils to his chin. His lips were pulled down in a perpetual slash of bitterness. His eyes were fanatical, were bloodshot from heavy drinking, and the lower lids were puffy and thick. His hair was streaked with gray and his body bore new scars to testify to the violence of his war.

He could not turn his head from the Mexican. Of the entire face of the tortured, dying man only the eyes were not covered by ants. The eyes, large and black and liquid as a woman's, stared back at him.

He drank in the agony of the Mexican as though it were strong whiskey. He reacted to each move of the head. His own lips worked convulsively with the screams. He wanted to see everything and to hear everything. It was something he needed, something that not even the whiskey gave him.

There had been many such scenes. As Cochise surrendered himself to this violence he had revived and recalled all the ancient forms of torture devised by his race. The ants were only one of them. He had had rawhide bands soaked in water until they were loose and stretched and then had bound them tightly around the skulls of captives and then had sat and watched while the sun dried the rawhide and then shrank it until the brains burst from the victim's heads. He had tied rawhide to the tails óf rattlesnakes and had bound prisoners just out of reach of the deadly fangs, out of reach, that is, during the day,

176

when the prisoners could look upon the struggling, angered snakes, until the sun set and the evening dampness spread over the earth and the rawhide grew moist and stretched just enough.

And still it was not enough.

Since he had sworn his vow of eternal vengeance he gave himself completely to outrage. He drank enough for ten men. He led his warriors in incessant attack upon his enemies and in the noise of strife, in the screams, in the thought-deadening extremes of violence, in the emotional baths of torture, he could blanket the voice.

But when it was ended and he fled into his own blackness and quiet, he still heard the voice, and when he slept the voice was plain, and sometimes his brother's face was behind the voice and he woke, shaking with sweat.

He had stripped himself until he could feel no emotion but the exultancy of killing. He killed now as a man breathes, to remain alive.

The eyes of the Mexican were glazed but they remained fixed upon him. There were torn parts in the skin where the ants had eaten. The Mexican closed his eyes for a moment and then he said in a tired croak, "I curse you, Cochise. Until the day you are dead, I curse you." Then the Mexican started to cry and he began to scream again and he began to pray and he begged for death. *"Madre mia,"* he sobbed between screams. "Please end it quickly, *Madre mia*, please kill me quickly, please, please, please, *Madre mia*," and then his prayer must have been answered because his head fell over a little and his eyes closed and there was no longer a sound from him.

Cochise rose and walked away. The curse of the Mexican stayed with him. He had been damned and cursed before but this time the words seemed like hot arrows in his heart. The people looked at him and said nothing. They had come to understand there was a sickness in their chief and when he passed they felt uneasy and sometimes frightened and there was no laughter in the tribe, not even when the fighting was most successful.

He entered his wickiup, walking past Tesalbestinay without looking at her. He picked up a bottle of Mexican whiskey and poured some of the fire into his throat. He kept hearing the curse and he drank off more of the whiskey.

He did not hear his son, Tahzay, enter the dwelling. Tahzay, now in his full youth, was tall and slender. He was quiet and thoughtful and he had some of the calmness of Naretena, although Cochise was beyond seeing this. As he stood there, he thought he could barely recognize his father. He could remember when Cochise laughed like other men, played games, gambled, became happy when he drank. He thought now there was no time when the bitterness was not written on his face like war paint.

"I do not like to be walked upon silently," Cochise said. His voice was grating.

"Pionsenay has returned," Tahzay said quietly.

"Bring him here." Cochise swallowed more of the whiskey. He threw the empty bottle away and called to Tesalbestinay to bring him another. She brought him a bottle silently. His torment had left a mark on her that was deeper than his. She had known and understood him for years and more than anyone she realized what he was doing to himself.

Pionsenay entered the wickiup.

"Well," Cochise said.

"He will give you the warriors you ask for." Pionsenay paused. "Up to two hundred."

"I asked for twice that number," Cochise said angrily.

"Mangas Coloradas is at peace with the people at the mine. He does not wish to send more than two hundred men away. He said the people at the mine would see and become suspicious."

"Now he is at peace with them," Cochise said sarcastically. "One day he is at war and the next day at peace. He has many colors."

"He is trying a plan."

"Always a plan." Cochise pulled the cork of the whiskey bottle with his teeth and put the mouth of the bottle to his lips. His face was darkened as he lowered the bottle.

"The men will be ready when you send for them," Pionsenay said. He shifted his huge bulk uneasily.

"Go," Cochise said.

Pionsenay left the wickiup silently. He joined his brother, Skinyea. He shook his head. "It is not right for him to live by himself that way," he said. "A man needs another man to speak his thoughts to. That is the way it is."

Tesalbestinay entered the wickiup. "Food?"

"No."

"You have not eaten since yesterday."

"No food." He lifted the whiskey to his lips and then lowered the bottle without drinking from it. He raised his fevered eyes to his wife. "Did you hear what Pionsenay said?"

"Yes."

"Mangas Coloradas has a plan," Cochise said with scorn. "He is getting old. His head is weary."

Tesalbestinay was afraid to remind him that he spoke that way himself before. "Eat."

"Stop talking about food."

178

"You will eat the emptiness inside of you with that poison water." She sat beside him. "You are not happy."

"Happiness is for the children and for the dead."

"It was not so before," she ventured.

His face tightened. "Quiet."

"There was not so much food but it was better then." Her aged ugly face was tender.

"Quiet."

"I speak of what I choose," she said with dignity. "Listen to me, husband. It is not too late."

"Keep quiet, woman," he said.

"It is not too late to undo."

He struck her. "Quiet."

She did not move. "Put on that face for the others," she said.

"Quiet," he said in a dull voice.

"Do not pretend with me. It has been too long."

"I will have to kill you, maybe," he muttered.

"Yes, you might have to do that. For all the others you have one face, but for me there is the other. You will have to kill me, maybe."

His head fell upon his chest and the hand holding the whiskey bottle loosened its grip. She reached out and took the bottle. Then she moved him to his pallet. She stretched him out and removed his high moccasins. His eyes were open and his face was blank. He lay there, not awake nor yet asleep; he lay in a half state and he stared at the domed roof of the wickiup and he heard the Mexican and he saw his face.

2

In June of 1862 there were some two hundred Americans working at the rich mines at Santa Rita del Cobre in the heart of the country claimed for his own by Mangas Coloradas. Their numbers were constantly increasing to the great displeasure of the Mimbres chief, and he decided they were too strong to be driven out by force. Since diplomacy was closer to his heart in any case, he bent his wily mind to discover a way to cause the Americans to leave.

When he thought he had evolved a plan he called in his chief lieutenant, Delgadito, and said, "The only thing the Americans want is gold. There is a place in the foothills of the Sierra Madres where there is plenty of the yellow iron. We can tell the Americans of this place and they will go there, maybe."

"They will not believe you," Delgadito replied. He was an Indian of middle height, with a broad, almost placid face.

Mangas Coloradas smiled cannily. He lifted his great head.

"Not if I tell it to them all at once. But if I tell it them one at a time, and make it seem that I am telling it to each man alone. What do you think then?"

"I do not understand."

"There are many things you do not understand," Mangas Coloradas said equably. "That is why I am chief of the Mimbres people. Listen and remember what I say. A man does not value something if it is offered to everyone at once. But if a man thinks he has something no one else has, he will consider it of great value. From time to time we will whisper in the ear of one of the Americans. One by one they will slip off and when they get there they will find that I have not lied and they will stay there, maybe."

"It is hard to say what Americans will do," Delgadito said suspiciously.

"You do not like Americans," Mangas Coloradas said blandly.

Delgadito flushed and walked away. His hatred and suspicion of Americans was based on an incident that had occurred some time before, one that no one permitted him to forget.

The Indians had learned the extreme range of rifles used by the Americans and during rest periods in the frequent encounters between the Indians and the Americans they removed themselves out of gun range, which was perhaps no more than two hundred and fifty yards, and then indulged in a favorite form of Indian insult. They lifted their loincloths, exposed their buttocks, and said offensive things.

The new type Wesson rifle had a considerably lengthened range, and one of the earliest pieces of this type was owned by John C. Cremony, who served as interpreter to the Bartlett commission. In addition to the rifle, Cremony had fitted the piece with a telescope sight. During one of the battle lulls Delgadito had stood off and had slapped his rear and shouted insults. Cremony, who was not a crack shot, handed the gun to one of the sharpshooters and this man took careful aim and fired and Delgadito leaped into the air and yelled with pain. The fight broke up but Delgadito could not mount his pony and had to run away on foot. He never forgot what he considered base treachery on the part of the Americans.

For the next few weeks after this conversation with Delgadito, Mangas Coloradas spoke privately to one white man after another. He said, "These are our hunting grounds. We have been here for many harvests. Now that you are here all the deer has been frightened away. The wild turkey has departed and the quail is scarce. You do not want to live here, but only to find the yellow iron that is in the ground. The yellow iron is no good to the Indians. We cannot drink it. We cannot eat it. It does not keep the cold from our wickiups.

180

Now there is a great deal of gold that is untouched in the Sierra Madre, five days' journey to the south, I will show you where it is and send men with you to help you find it."

The different Americans, thinking at first they were alone in being so informed, were interested. Then one day one man mentioned it to another, and soon they discovered that the Apache had approached no less than a score of the leading men at the mine. The miners decided that Mangas Coloradas was trying to lure them away from the mine to kill them, one at a time. The next time the Mimbres leader appeared, one of the miners said, "You're a pretty wise gent. You want to get us out of here to where your Indians can finish us off one at a time. But you picked the wrong men." Then the miner said, "Grab him, boys."

The miners tied Mangas Coloradas to a pine tree, face against the tree, and bound his arms around the trunk. Then they stripped off his cotton shirt and they whipped him, one at a time. They gave him a hundred lashes with a thick harness strap and they left him senseless, slumped against the tree, his feet in a pool of his own blood. They cut him free and one of the miners kicked him until he opened his eyes.

"You got off easy this time," the miner said. "Next time it won't be so easy. Go back and tell your people the men here know how to handle Indians."

Mangas Coloradas lost consciousness again. When the miners left Delgadito carried him away and brought him to a cool stream and bathed his back. Presently Mangas Coloradas opened his eyes. "Did you see?" he asked.

"I was in the forest. I saw," Delgadito said.

"No one must know of this. I am an old man. I have seen the seasons come and go sixty-five times but no one has ever done this to me. My people must never know this disgrace."

Delgadito nodded.

"Stay with me until I can move without pain. I cannot return to our camp."

Delgadito remained with him for ten days and then Mangas Coloradas said, "Go to Cochise. Tell him he is right. Tell him to join with me in killing every American in the mines and then we shall stay together thereafter in whatever he chooses." Mangas Coloradas gazed intently at his lieutenant. "You will not tell him of this."

"*Enju*," Delgadito grunted.

With a blanket around him to hide the shameful marks, Mangas Coloradas returned to his people, and Delgadito sped off to the west to deliver his message to Cochise.

Brigadier General James H. Carleton, commander of the First California Volunteers and military governor of Arizona, was an efficient officer who demonstrated his foresight and judgment as soon as he occupied the Old Pueblo. After declaring Arizona a territory of the United States and placing it under martial law, he inaugurated a system of commercial licensing to raise funds for the medical care of his soldiers. He charged ordinary merchants five dollars a month for the right to pursue their businesses; saloon-keepers and owners of gambling houses had to pay one hundred dollars a month for the same privilege.

A tall energetic forceful man, Carleton was a major in the regular United States Sixth Cavalry when he organized his column and led it into the Southwest to head off an anticipated attempt by Rebel forces from Texas to take over the silver mines of Arizona and New Mexico and then, if possible, to continue into the gold fields of California.

So far the volunteers from California had encountered no Rebels. On April 15, 1862, a small engagement between a few Californians and a few Confederates was fought near Picacho Pass, about forty miles northwest of Tucson. Three Union men were killed and a half dozen were wounded on both sides. This proved to be the sole engagement between Union and Rebel forces in Arizona.

When Jeffords was ushered into the general's office, Carleton was pacing up and down the room dictating a report to his superiors. He glanced at the dust-covered civilian and then continued with his report without pause.

"I am making every endeavor to get supplies together," he said in a deep resonant voice. "Meantime I shall try to straighten up matters here so that when a man does have his throat cut, his house robbed, or his field ravaged, he may at least have the consolation of knowing that there is some law that will reach him who does the injury. I shall send to Fort Yuma, for confinement, starting them today, nine of the cutthroats, gamblers, and loafers who have infested this town to the great bodily fear of all good citizens. Nearly every one, I believe, has either killed his man, or been engaged in helping to kill him."

Carleton continued with his dictation, pointedly ignoring Jeffords, who remained standing quietly. When he was finished the general seated himself in the decisive manner that characterized all his movements, and then he looked up at Jeffords. His manner was polite and without interest. His orderly repeated Jeffords' name and Carleton looked at Jeffords again. He saw a tall, spare man, his long red beard coated with white dust, his face almost floury, his clothing dirty, his boots peeling and torn. Of the man only his eyes, blue, cold, and clear, caught his attention. *"Captain* Jeffords?" he asked.

"Not a military title, General," Jeffords said.

"I am told you have some dispatches for me?"

"From General Canby."

Carleton frowned. "Canby? Have you come from New Mexico?"

"Yes." Jeffords reached into his pouch and took out his papers. He handed them to Carleton, who took them with some wonderment. After a moment Carleton looked up. His manner was changed.

"Sit down, Jeffords. You must be parched." He rang a bell and then ordered drinks. "Excuse me, please." He resumed his reading of the papers.

Presently he raised his eyes again. "Did you come alone, Captain Jeffords?"

"No, I started out with an old partner of mine. He got killed in an Indian fight. Apaches attacked part of a wagon train. I picked up a young girl, the only one left alive in the train, and came on in with her."

"You crossed Apacheria with a young girl and no other escort?" Carleton asked.

"You can generally make it with just one or two," Jeffords said quietly. "Either a couple of people, moving fast, or else a battalion. It's the inbetween parties that run into trouble."

"Where is this girl now?"

"One of your men brought her to the hospital for some rest. She was tuckered out."

The orderly entered with a bottle of whiskey and two small glasses. "I hope you have brought me some good news, Captain Jeffords," Carleton said, swallowing his drink.

Jeffords repeated what Canby had told him. As he spoke Carleton's eyes, set deep under a great forest of brows, began to animate, and when Jeffords finished he pounded his fist on the table.

"That is good news, Jeffords," he said in his ringing voice. "We have complete control of this territory—as far as the Rebels are concerned, that is. There is nothing to prevent the California Column from continuing eastward and joining forces with General Canby."

"He'll be glad to know that, General."

"I've already sent out a detachment of men to set up camp on San Simon. They had some trouble with Indians going through Apache Pass but their losses were not great and they are now encamped on the San Simon. My purpose was to have an establishment between here and the Rio Grande, complete with food, ammunition, and supplies, so that if we were ordered to continue eastward the troops might travel as lightly as possible. Now that I am informed of General Canby's requirements, I shall send out another detachment immediately to escort a military wagon train which will establish additional depots along the route, and then as rapidly as possible follow up myself with the larger part of the column." Carleton rubbed his hands eagerly and looked at a map for a moment. "I was afraid we would be ordered to stay here with nobody to fight but Indians," he continued in an excited voice. "It looks as though our luck has changed."

"I can start back for Fort Thorn and inform General Canby of your intentions," Jeffords said.

"You can do more than that, Jeffords," Carleton said. "You can guide the detachment that will escort the supply train."

"When do you want me to start, General?"

"Do you not need rest?"

"A night's sleep. A bath more than anything else."

"Excellent, Captain Jeffords. I will give orders to hasten the provisioning of the train. When you arrive at the San Simon you can continue with an escort from there. I will have the necessary orders prepared and send them with you to Colonel Eyre. That is Lieutenant Colonel Edward E. Eyre, who is in command at San Simon."

Carleton poured out two more drinks. "How is General Canby?"

"He seemed to be all right when I left him."

"Is he winning the war?" Carleton asked with a smile.

"He's doing his best."

"Lucky man," Carleton sighed. He swallowed the drink. "We've had nothing here but Indian trouble. No kind of fighting for a soldier. This would make ideal country for civilized warfare. Great open spaces, plenty of room for cavalry maneuvers, good weather. Instead we've had nothing but sneak encounters with these damned red savages. They fight like cats in the dark, killing without warning, vanishing when you line up soldiers to fight them."

"It must be annoying," Jeffords said seriously.

"The California Column was organized to fight for the United States," Carleton said vehemently. "Twenty-five hundred of the finest young men in California left their homes voluntarily to protect their country. Instead they've been saddled with Indian warfare. Damned treacherous savages. I tried to treat them nicely. I gave protection to half a hundred of them and one night they broke into my corral and stole half my horses. It's the damned Apaches. Nothing can be done

184

with them. Papagos, Pimas, yes. You can train them and make human beings out of them. But the Apaches, no. I'd like to see every one of them killed or driven out of the country." Carleton stood up abruptly. "You must be exhausted, Captain Jeffords. My compliments on the skill with which you performed your mission. I shall mention you in my reports to the War Department."

"That isn't necessary, General," Jeffords said quietly. "You might send along the name of Henry Thompson and the fact that he was on a mission for the government when he was killed."

"Very good, Jeffords." Carleton scribbled down the name. "Now what about this girl. What is her name?"

"Terry Weaver."

"What are you going to do with her?"

"I was hoping that you might suggest something, General."

"How old did you say she was?"

"Fifteen."

"No family?"

"No." Jeffords briefly told him of the details of the Weaver family.

"You say that seven of the wagons went on ahead? No train of seven wagons has come in here recently."

"Indians probably took care of them, too."

Carleton pulled on his beard and walked up and down the room. "There is hardly a place to send the girl," he said. "But I have an idea. There is a boarding house in town. It's called the Scat Fly. That isn't the original name but that's the only name it's known by now. It is operated by an old lady named Wilson. I believe she is from somewhere in New England. I think if you could prevail upon her to take the girl she would provide the most satisfactory home in Tucson. You know there are about five young ladies in town you could call decent. I think the girl might pay for her keep by assisting Mrs. Wilson."

"I'll look into it. It sounds all right to me."

"You get some rest. I will send word to Mrs. Wilson that you will be in to speak with her."

"Thank you, General. I could use some sleep."

As Jeffords left the room Carleton strode to his map and, humming happily, began to study it.

4

Jeffords got out of his clothing and threw himself gratefully upon the bed provided by General Carleton. Although he was exhausted, however, he found the heat too much to permit sleeping indoors. He tossed sweatily for several hours, dozing and waking, and then he rose, bathed, and brushed as much of the desert out of his clothes as he could, and went into the boiling streets, looking for the Scat Fly.

There were no paved streets or sidewalks in Tucson. There was no drainage of any kind and pools of stagnant water and collected garbage were everywhere. It was said that the history of Tucson could be read in the garbage strata, from the stone age on the lowest level, through the era of the *conquistadores,* to the playing cards, beer bottles, and tomato cans of the Americans on top.

There was no single water supply. Wells were dug anywhere a citizen desired and water drawn from them until the water filled with alkali and then the wells were unceremoniously abandoned without being filled in or covered and new ones dug. The city was pocked with these unused wells and at night unwary pedestrians tumbled into them. There were no lamps of any kind to light up the streets at night.

There were half a dozen saloons and all of them remained open continuously. The population, heavily Mexican, maintained its own customs and habits, in quiet contrast to the noisy, violent living of the Americans. A Mexican youth would serenade his lady a few feet from a gunfight where a man would be left dead and unattended on the street. A *baile* would be held in stately grace next door to a raucous all-night saloon and the singing of the saloon girls would make a curious obbligato to the ancient Mexican music of the dance.

The Scat Fly Restaurant was located in a long, narrow adobe building with a ceiling low enough to make a tall man stoop. The walls were washed with a neutral yellowish tint. The floor was packed earth. To keep out the heat strips of white muslin were stretched across the ceiling, making it lower than the builder intended.

Inside there were a dozen tables, all of different sizes, and they were covered with cloths, china, and glassware that made an unusual picture in the Southwest. Everything was immaculate. In the center of each table was the inevitable lead castor with a yellow glass vase and whatever desert flowers were available. On the wall facing the entrance was a large mirror, the pride of the establishment, and next to the mirror hung a wooden clock which never worked. The waiters were Mexicans and they wore white cotton jackets and white trousers and these uniforms were kept spotless.

The reason for all this unusual cleanliness in a town noted for its indifference to this virtue lay in the owner of the establishment, Mrs. Abigail Wilson, a New Englander born and bred, a tall, gaunt, white-haired lady, who, in the hottest weather, wore a pearl choker pressing against her firm, angular

186

chin. The spirit of Mrs. Wilson was everywhere: things remained cleaner, Mexicans actually moved quickly, food was served hot, and—and this was the greatest achievement of all—in some magical Yankee way this extraordinary woman had trained her Mexican waiters to carry—and use—fly swatters in one hand while they carried food in the other.

The popular name for her restaurant and the boarding house that was part of it was anathema to her. She had originally named the place Quincy House but her customers renamed it and after long protests she finally accepted the more suitable name.

How Mrs. Wilson managed the menu in her restaurant no one knew. One only came to marvel and enjoy. There was, in that incredible place, beef, bacon, chicken, mutton, and kid. Potatoes, which cost ten cents a pound, and were regarded as a luxury, were frequently on the menu, at a slight extra cost, of course. There were times when the usual desert grub was all that was available, but in some alchemistic fashion, Mrs. Wilson dissolved the jerky into stews and hashes so delicious that men could not believe what they were eating. There were always eggs and lettuce that was kept crisp by another magic secret, tomatoes that were as good as could be found anywhere. When the hostile Indians did not prevent it there was fresh fruit, brought up on burro trains from Hermosillo, honey, juicy oranges, sweet limes, quinces, and apricots. Upon occasion this unbelievable woman was known to floor her guests with fresh strawberries.

With every meal there would be chile, the sweet frijoles of Mexico, great velvety delicately flavored onions; guests remembered times when shrimp appeared from Guaymas.

It was into this establishment that Jeffords walked. He entered the dining room and sat at the first table he saw, only to have the proprietor of the establishment stride up to him, and in a clipped, flat-sounding New England voice, say, "This table is reserved for regular boarders, mister."

Jeffords rose immediately and bowed. "And where may a transient seat himself, madam?"

"Where you don't see napkins with a ring around them," Mrs. Wilson replied. She folded her hands across her lean bosom and contemplated the stranger. Starting with his worn boots and rising slowly up his equally worn clothing, her eyes, bold and calm, expressed disapproval, until they met his own and rested there for a moment and then dropped.

"Boston?" he asked politely.

"Not very far away," she replied.

"It stays with you," he said with a slow smile. "Even among the Mexicans."

"Are you from Boston, young man?" she asked.

"No, ma'am. Your ears are not as good as mine. Apple-knocker." He rapped his head lightly.

"New York State," she said, the ice melting.

"Chautauqua."

The glacier broke into a distant smile. Then the smile disappeared. "You have money to pay for your meal?"

"Yes, ma'am," he said courteously.

"It's an old trick around here," she said, unbending again. "Too many desert rats try to win a meal by talking about New England. Take a seat at this table, mister. It's the best view."

He bowed again and took the seat pointed to. It faced a large window in the rear of the restaurant. Outside the window was a cool-looking terrace, surrounded by flowers and plants that showed careful skill. "Pretty, isn't it?" Mrs. Wilson asked.

He looked up. She was standing in the same position, arms doubled with almost military stiffness across her chest. Her face, architecturally nothing but angles, was as relaxed as nature and habit permitted.

"Very pretty."

"Are you hungry?"

"As a bear."

"I'll see to it that you get a full dinner."

"Are you Mrs. Wilson?"

"Yes." There was a trace of suspicion in her voice again. Jeffords decided she must have a nature almost too soft to handle to have to cover it with that stony façade.

"My name is Tom Jeffords. I believe General Carleton was to speak to you about me."

"So you're Jeffords," she said. She looked at him again, as though she had not seen him properly the first time. "Well, eat your meal. I shall be here."

As Jeffords tore into the excellent and plentiful meal placed before him, the restaurant began to fill. Mrs. Wilson stood at the door and greeted almost each person by name, and each man, in turn, removed his hat and greeted her respectfully. The diners then proceeded to their regular places, and, without giving any orders, were served with food. Jeffords watched with some fascination as the waiters carried their trays, laden with dishes, and, at the same time and with great dexterity, swung their swatters at the interminable flies. Mrs. Wilson watched the efforts of her help and when one of the waiters was successful enough to kill his quarry she nodded violently.

When Jeffords finished and paid for his meal, he walked up to Mrs. Wilson and asked, "Do you have any free time now?"

"I never have any free time. Come into my office."

She led him down a long corridor, past a parlor in which the furniture, covered with chintz, and the walls, bearing lithographs of New England scenes, combined to give the atmosphere of a Sunday room in Boston, into a small office. "What can I do for you, Captain Jeffords?" she asked brusquely, seating herself at a huge rolltop desk. "General Carleton spoke to me of you, but I think you'd better start from the beginning yourself."

Jeffords told her about the girl and how he found her. Mrs. Wilson stiffened visibly as the story unfolded, and her lips compressed with disfavor. "You say you traveled night and day with this young lady?"

"Several nights and several days, Mrs. Wilson," he replied gravely.

"How old did you say she was?"

"Fifteen, ma'am."

"Captain Jeffords, I am running a respectable boarding house."

"I understand that, Mrs. Wilson."

"I can also smell a lie farther off than most people can smell a skunk."

"Fifteen is kind of young for me, ma'am," Jeffords said pleasantly.

Mrs. Wilson reddened. "You are shameful, young man."

"Yes, ma'am."

"I believe you," she said suddenly. "I will take the girl."

"Thank you, Mrs. Wilson," he said.

"She will have to behave like my own daughter." Mrs. Wilson paused and her face became strangely tender. Then she hardened it again. "That means you, especially."

"Mrs. Wilson, I am leaving Tucson almost immediately."

She looked down at her bony hands. "I did not quite mean it that way," she said.

"This child is without father or mother or any other relative that I know of except a brother who is fighting in the war. Her father asked me to get her to Tucson safely. It's a great relief to know that she will be in your hands. She has spirit and she is bright and I think that she can be helpful to you."

"I'll take good care of her." She looked up. Her face softened. "I've always wanted a daughter."

He rose. "I'll go to the hospital tomorrow and bring her to you."

"Where are you sleeping?"

"General Carleton has provided quarters."

"Stay here. I have softer beds than the Army."

She stood up and they looked at each other for several moments. "You look like you need refreshment," she said. "Go to one of the saloons and relax."

His eyes widened.

"I'm not the crab I look to be," she said shortly. "General

Carleton told me of the journey you have just finished. I think you deserve a drink, or perhaps several. The saloons all sell the same poison. The Quartz Rock is down the street. There is the Hanging Wall near it and on the other side of the street is the Golden West. The Congress Hall is as good a place as any, I guess. Don't drink too much. I don't like drunks among my guests. And don't gamble. You'll lose your shirt."

"Yes, ma'am," he said, feeling like a small boy.

"If you should happen to drink too much, just remember the name of this place, Scat Fly." She said the name with faint distaste. "Somebody will bring you here and I'll put you to bed." She blushed. "I mean I will see to it that you are put to bed."

"I'll try to make it under my own power," Jeffords said gravely.

"If you get into a fight, people here do not draw. They shoot from their holsters. Drawing is wasteful." She held out her hand and he shook it. He was surprised at the strength of her grip.

Jeffords, thinking about Mrs. Wilson, lit a cigar and walked through the corridor to the front door. A young man stepped out of the dining room at the same time and asked, "You are Captain Jeffords, are you not?"

"Yes." Jeffords looked at the man. He was tall and slender with fair skin and light hair.

"We met at Mesilla several years ago. My name is St. John. I was coming through for the Butterfield people."

"Of course. How are you?"

"Very well, thank you. Have you just arrived?"

"Got in this morning."

"Are you bound for a drink?"

"Yes."

"May I join you?" St. John asked courteously.

"Certainly."

"Do you have a preference for any particular place?"

"I've never been to any of them."

"The Congress Hall is not too bad."

The saloon was large and well filled. A score or more men, soldiers and civilians, were leaning against the long bar. Other men were seated at tables, drinking, playing cards. St. John nodded to a small table in a corner of the room and Jeffords agreed. They ordered whiskey.

"You are probably wondering about my arm," St. John said. Jeffords lifted his drink and inclined his head and then swallowed the liquor. He didn't answer the question.

"You are the first man I've made that statement to who did not immediately ask, 'Indians?' " St. John said. "I think I rather

190

expected you would not. As a matter of fact, I was attacked by three Mexican employees."

Jeffords signaled to a waiter.

"What have you been doing since we last met in Mesilla?" St. John asked.

"Nothing much. Looking into the ground."

"What brings you here?"

"I brought some dispatches to General Carleton." He lit another cigar. "And you, Mr. St. John?"

"I went East after my arm was amputated. I stayed there for a while and then I returned. You know how it is about this country."

"Is the Butterfield line out for good?"

"Probably. There is a shorter route farther north."

"That's too bad. This country needs communications."

"We were going along quite handily. The Indians were friendly, at least in the Chiricahua country. We had stations at the right places." St. John's face became eager and somehow younger. "They were exciting days, Captain Jeffords. Building that route through Arizona was a task a man could be proud of." His eyes fell and he sipped some of his whiskey. "It is too bad it had to fall to pieces." He finished the whiskey hurriedly. "We even had the Chiricahuas working for us, supplying wood. Civil War or not, it might have been a different story if it weren't for that tragic episode at Apache Pass."

"Bascom?"

"Yes. The poor young fool. The tragedy of it, I think, is that he never realized the wrong he did. According to his training what he did was proper, and the Army officially commended him for it."

"He was killed at Val Verde," Jeffords said.

"I hardly blame him for the whole affair. His just happens to be the name attached to it. It wasn't just Bascom. It was the military attitude behind him. He just happened to be the man there." St. John sighed slightly. "Ah well. There is no use going over that. It is only that I have a great deal of time to think. Being a cripple does that for a man. I frequently wonder how different the history of the Southwest might have been if it were not for that episode."

"Have you ever met Cochise?" Jeffords asked.

"Yes. He is an unusual man, Captain Jeffords. It is tragic that his inherent wisdom and leadership is now being directed against us. He might have made a very stout friend."

Jeffords looked across the room. St. John followed his eyes. "Will Oury?"

"I thought I recognized him."

"You have a long memory." St. John ordered drinks. "He is

with Jesus Elias, a Mexican who lived here before the American occupation. Those two men illustrate my point. Oury would give years of his life, I guess, to get Cochise. Elias is not much behind him. Will Oury is an extremely respected man here. He is honest and he is brave and I think I have a great admiration for him. But he has made a profession of hating Indians. It's almost a madness with him. And he is sincere. It's no pose. He believes that if it were not for the Indians this country would be a paradise. And the way things are going now he has many who agree with him." St. John laughed shortly. "Indian-hating is getting to be a cult here."

As they left the saloon, later, they walked past the table where Oury and Elias were seated. Oury, whose curly beard was almost blue-black, looked up. "Hello, Jeffords," he said.

"Oury," Jeffords nodded.

"It's been a long time."

"Yes."

Jeffords walked on. Oury stared after him and then began to talk to Elias. Outside the saloon Jeffords breathed deeply and looked at the sky. The heat was less oppressive.

"I think I'll try to get some sleep," he said. "I'm glad to have seen you again."

"Thanks, Captain Jeffords. I'd like to resume our conversation some time. Be careful walking back. People fall into well holes here and sometimes aren't found for a month."

Jeffords lit another cigar and strolled to the boarding house.

5

In the morning he rose early and bathed luxuriously again and carefully trimmed his beard. He enquired about the location of the military hospital and went over there. He had no difficulty locating Terry. He found her the sole occupant of a small ward. She was wearing a coarse, white military nightshirt and when she looked up at him she was very angry.

"Hi, Red," he said.

"Hi, Red, yourself," she retorted. "It's about time you came and got me out of this place."

"Don't you like it here?"

"Hospitals are for sick people. I'm as healthy as you are."

"Aren't they treating you well?" he asked solicitously.

"They're treating me too well. They act as though they never saw a girl before."

"They probably never saw such a pretty one before."

"Don't butter me up, Captain Jeffords," she said tartly. "Just arrange it so I can get dressed and leave."

"Where are your clothes?"

192

"I don't know. If I knew I would have been out of here before. They hid them on me."

"Hid them?" Jeffords fought a smile.

"I almost left here in this nightshirt."

He found the medical officer in charge and with some difficulty convinced him that the girl was not ill and had been sent to the hospital only to rest. He brought her the clothes. "I'll wait outside," he said.

"You look mighty handsome today, Captain Jeffords."

"I'm calling on a lady," he said.

When she joined him they found the entire staff as well as the patients who were able to walk waiting for them in the front room. Terry thanked them all graciously for their kindness, bestowing her smile and hand with queen-like imperiousness.

Outside the building she breathed joyfully and stretched her arms. "It's good to be outside again. I hate hospitals." Her hair sparkled in the sun. "Where are we going now, Tom?"

"I've made arrangements for you to stay here," he said.

Her eyes clouded. "Where are you going?"

"I have to go back to where I came from."

"You're not going to leave me here alone."

"You won't be alone." They were crossing the plaza. He found a shady place. "Let's sit down for a few minutes. I want to talk to you."

"It won't do you any good," she said. "You're not going to leave me alone."

He took her hand and smiled. "Carrot," he said, "I don't want to leave you alone. I would like to stay here. But I'm working for the government."

"You're not going back through that Apache country?"

"Not alone. I'm going with a party of soldiers."

"Take me with you."

"I can't, Terry."

"I can shoot like a man. I can take care of myself. Take me with you, Tom."

He looked at the tears forming in her eyes. He wiped them off carefully. "There is a war going on, Carrot. It's a funny kind of war. Northerners against Southerners. White men against Indians. But it is a war and when I accepted this assignment from General Canby I pledged myself to bring back a reply. And I can't take you."

The blood was gone from her face. "When will you return to Tucson?"

"I don't know."

"It may be a long time."

"Yes, it may be."

"It may be years." Her voice was dead.

"It may be," he admitted. "But I don't think so."

"And you'll forget all about me and meet some other girl and I'll never see you again," she said.

His eyes narrowed in some bewilderment and then he lifted her chin in his hands. "I won't forget you, Terry," he said tenderly. He thought he should be amused by this but he was not.

"You just think I'm a little girl."

"You are fifteen," he said soberly.

"Going on sixteen." She suddenly laid her head against his arm. "You remember what I told you that night? I belong to you, Tom. You just can't leave me and never come back."

"Listen to me, Terry," he said. "I have been in to see a lady named Mrs. Wilson. She owns a boarding house and a restaurant. It has a funny name. It's called the Scat Fly."

"That's a very funny name," she said without laughter.

"I told her about you and she is going to take care of you. You'll have a good home with her and I'm sure that you will grow to love her."

"All right, Tom."

"Don't say it that way, Carrot. You have to stay somewhere. I promised your Daddy I would see that you were safely settled in Tucson. This is no kind of town for a girl unless she has someone watching out for her."

"Yes, Tom."

"Perhaps I won't be away as long as you think. Let's try for a smile, Terry."

"There's no smiling in me."

He got up and helped her to her feet. "I'll take you to the place. It has a funny name, Scat Fly."

"You told me the name, Tom. It's very funny."

They were silent as they walked to the boarding house. Jeffords was conscious of the fact that passersby turned and stared after her. He wanted to tell them she was only a child.

In the Scat Fly, Mrs. Wilson came to greet them. Jeffords introduced them and Mrs. Wilson looked shrewdly at the girl and then at Jeffords. She put her arm around Terry. "You're going to miss him, Terry," she said. "And don't fear. He will miss you, too. But he will be back."

Terry looked up at her. "Do you think so, Mrs. Wilson?"

"Sure he will, child. He's not the granite rock he pretends to be. And meanwhile you'll be growing up into a beautiful lady with a head of red hair that he can see all the way from New Mexico."

Terry grinned. "Will you, Tom?"

"Sure," he said. He looked gratefully at Mrs. Wilson.

"This is war, child," Mrs. Wilson said. "In a war women remain behind while the men, fools that they are, go off and get themselves killed. But this one won't be killed. Not with those eyes. He'll be back to pledge you before you've properly begun to miss him."

"Goodbye, Terry," he said.

"I will be waiting here. Goodbye, Tom. Don't get hurt."

"I'm plenty grateful," he said to Mrs. Wilson.

"I'm the grateful one, young man," she said. "You heard what she said. Don't get yourself hurt. I wouldn't want to get that red hair angry with me."

He kissed Terry on the lips. "Be good, Carrot." He started for the door.

"Tom!" She ran to the door and put her arms around him. He ran his hand through her hair. He opened the door and left.

When he was gone she stared at the closed door and then she turned to Mrs. Wilson. "The time is passing already," she said. "He is already on his way back."

Chapter Eleven

Jeffords found General Carleton conferring with a young clean-shaven officer. The men looked up from a map as he entered the room. "Are you ready to start back, Captain Jeffords?" the general asked.

"All ready."

"Is your ward taken care of?"

"She is, General. And thank you."

"Nonsense. Good thing for the town. Jeffords, this is Captain Thomas Roberts. He is in command of Company E, First California Infantry. Roberts, Captain Thomas Jeffords, who will guide you across Apacheria." Roberts smiled pleasantly and held out his hand. "Roberts is going to start with a thirty-day supply of rations for Eyre's men. Eyre is at the mail station at San Simon, as I told you." Carleton picked up a pencil and pointed to a place on the map. "Jeffords, you may have heard of Captain John Cremony. He served as interpreter when the Bartlett people were working out the boundary difficulties. He commands a California cavalry company now. He has come across from Fort Yuma and now is camped up here at Antelope Peak, about thirty-five miles north. Roberts and Cremony will join forces here on the San Pedro, and then move eastward through Dragoon Springs, Apache Pass, and on to where Eyre is camped. Thirty wagons, loaded with food, ammunition, and supplies are ready. The plan is this: the wagons will be brought to Eyre. There they will unload and return to the San Pedro camp. By that time I will be there with additional supplies. The wagons will be reloaded and we will all move eastward. Do you follow me?"

"Yes," Jeffords said.

"I shall have some two thousand men to augment General Canby's forces," Carleton said, rubbing his hands eagerly. "You will accompany Captain Roberts and his men as far as Eyre's camp and then continue on, alone or with escort, whichever you choose, and convey this information to General Canby."

"Very good, General," Jeffords said.

Carleton looked at the map and toyed with his beard. "With luck we should be at the Rio Grande within a few weeks. I hope General Canby hasn't quieted things too much." He looked at Roberts and smiled. "Roberts will be in command of the expedition," he continued, "superseding Cremony on all military decisions. You are not a regular member of the armed forces, Captain Jeffords, but it is necessary that you consider yourself under Captain Roberts' orders. On the other hand, Roberts, Jeffords knows the country well and is thoroughly conversant with the ways of Indians. You will listen to his suggestions and ask his advice on all matters concerning Indians."

Roberts gave Jeffords a friendly smile. "I think Captain Jeffords and I will have no trouble."

"Good," Carleton said. "Is everything in readiness?"

"We are ready to depart immediately, sir," Roberts said.

"Godspeed, gentlemen. And good luck."

Outside the room Roberts turned to Jeffords. "We both heard what the general said, Captain Jeffords. Please understand that it is necessary for me to be in nominal command because of military regulations. Personally I do not hold myself as your superior officer. I hope we can consider ourselves as friends."

"Thank you, Captain," Jeffords said.

"May I compliment you on the journey you made from New Mexico. Please feel free to instruct me as we go along."

Roberts, Jeffords thought, must be in his middle twenties, of an age with himself. Yet with his eagerness and excitement he might be a schoolboy, getting ready for some contest. He wondered at the military attitude and he thought, as he had thought often before, that is was quite strange and quite wonderful. Whatever the system was, it produced men like Roberts and also men like Bascom. Whatever type they were, Carleton, Canby, Roberts, Bascom, they regarded their profession as some sort of game. They didn't like fighting Indians because Indians didn't play according to rules. It was almost as though the rules were more important than the causes and the results. He wondered how many professional officers on both sides in the war were fighting for the fundamental war goals and how many because they loved to utilize the technical knowledge of their profession, as a surgeon loves to operate.

The wagons and infantry troops were lined up in the military plaza in front of the *presidio*. The men were at parade rest, but at the appearance of Captain Roberts an order was given sharply and the soldiers came to attention.

The day was hot. It was not yet noon but the sun beat heavily upon the plaza. Heat waves made the air furry. The soldiers were in full uniform and carried full packs. The uniforms and equipment, Jeffords thought, were much too heavy. The men were equipped and dressed to march and fight in all climates; military regulations required them to carry numerous items useless in the Southwest. Jeffords compared the burdened men with the almost naked Indians and he did not wonder that American soldiers were virtually helpless against their red-skinned enemies. The soldiers, standing stiffly at attention, were streaming with sweat and the march was not yet begun.

Behind the line of men, drawn by mules, were two twelve-pound mountain howitzers. Jeffords looked at these weapons, novel in that part of the country, with interest. Roberts noticed his curiosity. "Brought them all the way from California," he said proudly. "Might find some use for them."

Behind the guns were the supply wagons. Everything was in order. Everything was assembled with neatness and precision. Jeffords and Roberts, together with several junior officers, took their places on horses in front of the troop.

The plaza was filled with spectators. Roberts nodded his head to the bugler and when the high, piercing notes sounded the crowd broke into a cheer and the people waved their hands. The drummer began to beat. A sergeant gave a curt order and the procession started.

Jeffords felt an inexplicable thrill as the troop moved across the plaza. Despite himself the sound of drums, and then the high shrill of the fifes, the pennants fluttering, the cheering of the people, stirred him strangely. They passed before the *presidio* and General Carleton, in full uniform, received the salute.

The contingent marched down the main street of the old mud city. In the crowd Jeffords made out the figure of Terry. She waved her hand and even at that distance he could make out the unhappiness on her face. He waved back, thinking, hell, the soldier is going off to the wars with all the trimmings, even a girl to cry after him and wave farewell. He felt a little silly and he felt unaccountably moved at the same time.

Out through the battered gate that once locked the town

fast within its adobe walls the company moved. Jeffords wondered idly how many similar forces of human militarism had similarly left Tucson, with cheering people behind. Once away from the town Roberts gave the order for route-step and the troops broke gratefully from their attention into the easier informal stride for the field.

2

The company proceeded steadily and without mishap throughout the blazing afternoon. The heat rose like something living from the desert. The sweat of the horses filled the air with a sulphurous smell. There was no visible sign of Indians.

At four o'clock they came upon horse tracks. They continued their march until Jeffords espied a pile of manure. He rode ahead and dismounted. He examined the droppings. Then he walked over to a patch of grama grass which bore signs of trampling. He studied the grass and then broke off a spire and felt for the amount of moisture of natural juice left in it.

"Indians?" Roberts asked.

"About twenty of them," Jeffords said. "They passed here maybe four hours ago, maybe a little sooner." He rose and looked back whence they had just come. "They know we are on the trail." He walked over to a small collection of stones that caught his eye. They were laid out in a straight line, with other stones arranged to shape the design into an arrow, the point toward the east. "Seems they have our plans figured," Jeffords said. "The rocks say a number of men are headed for the Chiricahuas."

"What do you suggest, Captain Jeffords?"

"You can see for miles in this country. No possibility of traveling in secret. But I think we are in sufficient strength to keep them away." He stood up. "They seldom attack a force this large. Not in the open anyway."

The men were alerted and the march resumed. At sunset the troop paused for a brief rest and meal and then continued again. Shortly after dawn the next morning after an all-night march, they reached the camp in the old Butterfield station on the San Pedro where Cremony and his cavalry were already waiting.

Roberts, assuming command of the joined forces, gave over the day for rest, and then called in the officers and Jeffords to plan the next move. With a map spread before them, Roberts said, "It is twenty-eight miles to Dragoon Springs. The question is whether there is sufficient water at Dragoon Springs to supply both companies plus the animals at the same time, or whether we are obliged to divide our forces again and arrive

198

at the springs separately. What is your opinion, Captain Jeffords?"

"The springs are never-failing," Jeffords said. "But this is a dry time. There hasn't been much rain."

"I agree," Roberts said. "I think I will go ahead with the infantry. I will leave a small detachment to garrison this station. I'll take some of your men, Captain Cremony, for scouts and couriers. Captain Jeffords, I should like you to accompany me."

3

News of the advancing company of soldiers was brought to Cochise soon after the troop had left Tucson. The Chiricahua leader was informed of the size of the column, its equipment, and its direction. When Cochise heard about the supply wagons his eyes glittered.

He knew that once the company headed east from the San Pedro they had to go to Dragoon Springs for water, and, if they intended to move farther east, they also had to stop at Apache Pass.

It was in the pass that Cochise elected to lay his ambush. With its series of interlocking hills and canyons, its rocky caves and ravines, Apache Pass presented a perfect place for a surprise attack. On this occasion Cochise planned something more complicated than an ordinary ambush. He had learned to respect the accuracy and fire-power of the soldiers' guns. It was his intention not merely to drive the soldiers away, but to kill and capture them, all of them, and to take the wagons as well.

While the troops were plodding across the desert, their progress rapidly made known to Cochise, he caused to be built in the rising ground above the springs in Apache Pass crude but efficient redoubts of rock, the rock fitted together to permit the Indians to fire through the notches. During the course of construction of these breastworks, he descended repeatedly to the springs below and viewed the works from there, and wherever he deemed the rocky strongpoints looked unnatural, were too prominent, he ordered them altered, and when he was finished his constructions were an integrated part of the hills and the rock piles looked no different from the natural scattering of boulders that had lain against the hillsides for thousands of years.

The work, backbreaking in the heat, caused some of the warriors to grumble. This preparation was not usual in Apache attack. Nahilzay, his eyes flaming with battle fever, urged Cochise to lead the warriors in a more normal pre-dawn attack, when the soldiers camped.

"Your temper has not cooled," Cochise said in the harsh manner that now was part of his nature. "I have tried to teach you for many harvests but you still think each attack is the same as the last. We will wait here and the soldiers will enter the pass and they will think of nothing but that water is here and we shall be above them and protected behind rocks."

While the breastworks were being constructed, Delgadito arrived with the message from Mangas Coloradas. He expected his information to be welcomed by Cochise, but the Chiricahua chief told him coldly that he had other plans and could not join Mangas Coloradas at this time. Puzzled, Delgadito borrowed a fresh horse from Cochise and started back to New Mexico.

Cochise watched him depart. He said to Nahilzay, "Mangas Coloradas becomes like a woman. He is hot and he is cold. When I asked for his help he promised and then did not keep his promise. Now that he has decided to fight he calls to me." His lips twisted. "If he wants fighting there will be enough right here."

"Do you think he will come here?"

"He is curious. Delgadito has seen what we are doing. He will be here."

He looked up and down the pass, at the bone, bleached white. Then his eyes turned in another direction. He looked at the oak tree where the Indians were hanged.

As Cochise had predicted, Mangas Coloradas was astonished at his refusal to join him in attacking the mines, and then, as Delgadito told of the strange doings of the Chiricahuas, he found himself consumed with curiosity. After much thought he decided to bring his warriors to Apache Pass to see for himself what was happening there.

At five o'clock on the afternoon of July 14, 1862, Captain Roberts, his infantry troop, less ten men assigned to garrison the former stage station, plus seven of Cremony's crack cavalrymen and three of the supply wagons, started out from the San Pedro River. Jeffords thought that he felt rain in the air and soon after the party left the station a storm broke over the plains. The rain descended in torrents and streaks of lightning crisscrossed the sky followed by rolls of thunder that echoed back and forth in deafening roar. The men had scarcely crossed the trickling San Pedro when the river, from a thin aimless creek, rose into a foamy, churning river and flooded over its banks.

The foot soldiers plowed through the wet sand miserably, the beating rain soaking them thoroughly; the ground became like soft clay and soon encased their legs, adding weight to their exhausted limbs. Jeffords tried to lift his face against the rain and see something of the country. The torrent made a gray curtain that obscured all view.

"There should be no water shortage now," Roberts shouted between pools of thunder. Jeffords nodded. The rain would provide water all right, he thought, but it prevented him from seeing any Indian signs, if any there were.

In the early hours of the morning the party reached Dragoon Springs and after verifying the availability of water Roberts dispatched two of the cavalrymen to Cremony with orders to bring up the rest of the men and supplies as soon as he could. At three o'clock in the afternoon of that same day, Cremony and his men with the balance of the wagons arrived at Dragoon Springs.

Roberts, again fearful that the supply of water at Apache Pass would be insufficient to accommodate the two companies at the same time, started out again at five-thirty in the afternoon, instructing Cremony to take to the saddle at daybreak the next morning with the wagons and to follow him to the pass.

The infantrymen trudged through the night. The rain ended soon after midnight. The sun broke hot and early and the damp clothing of the men began to steam in the blazing heat. They staggered on, sick with the brassy fire from above. Roberts ordered that water be conserved since there would be no replenishments until late that night. The men lurched forward.

Just before eight o'clock in the morning they reached the Ewell's station of the old stage line and there they rested briefly. They tumbled loosely like half-empty sacks on the ground· and were ordered to fall in again almost before their aching muscles relaxed.

The heat was such as no man had ever experienced. The soldiers did not appear to be only on a march. The men looked more like a defeated, broken unit, churning through the fiery sands. Several of the men collapsed. Precious water had to be used to revive them and then other soldiers had to divide their gear to lighten their loads. Into the hot daylight they drove themselves. Dry dust filled their throats like specks of fire, the rims of their eyes turned red and sore, the straps of their kits burned creases in their shoulders and backs.

Of all the men only the cavalry scouts were mounted now. Roberts had chosen to march with his men, refusing the use of a horse while his troops were on foot, and the other officers and Jeffords followed suit. Jeffords, more used to the scorching country than any of them, and encumbered with far less gear, showed less signs of fatigue than the rest. On one or two occasions he borrowed a cavalryman's horse and scoured the countryside for Indian signs. He found none.

By noon, despite Roberts' orders, water was almost out among the men. They moved on with throats like sandpaper, and they watched the ball of flame in the sky with fascinated eyes and counted each inch that the sun slipped toward the rim of mountains in the west. Roberts moved back and forth among the troops, encouraging them with cheerful words. The officer was indefatigable. Jeffords watched him with great respect as he spoke to the men by name, made small jokes, laughed with them. Wherever he passed men straightened a little and dragged their feet with greater strength.

High atop the walls of the entrance to the canyon Cochise lay and watched the approaching soldiers. In the transparent air his eyes, keen as an eagle's, saw the dust of the marching more than twenty-five miles away. He waited there, quietly, patiently, and watched the dust clouds grow larger. His warriors were ready. Each man was in his place. The Indians were rested and untired. Cochise knew what condition the soldiers would be in after their desert trek.

As he lay there, his mouth set in a vicious line, a scout came to him and told him that Mangas Coloradas and a large party of Mimbres Apaches were passing through the pass from the east. A short while later Mangas Coloradas appeared. He dismounted and joined Cochise. After a few minutes Mangas Coloradas asked Cochise why he had refused to join him in the attack on the mines and for an answer Cochise pointed to the west. "Soldiers from Tucson," he said tersely.

Mangas Coloradas looked at the nearing soldiers and then he looked around and saw the formidable rock enclosures behind which the Chiricahua warriors were waiting.

"They are like flies," Cochise said grimly. "They enter a trap. Join me now and later we will attack the mines together."

Mangas Coloradas agreed instantly and placed his men under the command of the Chiricahua chief. Cochise gave quick orders for their disposition among his own men behind the rocks and boulders. A short time later another scout ran up to Cochise and informed him that a small band of Americans was seen approaching the pass from the east, crossing the wide plain between the pass and the cienega. There were thirteen riders, he said, and he described them minutely.

"I recognize the description," Mangas Coloradas said. "They are miners from the Santa Rita del Cobre."

"Enju," Cochise said impassively. "You wanted miners."

"These men are dangerous. They are always well armed and they are experienced fighters. It may be that they will come through the pass from the east and interfere with your plans."

"They will never enter the pass."

These were his best times, Cochise thought. There was no

202

sound of the voice that he could hear at times like these. When he worked and planned, to meet challenges, to make quick decisions, and then the kill, the final kill, and the smell of new-spilled blood in his nose, he could not hear the voice. He was almost his old self again, as his mind worked swiftly and coolly and the sickness was almost not in him. He looked westward again. He had no concern about the approaching soldiers for a long while yet. He mounted a pony and bade Mangas Coloradas to follow him, and then he led a score of his warriors to the east approach to the pass. Several miles away he could make out the small party of miners.

"From the moment these miners enter the pass they will be alert," he said, as though he were expounding a lesson in tactics. "In the open country they are less careful. The wise thing then is to catch them before they enter the pass."

"That is open plain," Mangas Coloradas replied tolerantly. "How can you surprise them there?"

"This is Chiricahua country," he replied quietly. "There is no place in it that is not like the palm of my hand to me." He called his twenty braves to him. "A short distance east of the pass entrance there is a gully. You know it well. It was marked before for such a time as now. It is deep to the height of a tall man and twice as wide and its length would shelter a hundred warriors. This gully cannot be seen by a man on horse until he is almost on it. You men shall be there when the miners come to it."

With no further word from their chief, the Chiricahua warriors gave Mangas Coloradas a lesson in training. They stripped themselves of everything except their breechcloths and moccasins and then they rolled bodily in the thick alkali dust. They rose covered with a gray film, their red, painted bodies and faces now a neutral color that blended perfectly with the desert. Still without a word of command they scurried silently with their weapons down the side of the pass and in a few moments they were lost to sight. Mangas Coloradas watched them disappear and his face was serious and thoughtful.

The miners approached. Their rifles rested in the slings across their saddles. Their pistols were in holsters. They watched the great opening to the pass in front of them and they rode carelessly, feeling secure in the flat, bare country where they could see clearly for miles in all directions.

When they were forty yards from the gully the Apaches opened fire. In the first volley six of the miners fell dead. The rest, in a panic from this attack which seemed to come from the bowels of the earth, turned and fled. They were massacred before they moved fifteen yards. The Chiricahuas came out of their concealment and gathered in the horses and then stripped the dead miners of their weapons and ammunition. One of the

Indians found a leather pouch filled with gold dust to the value of fifty thousand dollars, the records show, and knowing well the value of this yellow iron dust, took the pouch with him.

While the attack was in progress, Mangas Coloradas lifted his huge head to pay Cochise a compliment on the masterliness of his tactics and the efficiency of his men. He never spoke the words. He looked upon the face of Cochise and held his tongue.

Mangas Coloradas had lived long and at one time or another had lent himself to ruthlessness as great as any Indian of his time but he thought then he had never before seen hatred such as he saw now. The Chiricahua chief's face was twitching with an internal ecstasy; his eyes were ablaze and his jaw muscles pulsated. There was a madness there that made the old Mimbres chieftain shudder slightly. He knew violence but this was something beyond human violence. Cochise lay there as though he were alone in the world. His fingers coiled and uncoiled and he breathed heavily as though the efforts of his men drained his strength. Mangas Coloradas remembered then the reasonable and thoughtful Cochise who had urged peace and co-operation with the white men six years before.

When the last miner fell Cochise sighed and the tumult left him and he relaxed on the ground exhausted. Mangas Coloradas thought that there were things he himself knew nothing of and that his time and way of thinking were past. Mangas Coloradas suddenly felt old and tired.

4

It was soon after two o'clock in the afternoon that the soldiers came to the cleft in the hills that was their objective for the day. The men moved like sleep-walkers. The terrible heat and their thirst robbed them of decision. They walked automatically, their legs weighted as though their boots were filled with lead. Their necks and wrists were bleeding from the chafing uniforms. They slipped on small stones and regained their balance painfully and stumbled on. Three or four men were delirious and had to be supported by other men.

Roberts halted the troop at the pass entrance and sent his cavalry ahead on reconnaissance. Jeffords looked into the pass through field glasses. Shadows already crossed its steep slopes and in contrast to the unshadowed portions, glaring in the brilliant sunshine, the dark parts seemed black. It was cool and quiet ahead. A slight breeze drifted out of the pass and the men gulped in the air as though it were water. Their tongues hung out like the tongues of exhausted dogs.

Jeffords felt a slight uneasiness he could not explain. The pass seemed almost too quiet to him, and yet, if it were empty, there was no reason why it should not be quiet. He played the glasses back and forth. Nothing moved. He told himself he was conjuring fears out of nothing. The cavalry returned and reported the pass untenanted. Jeffords shook his head and decided he was tired. The men cheered weakly at the news and Roberts ordered the march into the pass. He told his men to hold their rifles at the ready and with himself and Jeffords in the van the company moved forward.

The men walked silently. They looked wearily around them. The thought of the water that lay ahead and the rest they soon would get spurred them beyond their strength. The breeze came cooler and then the walls were on either side of them and the men stumbled on and then from both sides of the gorge came a barrage of bullets and arrows and the canyon was silent no longer.

The men returned fire in all directions, their exhaustion forgotten. They could see no enemy. They turned and fired aimlessly everywhere. There was nothing human in sight on the hillsides. But from every rock, every tree, every natural declivity and shelter there came bullets and the whining song of the arrows.

Roberts ordered the bugler to sound retreat. He prayed that the soldiers would still retain enough discipline to respond. Then he said, "Thank God, thank God," and a lump rose in his parched throat as the soldiers obeyed instantly and retreated, firing at their invisible host as they moved backward away from the water, back into the open valley.

At the pass entrance Roberts reformed his men when they were outside the enemy range. His men were soldiers now. The heat and the long march were forgotten. "We've got to get in there," Roberts said hoarsely. "We cannot march back over those forty miles without water. We'd leave three-quarters of the men dead of thirst on the desert." He lifted his glasses and looked into the pass. "Jeffords."

"Yes?"

"Is there any way to the water except through the pass?"

"No, none that I know of."

"We've got to get in."

"Why not try sending skirmishers over the hills and try to get behind the Indians?"

"It was a beautiful ambush," Roberts panted.

"Cochise," Jeffords murmured.

Roberts ordered skirmishers out and then he pulled up his howitzers and sent in a small detachment of soldiers to draw the Indian fire.

From his vantage point Cochise watched the activities below. He wet his lips and tasted the pleasure of the initial setback. He looked on curiously as the soldiers pulled up the strange guns on wheels. He had never seen anything like them before. He saw the small group of soldiers start back into the pass and his eyes narrowed as he tried to understand what his foe was attempting.

The Indians again opened fire as the bait approached them and then the howitzers blasted an answer and the great bursting shells fell among the Indians. The Apaches took on a sudden panic and their fire was stilled and then the company again moved in from the valley to join the vanguard. The howitzers were fired again, and again the flaming shells churned the sides of the canyon and the Indians shrieked in their terror. Then the skirmishers cleared the crests above and behind the Indians and opened fire from the rear. The Indians were caught between the shell fire and rifle fire from below and the rifle fire from behind them. Clearing a passage yard by yard as the afternoon wore on and the Indians fought grimly, Roberts finally brought his troops to the old Butterfield station and they took shelter behind the corral walls.

Cochise, furious at the unexpected turn of events, ordered the Indians to move to their prepared positions in the stone redoubts on both sides of the springs, leaving dead and wounded behind them. He was the last to leave. He looked on the destruction and a great bitterness filled him. He saw boulders shattered and great holes torn in the earth. His ears still ached from the explosions of the fire-wagons. The sun was setting behind the far western hills and as he hastened at last to join his men he knew that he had seen the end of the old way of fighting and the beginning of something new.

The station depot provided temporary protection for the soldiers but they were still without water and the springs were six hundred yards away. Night was falling to add darkness to their difficulties. They had fought for more than five hours and before that had marched for almost twenty-two hours across the desert. With the end of the fighting their energy again left them and the thirst returned and with it a dangerous lethargy.

Roberts gave his men scarcely time to catch their breaths. With Jeffords to guide him he again led them from the station toward the spring. From their entrenched positions behind the stony walls the Apaches again opened fire. The muskets of the soldiers, three or four hundred feet below, were useless.

Jeffords crept away from Roberts suddenly and ran swiftly, catlike, up on the hill to the right of the spring. There he found a boulder and lay down and watched for several minutes while the Indians fired volley after volley and the soldiers discharged their futile return. Then he hurried back to Roberts. "Those Indians are not scattered above the springs the way they were scattered at the pass entrance," he panted. "Their fire is coming in concentrated bursts. Apaches don't fight in groups normally. They must have built themselves some kind of protection."

"The howitzers," Roberts said instantly.

"Carbine fire is useless. If you can land shells in the right places you will be able to kill them in bunches. Maybe they outsmarted themselves."

Roberts ordered the howitzers brought into position. "Watch carefully," he said to the artillerists. "Hold your fire until I give the order. Find out where the Indian fire is coming from. Then dump the shells there. Every shell has to count."

Each gun was positioned to cover one side of the springs. Roberts ordered the men to fire their muskets and there was an immediate reply from the Indians. Then Roberts signaled to the artillerists to let go. The gun on the left found a target immediately and the Indians who were not killed screamed in fright and pain. The gun on the right was less well handled. Unaccountably the howitzer was overturned. The men manning it were driven off. Then six men and a sergeant rushed to the piece. Under the most concentrated attack they righted it and turned it again to the enemy. At that moment a multiple burst of Indian fire revealed a stone enclosure. The howitzer was fired immediately. The shell found its target. Now both field pieces had the range and fired shell after shell into the hills. The redoubts were blasted open and the Indians rose hysterically and fled in all directions.

And suddenly the canyon was quiet. The hills above sounded a noisy silence. It was as though the silence could be heard, felt, almost seen. The men rushed to the springs and fell on their bellies and put their faces into the cool water and they drank.

A half hour later the troop was back in the corral. Their thirst was quenched. Their canteens were filled with water. They lay on the ground and stretched out with an almost painful luxury and let the cool night air rest upon them.

Roberts gave them permission to build fires and prepare food, and then he ordered his junior officers to select half of the men, those who were most physically able, and to await orders to march again.

He ordered five of the cavalrymen to go back and find Cremony. "Tell him to park his wagons wherever he is and take every precaution for safety. Tell him I will join him with half of my company tonight. He is not to attempt to come through the pass with his wagons."

The men departed. Among them was a soldier named John Teal. His name is remembered for what happened to him that night.

Soon after the cavalrymen left the pass they were set upon by Indians who shot three of the horses from under them. Two of the men on foot climbed up behind their mounted comrades. Teal was lost. The four men on two horses rode as far as Ewell's station where they found Cremony had arrived with the balance of the cavalry company and the supply wagons. They reported what had happened in the pass and gave Cremony Roberts' instructions. Teal was abandoned for dead.

At one o'clock in the morning Teal walked into the station house. He carried his saddle, blankets, saber and pistols. This is the story he told as Cremony recorded it:

"Soon after we left the pass we opened upon a sort of hollow plain or vale, about a mile wide, across which we dashed with speed. I was about two hundred yards to the rear and presently a body of about fifteen Indians got between me and my companions. I turned my horse's head southward and coursed along the plain, in the hope of outrunning them, but my horse had been too sorely tested and could not get away. They came up and commenced firing, one ball passing through the body of my horse, just forward of the hind quarters. It was then about dark, and I immediately dismounted, determined to fight it out to the bitter end. My horse fell, and as I approached him he began to lick my hands. I then swore to kill at least one Apache.

"Lying down behind the body of my dying animal, I opened fire upon them with my carbine, which, being a breech-loader, enabled me to keep up a lively fusillade. This repeated fire seemed to confuse the savages, and instead of advancing with a rush, they commenced to circle round me, firing occasional shots in my direction. They knew that I also had a six-shooter and a saber, and seemed unwilling to try close quarters. In this way the fight continued for over an hour, when I got a good chance at a prominent Indian and slipped a carbine ball into his breast.

"He must have been a man of some note, because soon after that they seemed to get away from me and I could hear their voices growing fainter in the distance. I thought this was a good time to make tracks, and divesting myself of my spurs, I took saddle, bridle and blanket from my dead horse and started for camp."

At two o'clock in the morning, while Cremony was still listening to Teal, Roberts returned to Ewell's station, having left half the troop to garrison the depot in the pass. Three hours later the entire force left Ewell's station and moved eastward. Half the cavalry was sent on ahead and half formed a rearguard. The infantry flanked the wagons on both sides. In this formation, without further encounters with Indians, the

208

party, intact, reached the Butterfield station in the pass at ten
o'clock in the morning.

"I think," Roberts said to his men, "that you now may rest."
His young face was grimy and he appeared a dozen years older
than the clear-faced youth who had led his men out of Tucson
to the sound of fife and drums. He looked around him. His
men had marched forty miles over desert without food and
with almost no water, had fought some seven hours against a
force six times their numbers; half of them had then marched
back fifteen miles and then returned those fifteen miles. "There
is almost no need for me to say it," he said soberly. "I'm proud
of you."

Reveille was sounded before dawn the next morning. Campfires were lighted. The smell of bacon and flapjacks filled the
air. An hour later the soldiers again took to the field and
marched through the pass. On the other side they found the
bodies of the thirteen miners. At four o'clock in the afternoon,
the men reached the camp on the San Simon after a quiet day.

Jeffords rested briefly and then, with a token force, continued to Fort Thorn where he gave General Canby the welcome news that Carleton and his Californians were on their
way.

5

The utter defeat of the Indian forces in a major engagement
in which everything had been prepared in favor of the Apaches
was a shattering blow to Cochise. The introduction of the
howitzers into combat was revolutionary and the Chiricahua
leader realized his warfare now was obsolete if more of the
deadly fire-wagons were available to the Americans. During the
catastrophic engagement at the springs he had felt a consummate weariness overcome him. It was as though his mind
locked and he could not think. Superstitiously he attributed
the success of his hated enemy to disfavor from above. The
voices sounded noisily within him, and then, in his torment,
he saw the face of the Mexican again and heard his agonized
voice.

To Mangas Coloradas and to many of the younger warriors,
the rout vindicated the ancient method of Apache warfare.
With satisfaction Mangas Coloradas informed Cochise from
the superiority of his years that Apaches were successful if they
attacked their enemy at dawn, as always, and not behind rocky
buildings that the white men could blast out.

In an attempt to win some victory from the calamitous day,
Mangas Coloradas set forth with a group of his Mimbres warriors, and it was he who led the attack on the five cavalrymen

sent out by Roberts to find Cremony. And it was Mangas Coloradas who was shot down by Teal.

Weak from his freely running wound, Mangas Coloradas was taken by his men to the small town of Janos, in Mexico, and there they surrounded the town while Delgadito and Victorio found a physician. They carried the heavy, semi-conscious body of their chief into the doctor's home and with knives drawn, ordered the terrified Mexican to operate upon him to remove the carbine ball from his breast. "If he dies," Delgadito announced, "so does everyone in Janos, down to the last woman and the smallest child."

The villagers gathered around the doctor's house and led by their priest began to pray for the life of Mangas Coloradas, for whose death they normally would have celebrated a joyous *Te Deum*. With a dozen Indians, some of them still bearing marks of the shell bursts, all of them showing signs of the battle, watching his every move, the Mexican doctor removed the ball. Mangas Coloradas fainted from weakness and pain. The Indians began a vigil. The villagers continued their prayers. By noon the next day Mangas Coloradas recovered consciousness. By evening he was strong enough to remount his horse and ride away. The doctor was hailed as the village savior.

In the third week in July Mangas Coloradas reached his home at the Warm Springs in New Mexico. He was a sick and tired old man and he was glad that he was close to the end of his days because he understood now, and for the first time, what Cochise had sought to tell him six years earlier and he was not unhappy that he would not be present to witness the ultimate subjugation of his people.

In Apache Pass the Chiricahua people gathered in their dead. The bodies of sixty-three Indians marked the worst defeat the Apaches had ever suffered in single battle. There were those who died later of their wounds, and still others who lived but who would never fight again.

When the last man was buried Cochise brought the rest of the tribe to the West Stronghold. News of the debacle had preceded the warriors and the women were waiting silently. The silence changed quickly into a chorus of mourning that filled the canyon from one end to the other. Where Cochise walked he saw faces seared with sorrow. His people withdrew from him sullenly as he moved among them. He saw the blackened faces and the shorn hair and listened to the widows' wails and he felt then that he needed his people more than he had ever needed them before but he could not touch them. His brain felt as though it were being consumed by a fire and the voice was with him always. From the time he had assumed the

210

chieftainship of the Chiricahua Apaches he had felt that his people supported him, quietly and steadily, as the earth supports a tree, but now he felt that support was not there and he felt a stranger among his own followers. He was torn inside, but the more his heart ached within him, the colder and harder he grew on the outside. As the people retreated from him, so he retreated from them, hiding his grief behind his remoteness.

There was no one he could talk to. Nahilzay, Juan, Skinyea, Pionsenay, all of them were brilliant and brave men in war, but no one of them could think further than the next moment. Tahzay? He was quiet and thoughtful, but his thought was still that of an untried youth. He needed Naretena, he thought bitterly. He needed Naretena to listen to him and to advise him.

The stillness penetrated even his own dwelling. Tahzay was silent and Nachise, who was now nine, was caught in the silence. Nalikadeya longed to soothe him but she knew of nothing to say and waited quietly until the time when he needed her bed. Tesalbestinay alone indicated her compassion and, since they were almost old companions now rather than husband and wife, Cochise felt her warmth and understanding with gratitude though he could not show it externally, to a woman least of all.

He tried to eat but the food tasted like ashes. He sat in the wickiup and felt the voice rocking in his head, and he looked at Tesalbestinay and said, "Speak, woman. I know your tongue is heavy with words."

Tesalbestinay shook her head.

"Speak," he commanded.

"Listen to the mourning of your people," she said. "That is speech enough."

"Battles have been lost before," he said dully.

"There is no joy in that sound. Listen. The cries of your women are like the wind."

He was silent.

"Let the sound reach your heart," she said. She fell on her knees before him and took his hand. Her old, ugly face was filled with pain. "It is not too late to undo. There is food in our homes. There are weapons and fine horses. There is even yellow iron, though what an Indian needs of yellow iron I do not know. But there is also death among us. There are less of our young men to enjoy these things. There will be less and finally there will be a camp filled with old men and women and children to enjoy them."

He looked at her somberly.

"It is not too late to undo, Cochise," she said.

"It is too late," he said in a voice that seemed to come from the earth.

"It will be too late only when no man who bears the name of Chiricahua Apache walks alive," she said. "It is not too late, Cochise."

He stood up suddenly and walked from the wickiup. He strode through the camp, again feeling as a stranger, until he came to a small hillock that stood alone. He sat down on top of the rise. The sun was far to the west. The near hills had caught the first color; the distant mountains to the east were already blue. Birds chattered in the trees and small things ran swiftly on the ground. And from the camp he could still hear the dirge of the widows.

He lifted his arms upward and prayed for guidance. The voice was very loud in torment within him. He knew, as he had known deeply from the beginning, that peace was the only solution. But where could he go to find this peace? What white man had power to make it? Which white man had the honesty to fulfill it? Other Indian leaders had attempted to come to terms with the invaders with disastrous results. Indians had sat down to confer with white men and had been poisoned as they sat there. Less than three months before the white man had called together several young Apache leaders from other tribes into a small natural amphitheater on the promise of making peace, and had had the Indians slaughtered from behind.

It was death either way, he thought. He looked at the dying sun and his eyes roamed over the reddened country that he loved. What had his people done to bring this upon them? Was it better to die fighting, like the men who were now underground in Apache Pass? Or was it better to still seek peace?

He sat there until the darkness covered him like a blanket and he thought at last that he would again try to find among his enemies a man of honor with whom he could come to terms with dignity.

The decision made, he felt as though a weight was taken from his heart and the air smelled good to him again. His mind began to work; he began to think of plans, testing them, rejecting them, thinking of others. He could not make overtures immediately, he decided, because his overtures would be interpreted as the direct results of the Apache Pass catastrophe, as though they were a surrender. The moves would have to be made slowly and with great care so that when he offered peace it would be as welcome to the white men as it would be to the Indians. He would have to continue as before for the time being until the stigma of defeat was washed away and then the Indians could treat with the Americans as equals. And he would have to keep his decision secret lest word of it reach the Americans before he was ready.

Then, for the first time in his long leadership of the Chiricahuas, he was assailed by doubts. Could he lead the people in victory again? Were the Americans now so powerful, so cunningly armed, so numerous, that the next encounter would result in even greater defeat, and the next move more than that? He had never before doubted the ability of his people to wage successful war. That he now considered failure came as a shock. He stared into the darkness with thoughtful eyes and listened to the endless cries of the women.

6

General Carleton left Tucson on July 23 to join forces with General Canby and drive the Rebels out of New Mexico. Carleton decided at the same time to end, once and for all, the menace of hostile Indians in Arizona and as he progressed westward he formulated plans to accomplish this end. He was deeply impressed when he reached Apache Pass on July 27 at the skill displayed by Cochise in setting the ambush, and realized that were it not for the unexpected success of the howitzers the story might have had a different ending. As a defense directly aimed at the Chiricahua Apaches, he ordered a fort built in Apache Pass and left behind Major T. A. Coult, Fifth Infantry, California Volunteers, to supervise the construction and then command the garrison.

Work was started on the same day, July 27, and was finished in the incredible time of nine days. A total of four hundred and twelve feet of protecting wall, from four to four and a half feet high, and in thickness of from three feet at the base to two feet at top, was raised. The walls were constructed of stones, some weighing as high as five hundred pounds. By August 4 the walls were completed and some of the buildings inside of them were erected.

Major Coult's orders were explicit. Apaches were to be attacked whenever seen near the camp and no male adult Apache was to be taken alive. Women and children might be spared but, in every case, Apaches of fighting age were to be killed on the spot, regardless of the circumstances. Additionally Coult was ordered to escort all trains and couriers through the pass and well out onto the mesas on either side. He also was empowered to send out detachments of soldiers to protect travelers in any direction whenever he deemed it wise to do so.

Fort Bowie made the pass unhealthy for the Apaches at the beginning and Cochise resumed his tactics of roaming over the vast country, attacking, slaughtering, burning, pillaging. There was no thought, for the moment, of seeking peace, because the instant white men and Indians saw each other now there was fire.

In September after a month of violence by which Cochise

213

hoped he demonstrated that the Chiricahuas were far from defeated, he ordered that all fighting on the American side of the border be ended. There was a brief, bloody running fight between Chiricahua Apaches and a patrol of soldiers under the command of Captain E. D. Shirland and then it was as though the Apaches had disappeared. Raids were conducted frequently and at will in Mexico during the last quarter of 1862 but there was no important conflict in Arizona after the Shirland engagement.

Chapter Twelve

Encouraged by the unusual quiet that had spread through the Chiricahua country in Arizona, and attributing it solely to his show of strength in establishing and manning Fort Bowie, General Carleton at the beginning of the new year of 1863 determined to destroy the Mimbres Apaches who clustered around the headwaters of the Gila River near the Pinos Altos gold mines in New Mexico. The fighting against the Rebels had proved disappointing and Carleton, to his despair, found that he had only his old Indian problem on his hands.

He ordered General Joseph R. West, under his command, to arrange for the capture of Mangas Coloradas as the first step in his campaign, and West, in his turn, sent out Captain Shirland, the same officer who had last fought with Cochise, to make the capture. "You will take him dead or alive. You will get him by force or strategy," West ordered.

In groping around in the hills for Mangas Coloradas, Shirland came upon a party of civilian prospectors led by a former Confederate officer, now a prospector, named Jack W. Swilling. The civilians and soldiers joined forces and on a mountainside near Pinos Altos located Mangas Coloradas with a considerable body of men. The opposing forces eyed each other with hostility and then Swilling, with great bravery, walked to a clearing between the two forces and announced in a loud voice that General West desired Mangas Coloradas to visit him for a peace talk. Delgadito and Victorio argued against it, but Mangas Coloradas, convinced now of the ultimate futility of resistance, and confident of his own powers of diplomacy, lay down his arms and walked over to Swilling, saying that he too wished to make peace. He ordered his warriors to remain quietly in the hills until they heard from him and then he said he was ready to see the general. "It is humiliating to surrender," Mangas Coloradas said. "I am an old man.

214

I have one desire. I will walk by your side to the fort. I will not be bound. I will not walk behind you."

"It is agreed," Shirland said with respect. "You are not my prisoner."

Mangas Coloradas was brought before West and the two men were closeted in the general's headquarters. Mangas Coloradas began to speak of a peaceful agreement between the Americans and the Mimbres Apaches when West cut in suddenly, "You have lived a life of crime and terror. For many years your warriors, under your leadership, have made life impossible for peaceful settlers."

Mangas Coloradas' great face was impassive. Through barely moving lips he said quietly, "There has been little honor on either side. The Americans have not looked for a fair peace with my people."

West banged his desk. "I am not going to argue with you about who is right or wrong," he said angrily. "You are a prisoner. You will remain a prisoner for the rest of your life. Your people will not take to the warpath so easily without you to lead them, maybe."

"I came here freely," Mangas Coloradas said tonelessly.

West called for an orderly. "Send the Sergeant of the Guard in here," he ordered. Then he said to Mangas Coloradas, "You will be held under guard tonight and then moved to a permanent prison tomorrow."

"The white flag of the Americans is the same color as that of the Mexicans," the old Indian said.

"Honor is for honorable men," West retorted. "You have little reason to expect to be treated with it." A sergeant entered the room. "Take this man and keep him under guard all night," West said.

"Yes, sir."

"I hold you responsible for his presence here in the morning," the general continued. "I want him here in the morning." He looked intently at the sergeant. "Dead or alive."

"He will be present," the sergeant said.

The sergeant pushed the point of a bayonet against Mangas Coloradas. The Mimbres chieftain looked long and quietly at West and then, with no change of expression, he walked silently out of the room. A small trickle of blood crept down his side where the bayonet had pierced.

He walked slowly and with great dignity through the camp, refusing to be hurried by the incessant pricking of the steel point. He was directed to a wall and there left for a while as curious soldiers and civilians walked up and stared at him. He stood erect with his arms folded and looked at no one. When it was night a fire was lighted. He was pushed toward the fire and

215

told he might lie down and sleep. He obeyed. He was bound quickly, his hands tied behind him. He did not protest. When he finally was left alone he curled as closely to the fire as he could and he slept.

While he slept three soldiers put their bayonets in the fire and held them there until they turned red. Then they lay the bayonets on the bare back and legs of the sleeping Indian. Mangas Coloradas opened his eyes but did not move. The smell of his burning flesh rose. Again the soldiers heated their bayonets and again laid them on the Indian's skin.

Mangas Coloradas raised himself painfully on his elbow. "I am a prisoner," he said, "but I am not a child to be played with."

The soldiers lifted their muskets and each soldier fired once. They put down their muskets and drew their six-shooters and fired them twice. Mangas Coloradas fell back on the ground in the same position he had lain in sleep.

In the morning the guard reported to General West that Mangas Coloradas, chief of the Mimbres Apaches, had been killed while attempting to escape from his confinement. A soldier, using an axe, removed the scalp from the head of the dead Indian for a souvenir. Then the body was buried.

A few days later a surgeon for the troops exhumed the body and severed the head. The head was sent to Washington. The brain was found to weigh as much as that of Daniel Webster and the skull was larger. The skull was sent to the Smithsonian Museum and placed on exhibition.

Three days later Delgadito and Victorio captured a Mexican and under torture elicited from him the story of the assassination. Delgadito immediately set out to carry the word to Cochise in the Stronghold in the Chiricahua Mountains.

2

Snow had fallen during the night. From the center of the domed roofs of the wickiups thin trails of smoke climbed vertically. Delgadito arrived in the camp and went immediately to the wickiup of Cochise. He seated himself silently and Cochise read in his face that some tragedy had occurred.

"How does it fare with my brother, Mangas Coloradas?" Cochise enquired at last.

"He is dead."

Tesalbestinay, fashioning a new pair of moccasins for Cochise, paused in her work, the bone needle in one hand, the deerskin in the other.

"He was an old man. He was filled with many years," Cochise said.

"He did not die of his years," Delgadito replied.

Tesalbestinay did not stir.

"He was ever in the forefront in battle," Cochise said.

"He did not die in battle."

Tesalbestinay, sister to Mangas Coloradas, leaned forward. Her eyes alone were alive. "How did my brother die?" she asked.

"He was shot in the back by American soldiers after entering an American camp under the white flag to confer with an American general," Delgadito said slowly, spacing his words.

"Speak," Cochise whispered. "Omit nothing."

With a note of deep reverence, Delgadito, who loved his leader more than any man, related the story. As he spoke Cochise's face formed into a craggy mask and the pupils of his eyes became as flat and shallow as pieces of obsidian. When Delgadito finished with the last detail of the treachery, Cochise asked, "The parole was given when Mangas Coloradas agreed to parley?"

"Yes."

"You are certain?"

"I was standing only a short distance away and heard everything."

"The order for the slaying was given by the general?" Cochise pursued.

"It is not known who gave the order. All that is known is that he was invited to the camp to talk peace and he went freely and within five hours was dead."

"Return to your people," Cochise said. "Find a cave in the land and in it place his possessions and it will be as though he himself were there."

When Delgadito left, Cochise sank deep in thought. He lifted his head after a little while and said to Tesalbestinay, "It is the end. These people want no peace."

Tesalbestinay pulled herself over to him until she was at his feet and she pressed her face on the earth and her hands found the ankles of her husband and she held tightly to them as though she feared slipping away. "We are the same now, husband," she said.

"Yes."

"We have each lost a brother and we are the same."

He placed his hand gently on her head. "Cry."

"I cannot."

"Cry," he repeated softly.

"I have forgotten how to cry."

"There is no ending," he said. "There are only beginnings, always beginnings."

She lifted her dry-eyed face to him. "Will it be the same, an empty grave, with only the things he owned and touched?"

"It will not be the same."

During the next few weeks Cochise isolated himself and spent hours in meditation. He tried to make himself understand what was happening. It did not seem possible to him that men who fought as bravely as the Americans could also be so treacherous. But the facts answered him. It was so and there was nothing he could do to change it.

In the third week a delegation of men arrived from the Warm Springs. They informed him that Victorio had been chosen the new chief of the Mimbres Apaches, and then they told him that it was the desire of the men that Cochise take over war leadership of the Mimbres nation.

Cochise listened gravely, and then he said to the delegation, "We will join forces, but I tell you this: our cause is lost. Together we will last a little longer, maybe, but in the end it will be the same."

The delegation declared that with the Mimbres and Chiricahuas fighting side by side the white men would be driven from the land.

Cochise shook his head heavily. "It is not so. Our time is passing. People have lived here before us and something was decided and they no longer live here and there is nothing of them that remains, only the signs in the stones." He looked at the men bitterly. "The time has come for us. We have left nothing in stone and the forests will grow and the rivers will flow and the sun will heat our earth and the rain will wet it and the day will be followed by night but there will be nothing of us.

"No, we leave no markings on the stones and no empty dwellings in the cliffs to show that once we were a people and lived here upon this earth. But we shall leave behind us bones and a memory and when we are gone and we have taken as many of our enemies as we can for companions on our journey, it will be said that no one fought braver than the Apache and that no one held out longer against the foe and our markings will be in the hearts of the people who have come to our land so that forever afterward our people will not be forgotten.

"I will be your leader and henceforth you are the same to me as our people. But we are doomed and we join hands together with that knowledge."

The Mimbres leaders swore fealty to Cochise and pledged themselves to follow him to the death. At his first order, he instructed them, upon their return to their own land, to seek out Navajo leaders and ask them to join them in war.

"It will not change things," he said. "But it is better for us to die together. We shall die, all of us, singly and together, by tribe and by nation, but we shall not die alone." His eyes were vacant and his voice distant. "When we are gone there will be a great hole where we stood and in this emptiness there will echo again and again, Apache!"

3

General Canby was recalled soon after the arrival of General Carleton, and Carleton assumed command of the military departments of New Mexico and Arizona. The Rebels under Sibley soon were driven from the country and Carleton concentrated thereafter on Indians.

Indian warfare took on a new complexion. From scattered uncoordinated raids it became a single, organized operation. The Mimbres and Chiricahuas, joined by many Navajos, fought a savage, ruthless war, led by Cochise with a despairing brilliance that gained in audacity from his conviction that his war was lost before it had begun. In the spring of 1863 Carleton assigned the Indian scout, Kit Carson, who was serving as a colonel on his staff, to the task of wiping out the Navajos. After almost twelve months of fruitless effort, Carson succeeded in persuading a large number of Navajos to surrender and accept protection on a reservation in the Bosque Redondo. In his ignorance, Carleton also settled on the same reservation a large number of Mescalero Apaches, ancient enemies of the Navajos, believing the tribes would intermingle. During the next two years, through inept management by Carleton, through failure of crops because of cutworms, through fighting between the two tribes the Indians starved and froze, and the Navajos, who were regarded as the greatest makers of blankets among the Indians, were without blankets for themselves.

When they protested to the authority, Carleton told them to be "too proud to murmur." They continued in hunger and cold until 1868 when the government realized that the Bosque Redondo would never sustain the thousands of Indians held prisoner there. In that year they were returned to a reservation on their own lands, and it was not until 1876 that they were reported as self-supporting.

The Navajo assistance, then, to the Apache war, was short-lived, and Carleton won a manner of peace in New Mexico, but throughout the Civil War Cochise dominated Arizona and he used his men and resources in a degree that had never before been equaled. No white man saw him and remained alive to tell it. His doman stretched from the Mimbres country in New Mexico across almost all of Arizona, and from the Gila River in the north to as far south as his men cared to venture. He turned into a legend of death and horror. He was reported dead, insane, wounded, deposed. He scattered his men throughout the country he claimed for his own and used them as small shock units, abandoning the large concentrations, such as had proved so disastrous at Apache Pass. He knew he could never meet the white soldiers on open field of battle: they were too heavily armed and too numerous. But against sudden early morning raids, followed by quick retreats, the soldiers were helpless. In groups of twenty and forty the Apaches roamed at will, and wherever they passed they left their mark, as Cochise had sworn, in the bones and the memories of his enemies.

4

In the fall of 1864 Jeffords, who stayed on with Carleton as scout, returned to headquarters in Santa Fe, New Mexico, from a brief mission and was handed a letter, brought in by a military courier from Tucson. He looked at the neat, even writing, and then he went to his quarters and poured himself a glass of whiskey and before he opened the letter he swallowed the liquor and thought of the girl with the red hair. The two years seemed longer than two years. He broke open the letter.

September 20, 1864
Tucson
Dear Tom:
I received word today that a courier was about to leave for General Carleton's headquarters (don't ask me how I found out. I have grown into a young lady who is not regarded as unattractive by some and learn many little things, especially at the dances that are held here) and hoping in some way that this courier could reach you, I asked him to carry a letter from me to you.

Jeffords grinned and poured himself another drink. Then he continued.

I kept hoping during all these long months that one day or another would bring some word from you. I know that men are fighting for their country and you too are fighting even though you are not in uniform (or have you joined the Army and do you wear the dashing blue uniform of an officer?) and have very little time to write
220

letters, especially to little girls they have rescued from Indians. You have not rescued anyone else, have you, Tom? I would hate to think that your life has been just one bold rescue after another.

Anyway, no letter from you has ever come, but I have, in one way or another, managed to keep up somewhat with your doings. Officers and soldiers pass back and forth and every time I meet someone new I ask for news about you. You have become quite a famous man, because most everybody has heard of you, and I've been told of some daring things you have done, especially against the Indians.

I guess that you have never written because you still think of me as a little girl (although I kept insisting that I was not, even then) but now I am eighteen years old and even you cannot say I am a child any longer. I have even had some proposals, Captain Thomas Jonathan Jeffords, but I have not accepted any, don't worry. (Or would you worry?)

I have grown up considerably. I wear my hair in a new style, which a lady who recently arrived from San Francisco designed for me, saying that it is the latest style from Paris, France. It is up on my head now instead of hanging down as it was when you saw me last, and it makes me look even older. I went to a *baile* the other night and several officers told me I was the prettiest girl there.

I have been learning lots of things from Aunt Abigail. I love her dearly. I think she loves me too. I help her in managing her restaurant and boarding house and she says she doesn't know how she got on before I came. She just says that because she is so nice but I do think I am of some small help. She has taught me many things, about cooking and running a home and buying food. She says that some day I will make a wonderful wife for some man.

I seem to be talking only about myself, Tom, but that is only because I want to tell you of some of the things that have happened to me. I feel that I owe everything good that happens to me to you, because if it were not for you I would be dead or maybe the wife of some smelly Indian now and that would be awful.

I think of you all the time, Tom. Sometimes I ride out into the desert (when the Indians are not around) and every time I smell the sage I think about our trip here together and how good it was and how happy I was even though we never knew if we would ever get to Tucson alive. I have begun to understand some of the things you said about the desert, even though I still think it lots nicer to live in town with your friends. I have made some studies of the different kinds of things that grow in the desert and I think I can talk about them almost as well as you can. I have a little dog (given to me by a nice young officer) and the other day he walked through some cholla cactus (the dog, I mean, not the officer) and I got the needles out of him with a stick, just as you taught me. I never touched them with my hands.

Oh, Tom, when are you coming back? Do you ever think about me? If you do, in the future try to think of me as eighteen with my hair done up in a Paris, France, style, and able to cook and manage a house. Don't forget the girl you brought across the desert, but please remember that more than two years have passed and she has grown up.

I think you would hardly recognize Tucson. It is growing bigger all the time. There are new stores and the names of some of the streets have been changed from their Mexican names to American names. There is not so much fighting, but there is still some, and if that is what you need I think you could find enough to satisfy you here.

I know how important you are and how busy you must be but still, could you find some time to write a short letter to me (a long one if you really could) and tell me something of what you are doing and whether you will ever come back here and when it will be?

I miss you so dreadful much and it seems that I know you more than it would seem possible in the little time we were together. I was telling that to Mr. Silas St. John, a friend of yours (who always speaks so warmly of you) and he said that time doesn't count at all, it is what happens during the time, and I think he must be right because it seems I know you so well and spent so much time with you, and actually we don't know each other at all and spent only a short time together.

But, please, please, Tom, write to me. Everybody is so wonderful to me here, but sometimes I get so lonesome thinking about you and worrying about you. Haven't you done enough fighting and can't you come back here soon?

He looked at her signature and smiled again. It seemed, reading the letter, he could almost hear her. There was another sheet of paper with more writing, this time in a bold, angular hand. He glanced at the signature and saw the name, Abigail Wilson.

Captain Jeffords:

The girl is fine, although she is no longer a child but a young lady. She is quite in love with you, which I cannot understand. She is a sweet, chaste, lovable creature, and when I get through with her she will be a New England house-mistress, which is the highest goal any decent young woman can hope for.

Why do you not leave off with your Indian fighting and return? Surely there must be other men who can hunt down red savages. Try to write a letter to the girl. It would make her very happy. It would make me happy as well.

When he finished he laid the letters down on his cot and filled his pipe slowly. Then he reread Terry's letter. For the first time in his life he felt a sudden loneliness. He had frequently seen men at war who were lost on the depths of their being alone, but he had never felt there was anyone he was alone from, and had never, until then, felt the tight hard weight inside that is the occupational ailment of almost every soldier who ever lived.

It was a pleasant feeling, this sudden unhappiness, and he enjoyed it to the full. And then, feeling very young, he borrowed some paper and a pen from a friend, having neither of his own, and he sat down on his cot. He had almost forgotten how to write letters, particularly to young women.

"I would love to see you with that red hair of yours done in the latest style," he wrote. "I'm certain that it must be as becoming as you say, and I do realize that time has passed and that you must be a lovely young lady. I have often thought about you, Terry. . . ."

His pen scratched on for several hours and it was early morning when he finally stretched himself on the cot and slept.

THE THIRD BOOK

TUCSON

———◆———

Chapter Thirteen

In September of 1865, some five months after the end of the
Civil War, Jeffords resigned his commission as government
scout to Carleton. He went to Mesilla and remained there idly
for several weeks and then tied on to a train of fourteen covered wagons coming from Kansas and bound for California.
The train was led by a Kansan named Jed Hawkins and Jeffords volunteered to accompany the wagons as far as Tucson.

He rode along silently, grateful that he had no friends
among the travelers, filled with old thoughts as the landmarks
appeared before him. It was almost four years but the route
remained familiar. From time to time he almost expected to
hear the querulous voice of Hank Thompson.

He thought about what Carleton had said to him when he
attempted to dissuade him from resigning. "I know what you
mean when you say it's quiet here, Jeffords," Carleton told
him. "War does that. It's dirty business while it lasts but it gets
into your blood and when it's finished something seems to go
out of your life." Carleton hadn't quite understood him at that.
New Mexico was quiet, but that wasn't the whole reason. Jeffords himself didn't know the whole reason, nor entirely why
he was returning to Tucson. Carleton had made him a very
attractive offer to remain with him in a civilian capacity.

With the end of the war Carleton's men had begun to
grumble. They wanted to go home. The war was ended and
they had no liking for their jobs supervising Indians. Carleton,
striving to keep his volunteers together, thought of a novel in-
ducement. He allowed his men, to the numbers of one-fourth
his army at a time, to spend a month prospecting for gold on
their own account in the Pinos Altos region. When Jeffords

tendered his resignation, Carleton suggested that the scout and the general might team up in a private way to look for some gold for themselves. Jeffords declined the offer with thanks and said that he planned to go to Arizona, for more than two years now a Territory of the United States. Since the military department of Arizona had been taken from Carleton's command, because of his inability to stop Indian depredations, and had been transferred to the military department of California, Carleton was extremely touchy about all mention of Arizona and he did not pursue his offer.

The wagon train passed near the place where Hank Thompson was killed and Jeffords rode off to look at the grave. He found it with difficulty. The cross was long since gone and the slight rise in the ground was barely visible. Jeffords dismounted and squatted next to the grave. He looked up to see Hawkins gazing at him curiously. "Looks like a grave," Hawkins said in his Midwestern drawl.

Jeffords stood up. He felt oddly embarrassed. Hawkins looked around. The remains of the wagons and the signs of the fight were still to be seen. "Looks like an Indian party here," he said.

"There was," Jeffords said shortly, getting back on his horse.

"Looks like the white folks were pretty well wiped out."

Jeffords rode back to the train. He created some work for himself, riding back and forth, suggesting a slightly different disposition of the train scouts. He thought about Terry. He had heard from her a second time but had been starting out on a scout at the time and he had never answered. He was curious about her. He wondered if she were the reason he was going to Tucson. He felt some responsibility for her, he supposed. It was hard to think she was nineteen. She was a pretty good trail partner. He thought how good trail partners were hard to find. Hank was perfect. Men together on trail get into each other more than any other place. Whatever rubs wrong rubs harder than any other place. Men on trail had to understand how to leave each other alone. It was something not many of them knew entirely. If they felt the right way about the desert they never needed anything else. He didn't know it much himself, at least not to explain. He knew he felt better alone in the desert than anywhere else. He often had envied, in a way, the kind of religion some people could find in a church. He never could feel that kind. Religion was not the right word, but whatever it was, he could only feel it out here where it seemed to him that things were still new. New and old, together and at the same time.

Riding now, a short distance apart from the other men, he began to feel again something that had stayed with him during the war. He was never quite at ease with people; he had no command of small talk that exchanged no information. Around the campfires during the war, he had most often sat quietly and listened, answering only when spoken to directly. He supposed there was something wrong with him, but he preferred to be alone, and now, with the war ended, with New Mexico filling with settlers, there was nothing for him to do but move on. He would have liked to have had Hank Thompson with him but Hank was dead and beyond regrets and he probably would have been too old then anyway.

Hawkins rode up to him excitedly. "Looks like we might get some fresh game. There it is again. Listen."

What appeared to be the sound of a wild turkey came to him from about a quarter of a mile ahead.

"Nothing tastes so good as fine wild turkey," Hawkins said. "Want in on a little shooting, Captain Jeffords?"

Jeffords listened again. "That's not turkey. That's an Indian."

"Indian?" Hawkins laughed. "I know the sound of turkey."

There was a rocky canyon that cut down ahead of them. "The Indians know that," Jeffords said drily. "They can imitate the turkey call so expertly they fool turkeys. They're trying to get us into those rocks and brush. We're carrying breechloaders and they're afraid to come into the open."

Hawkins looked at Jeffords for a moment and then lifted his head and roared. "You Westerners sure got a sense of humor," he said. "We're not that green, Captain Jeffords. I can tell a turkey gobble when I hear it. I guess you folks out here try to play all us travelers for fools."

Hawkins rode off. "Hold it," Jeffords said quietly.

Hawkins looked puzzled. Jeffords rode past him. He listened intently and then turned his horse slightly to the right. "It's almost noon. Wild turkeys gobble on the roost. Never as late as this in the morning. If we had frightened turkeys they'd be off in the bush, out of reach."

"A joke is a joke, Captain Jeffords," Hawkins said peevishly.

"They want to draw a couple of men ahead of the train," Jeffords said, ignoring the tone in Hawkins' voice. "They'll have them shot and stripped and be away before anybody could stop them."

"You folks are always talking Indians."

Jeffords lifted his rifle and fired. There was a howl of pain. An Indian leaped up from behind a bush. Two other Indians rose from behind rocks and scurried up the canyon. The wounded Indian tried to follow them. Jeffords fired again and he fell.

Hawkins blanched. "Holy Moses," he said, rubbing his face. "Holy Moses."

Jeffords rode to the Indian. He was dead. "Navajo," he said when the other men joined him. "Probably one of the boys who wouldn't accept Uncle Sam's hospitality."

"Holy Moses," Hawkins repeated. "I thought you were joking, Captain Jeffords."

One of the men dismounted and drew a long knife. "What are you going to do?" Jeffords asked.

"Scalp me an Indian. Fellow tells me you can weave their hair good for a saddle decoration."

"Forget it."

"He's dead, ain't he?"

"Forget it. Get back on your horse and let's move."

"You ain't the boss of the show," the man said angrily. He continued to walk toward the dead Indian.

"Get back on your horse," Jeffords said. His voice was almost a whisper.

The man half knelt before the Indian and then he slowly stood up and walked back to his horse. "Every Westerner I ever heard of has scalped his Indian."

"You're not a Westerner yet," Jeffords said. "Let's move. There may be other Indians around."

"Who the hell is boss of this outfit, Jed," the man asked.

"Do what he says," Hawkins said. "Get back into your place. I'm asking your pardon, Captain Jeffords. I guess we are all a little green."

At the east entrance to Apache Pass a troop of mounted soldiers rode out. A young lieutenant explained that military protection would be necessary to insure safe passage through the pass. The soldiers spread out on both sides of the train.

"Those Apaches raise the very devil with us," the lieutenant said pleasantly. They rode past the gully where the Chiricahuas had ambushed the miners. The bleached bones still were scattered on the earth. "You'd think with a place like Fort Bowie here they would keep away. But they come down to the fort, right to the walls, if we are not alert. They've stolen cattle and horses from right under our noses, so to speak. They've attacked travelers not a hundred yards from the walls."

The train stopped to rewater at the springs. Jeffords, with strange feelings inside of him, looked at the fort for the first time. He thought of Roberts and he wondered what had happened to him. It seemed another time entirely now.

"First time you have seen Bowie?" the lieutenant asked.

"Yes."

"They used to have some brawls around here."

"I know," Jeffords said.

The patrol stayed with the train until they were well out of the pass on the west and then the lieutenant told them they would be safe from there on in. Soon the train was in the Santa Cruz Valley and in the distance Jeffords could make out first the high church edifice and then the lower buildings in Tucson. He felt a curious excitement. A few miles from the town another small mounted troop rode up to them and the sergeant in charge reported that earlier wagon trains were stretched out the length of the main street in the town. "You people will have to remain outside the walls until tomorrow," he said. "It will be perfectly safe. If you want to park your wagons and come on in, you are welcome. There just isn't enough room for a wagon train this size until one of the other parties move on."

Hawkins directed a circular park outside the town. Jeffords received his thanks and then rode on into Tucson alone. He tied his horse outside the Congress Hall and went inside. He finished his third drink and then he left. He untied the horse and walked slowly to the Scat Fly.

Tucson had changed, he thought. Not much on the outside but he could feel the difference. There were a few stores, a few more gambling halls and saloons, the streets were still unpaved, and the garbage piles were as high, or higher. But the place breathed more American than he remembered it.

He came to the Scat Fly. It was only four o'clock in the afternoon but the door opened and closed several times as men passed in and out. He tied up his horse and entered. He walked through the long corridor to the office. He pushed open the door and walked in. The color of her hair had not changed either, and she was right, it did look better fixed up on her head. Her face was in profile, bent over the desk. She was working on a book. He listened to her pen scratch. She turned around with an automatic smile, saying, "Yes?" and then she slowly put down the pen and said, almost again in a question, "Tom?"

"Hello, Carrot."

"Tom," she said again. She stood up slowly and he saw that she was taller and quite nineteen. "Tom." She walked over to him and put her hands on his cheeks. Then she clutched his arms and kissed him on the lips.

"Funny redhead."

"Your beard tickles," she said. "I knew it would. I was always afraid to tell you that. They said you would never come back and I said you would come back with your red beard."

He stroked her hair.

"How long will you stay? Are you passing through?"

228

"I think maybe I'll stay for a little while. If you have room for me. I hear people are sleeping in the plaza."

"Lock the door, Tom," she said. "I'm going to cry like a fool. I feel it coming on good. I don't want anybody to see me crying." She touched his cheek. "Desert dust. This will be the first good cry. I've had bad cries but this will be a good one. Lock the door, Tom. I've waited so long for this cry."

"On business time, Carrot?"

"If you knew how long I've been saving for this. You're thin and you look tired and there's a little gray in your hair and there are lines around your eyes. Maybe I won't cry. Come here and kiss me again."

"I've got all the dirt of Arizona on me."

"I haven't had desert dirt on my face in a long time. How long is it, Tom? It's almost four years."

She sat down. She was trembling. Her face had lengthened a little, he saw. And there were no more freckles.

"Tom Jeffords," she said. "You big hero Captain Thomas Jonathan Jeffords." She wiped her eyes. "Do you know how often I've said your name? Have you thought of me?"

He nodded. "Yes."

"I know this is no talk for a man," she went on swiftly. "I know you don't want to talk like this. You want something to drink and something to eat. You want to wash up and rest and then, perhaps, later, little by little, tell me what's been happening to your life in four years. But it has been four years and please let me have a little of it now."

He sat down.

"I don't have to hold back any more, do I, Tom?" she asked in the voice of a small child. She started to cry. There was a knock on the door. She took out a tiny handkerchief and blew her nose. "Who is it?"

"Who would it be?" Mrs. Wilson asked loudly. "Why have you locked the door?"

Terry ran and opened the door. "What's the matter here?" Mrs. Wilson asked. Then she saw Jeffords. "Hello, Jeffords. You picked a good day to arrive. We have fresh meat. Go on up to your room and wash."

"Somebody is in that room," Terry said, blinking.

"Won't be in five minutes. Whoever it was slept in the plaza the night before last and he can do it again. All he has in the room is a saddle."

"Any room will be all right," Jeffords said. "I don't want to put anyone out."

"You are not being asked what you want, young man. Terry, tell one of the boys to put that horse furniture out of the room and to clean it up."

"Yes, Aunt Abigail," she said. "Tom. Oh, Tom!"

"Terry," Mrs. Wilson said. The girl left the room. "I'll heat up some water. You look dirty as a pig. There are some clean clothes for you. Why are wars always so dirty?"

"Clean clothes?"

"They've been here for two years. You better like them. She picked them out when a freight load came in."

"I will like them," Jeffords said.

"Go on and take a bath. You smell of horse."

"Yes, ma'am." He started to walk out of the room.

"I'm glad you are still alive," she said.

"Thank you, ma'am," he said.

2

When he emerged from his bath he found the clothes laid out on the bed. There was a blue checked shirt, a pair of corduroy pants, and a new pair of boots. On the dresser there was a new Stetson and a red kerchief. While he was getting dressed he heard a knock on the door. "Who is it?"

"Terry."

"Wait until I get my pants on."

When he opened the door she rushed in. "Do they fit, Tom?"

"Just as though a tailor made them."

"I was so worried. I couldn't remember your size. I kept thinking you were bigger than you are."

"Bigger?"

"Oh, I know. You're over six feet, but you seemed bigger as I remembered you. I ordered things and Mrs. Wilson said they were too big and she finally picked out a man she said was your size and I got everything to fit him."

"She had a good memory." He pulled on the boots.

"Are they all right?"

"They're fine." He picked up the red kerchief and looked at it dubiously. Then he saw the eagerness in her face and he carefully tied it on.

"You look exactly as I thought you would," she breathed. "Come downstairs. I want you to meet my friends. We're going to have a celebration."

"Do your eyes always shine that way, Carrot?"

"Every time you come back after being away four years. I think I must be shining all over inside me. It must be showing through."

"You look very pretty," he said.

"Do I? I used to ask Aunt Abigail whether I was pretty. She wouldn't tell me. She said it would make me vain."

"Ask me next time," he said.

They went down to the dining room. It was unchanged. A

230

Mexican waiter, carrying a tray of food, swung his swatter as they entered the room. "Didn't they get that fly yet?" he asked. The large table was laden with food. Several men were seated around it. One of the men rose immediately and held out his hand.

"Hello, Captain Jeffords."

"Hello, St. John."

"Good to see you back."

Jeffords nodded. The four years now seemed only a little while ago. He was introduced to the other men. One of the men, Milton Duffield, an enormous figure with broad shoulders and a massive body, caught his eye. When he rose to shake hands with Jeffords he stood several inches above him. His face was dark and swarthy and his eyes were black and keen. "Seems I heard of you somewhere before," Jeffords said. "Didn't you come out here as marshal to the governor?"

"That's right. I resigned. I'm mail inspector here now." Duffield's voice was rich and loud.

"Mail?"

"Does that surprise you, Captain Jeffords? Well, we do have mail. Of sorts. We have a route running north and south and expect to start the overland route very shortly."

Mrs. Wilson, at the head of the table, ended the introductions by announcing the meal was getting cold. Jeffords sat down with Terry next to him. The meal was sumptuous. There were fried steaks, potatoes, and several kinds of Mexican dishes. As soon as the men began to eat they concentrated on the job and forgot all else; they stopped asking questions of Jeffords, for which he was grateful. When the meal was ended and the men had lighted their cigars, St. John said, "I hear you had some trouble with one of your postmasters, Duffield."

Duffield slapped the table so violently it shook from end to end. "There won't be no more trouble with him," he roared.

"What happened?"

"Can't blame the poor hombre too much, I guess," Duffield said. "They get paid twelve dollars a year and I think maybe they get a little finger itch now and then." He bit off half of a long, fat cigar and put the other half in his mouth. "One of the boys was helping himself now and then. I rode up there and I said to him, 'You see, it's just like this, the postmaster general is getting mad because there's thieving on this line and I'm getting tired at his growling and I want to get the business off my mind. I think you better pull out of here without any more nonsense.' " Duffield applied a match to the cigar stump. "The hombre was gone inside of twelve hours and there hasn't been no more stealing on that line. Either the rest of the twelve-dollar-a-year men are turned Christian or else they don't want me paying them no visits." Duffield roared in satisfaction and blasted out a great cloud of smoke. Then he rose and bowed with great courtesy to Mrs. Wilson. "The meal, ma'am, was up to your usual sky-high standards. I beg to be excused." He paused by Jeffords' chair. "I'm mighty proud to meet you, Captain Jeffords. Consider Milt Duffield your friend." Trailing a stream of smoke he strode heavily across the room, slapping the backs of his friends. The men so honored were almost driven across their tables. At the door Duffield picked up a black silk plug hat, put it on his head at a rakish angle, and thundered out.

"Are they letting hats like that walk around Tucson now?" Jeffords asked.

"Nobody would take a shot at Milt Duffield," one of the men said.

"I guess he is the only man in the Territory of Arizona who could get away with a silk topper," St. John laughed. "He says the black band around it is crepe to commemorate his departed virtues. He comes from New York. They say Lincoln discovered him. He shot some rioters who were chasing a Negro. He's supposed to be the handiest man with a gun out here. He likes to put the point of a tenpenny nail into an adobe wall and then shoot the nail through the wall."

"Good man to have on your side."

"He's been very decent to me," St. John said. "I'm working for the mails. He blusters and he gets into fights but he makes a good friend."

Terry and Jeffords walked out into the patio. He lit a pipe. "I haven't had a meal like that since the last time I was here," Jeffords said comfortably. "I hadn't realized how much I missed good food."

"Tom, I can't believe yet that you're back," she said. "What are your plans?"

"I don't have any."

"You came back just at the right time. Tucson is growing so fast. You can get started in almost anything and make a success."

"Do I have to be a success, Carrot?"

"You know what I mean, Tom. You've been wandering around so much by yourself. Always out there on the desert, liable to be shot any time. When I used to hear those terrible stories about the Indians killing people I used to wonder if I would hear one day that you were one of the victims. Oh, Tom, it's been awful. Men would eat here and leave and the next thing we'd know they were found dead on the desert. People you just spoke to a few hours or a day before. Isn't that over with, with you, Tom?"

"I haven't thought about it." He was amused at her eagerness.

"There are some fine people here in Tucson," she said. "Any one of them would be proud to take you in with them. I've spoken to several of them. Everybody thinks Tucson is going to grow faster than any other place in the Southwest. We have the climate and now that we are a separate Territory in Arizona maybe the capital will be changed from Prescott to here."

"You sound like a booster all right, Carrot," he grinned.

"I love it here. If they only find some way of getting rid of the Indians so people can come here safely. It's only the Indians who prevent people from settling outside Tucson. Why, with the mines and the grazing land this ought to be the most popular place in the country."

"Let's hope not," he murmured.

"You could do most anything, Tom. Ranch, perhaps. A fine big ranch with lots of cattle. Or maybe join one of the merchants here. The stores are all developing so rapidly. And when the freight trains get past the Indians they have such fine things to sell."

"You've turned into quite a little business woman."

"Oh, I am, Tom. Aunt Abigail says I have a man's head on my shoulders."

"Awful pretty for a man."

"You're teasing me again. I guess I wouldn't know what to do if you didn't tease me. But seriously, Tom, I did speak to several of the important men in Tucson about you. I spoke to two of them at dinner tonight. They would like to see you tomorrow."

"I don't want to see anyone tomorrow."

"No? Well, perhaps you're right. You just arrived here and you deserve a little rest."

"I think I might want to ride out on the desert tomorrow."

"You just rode across the desert."

"With a wagon train from Kansas."

"It's not safe to go alone," she said.

"Want to come with me, Red?"

3

They rode south from the Old Pueblo and presently they came upon the old mission of San Xavier del Bac. "This is such a wonderful old place," she said. "They are doing so much good for the Indians here, teaching them to have pride in themselves and to be self-sustaining."

"I never noticed Indians lacking in pride in themselves," he said dryly. "And before we came out here they managed to sustain themselves pretty well."

"Oh, you know what I mean, Tom. Self-respect and responsibility and a realization of their proper place in the new order of things."

"You didn't make that up. Who's been teaching you things?"

"Teaching me?"

" 'Realization of their place in the new order of things.' That's not you."

"Nobody's teaching me things," she flared, in the old manner. "The best people in town eat at our place and I listen to them and learn."

"The best people?"

"Only the other night Mr. Oury said that civilization could not take firm hold in Arizona until every last Indian was dead or on a reservation. He said that the Indians had come to the end of their careers as murderers and thieves and that now there were new and greater people on the land and that the Indians had to submit and go to reserves or else be wiped out."

"Oury."

"And he should know," she said vehemently. "Mr. Oury is one of our most important men. Why, when Governor Goodwin first came through Tucson he appointed Mr. Oury Mayor, and Mr. Oury has been trying to make Tucson as safe a place in which to live as anywhere in the United States. He has organized dozens of expeditions against the Indians, he and Mr. Elias and Mr. Williams."

"Williams? Duke Williams?"

"Yes, and don't you tell me that he poisoned Indians." Her eyes sparkled in her anger. He thought she looked very beautiful, angry. "Mr. Williams said he never put any strychnine in any pinole he gave to the Indians. I am sure he wouldn't do any such thing. He is a gentleman."

"Mr. Williams," Jeffords replied quietly, "is generally credited with playing one very lousy trick on those Indians after he got them collected under a white flag for a powwow. The way I heard it those Indians fell over like logs with that poison in their guts."

"I don't believe it."

"A friend of mine was there. He said they died smiling."

"Smiling?"

"Carrot, strychnine does that."

"Well," she said, "after some of the things those savages do I think anything is fair."

"Let's not talk about Indians."

Her anger evaporated. She smiled and the bright sunlight glinted on her teeth and turned her hair into fire. "After four years we should have something better to talk about."

"I stopped at your Daddy's grave, Terry."

"I was wondering if you ever would. I was hoping you might."

234

"Your Daddy and my partner ought to know each other pretty well by now. Hank never talked much. I hope your father is a good talker. Hank was more the listening type."

"My Daddy was a wonderful talker," she said. "He could sit around the campfire and tell stories by the hour."

"Good. Hank always used to complain I never told him things. I guess he's finding your father better company."

"It seems like such a very long time ago. Do you remember those few days?"

"Yes." The word was long in coming out of him.

They found some shade and dismounted. There was something wrong. He realized that somewhere very deep he must have cherished those few days four years before and she wasn't any part of it now. He had no idea of what he expected, but she was nothing of it. He was with a very lovely young lady, really a beautiful young lady, and a stranger. He wondered if that was what he had come to Tucson to find out. "How do I seem to you, Terry?" he asked suddenly.

"Wonderful."

"Have I changed?"

"Not really. You're quieter and you have a look in your eyes sometimes that you didn't used to have, as though you were going off somewhere inside of your head to some place far away. But not really changed." She stopped. Her eyes opened wide. "I didn't quite understand, Tom," she said quietly. "I've changed. Is that what you are trying to tell me?"

"You're a grown-up young lady now," he said. "You told me that yourself."

"That isn't what you mean, is it, Tom? It's different now, is that what you mean?"

"I'm not used to being alone like this with anyone as pretty as you, carrot," he said. "I'm lost a little, I guess."

"Where do you wander to?"

He tried for a grin. "You make me sound like a crazy man."

"It's all right, Tom. It really couldn't have been any other way. I was a child then, even though I kept getting angry when you called me one, and I'm not a child now, and there had to be a break somewhere. I'm glad it came right at the beginning, because now we can start fresh, and here I am, just as you see me, and I guess I'm in love with you. That's the same now as it was before. Maybe the only same thing."

He didn't say anything.

"I know how you must feel," she said. "I'm not stupid. Men are supposed to need some self-adjustment after a war. There must be many girls and men going through this now."

She understood it all, almost uncannily, in a way he never expected, he thought, and yet she didn't understand anything.

235

"I'm going back alone," she said. "You want to stay out here."

"It's too dangerous."

"I've come out this way before. It's not dangerous on this mission road."

"I'll ride back with you."

"Do it quickly then. You can bring me to within sight of the town and then go off by yourself."

A half mile from Tucson she reined in her horse. "I shall be perfectly safe from here on," she said.

"I have the feeling that I ought to be sorry," he said.

She leaned down from her horse and broke off a piece of sage. "Smell it, Tom." She held it under his nose and then she tossed it away. "I shall see you at dinner. Getting to know each other again will be like a game, won't it? An exciting game."

She dug her spurs into her horse and galloped off. He sat there for a long time, until she disappeared through a break in the ancient wall.

4

When she got back to the boarding house she went directly to her room and flung herself on her bed. A little later Mrs. Wilson sat down beside her. "It came very quickly," the old lady said.

"He's a different person," the girl wept. "He's not Tom at all. I felt we were almost strangers."

"You are strangers, child."

"You knew?"

"You are still a child. Did you expect to just pick up where you left off four years ago?"

"You never said anything."

"I never said anything. Nobody believes what old ladies say."

"It was horrible. He kept shifting and wanting to be away from me." She looked up. "Away from me."

"He's got a shell of brass but underneath he is a man, which is the same thing as saying he is a sentimental idiot, although he would shoot me for saying it. No man can ever reconcile himself to change. He expected you to be exactly the way you were the day he left. When he found out that you have lived four years, the same as he has, the shock was too much for him."

"You make it sound very simple, Aunt Abigail."

"It is simple. People do not realize how simple many things are. Most things are simple, if you'd let them be."

"You mean it will be all right?"

236

"Unless he's a bigger fool than I think. You are as pretty as a picture. Never told you before, but you are. He'll be around, acting like a fool man, which means less sense than an average horse. Give him a little time. He has to get some war out of his head."

"I told him that but I didn't really believe it myself." She shook her head. "We argued about such silly things. About Indians. I remembered the time he saved me. The first thing we argued about then was Indians. He feels differently about Indians than anybody I ever listened to."

"There is something about Indians that makes men think that way," she said. "People used to talk about the Negro slaves that same way."

"Thank you for coming in to see me." She sat up and wiped her eyes.

"Thank me for nothing," Mrs. Wilson retorted tartly.

"I shall wash and be downstairs shortly."

"That is a pious idea. Don't moon like a sick calf. Men can't stand that."

"How do you know so much about men?"

"I lived with one for thirty years. I know the breed."

"Were you happy for those thirty years?"

"Certainly I was happy. They do that."

Terry grinned. "You are a wonderful old lady," she said lovingly.

"Wash your face and change your clothes. There is work to be done." She stood up and straightened her dress. "He will come around. Maybe take a little longer with him than with most of them. There is an odd streak in him. But if you have patience he will come around. He returned to Tucson as quickly as he could."

"Do you think he came for me?"

Mrs. Wilson snorted. "Certainly didn't come here to see me." She walked briskly from the room.

Terry slowly removed her clothes. She stood nude and looked closely at herself in the long mirror over her dressing table. She stretched her arms and smiled and she examined herself from her head to her feet. Then she went to her bath. While she was bathing she thought that before dinner she would go over to see Mr. Estevan Ochoa, the merchant, and explain to him that Tom Jeffords would wait a few days longer before visiting him with reference to a job. Mr. Ochoa was a very kind gentleman and he would surely understand how a man fresh from almost four years of war needed a little time to adjust himself before settling down to business. She stretched herself as much as she could in the little tub and she had a sly thought that made her giggle and then blush. She wondered how Tom got himself into the tub with his long legs.

237

For several weeks Jeffords did very little. He lounged around during the day, spending his time at one saloon or another, and in the evenings he sat for hours playing poker in the little rooms behind the saloons. He slept late and ate when he pleased. There was nothing in particular he wanted to do and he loafed and watched other people work. But he was not content, or very relaxed. He found himself tired all the time, which puzzled him. He had seldom been physically weary during the years he served as a scout, at least not physically weary beyond the revivifying power of a night's sleep, but now, doing nothing, seldom on his feet, he was almost always drowsy and without energy.

He also was bored. He had moved in some degree of danger in the war years and he discovered he was unable to slow down easily. He frequently became irritable and surly. On two occasions, when he had been drinking heavily, he had got into quarrels in saloons, quarrels that were stopped short of shooting in each case by the quick intervention of Silas St. John who accompanied him often.

During this time Terry, guided by Mrs. Wilson, did not again bring up the subject of his beginning to work. She pointedly ignored his gambling and drinking. She was pleasant and sweet when he came to her. She asked him to take her to a *baile* given by one of the old Mexican families; he did and they enjoyed themselves in the formal, traditional atmosphere. They went riding together two or three times and each time she carefully avoided anything but the most innocuous conversation.

It was almost two months after his return to Tucson that Terry returned to her urging. One evening after dinner they went out into the patio. He sprawled out lazily and smoked his pipe.

"Do you mind my asking you out here for a little while?" she asked.

"Of course not."

"I know you want to get to your poker game," she said with forced lightness. When he did not answer, she said, "Mr. Ochoa was asking for you."

"Ochoa?"

"Don't pretend you don't know who I'm talking about," she said. "He is one of the most prominent business men in town."

"I guess he doesn't play poker," Jeffords murmured.

"I spoke to him about you months ago. I told him you would be in to see him about going to work for him."

"I'm not a business man, Terry."

"He has freight lines running all over the Southwest," she said. "You would be invaluable to him with your knowledge of the country. Oh, Tom, he would make such a success out of you."

"Must I be a success, Terry?" he asked.

She shook her head in sudden fury. "You make me so angry, Tom Jeffords. Are you determined to just let yourself become one of those men who live in saloons? I'm not a Puritan but so many things are happening here and you are just standing on one side and watching them go by. Everybody who puts his hand to it is growing with the town. And you, who have so much more than any of them, spend your time drinking and gambling." She sat down next to him, and took his hand. "I'm not forgetting what you've done these last few years. You've been magnificent and I know it and everybody knows it. But the war is over now and you have to be making plans for the future. Oh, Tom, I've been so proud of you, and I want to be prouder of you yet."

He emptied his pipe and then refilled it slowly. When he thought about it, he said to himself, she was really quite right.

"Have you thought at all about what you want to do?" she asked.

"I might do a little mining."

"Good," she said happily. "One of the gentlemen who is connected with the Paragonia Mines in the Sonoita is a very good friend of mine. I'll speak to him. I'm sure he could make a fine place for you."

"I'm not interested in Paragonia Mines," he said. "I mean prospecting by myself. Alone."

"Alone?" she echoed. Her voice turned flat. "Do you mean that you are going to start drifting around by yourself again?"

"I don't mind my own company," he said cheerfully.

"You infuriate me!" She rose and began to walk up and down the patio. He watched her, amused. He could almost feel her bristling. "Don't you ever intend to grow up? You act just like a spoiled child." She paused and shook her head and said more quietly, "Listen to me, Tom. I know how you feel about wandering around alone. I think I understand you." She sat down again and looked at him earnestly. "I do understand you, you know. I've thought about you so much that I think I know you better than anyone else. But the time has passed for men to wander around by themselves hoping to strike pay dirt. It doesn't work that way any more. Men have to get together, work together. Besides it's too dangerous to go out into the mountains by yourself."

"From the number of posses that go out from this town

you'd think there couldn't be a live Indian within a hundred miles," he said dryly.

"That's another thing I wanted to talk to you about. Three times now you've refused to join the posses. People are beginning to think it's strange. Why, you're a natural one to guide these posses, if you would."

"I thought you didn't want me to get killed, Carrot."

"White men don't get killed on posses."

"They seldom find Indians," he agreed.

"It's the idea of it more than anything else," she said. "The best people in Tucson are behind these posses."

"Sort of like a fox-hunting set?"

"Everybody agrees the Indians have to be wiped out," she went on, ignoring him. "Why must you be different?"

"Maybe I'm afraid of Indians."

"Tom Jeffords, you can be the most tantalizing human being who ever lived. You're not afraid of Indians and you never were. Why don't you help clean the country of them?"

"Maybe I could join your friend Duke Williams."

"There's nothing the matter with Mr. Williams."

"Which one of your big merchant friends supplies him with his poison these days?" he asked pleasantly.

She became so enraged she could not speak.

"Temper, Carrot," he warned. "You look like you're fixing to burst."

"Tom Jeffords," she said at last. "You are just a no-good, lazy, useless loafer. I've tried to help you get in with the right people and you've done nothing but laugh and make fun of me. You can live alone and be alone and do anything you please." She stood up. She started to cry and she was furious with herself for that. "Go and get yourself shot," she said. "Go out and let Indians catch you and burn you to death. I don't care what happens to you." She fled from the patio.

6

A week later he got a kit together and went out into the hills. Terry avoided him and refused to say farewell and when he was gone he did not know she spent half the day in bed, weeping for him, nor that she prayed morning and night while he was gone for his safe return. The only church in town was Catholic. She was not a Catholic but she slipped into the cool, semi-dark building and whispered words that she had almost forgotten. He returned a week later, alive but unsuccessful. She was as cool to him as she had been before he left.

The solitary journey into the mountains seemed to have restored something that he had lacked. He felt calm and rested upon his return. He went to the Congress Hall that evening

240

with St. John and he was more cheerful and relaxed than he had been for weeks. He was animated and amusing as he told St. John of some of his experiences. Then he questioned him about Arizona and how it had progressed since it was made into a separate territory.

"There has been very little change," St. John said. "The main subject here now, as always, has been Indians. People talk about Indians out here the same way some people talk about sex. It enters every conversation, dominates every discussion. All plans and projects are predicated upon the presence or absence of Indians."

"What are they doing about it, outside of sending out these useless posses?"

"Worse than nothing," St. John said. "I had hopes when we were separated from New Mexico that we might pursue a calm, intelligent course of action. But I think, if anything, it's worse. The first thing the governor did was proclaim Indians the greatest menace to the territory. From that time on the territorial legislature has done very little but memorialize Congress in Washington to send troops and money out here to wipe them out. We've pestered the military people in California the same way. I think they must be sick and tired of our constant whining. The military comes and goes. New leaders come with great threats and promises and pretty soon the generals and the colonels discover they can't do anything and the people begin to abuse them and out they go and new ones arrive. And meanwhile, of course, the Indians keep on."

"Has no one attempted to come to decent terms with the Indians?" Jeffords asked.

"No. When General Mason took over here he went to Bowie and tried to get to see Cochise. Maybe he was trying to make an honorable peace. Only he had as a handicap the fact that the last five times that military authorities or civilians tried to get together with the Indians for a parley the Indians were poisoned or shot. Cochise wouldn't see him and Mason went off more of an Indian-hater than ever."

There was a commotion near the bar and the two men looked up. Duffield, half drunk, was, as usual, showing off his astounding strength. He had gathered a large circle of his admirers around him. He removed his long, black coat and had elaborately rolled up his right sleeve. He grasped a heavy chair by its leg. Then he lifted the chair and held it at arm's length while the crowd cheered.

"Let's see you lift a body," a man shouted.

"Try a gal!"

"A gal is too light," Duffield pronounced. He looked around. "Hey, Jeffords, come on over here." When Jeffords didn't move, he shouted again, "Did you hear me, Jeffords?"

"Better humor him," St. John said. "He turns mean."

"What were you saying about the military?" Jeffords asked quietly.

Duffield walked over to him. His dark face was flushed and his eyes looked dangerous. "I called you."

"I heard you."

"People come when I call them."

Jeffords finished his drink. "When did you leave off being marshal?" he asked pleasantly.

The crowd suddenly quieted. Duffield looked down at Jeffords, sitting carelessly, his long legs stretched out. Then Duffield laughed and slapped him on the back. "Folks here want to see if I can lift you by your ankles," he said.

"Sure, Duffield," Jeffords smiled.

"If I do it I'll buy you a drink. I mean if I don't do it I'll buy you a drink."

"Sure," Jeffords said. He stood up. Duffield squatted and took his ankles. He started to lift. His face got red and the veins stood out on his forehead. The crowd leaned forward and then he bunched his massive muscles and lifted Jeffords two feet from the ground.

"Reckon I did it," he said, standing up, panting.

"Reckon you did. Sit down and have a drink."

Duffield sat down, still breathing heavily. His eyes, fixed on Jeffords, were clear and penetrating, and Jeffords had the sudden understanding that he was far less drunk than he had appeared. "Here's to you, Jeffords," he said, lifting his glass.

"To you."

"I'd like to see you some time tomorrow," Duffield said in what seemed to be an unnaturally quiet voice.

"Any time. I'm doing nothing these days."

"I need you, Captain Jeffords."

"Need me? For what?"

"The government needs you," Duffield said. He waved to a waiter to bring another round of drinks. "The mail situation here is run all to hell."

"What have I got to do with the mail?"

"This is no place to talk. Will you come over to my office tomorrow?"

"Sure."

Duffield twisted his whiskey glass around in his hand. "I didn't fool you a little while ago?"

"No."

"I have my own way of trying to size a man," Duffield said.

"I'll be around tomorrow."

Duffield rose from the table and he changed his manner instantly. He walked heavily over to the bar and again seemed to be drunk. He was telling a story about something that happened to him back East when a man ran into the saloon and looked around for a moment and then rushed over to Duffield. "They's a hombre just pulled into town from Texas," he said. "Name of Waco Bill. He's hunting around for you in the saloons. He's got half a load on."

"Why, thanks," Duffield said. "I believe I recall the man." He resumed his story. A half an hour later a huge, red-faced man entered the saloon. He lifted his head and shouted, "Where's Duffield?"

Duffield kept his back to the door and went on with his current story. He seemed unaware of the fact that no one listened.

"Where's Duffield!" the man shouted again. He jammed his thumbs in his cartridge belt and pushed his way to the bar. The crowd parted until Duffield was standing alone. He looked subdued and quiet in his black clothes and black silk full-blown tie.

"Where's Duffield?" the stranger shouted. "I want Duffield! He's my meat!"

Duffield finished his drink without turning and placed the glass carefully on the polished bar. Then he slowly faced the stranger and his fist moved and there was a heavy, thick sound and the stranger was flat on his back. The stranger reached for his gun. Duffield shot him casually from the hip. He bowed politely and said, "My name's Duffield, sir, and that's my visiting card." He ordered another drink which he drank slowly and then he nodded pleasantly to his friends and walked out without glancing at the floor. A few moments later the body of the dead man was carried out.

Duffield looked up. He was freshly shaven and his black sedate suit was immaculate as usual. "Sit down, Captain Jeffords," he said. "I'm mighty glad to see you this morning." He offered Jeffords a cheroot and then lighted it for him. "I told you last night I needed a man bad. I say it again today. I got a job for you to do. It ain't worth a damn for money. You could pick up loose change like that in half an hour digging somewhere. But it's a job that needs doing."

"Go on."

"The mail situation is plain lousy. What with Indians and clerks who line their pockets and one thing and another this place might be an island in the Pacific Ocean. The government can't hire riders. Too much Indian trouble. Mail takes months to get here, months to get out. There's no schedule. Nobody keeps things organized. I got to keep on the move to see that the damned clerks at one place or another don't run off with government money. How would you like the job of supervising the mail between here and Bowie?"

"I don't know anything about mail,"

"Ain't nothing to know about mail. St. John knows about mail and he's doing as good a job as he can. But this job needs a man. Mail riders are worse than mules. St. John's a cripple. He can't handle them. Nobody else in this damned town will do it. Everybody is too damned busy making a million dollars and trying to kill Indians. Want the job?"

"Why me?"

"I know men. You ain't about to become a clerk over to Tully and Ochoa. You ain't about to go to work for one of the mines. I don't think you have the look of a cattleman."

"Since I don't seem to be able to make a living you think I'm fit to work for the government."

"I'm working for the government, Captain Jeffords," Duffield said with sudden pride. "Somebody has to keep government business moving in a god-forsaken place like this. Do you want the job?"

"I'll try it."

"You're working as of now." He turned his head. "St. John, come in here." When St. John entered the room, Duffield said, "Jeffords is going to take over operating this station. Starting now."

Jeffords grinned. "Duffield seems to think I'm turning hobo. He's saving me."

"Put exactly right," Duffield said. "St. John will tell you how this damned office doesn't run. You make it run." He paused. "You understand, Captain Jeffords, when I say I want it run right I'm speaking for the government."

"I've been a good Democrat all my life," Jeffords sighed. "Now I'm working for a Republican Administration."

"You are working for the United States," Duffield said. "I need refreshment." He picked up his black silk hat and clapped it onto his head at its usual angle. "After St. John acquaints you with conditions here, I daresay you will be in a mood to join me at the Congress Hall."

St. John watched him walk down the street. "I think he's not quite the bully boy he pretends to be. I'll never forget how he took the killing of Lincoln. You know he was a close friend of Lincoln's. We received word here a couple of months after the assassination through a courier who came down from Utah. He wasn't sure of it. He said he had just heard it. When Duffield got the word he didn't move out of his chair here for three hours. Finally he said it couldn't be true, that nobody would want to shoot Abe Lincoln, and he forgot about it, except he got in a fight that night and then broke open a rancher's skull with a chair. A few days later we got definite word and Duffield locked himself in the office here and when I came back in the evening to do some work I found him sitting with his hands straight down at his sides and the tears coming down his face. I became embarrassed, thinking how a man wouldn't want another man to see him cry and I started to go out and he called out, 'St. John, come in here,' and I didn't recognize his voice. When I went in he looked at me with his eyes wet and it didn't seem to bother him, me seeing him that way. He said, 'Jesus, he was such an ugly old bastard,' only the way he said 'bastard' it was the greatest compliment I ever heard. Then he said, 'He was too god-damned good for this lousy country,' and then after a while he went out to church. I never saw him go to church before that or after it either."

"Tell me about the mail business," Jeffords said.

"Of course," St. John said. "Let me begin by telling you how glad I am that you are coming in with us. We're running mail out of here in four directions, up north, down to Mexico, west to Yuma, and east to Mesilla. The trouble is east and west, and mainly east. The route goes through Apacheria. We are using the old Butterfield stations for depots but the country in between stations is rough. The riders are attacked regularly. They get paid one hundred and twenty-five dollars a month, but very few of them ever collect. There are mail pouches scattered all the way between here and Mesilla."

"That's a lot of money, a hundred and a quarter a month."

"There aren't a half-dozen men who've ever collected."

"How about military protection?"

"Part of the way. Through Apache Pass. Whenever a patrol happens to be going in the same direction we tag on. But there are not enough mounted soldiers around here to make a permanent escort. Riders go out alone, sometimes with pack mules."

"How often does the mail go out?"

"It is supposed to move in and out once a week. It never does."

"When is the next load due to go?"

"It ought to go out in three or four days. The mail due in is what's causing me worry right now, with its Christmas load."

"Christmas! I forgot all about it," Jeffords said.

"I thought you might have," St. John said. He looked at Jeffords strangely. "I was going to tell you Terry got you a saddle from Texas. A fancy one with silver mounting."

"Holy smokes," Jeffords said. "What's today?"

"The twentieth."

"I suppose the local emporiums are sold out. What the hell am I going to do now?"

St. John went to the government safe and twisted the dial. He swung open the door and removed a small package. He unwrapped it carefully. In a small box was a tiny, exquisitely made watch on a long gold chain. "Here," he said.

"What's this?" Jeffords asked, taking it.

"It used to be owned by some French countess in Mexico. Somebody attached to Maximilian's court." He smiled. "It's yours."

"I'll buy it from you."

"I won it in a poker game."

Jeffords dangled the watch on the chain. "You were going to give her this yourself."

"No. I've had it around for a long time."

Jeffords smiled. "Thanks, Silas," he said. "I'll find something else. Give it to her yourself." He put the watch on the desk.

"That girl has talked about no one but you for years, Jeffords," St. John said quietly. "I've watched her grow up and I'm crazy about her, but not the kind of crazy you might think. She'll be hurt real bad if you forget to get her something and you can't buy anything in town at this time. You'll be doing me a favor. I feel like her big brother, and I mean exactly that."

"All right," Jeffords said.

St. John carefully rewrapped the watch. "Women wear a thing like this around their neck. They tuck the watch into their dress belt. There's no more talk about paying for this."

"Thanks," Jefford said. "Now tell me more about the mail."

7

Christmas was celebrated with great extravagance at the Scat Fly. Firearms were checked and the men ate stupendously and then, on this special occasion, drank their liquor in the dining room. Mrs. Wilson, who allowed herself to drink several glasses of blackberry cordial in honor of the season, became involved in a detailed description of a Christmas in New England. "I never feel that it's Christmas here," she said, her angular face softened with sentiment and cordial. "There is no snow and no sleigh bells and no holly and no tree." She wiped her eyes and blew her nose. "It has been so many years since I've seen a tree. We used to have such beautiful trees back home. My father and brothers would go out and pick one out —my father was very particular about his Christmas trees— and then cut it down and bring it home and we would decorate it and it would be so beautiful, with candles all lit and the presents lying under it. I can stand it here as well as anyone during most of the year but Christmas here just doesn't seem right."

"There's snow in the mountains," Duffield said loudly. "I'll go and bring you some." He half rose from his chair, his heavy face flushed with liquor.

"Now you just sit down and relax, Mr. Milton Duffield," she said. "You'll get yourself hurt by those Indians."

"Hell, lady," Duffield boomed. "Indians wouldn't shoot a man on Christmas Day." Mrs. Wilson walked over and pushed him down. "All right," he grumbled. "I'll get you a tree next year."

"You say that every year," she said softly, "and remember when it's too late." She began to sing a Christmas carol and several of the men attempted to follow her. Terry beckoned to Jeffords and he followed her out of the room.

"I have a surprise for you, Tom," she said excitedly. "It's in your room."

"Why, I just left that room a little while ago," he said. "There was nothing in it then but an old bed and dresser and a dirty pair of boots."

"Look now," she said.

They went upstairs. The saddle, beautifully tooled and mounted, lay on the bed. "It's beautiful," he said.

"Do you really like it?"

"It's the most beautiful saddle I've ever seen," he said honestly.

"Get on it."

He strode the saddle, his legs dangling over the sides of the bed. "Fits perfect." He cupped her chin in his hands. "Thanks, Carrot."

"I've been wanting to give you a Christmas present for years," she said. "Every year at this time I would try to imagine where you were and I would want to send you a present."

He took out the little package and gave it to her.

"You remembered, too," she breathed. "I never thought you would remember." She unwrapped the package quickly and then squealed. "Oh, Tom, it's so beautiful."

He started to be honest with her but the happiness in her eyes stopped him. It was a little lie, he thought, but a very little lie.

She threw her arms around him and kissed him. "I'm so happy, Tom."

"Are you, funny redhead?"

"I heard about your taking over the mail. At first I was a little disappointed. I thought the job was beneath you. But Silas told me how important it was and how much you were needed and how nobody else around here could fill the job and I began to be proud of you all over again. And the main thing, my darling, is that you are taking a job, that you are accepting your responsibilities."

"Yes," he said.

"I want everybody in this town to respect and love you," she went on. "They can't love you as much as I do, but I want them all to look up at you. Oh, I want to be so proud of you." She moved away and looked intently at her watch. "I want the name of Jeffords to be the most respected one in Tucson."

"Why are you so interested in the name of Jeffords?" he asked, lifting his brows.

She turned scarlet. "Tom."

He kissed her on the lips. They were very soft and warm. She smelled sweetly of lilacs. He kissed her again. "You're beautiful, Carrot."

"I don't know what I would do if you didn't think so," she said, lifting her face to him.

8

A patrol of six soldiers from Fort Lowell just outside of Tucson rode up to the mail office and called for Jeffords. When he stepped out into the sunlight the sergeant handed him a torn leather pouch.

"Where did it happen?" Jeffords asked.

"About fifteen miles out. We found the rider's body. What there was left of it."

"Burned?"

"To a crisp. Nothing left but bones. We found some of the mail scattered around and then this bag. Looks like they cut it open and then threw it away. Never saw a bag thrown away before. Apaches like to keep these things for themselves."

"Thanks, Sergeant."

"Looks like old Cochise ain't fixing to let any mail go through. Last rider, before you took on, was handled the same way."

As Jeffords reentered the office with the torn pouch St. John looked up. "Another one?"

"Yes."

"That's the last three out of four," St. John said. He looked curiously at the pouch. "Funny they didn't keep that. They say the Chiricahuas are well supplied with government mail pouches. They use them to store dried meat."

Jeffords filled his pipe and lit it slowly. "I wonder if this is some kind of a greeting to me."

' You might have something there, Tom. You can bet Cochise knows a new man has taken over. Nobody has ever found how he does it, but he seems to know what's going on almost before it happens."

Jeffords blew out a mouthful of smoke. "This looks like a gesture of contempt. Indians don't waste things."

"Maybe he's trying to show that he has so many of those mailbags he doesn't need any more," St. John laughed grimly. "God knows, everybody in the Chiricahua tribe down to the last little papoose must have a government mail sack."

Jeffords stuffed the recovered mail in a new sack, already half filled with letters. He examined his revolver and then took his carbine from a wall-rack and looked carefully at it.

"You're not going out yourself," St. John said.

"I need a little air."

"That's not your job."

"The west-bound rider ought to be at Bowie, don't you think?"

"If he is alive."

"I'll swap pouches with him." He hefted the pouch. "Not much in it. I don't think I'll need a mule."

"Andy MacDowell is over at Congress Hall. He's ready to go," St. John said.

"He just got paid, didn't he?"

"Yes."

"Let him enjoy it. He'll have to make the run soon enough." He swung the pouch over his shoulder. "Be seeing you."

"I think you're crazy, Tom."

"I don't like to tell men to do something I don't do myself."

"Shall I tell Terry anything?"

"Tell her I'm trying out her Christmas present."

He reached the Apache Pass station the following afternoon without sign of Indians. After a short rest he started back again with the pouch of mail from the East. He rode slowly, resting his horse frequently to keep him from overtiring. He rode all night. There was a full moon. The country was well lighted. He rode easily in his saddle and the silver trim glinted in the moonlight. He supposed they probably should get married, he thought. He'd had a long life alone and that was all over with. The war was over and the country was changing and he probably was out of step. Things were settling down all over and he probably ought to do the same. There was no place to go anymore. Arizona was probably the last place of its kind. And it wouldn't be too long. The Indians had cards stacked against them and in a few more years it would be the same here as it was everywhere else. He felt himself an anachronism. He had kept just ahead of it for a long while now and it was finally catching up and there was no place to go. What he ought to do was call it quits, get married and raise a family, and when his kids got old enough, spend his time in the evenings telling them what a hell-raiser he was in the old days. He thought of what Carleton had said. There was a hole left, all right. He wondered if he was in love with her. He didn't know how he would know.

There was a faint reflection of light on the trail ahead of him and he turned in his saddle and saw the dawn lying like a broad bright paint streak in the east. It was very quiet. There was no sound except the horse's hooves on the flinty ground and the crunch of leather under him. He breathed deeply. There were good smells. The acrid smell of the horse and the rich smell of the leather under him and the outside smell of the country that was made of all things alive in it. It got brighter. The sky was stainless. He was a little tired. He was passing through the Santa Cruz now and it would not be too long.

The valley lay before him and he thought it was the most beautiful thing he had ever seen. The air was sweet and fresh and the sun rose slowly and woke up everything and he thought how each day was new here, each day a beginning, with what happened yesterday gone and ended. Nothing carried over here, he thought. You could sleep and wake up and it was new. Some people resented the fact that the country was remote. They said you couldn't get close to it, the way you could to places back East. Maybe that was what he liked most about it.

There were several large boulders in the distance ahead of him and before he translated their strangeness into his mind he automatically kneed in his horse. There was something flicking in him as he looked at the rocks, lying so naturally next to the trail. He felt his wrists tingling. He thought those boulders did not belong there. He lifted his rifle and fired and one of the boulders let out a scream and the boulder became a gray blanket and the Indian under it rose and started to fall. He fired again and twisted his horse and slid down its side, riding so the horse was between him and the Indians and he jabbed his spurs into the horse's side and he heard the whine of bullets come past him. He lay low on the far side of the horse and fired under its neck and when he looked back, afterward, he could see several Indians. They were on foot. There were no horses near them. He reined in and looked around swiftly. He could see no horses anywhere. Then he felt a pain in his side and another in his arm. He heard the hum of other arrows. There were three Indians behind a clump of palo verdes. He fired again and broke his horse into a gallop again and then he was in the clear. He felt wet on his right side. He reached back with his right hand and pulled out the arrow. When he bent his right arm he saw the tail of the other arrow stuck in the soft part of the arm. He held the reins with his right hand and pulled out that shaft. His face broke into sweat. He opened his leather jacket and then his shirt. Looking down he could make out the cut in his side. It was not too deep. He jammed a handkerchief against it and kept his right elbow pressed against it from the outside. His arm was bleeding and the blood ran down inside his sleeve and out over his fingers. The horse smelled the blood and snorted nervously and then galloped faster.

Jeffords wondered about poison. The Apaches used poison when they meant business and Cochise meant plenty of business. They used poisonous plants and mixed the poison with deer's blood. They had another way, mixing poisonous insects with putrefying liver and dipping the arrowhead into the mess. Then there was the formula that called for a mixture of deer stomach, blood, and thorny plants, all allowed to spoil together.

He ought to know pretty soon. With the jouncing the horse was giving him if there was any poison at all it ought to be all through him before very long. One kind made a man's finger start to itch from the inside, so he couldn't scratch it, and then the itching changed to an ache and then the man keeled over. That worked pretty fast. Another kind just made a man's head get so big inside it felt as though it would burst. That took a little longer.

After a while he decided that if it were poison it wasn't the itching finger kind. His fingers felt all right except that his right arm was getting stiff and hurt like hell. He felt tired and then sleepy, but it was not the poison kind of sleepiness. The blood was running down his arm in a stream and then divided into three streams and ran between his fingers. He looked back. There was nobody near. He ripped open his shirt and made a tourniquet and twisted it around his arm, not too tightly, just above the wound.

Presently he could see Tucson and he was very glad to see it. He was getting very tired and he felt himself swaying on the saddle and he knew he couldn't shoot very straight if he had to shoot. He started to sweat hard and he could taste the salt sweat at the corners of his mouth. By God, this was lousy melodrama. He hated melodrama and it kept clinging to him. The wounded man bringing in the mail. He started to sing, "The mail must go through, you, the mail must go through." He tried to think of something to rhyme with Cochise, but all he could think of was, "like grease, old Cochise." Cochise. The name sounded like a shot. He remembered an officer once who said it sounded like a sneeze.

He was almost at the gate now. He was very sleepy. He loosened the tourniquet. His arm started to bleed immediately. He flexed his fingers. There was a dull ache in his side. He entered the town and rode up to the mail office. He tried to yell, "St. John," but it wouldn't come out very loud. He slid

251

slowly down the side of the horse and fell on his knees. He was bathed in sweat. Then he felt someone picking him up and he went out.

When he opened his eyes again it seemed a long time later. He was seated in his chair in the office. "Get me a drink," he said to St. John. "There's a bottle in my desk drawer."

"Somebody went for a doctor."

"Get me a drink before he gets here. He'll tell me not to have one." He swallowed from the bottle and felt stronger.

Terry ran into the office. Her face was white and he thought how red her hair looked. "You idiot," she said. "Tom, my God!" She looked at St. John in panic. "Is he hurt badly?"

The doctor entered and went to work. Jeffords felt him probing from a long way away. He felt sleepy again.

"Will he die?" he heard Terry ask from a great distance.

"Die? Him?" he heard the doctor say.

9

He was up and around in three days. He discovered he was something of a town hero. Strangers walked up to him and congratulated him. He got his old feeling of embarrassment. It made him a little short when he answered. Nobody seemed to mind.

The next rider got through. The one after that disappeared and was never heard from again. The one after that was shot at but got through. The next two were shot and killed.

Then Jeffords began to take his afternoons off. He explained nothing. Regularly he disappeared for an hour or two in the afternoon. St. John looked at him questioningly once or twice and then when he saw that Jeffords didn't want to talk he kept silent.

The riders continued to be attacked. Jeffords tried sending them out in pairs; that helped a little but not much, and it ran over the budget the government allowed. By summer six more of the riders were killed or wounded and two were missing.

Then one day Jeffords called St. John into his office. "I'm going up to see Cochise," he said.

"I thought you would, eventually," St. John said, after a long pause.

"You've been wondering where I've been going afternoons these last few months," Jeffords said. "I've been learning to speak Apache. I found an Apache boy named Juan down the San Xavier Mission. He's been teaching me. He told me yesterday that I speak it like his brother."

St. John nodded. "You are going at it right," he said.

"Not only the language," Jeffords said. "But the customs

252

and the manners and the traditions and everything else Juan remembered. It's not a bad language, Silas. I spoke a little of it before, but it's quite a language. I think some of our friends around here might be surprised at some of the things I've discovered. The religion is a beautiful thing. I've got a different idea of our red friends." He filled his pipe. "Juan told me Cochise is camped up in the Graham Mountains. He said he would take me part of the way."

"Can you trust him?"

"I don't know. I think so. He is pretty proud of his race and it wasn't hard for me to let him know I shared his pride." Jeffords puffed slowly. "They are quite a people."

"You know that for more than five years now no white man has seen Cochise and lived."

"I thought all about that, Silas," Jeffords said. "Somebody's got to get to him and try to get things straightened out. People can't go on killing each other forever. I think maybe Cochise is human. I'll gamble on it."

St. John smiled faintly. "I think I somehow always knew that Cochise and you would get together one day."

"Tell me what you remember about him. I'll need all the information I can get."

"It's an odd thing, Tom," St. John replied. "But I have never been able to reconcile my own memory of Cochise with the man who has been causing all this trouble. I don't know how to say it exactly. He affected me very strongly. I probably could get lynched for my opinions in Tucson but I've never forgotten talking to him. He has something that keeps you seeing him and hearing him for a long time afterward. I'd like to see him again. Even now."

"No."

"I know. I wouldn't do much good."

"It's not that." Jeffords raised his eyes. "Hell."

"Jim Tevis knows him."

"I better not talk to him. It will be all over town."

"Tevis got to like him. Cochise and he got into a fight about something once and Cochise threatened to kill him. He had the chance to do it twice and let him go. Tevis has no lost love for him, but he does have a kind of strange admiration. It's hard to explain. Cochise did that to people who knew him in the old days. Another thing. He used to be a man of honor and I don't think the last few years changed that. If he gives his word I think you can depend upon it."

"You can with most Apaches if you keep your own word." Jeffords relit his pipe. "Another thing. I don't want Terry to know about this until after I'm gone."

"Of course. When do you plan to leave?"

"Tomorrow morning. Juan is meeting me at the gate."

253

St. John looked out of the window. His fine, sensitive face looked tired. "I guess I think things out as much as I can," he said. "Having one arm stops me from doing things and gives me more time to work inside my head. You remember your Greek dramas in college? Everything in them had to be. Each little thing had to take place. I've thought about all the things that have happened out here and I get the same feeling. There were a dozen factors in the Bascom incident—the original kidnaping of Jesus Salvador, the kidnaping of the Ward boy, the kind of man Ward was, the kind of man Colonel Morrison was, the kind of man Bascom was, the fact that Bernard and his veteran dragoons were present—all of those things added up to what happened. If a single item had been missing, the thing might never have been and the whole history of Arizona might have been different. When you arrived here and then took this job I got the feeling that this was another inevitable step." He looked up and reddened a little. "If you believe in that sort of thing," he added.

Jeffords didn't answer.

"After I met Cochise," St. John said, turning to the window again, "I felt that I knew him better and less, at the same time, than anybody I ever knew. Some people have something. Cochise has." St. John paused. He felt himself about to say that he thought Jeffords had it, too, but he couldn't to his face. "You know there is less than a fifty-fifty chance that you will get as far as seeing Cochise?"

"Yes."

"And if you do stay alive that long, there is still less chance that you will leave his camp alive?"

"What the hell."

"Let's go have a drink," St. John said.

After dinner that evening he sat in the patio with Terry. It was a warm clear night. Somewhere in the distance someone was picking on a guitar. "It's a lovely evening," she said. "The stars almost hurt my eyes."

"I hope he makes the grade," he said.

"Who makes what grade?"

"That guitar player. He's standing in front of a window singing his heart out. He's singing as though his heart is tearing to pieces but if the lady breaks down and gives in he gets scared and runs away. I guess they have more fun having a broken heart than having the lady."

"Tom, you're terrible."

"It's true. If she opened the shutters and leaned out and said, 'All right, Juan, or Pepito or Jesus or Santiago or whatever your name is, come on in, the old man is down in Chihuahua and the old lady is out drunk somewhere,' why the little Mexican would scoot off so fast she wouldn't see him for dust."

She giggled.

"Mexicans love to be heartbroken. Makes them round-eyed and sad and they love to be round-eyed and sad."

"It's a very beautiful song," she said. "It would make almost any lady tender."

Her face was pale in the night. He thought how very close to him she was, how, slowly and without effort, they had moved together in the months that he had been back. It had become part of his life, in an easy and graceful way, and it was comforting and pleasant. Then he thought he felt that way because of what he was going to do the next day and he felt himself hardening. "I think I'll go get a drink," he said. He could feel the unhappiness that filled her. "I'll see you later." The air was full of smell from the oleanders and he had to get out. "I might stay at the Congress Hall for a while." He stood up. She looked up at him. Her face was beautiful. "Going inside?"

"No," she said. "I think I will stay out here for a little while."

He leaned down and kissed her briefly. He let his fingers rest on her cheek for a moment and then he quickly entered the house.

He rose before dawn the next morning. Juan was waiting. "Are you ready?" Jeffords asked.

"Yes, *Nantan* Jeffords."

The two left town.

Chapter Fourteen

Cochise had established a temporary camp about eighty miles northeast of Tucson in the foothills of the Grahams. Juan led Jeffords through the mountains to the north and east of Tucson. The boy rode ahead steadily and with assurance and Jeffords let the reins hang slack and followed him. At dawn they were deep in a precipitous canyon. When they climbed out of the gorge the sun was well up. Juan increased his pace, riding his horse almost recklessly.

In the early morning the mountains with their gullies and sharp clefts still in shadow looked tortured. The men descended the eastern slopes and then entered a level plain and then, shortly before noon, they came upon the San Pedro River and here Juan said he would go no farther.

"Apaches who have made their peace with the white men are not loved by their people," he said quietly. "It would go

255

worse with me if I were to be taken by Cochise than it might with you."

"You have done good things," Jeffords replied. "If there is any success in this journey much of it will be due to you." He leaned over and embraced the boy.

"I wish you luck, *Nantan* Jeffords. It is said that Cochise is the cruelest of our race and yet it is also said that there is nothing he admires more than bravery." He lifted his right arm gravely and then he galloped off. The dust soon settled again and he was lost in the mountains.

Jeffords dismounted. He looked around him. It was quiet. He could see no living thing and yet he knew, with that sense that told him of these things, that he was being watched. He set to work on the first part of his plan. From his saddle he untied a small bundle of evergreen branches he had cut while crossing the mountains. He built a small fire and placed part of the bundle over the flames. Then he spread his blanket over the fire and suddenly lifted it so that a great cloud of black smoke columned upwards. He blanketed the fire again and after a moment lifted it and permitted another smoke shaft to rise into the still air. He removed the blanket and five minutes later repeated the performance.

His smoke signal could be read for many miles. With it he was announcing that he was traveling alone and that his mission was peaceful. To reach Cochise alive he had decided, in planning his expedition, that he had to arouse the Chiricahua's curiosity and he thought the most audacious way to do that was to send his own signals ahead, before the Indians would do it for him.

He had decided also to travel openly, making no attempts to cover his tracks or hide. He planned on the novelty of his actions to be his passport.

He extinguished the fire and mounted again. He scanned the sky as he progressed. There was no other smoke signal he could see. He hoped he had the Chiricahua videttes off balance.

He rode steadily through the afternoon. He reached the foothills of the Saddle Mountains and skirted to the south of them and then he again entered a flatland. In the distance ahead of him he could make out the Graham peaks. He dismounted again and sent out another signal. He was deep in Indian country now. He rode slowly, almost casually, and then he came to the foothills of the Grahams. The sun baked the hard rocky earth around him and the terrible heat came from everywhere. His horse shivered nervously. The country was filled with rocks and boulders of all sizes and Jeffords knew that there must be Apaches behind many of them and that their fingers must even now be resting lightly on triggers or clutched tightly on the feathered tails of their arrows.

He climbed down from his horse. His fingertips tingled. He started another fire and sent up a final signal. He knew this last was a gesture. He needed no smoke to announce himself now. He knew that there must be eyes on him from all directions. He moved calmly and with deliberation. He did not want to excite any of his watchers.

There was the quiet of the grave. He got on his horse and rode again, slowly and erectly, his rifle plainly sheathed in its scabbard, his elbows high, and his hands plainly on the reins. So far, he thought, his bluff had not been called. He had to keep on, just as he was going.

There was no sound except for the ring of the horse's hooves on the hard earth. Then the horse whinnied. He touched its neck to calm it. He rode on, his eyes straight ahead, and he felt invisible doors closing behind him.

He rode up a straight narrow wash and then the dried gully turned sharply to the right and he followed it and he was in the camp of the Apaches and they were around him. They appeared noiselessly with a strange shock as though they had formed themselves of the air and they looked at him incuriously and their silence was louder than any noise. Their faces were around him, as though in a dream, remote and without substance and yet hard-seeming as the rocks that tumbled crazily down the mountains, and their eyes were blank and expressionless. He felt as though his appearance had suddenly arrested all life within the camp and yet he knew that he was not unexpected.

He moved on to the center of the rancheria and he leaped lightly from his horse. An old woman walked up to him. Her face was as inscrutable as the others but he felt she was trying to convey something to him, through the wall of nothingness. He handed her the reins. She took them silently. He unbuckled his cartridge belt and handed it to her, the holster heavy with its revolver. He pulled his knife from his sheath and gave that to her. He felt in everything that he was doing he was performing some esoteric ceremony. Then in a voice as calm and even as the eyes that lay upon him from all sides, he said, in perfect Apache, "Hold these things for me. I will need them when I leave."

Those were the first words spoken since his arrival. They fell upon the broad silence loudly, almost peremptorily. The woman did not answer him. She walked away slowly and silently, her right arm holding his weapons, her left arm leading the horse. The horse suddenly neighed loudly and reared. The woman pulled on the reins with a strong gesture and continued to walk away.

A tall Indian, naked except for loincloth, his broad and heavy chest covered with the symbol of the sun in red and with the sign of Lightning in yellow, his arms hidden from his wrists to his elbows with bands of silver and leather, walked up to Jeffords. "What makes you think you will leave here alive?" he asked in Spanish, although Jeffords knew he had heard him speak to the woman in Apache. The Indian lifted his eyes and looked Jeffords full in the face and he knew that Cochise was facing him.

Jeffords felt a curious calmness come over him. He returned the stare not boldly, but tranquilly. The two men remained silent and Jeffords felt himself breathe in and out six times, and then he said, "It is known that the chief of the Chiricahua Apaches is the greatest Indian leader. It is known that he respects bravery as he respects truth."

The words might not have been spoken. There was not a flicker in the eyes of the Indian to indicate he heard or understood. Jeffords waited quietly.

"You are a brave man," Cochise said. "I will listen to you."

He turned abruptly and walked away. Jeffords followed him. The encircled Indians opened their ranks to permit Cochise to walk through and they remained apart as Jeffords followed. He kept his eyes level and straight and looked neither to the right nor the left although the Indians were close enough for him to touch them without fully stretching his arm. He walked behind Cochise and he saw the great muscles of his back move under the flesh, covered with scars, and he remembered the harshness of his face, a permanent astringency written by the shape of his mouth and the set of his jaw. He remembered then what St. John had said.

2

Cochise walked to his wickiup and entered. Jeffords followed him in. A small black and white dog, hardly more than a puppy, barked happily and wagged its tail. Cochise reached down and tugged its ear and then he sat silently on his haunches. Jeffords sat down facing him, his own legs doubled under him. The woman who had taken the horse and weapons appeared with two flat clay plates filled with a hot meat stew. Without speaking Cochise began to eat, picking up chunks of meat with his fingers. Jeffords did the same and discovered he was hungry.

When they finished eating the woman entered again and took away the plates. "Speak," Cochise said. It was the first word he had uttered since the initial colloquy.

"I am the boss of the white man's mail that is centered in Tucson," Jeffords said. "Mail is signaling that the white men use. Things are told on pieces of paper and when someone

258

else receives the paper he can understand what is being said to him, the same as a smoke signal. This mail"—he used the English word since there was no Apache equivalent—"is carried by messengers. They have no interest in the messages. They do not know what the messages are. They are poor men who make their living bringing the signals back and forth. They do not seek trouble. They do not cause trouble. They are like the air which carries the smoke signals of the Apaches. Yet these men have been killed again and again by the warriors of the Chiricahua. I am come to you to ask that you permit them to travel their way in safety.

"I have come alone. I come without presents. I have not brought the chief of the Chiricahuas tobacco or horses or blankets or clothing. I come only with a straight tongue to ask him to relent in his attacks upon these men."

"These signal carriers carry signals for the white men in the war against Apaches," Cochise replied.

The statement, uttered half as a question, surprised Jeffords. He began to understand something of the incisive mind of the Indian sitting opposite him. "No. Such signals are carried by the military in special ways. I know of that because I carried such messages."

"You say this of yourself?"

"I do not hide anything. I have come to you alone, to speak to you, with a straight tongue, as a man speaks to another man. During the war between the white men I carried signals for the military. That war is ended. I was a servant for my government. In a war a man has to take sides. He cannot sit and do nothing. The messages now carried by the men who work for me are messages of peace, between the white men and their brothers in other places. They are messages that do not act against the Indians."

Cochise was long in replying. His black eyes seemed to look at Jeffords from across a great distance. This distance was the difference between the two of them, Jeffords thought, and had to be crossed. He had to get to Cochise, where he was.

"You are a brave man to tell me of this," Cochise said at last. "You speak with a straight tongue, maybe."

"There is no fork in my tongue," Jeffords replied. "I have come to you not knowing whether I would return to my own people. The end of my time may be today or tomorrow. I have never spoken with a double tongue and I do not begin now."

"Why should I do anything to help the white man?" Cochise asked suddenly. His voice lost its iciness and seemed to become human. Jeffords felt a sudden glow of hope. "For many harvests I was their friend. I protected them against bad Indians. For my actions I received treachery. For the lives I saved I

259

was paid in death. I am not alone. Everywhere the treachery of the white man writes itself in death. It was so from the earliest days."

He spoke rapidly, so that Jeffords was hard put to follow him. He told story after story of the American's betrayal of the Indians. He started with the old story of Juan Jose and told of the Bascom affair and of the slaying of Mangas Coloradas. He told of the many times the white man had gathered the Indians together promising to make peace and then poisoned or shot them.

When he finished Jeffords replied, "You do not yet tell the whole story. There are other stories. You are right and just in your hatred. I could tell you as many more as you have already told me."

"You come to me and ask me to spare the lives of these white men."

"These men have caused you no harm."

"There are Indians who caused your people no harm and they were hunted like animals and killed. Do the white men try to find which Indians are good and which are bad?"

"No."

"You ask me to be better than the white men?"

"I ask you to be greater than the white men."

Cochise gazed at him in bewilderment. "You are a strange man and you ask strange favors."

"A man can give favors only according to his own size," Jeffords said.

Cochise stood up and walked out of the wickiup. Jeffords followed him until they stood on the edge of a cliff looking over the valley. "It is quiet here," Cochise said.

"Yes."

"It is a good place."

"Yes."

"This is the country of the Chiricahua Apaches. This is the country where the Chiricahua Apaches belong. The mountains and the valleys and the day and the night belong to the Chiricahua Apaches. It was so from the memory of the oldest man and that memory came from the oldest man ahead of him. There was nobody but Indians here and the land was filled with food and the Indians could make a living for themselves. The men with the steel came and tried to take it from us and we defeated them. The Mexicans came and we defeated them. Now the Americans and none is more treacherous than the Americans and none more arrogant. The Americans think they are better than any other men. They make their own laws and say those laws must be obeyed. Why?"

"You say nothing I have not myself said before," Jeffords said.

260

"I know your face," Cochise said. "We have fought against each other."

"I fought in the great battle of Apache Pass before the fort was built," Jeffords said calmly.

"The day the wagons that fire were used against us," Cochise said. "I remember the red beard. You were not a soldier. We would have won that fight until you turned the fire-wagons on us."

"I directed the use of the gun on wheels," Jeffords said.

Cochise stretched his arm and touched Jeffords' shoulder. There was an expression of serenity on the Indian's face. "Tagliato," he said, using the Apache word for redbeard, "I respect you."

Although the touch on his shoulder was light, Jeffords felt fire course through his body. He felt a great peace come over him. He knew without understanding how he knew that Cochise was a man of loneliness, and that the outstretched hand was a bridge to cross the abyss. Jeffords felt secure and very alive. "Men may touch each other," he said, trying to put it into words. "If they lift their heads and reach out, they may touch each other."

"Tagliato," Cochise said in a stirring voice, "we are friends."

"Yes."

"I will grant your request."

"Yes. We do not lie to each other."

"No."

"It will be a strange friendship," Jeffords said after several moments. "There are many things between it. My people will not understand and your people will not understand."

"I do not speak of people," Cochise said, his voice hardening slightly. "And you are not the same as your people."

"I do not think so, Cochise."

"We will speak the truth always and we will talk often and our talk will have nothing in it of anything else we may do. Your life is safe among my people always."

"I cannot promise you the same," Jeffords replied softly.

"I lead the Chiricahua Apaches," Cochise said ringingly.

"There will be a day when you may walk among my people in safety."

"There is no value in many persons," Cochise said. "Through his life a man is lucky if he finds a friend. For that one friend a man has more luck than he can have with hundreds of others."

It was night. The men sat wakefully through the hours and talked. They were still talking when it got light.

"How long do you rest among us?" Cochise asked.

"I find it good here."

"We will rest. The night has walked its way across the sky."

261

Jeffords threw himself on a pallet in one of Cochise's wick-iups. He felt that it was longer than a single night that he had been in the Chiricahua camp and longer than that that he had known its leader. Everyone found his sanctuary, he thought, and it went along with the other things of his life that it was his lot to find his in an Apache camp. He thought of the people he knew, before he fell asleep, of Terry and St. John and Duffield, of the others, of Carleton and Oury, and the names sounded in a foreign tongue in his mind as though they were people of a strange land.

3

In the late afternoon, after a long sleep, Cochise told him there was a ceremony to be held that night. "A young girl who came of age a long time ago was captured by the White Mountain Apaches and is now returned to her family and they are making a ceremony for her, one she should have received before. The people will have a good time through her."

"The puberty rite?" Jeffords asked.

Cochise looked at him intently. "One day, Tagliato," he said, "you will tell me where you learned so many things about us. This visit was not decided yesterday or the day before. It is the puberty rite. The girl is now eighteen and she is still a virgin and though it is many years late and not usual, a ceremony has been arranged for her. If she had no ceremony she would not be healthy nor live long. As long as she is not known of men it will be all right."

While they ate roast meat and corn cakes, Cochise told Jeffords the story about the girl. Her name was Sonseeahray, or Morning Star, and she was daughter to an uncle of Cochise's. Almost six years before, she had become a woman and her parents ordered the ceremony. While preparations were being made the girl was kidnaped and never heard from thereafter.

Recently a small party of White Mountain warriors joined Cochise in his war against the Americans and, as a gesture of good faith, the sub-chieftain who led the contingent into the Chiricahua ranks returned the girl to her people. The story she told was strange.

Soon after she was kidnaped, she related, the son of the chief of the White Mountain clan where she was held prisoner was bitten on the thigh by a snake. She had quickly opened the puncture and had sucked the venom dry. From then on she held a special position in the White Mountain clan. She was still a prisoner because to return her to the Chiricahuas would have constituted an apology, a loss of face the White Mountain warriors would not have tolerated. But she was not molested and she came to hold an almost religious status and she was loved and respected for her good ways. Upon her word not to attempt to escape she was permitted all freedom.

Her return to her family caused the greatest rejoicing. She was welcomed as one returned from the dead. When she informed her parents she was still virgin their happiness was even greater and so, at the age of eighteen, five or six years later than was normal, her parents had ordered a ceremony marking her emergence into womanhood, in the rite considered the most important event in the life of an Apache woman.

The preparations had been under way for several days. The ceremonial dress was made. Five buckskins were needed for the dress, two for the upper part and two for the skirt and the last for the high moccasins.

For two months while the costume was fashioned a woman learned in the ceremony of holy songs sang over the skins. The morning star, which was the symbol for which the girl was named, was set in the center of the outer blouse by a circular piece of pure silver and strips of silver radiated from it. Under the star there was a crescent moon made of white stone. A sun was depicted in red paint, and buckskin fringes, dangling in all directions, were the rays. There were colored arcs indicating rainbows and then the costume was painted yellow, the color of pollen, for fertility.

When the ceremony was ordered, Sonseeahray chose Tesalbestinay to be her attendant, presenting the wife of Cochise with an eagle feather. From this time on Sonseeahray would call Tesalbestinay mother and Tesalbestinay would call her daughter and they would be close to each other throughout their lives.

Cochise had ordered Nochalo, his chief shaman, to conduct the rite, and this double endorsement from the war leader of the tribe and its highest religious authority soothed the uneasiness of those who were concerned with the unusual aspects of this particular ceremony, the origin of which went back to White Painted Lady and Child of the Water and the beginning of things.

Tesalbestinay was busy with her duties for the ceremony so Cochise summoned Nalikadeya to explain the origin of it to Jeffords. In the beginning, she told him, a young girl began the flow that marked her entering womanhood, and to give her a good life White Painted Lady, the mother goddess, and her son, Child of the Water, conceived immaculately, directed that certain rituals be performed. The first child was identified with White Painted Lady and referred to by that name alone during the ceremony, and for the length of it was regarded as the earthly symbol of the deity; the costume designed for her was

263

copied from the clothing worn by White Painted Lady when she was on earth. And the ceremony was conducted in exactly the same manner from that time on.

The ceremony itself had started while Jeffords and Cochise slept. The girl washed her hair in yucca-root suds and went to the special wickiup erected for her and there was greeted by Tesalbestinay, who put pollen on her face for fertility, and then knelt and prayed for her. Then Tesalbestinay dressed the girl in ceremonial costume and while this was done Sonseeahray faced the sun and when she was dressed she was called White Painted Lady by Tesalbestinay and would continue to be so called by everyone until the ceremony was finished.

Sonseeahray stepped out of the wickiup and lifted her arms to the sun. The rite had greater meaning for her because it was performed, due to her unusual experience, at a time of her life when she was mature enough to comprehend its significance. Her face was radiant and serene as she assumed her role as the living goddess on earth.

She was a girl of more than medium height. Her face was shaped like a heart and her lips were full and rich. The years she had spent with the White Mountain people had left their mark: her beautiful lips were turned down at the corners, her eyes were somber and thoughtful, her voice was low and filled with restraint, and her movements were unhurried. The ancient costume, designed for a child of twelve or thirteen, covered her woman's figure with a strange grace. Her full breasts rose and fell under the decorated shirt in the intensity of her feelings.

"You are very beautiful, my daughter," Tesalbestinay said in a low voice. "Your body is straight and strong and your breasts are ripe and soft and your thighs are shapely and your legs are slender. You now are White Painted Lady and what comes to you from now until the ceremony is ended will be the measure of your life. The things that you feel now in your heart will mark your feelings henceforth. What you like now you will like until the end of your days. If you eat well now you shall always have plenty to eat. Watch carefully and study yourself for you now have the opportunity, for the first and last time, to know yourself and what lies within you, in your body and in your heart."

Sonseeahray held her hands together; her lips quivered. "Yes, my mother," she whispered.

"You must not speak overly much because then you will become a talkative woman. You must not laugh because then your face will become old and wrinkled before its time. You must not wash before the ceremony is ended because you are now the living White Painted Lady for your people and if you wash it will rain and if it rains and you get wet it will rain

264

harder and will spoil the good time of your people. You must not even look at a spring of water for then the rain clouds will gather."

"Yes, my mother."

"You must listen to what the singer tells you and believe him. If you do not believe in your heart what he says it will be of no benefit to you. You must not become angry or use bad language, for if you do, such will be your nature for the rest of your life."

Tesalbestinay placed her hands upon the girl's head and said, "Now I must ask you this: No man has entered you and made you unchaste?"

"No, my mother," the girl replied with a solemn ecstasy.

"You must speak the truth," Tesalbestinay said sternly. "If you lie the curse will strike you and your parents and the people of your tribe who give you this ceremony."

"No man has touched me."

"You are ready then," Tesalbestinay said.

In a clearing Nochalo supervised the raising of the ceremonial structure, singing,

"Killer of Enemies and White Painted Lady caused it to be,
They have caused the poles of this dwelling;
The blue stallion stands for long life."

When the poles were erected and the tips inclined until they met in a point at the top, Nochalo sang,

"This is the home of White Painted Woman,
Her home for the ceremony of long-life,
Her home for the ceremony of long-life,
So it was ordered by Killer of Enemies."

From the long cooking wickiup nearby, women emerged with clay trays filled with mesquite beans, boiled meats, yucca fruit, mescal, and other things. The food had been prepared in great plenty, as a compliment to the deities, to indicate they had provided well for their children, the Chiricahua People of the Woods.

Now Tesalbestinay came forward with Sonseeahray walking slowly behind her. Tesalbestinay lay the skin of a deer in a position to the southeast of the structure and the girl knelt on the skin and received a basket filled with ritual objects. Sonseeahray offered pollen to the directions and, after performing other details of the ceremony, entered the dwelling.

She was now entered into the holiest moments of her life. She was believed possessed of supernatural powers at this

265

time and the sick and the ailing of the tribe came to her in her virginal purity and sought relief. Other Indians began to eat of the food that was laid out and to sing and jump around joyfully.

It was into this gathering Cochise and Jeffords came. "Do you have a sickness?" Cochise asked.

"No," Jeffords replied.

"No old wounds?"

"Just two arrow wounds given to me by your braves."

"Where were you wounded, Tagliato?"

"On the side and in my right arm."

"An arm wound is bad. A man needs his arms to fight with. Go in and see the girl inside. I will go with you. I too have old wounds. From bullets."

In front of the dwelling there was a line of supplicants. The people moved back respectfully as Cochise and Jeffords walked up to the entrance to the conical structure. Inside it was cool and dim after the hot afternoon sun. The girl was seated on a leather pallet. Her eyes were away, as though she were viewing distant things.

"Give her your arm, Tagliato," Cochise said. "It has an old wound, White Painted Lady. Return to it its strength."

Jeffords slowly extended his right arm. Sonseeahray seemed to see him for the first time. She took his arm in her hands. She moved it to her breast and held it there, inclining her head over it. "Does it ache often?" she asked. Her voice was filled with pain.

"It will never ache again."

"It will never ache again," she repeated. She lifted her head and looked at him and slowly relinquished her hold on his arm. He watched her fingers open, one at a time, and then his arm was his again and he took it away.

"Do you hurt?" she asked.

He shook his head.

"You will live long." Her eyes closed slightly and she seemed almost in a trance. "The good things will be yours. The sun will shine for you and the rain will cool you and the nights will rest your weariness and your days will be as the stars, as bright and as many."

Then she turned to Cochise. Her face filled with adoration.

"You are the greatest leader your people has known, O Cochise. The wounds you have suffered have been many and each scar is a mark of love for those who follow you. Your judgment will be ever good and the path of your people is stretched long behind you and you are the head and you are the heart and you are the blood."

Cochise, his face a mask, leaned forward and she put her

266

arms around him and placed her head upon his chest. "Killer of Enemies is your father and you are his son."

She relaxed as though exhausted and Cochise rose and walked from the dwelling. Jeffords followed and his throat was as dry as though he had been long without water. He wondered if he would ever lose the feeling of his arm resting against her breast.

Inside the dwelling Sonseeahray remembered the words spoken by Tesalbestinay and she said in a dead voice, "White Painted Lady, whose name I bear, please help me. There have been strange things in my life and this is the strangest. When he goes back to his people he must not take any part of me with him."

When the sun began to set the men who were to serve as masked dancers walked off into the hills where a brush shelter had been erected for them. There they stripped and put on their ritual shirts and moccasins. Nochalo rolled a leaf of tobacco and puffed smoke to the directions and asked the dancers to face east. "The great Black Mountain Spirit resides inside Big Star Mountain," Nochalo said. "He can be seen to the east under the heavens. The design of his body is fixed and unchanging and the big stars have created the uprights of his headdress. The Mountain Spirit rattles his headdress as he dances around the fire and drives away diseases. He sends away all evil and brings good."

The dancers painted themselves and Nochalo continued,

"*The Holy Mountains,*
The Holy Mountains,
There it is and
In its middle, in its body,
There stands a brush-built hut.
This brush-built hut is for the Mountain Spirit.
This is what he says,
This is what the Mountain Spirit in his brush-built hut in
the Holy Mountain says,
'In these moccasins flash Lightning,
'I am Lightning flashing and blazing,
'There is life here, in this headdress,
'In the noise of its pendants there is life,
'The noise is heard and it sounds and my song is around
these dancers
'And protects them.'"

The dancers ate the special food prepared for them and then put on their masks. These were soft pliable helmets with drawstrings around the necks and two slits cut for eyeholes.

The hoods were painted in all colors. Built into them on top were strips of slats, pointing up vertically and at angles and bound together across their tops by other slats, the super-structure rising more than a foot above the dancers' heads. Hanging from the ends of the slats were loose pieces of wood which rattled loudly as the dancers moved.

Nochalo led the hooded men, who symbolized the good and evil Spirits, down to where the people were seated in a great circle around the ceremonial dwelling in which the girl was still seated. Just before the dancers reached the circle they sounded their ululating call and the people answered them with cries and prayers and then the dancers burst into view, leaping to incredible heights, twisting and contorting their bodies in the flickering firelight. The people shrieked in delib-erate fear and the masked figures catapulted themselves in gigantic leaps, their faceless heads giving them unworldly anonymity, the clatter of their head rattles making sounds from dark places.

Cochise sat next to Jeffords, directly to the east of the ceremonial dwelling. Jeffords responded effortlessly to the mass hypnotism of the chanting and the frenetic dancing. His blood beat with the drums. The Indians were lost in their own surrender and paid no attention to the stranger.

He shuddered in the violence of the assault on his ration-ality. The gyrations and weird intermingling of lights and shadows, of noise and silence, of grace and violence, fell upon him like blows.

The dancers worshiped the fire from the four directions, blowing away evil and sickness. From one side of the gathered people came a steady beating of drums and rattling of gourds. Then Nochalo began to sing, in a low, penetrating voice; his song had no rhyme and seemed composed of the moment, and yet it told of all the beliefs of the people, of the things they feared and held holy. Then he sang of the girl and told of her childhood, and he spoke of the sweetness of girl-hood, likening it to the first opening of the flowers under the sun. He led her through gardens of flowers in his song and through all the seasons. He told of the full cycle that was given to her, from the sprinkling of the pollen to the final fruition of nuts and fruits. He sang,

"To White Painted Lady I have come,
To her blessing I have come,
To her good fortune I have come,
To her long life and the grace of her days I have come.
This is the song of her long life,
This is the song of her life in the sun,
With this holy truth I have come to her."

268

At midnight the dancers left and when they disappeared into the blackness, the people began social dances and the songs were lighter and some of them were comic and referred to things that made the people laugh. Old love affairs were told by witty singers, old battles were recalled, old victories and defeats recounted. Throughout the night the people danced and sang and ate. They were tireless and their legs never faltered and their throats never became hoarse.

With the first rays of the morning sun the singing changed and became quieter and had a sadness. The girl stepped from the dwelling. It was her first appearance. She lifted her face to the morning sun and closed her eyes, and a single voice sang,

> "The girl is here and I see her again,
> And then I become with her, like this.
> I see her and she is my sweetheart,
> And then I become with her, like this.
> Maiden, speak softly to me, speak softly,
> I will never forget your voice,
> I will never forget the words,
> I will remember you always, always,
> Your words are as soft as falling rain,
> I shall surely remember your words, always."

The girl's face had in it an exhaustion that seemed not to be of life. She stood with her hands crossed on her breasts and the light filled her face. Then she returned sightlessly into her dwelling and the first night of the ceremony, which would last four nights in all, was ended. The people rose from the circle and walked slowly to their wickiups and the dancers drifted away and the drummers stopped their beating and there was silence and only the sounds of morning and the awakening of birds.

"I must return to my people," Jeffords said. "There is only so much a man may see at one time."

"You will come back. Your home is wherever I am," Cochise replied.

The two men rose. They were alone in the clearing. Jeffords looked at the ceremonial dwelling.

"I will order your horses and weapons," Cochise said. "And I will send two men with you so that no harm befalls you."

When Jeffords climbed into his saddle, Cochise said, "There is food in your saddlebag."

Jeffords leaned down and touched Cochise's shoulder.

"Return, Tagliato."

Jeffords rode slowly down from the mountain. He felt he was wakening from sleep.

4

After a while the escorts left him and he rode alone and waited for the moment of clarity. The whole episode must move into proper perspective. Soon Cochise had to lose his dynamism in his memory. Soon he would forget the exaltation of the girl. Soon everything would lessen in size.

He felt he was in a strange country. The mountains and desert took on the appearance of a landscape on the face of the moon. He thought suddenly it would be good for him to see something familiar. As the day wore on he got drunk on exhaustion. He felt he had to keep riding. He could not pause to rest. He had to put miles between him and the Apache rancheria and get back to his own people. He heard the sound of the drums in his ears keeping time with the clump of his horse's hooves. He heard the penetrating monotones of the songs.

It was midnight when he entered Tucson. He tied his horse in front of the Congress Hall. He drank three straight whiskies at the bar. A powerful lassitude came over him; he drank another whiskey. He felt that men were looking at him and he paid for the drinks and walked out. He walked to his room in the Scat Fly and fell on the bed without undressing and as soon as his face touched the pillow he was asleep.

It was fully noon when he opened his eyes. He swung his feet out of bed. His boots had been removed. He picked up the pitcher of water on the dresser and drank a great draught. He bent his head over the basin and poured the rest over him. He went downstairs. The dining room was filled. There were too many people there and too much talking. He went into the office. Mrs. Wilson was working on her books. "Well, you have come back," she said. "It's a wonder."

"How about some coffee?"

"There is a dining room."

"It's too noisy."

She looked at him with disapproval and rang a little bell. When a Mexican boy came into the room she told him to bring Captain Jeffords some breakfast.

"Not breakfast, just coffee," he said.

"You heard him," she said tartly. "Just coffee." When the boy left she said, "It is indeed a living wonder you are back here, Captain Jeffords. Gallivanting around with those crazy Indians. Nobody thought they would ever see you again, alive or dead."

"I'm sorry to be such a disappointment, ma'am."

"Never mind your sassy answers. A body has enough to

270

do around here without having to take time to worry about a no-account like you. I don't think that little girl has closed her eyes to sleep since you went away. You ought to be ashamed of yourself, Tom Jeffords, just riding roughshod over people's feelings that way."

The boy brought the coffee and Jeffords drank it hungrily. "Where is Terry?"

"She is at the market."

He finished the coffee and stood up.

"Where are you going?" Mrs. Wilson asked.

"To work."

"I thought you might be going to pay another visit to your Indian friends," Mrs. Wilson snapped.

He walked down the street to his office. Everything looked different, as though he had been away a long time. He saw Terry walking up the street. When she saw him she started to run. Then she slowed and walked to him. "Hello, Tom," she said.

"Hi, Terry." She was changed too.

"I came into your room this morning and pulled off your boots. I hope you don't mind." She looked tired.

"Thanks, Carrot."

"I don't have to say how relieved I am to see you back safely. Why do you do these things, Tom?"

"Somebody had to call off the wolves."

"Why do you, always you, have to do those things? No one else does things like that."

"Too many riders were being killed," he said, as though speaking to a child.

"Don't give me a reason like that. Not me. It isn't that."

"What was it then, Terry?"

"It's what's inside of you." When he smiled she said wearily, "Don't be charming with me. I haven't slept since you left. I can't take charm now."

"I am very sorry, Carrot."

The rims of her eyes were red. "Will you always keep doing things like this to me, Tom?"

He didn't answer.

"I am very happy to see that you are back and that you are alive." She looked at the ground. "How long do you think I can live if you keep doing these things? How often do you think I can stand times like these last few days?"

"I think you are taking this too hard."

"In the last two days Apaches attacked a wagon train just forty miles east of here and killed every person in it and another band of Apaches attacked Pete Kitchen's ranch and killed three men and a boy there and another band drove off fifty head of cattle from practically outside the walls here and another band fought a military patrol near Bowie and killed three soldiers. And you think I am taking it too hard."

She walked away abruptly. He looked after her and then he went on to the mail office.

"Terry told me this morning you were back," St. John said. "I'm glad to see you."

"I saw Cochise. He promised to let the mail riders go through."

"Tom." St. John pounded the desk. "How did you find Cochise?"

"All right."

"He is quite a man, is he not?"

Jeffords nodded.

"When you get around to it," St. John said, "I'd like to hear the details." He looked at Jeffords with understanding. "I believe you must have a great deal to straighten in your mind."

"Thanks, Silas," Jeffords said gratefully.

"We are ready with a load."

"Send it out."

He left early that day. He felt a sudden hunger. He went to the dining room. People at the tables looked at him curiously. He knew they were talking about him. He felt uncomfortable. He hated being conspicuous. He thought of how the Indians had acted. They must have been far more curious than these people. He wondered why the hell Americans couldn't have the good manners of Apaches. He ate a big meal alone and in silence and then went to the Congress Hall.

As soon as he entered the saloon he again felt the eyes and he could almost hear the discussions. The bartender looked at him strangely as he pushed a bottle of whiskey and a small glass toward him. He poured himself a drink and lifted the glass to his lips. A great clap on his shoulder made him choke on the drink.

"By God, Tom Jeffords," Duffield bellowed. "I'm the happiest man in this damned country to see you back. I want to buy you a drink and tell you you got more guts than a rattler's got rattles."

Jeffords wiped the spilled whiskey from his shirt.

"By God, any man who'd go alone to the camp of old Cochise is a man in my language and anybody that says different has Milt Duffield to answer to." Duffield, half drunk, glared around him belligerently. Nobody was inclined to contradict him. Instead the loud announcement broke the tension and drinkers clustered around Jeffords, asking questions together.

"What happened, Jeffords?"

"What was it like?"

272

"Old Cochise try to grab off your scalp?" This brought laughs.

Jeffords couldn't pay for his whiskey. That day every man was his friend and every man extolled his courage. Duffield ordered silence in a voice that must have echoed against the nearer mountains. "Seems as though everybody is doing the asking and nobody is giving this man a chance to do some answering. Now I say everybody close up and let the man speak."

There was instant silence. Jeffords shifted uneasily. He poured himself another drink and finished it quickly. "There's not much to tell."

"Don't hand out that," Duffield shouted. "You saw old Cochise?"

"Yes."

"What did he tell you?"

"The mail riders will no longer be attacked."

Murmuring rose in the room like the heavy ruffling of leaves in the wind. Even Duffield's furious facial contortions could not end the whispering. Jeffords had made the statement in a matter-of-fact voice, but when the words were past his lips he realized what implicit faith he had in Cochise's promise. He thought he should have kept silent and see what happened to the mail and then he knew that that was not necessary.

"So the old cutthroat promised immunity to the mail riders," a deep voice said. The body followed the voice and Jeffords looked into the face of Will Oury.

"That's what I said, Oury," Jeffords said, standing straighter.

"I want to listen," Oury said harshly.

"This is a public place."

"Cochise is going to make an exception for your riders?"

"Seems to me that was already said, Oury," Jeffords said. "Got any other questions?"

"Do you believe him?"

"Yes."

"Folks say you know Indians," Oury said sarcastically. "Did you ever know an Indian to keep his word?"

"No one you ever knew, Will," Jeffords said evenly.

"Would you like to back up that great faith you have in that lying murderer?" Oury asked.

"Sure, Will."

"Say a hundred bucks?"

"You have it."

"Cochise misses some of them," Oury said.

"Since I been running the mails there haven't been three

riders in a row to go through," Jeffords said. He poured another drink and emptied the glass. "The bet is that five men will leave here and five men arrive here without Indian trouble."

Oury pulled on his black beard. "You got a bet, Jeffords." Jeffords turned his back. He poured a drink again.

"That's a mighty risky wager," Duffield said.

"Do you think so?" Jeffords asked, lifting the glass. He was weary of the crowd around him and of the questions and talk.

"Chances are Cochise will forget his promise as soon as you got away. Chances are if he remembers, some of those crazy fighting men of his will not obey. If he keeps his own galoots in line, maybe there will be other Indians around who don't like white men."

A man walked up to Jeffords. He introduced himself. "My name is Jim Tevis. We met once or twice. If Cochise gave you his word your worries are over. I know Cochise. His word is like a bank bond. I ain't never known him to break it."

Jeffords nodded.

"How was it?" Tevis asked. Then he shook his head. "No, you can't answer that right off, like that. When you talk about him, you got to talk slow, and for a long time."

After a while Jeffords left. He felt he had to get somewhere where people did not stare at him. He went back to the Scat Fly and walked out to the terrace. He sat down and lit a cigar and he looked at the sky and he thought the same sky, the same stars, were over the camp and that this would be the third night of the ceremony and the Indians would be dancing and the drums would be sounding again and she would be sitting in her dwelling.

He heard footsteps. "Hello, Terry."

"I'm sorry about the way I acted this noon. I was distraught and tired and I didn't know what I was saying."

"I understand."

She sat next to him. "I *was* so worried about you and I *am* so happy to see you back safely."

"I'm rather pleased myself," he said.

"I'm sorry I made a scene."

He wondered what he could say to her.

"Tell me about it, Tom. It must have been very exciting."

He couldn't think of the right words.

"I guess you are the first white man in the world who ever visited old Cochise's camp and came out with your skin whole. Everybody is talking about you, Tom. It was terrible while you were gone but I am proud of you. Mr. Duffield said he never heard of anything like it. There were some military gentlemen in for dinner one night while you were gone and they were so flabbergasted when they heard where you were they could barely finish their meal." She giggled. "I would have thought it was funny at the time if I weren't so frightened."

"What did your friend Mr. Oury have to say?"

"Well, he was heard to say that you always did make friends out of Indians."

"Ah."

"Now tell me about it. Did you see a lot of Indians? Were they all painted up in their crazy colors?"

"Let's talk about it some other time."

"I understand some of their dances are quite wild. They are like animals, aren't they?"

"Another time, Terry."

"Are they as filthy as everybody says? Do they live in grass huts and act like beasts?"

He didn't answer.

"You do refuse to talk about it," she pouted. "But you must tell me the whole story one of these days."

"Yes." He could almost hear the chanting.

"Maybe you could write a story about it for one of the magazines back East."

When he closed his eyes he could see her as she stepped out of the dwelling.

"There is a *baile* this Friday evening. Will you take me to it?"

"Sure," he said.

"Mr. Ochoa got some new dresses in and I bought a beautiful one. Oh, I love to dance."

A sudden pain went through him. He liked her very much. "You're a sweet person, Carrot," he said tenderly.

The first rider reached Mesilla and the west-bound rider arrived in Tucson with a report of complete quiet on the trail. Jeffords sent out the next man. He too was unmolested and the second west-bound rider arrived safely. During the next few weeks the Apache attacks on other Americans continued at their usual rate. Troops reported Indians raided trains, ranches, farms, travelers everywhere. Reports from Mexico told of villages raided. A patrol of thirty infantrymen was attacked on the open plains by a large body of Indians led by Cochise himself and was soundly trounced. But the mail couriers remained untouched.

And in those weeks Jeffords found himself undergoing a profound change. The clear moment never came. He began to remember his time in the Apache camp no longer as a dream but as reality, and Tucson became the dream and the people, his own people, became the inhabitants of this dream, and as distant and unreal as dream figures are. He saw Tucson as a small noisy dirty place and the voices around him seemed raucous. He was an established celebrity now and was used as such. The arrival of each rider was hailed and there were many side-bets of the same nature as the wager he had made with Oury. The mail office became the town hangout. Ranchers came in from miles around to watch the outcome of the wager.

To all of these people Jeffords became aloof and inaccessible. He became more ingrown and he spoke less than ever. Of all the people St. John was closest to him and during those weeks the crippled assistant displayed a rare understanding and tact. Duffield stalked around the mail office, sometimes drunk, embarrassing him with compliments. He felt strangest of all to Terry; he felt in a peculiar way that he was being unfaithful to something they had between them. This angered him; there was no reason to feel that way, he thought. Nothing had happened that way in the Indian camp; still he felt wrong when he was with her and he hated himself for it and he disliked her for making him feel that way.

There was no place in Tucson where he could find repose. He rode out into the desert but now the desert too seemed a strange place and its emptiness was not one of peace.

The day the fifth rider left there was a great crowd in front of the mail office. Jeffords somehow now felt ashamed of the bet he had made with Oury; he felt as though he had in some way traded on Cochise's honor. The men, some of them already drunk, lounged around the office. Then, at twilight, someone shouted he saw dust in the distance, and then, later, the fifth rider entered Tucson. Duffield, who had appointed himself referee, yelled, "Any trouble on the road?"

"Quiet as hell," the rider announced.

"No Indians?"

"Nary a sign. That trail is so quiet I got plumb tired."

Duffield raised his huge arms. "If nobody has got no objections I will just announce the contest ended and say that Cochise has kept his word. Gentlemen, pay your bets!" He opened the door to the mail office. "Jeffords!" he bawled. When Jeffords came out, he said, "Looks like you won some money, son. Here's your fifth man, as safe and sound as though he was in the arms of his best gal. Safer, I guess, knowing who his best gal is."

Oury walked up to Jeffords. He handed him a small bag of gold. "I guess you still know your Indians," Oury said.

"What do you mean by that," Jeffords asked.

"You won the bet, didn't you? That makes you a greater authority on Indians than I am."

276

Jeffords tossed the pouch to Duffield. "The priest down the road needs some cash," he said. "Give this to him when you see him, will you, Milt?" He walked back into the office.

"Now there is a great man," Duffield said. "Think of all the liquor this'd buy and there he goes handing it over to God Almighty."

Jeffords sent for Juan. When the boy arrived, he said, "Find out where Cochise is camped now."

"Yes, *Nantan.*"

"You've been a good boy, Juan." Jeffords took down a shotgun from his rack. He handed it to the Apache youth.

Juan took it. His eyes shone. "Apaches are not liked to have weapons, *Nantan* Jeffords."

"If anybody says anything, tell them I gave it to you and to make any complaints to me," Jeffords said.

5

Jeffords rode toward the Stronghold. The East Stronghold, he thought. It was something that Cochise would have. The East Stronghold is very big, Juan had told him. The West Stronghold is small but it is better to fight from inside of it, he said.

Tahzay lifted his hand and pointed. Ahead Jeffords could see the great rock walls. "That is our home," Tahzay said. He tried to get the repressed quality of his father's voice into his own but he betrayed pride.

It was a place to be able to point to and call home, Jeffords thought. He followed slowly behind Cochise's son. He had sent up a signal from the valley and had received an answer to wait and soon Tahzay had come to lead him to his father and he understood the honor. He studied the youth to better comprehend Cochise. At twenty Tahzay was tall and he spoke with a quiet thoughtfulness that was impressive. He had little of Cochise's dynamism, Jeffords thought; Tahzay won respect, rather than devotion. Perhaps, Jeffords mused, nature arranged properly for these things. Perhaps when it would be time for Tahzay to assume leadership of the Chiricahua people it would be a time for Tahzay rather than Cochise. The fires slowly were being put out, he thought.

He thought suddenly of Terry and how she had reacted to his statement that he was going back to see Cochise. He had expected arguments, but, womanlike, he thought, she had confounded him again. She had told him she had expected he would soon be returning to the Indians and asked only that he take her. "I'll be very quiet," she had said, "please don't make new places where I can't follow." And when he told her he

277

could not take her she nodded as though she had expected that too.

As he rode up the long steep slope on the north side of the East Stronghold he again felt his nerves loosen and a restful lassitude came over him. He felt not that he was passing into another world but into another time. The great vertical rises of rocks with the scattered scrub oak and juniper jutting arrogantly against the steel sky were at once older and newer than now. He felt the rocks, not only on his eyes but within him; they had a demanding quality and he felt himself responding to them. He felt an excitement, a relaxed excitement, devoid entirely of tension. He had a strange feeling that he was coming home, that he was returning to his own after visiting with strange people.

Tahzay turned and smiled. It was a pale, almost fragile smile that gave light to his young serious face. He was conscious, too, of the honor of having been sent by his father to escort Jeffords to the camp. He led Jeffords into the heart of the rancheria in a little vale filled with trees. Here the wickiups were laid out in an orderly arrangement, not unlike an Army camp; the dwellings were sturdier and of a more permanent type. Indians moved quietly among them, working, talking, gambling, idling. They glanced at Jeffords but evinced no surprise.

He succumbed slowly to the mood of the camp when suddenly he realized that these cool, unhurried men were slayers and torturers. He looked at a tall, muscular warrior who was restringing a bow and wondered how many white men he had killed. Among these men were those who had shot at him, and he had the scars to show for it. Among these men were men kin to Apaches he himself had killed.

His presence among these Apaches seemed then a monstrous thing. His good feeling turned sour in his mouth and he thought of the word renegade.

Tahzay stopped at a wickiup somewhat larger than the others. He called out to his father and Cochise stepped out immediately. His face lighted when he saw Jeffords and he embraced him as he dismounted. Then he stepped back and looked at him keenly; his eyes moved rapidly over his face. "You are troubled," he said. He reentered his dwelling and seated himself. Jeffords squatted in front of him. He looked around the dwelling. It was more lavishly furnished than the wickiup in the Graham Mountains. Finally he looked at Cochise. The Indian's face was impassive. When Jeffords sat long in silence Cochise said, "You feel you are a traitor, Tagliato. It is not good to come as a friend to the camp of the enemies of your people."

Jeffords was startled. "Your eyes see deeply, Cochise," he

278

said. "I felt a cleanliness in me and a peace until I entered your rancheria."

Cochise nodded shrewdly. "Then you felt you should be killing Apaches instead of walking among them as friend."

"May a man put himself apart from his own?" Jeffords asked unhappily. He again felt the powerful attraction of Cochise's personality and his penetrating intelligence and yet his mind protested that it was wrong.

Now Cochise rose and walked from the wickiup. "Come," he said quietly. He walked to a huge boulder that rose a dozen feet from the ground and made a stone platform; in its side were niches, worn and chipped into footholds. Cochise climbed lightly to the top and Jeffords followed him more slowly. Below them lay the camp. Around them were the overpowering rocks. "How long do you think these rocks have stood, Tagliato?" Cochise asked.

"From the beginning. Or only since yesterday."

"They create a world," Cochise nodded. "They are filled with many things that live. There are trees that you can see. There are birds in the trees. Listen, Tagliato, you can hear them. Watch, you can see them. There are rabbits. There are squirrels. There are smaller things, insects, worms. There are snakes. And within the world made by the rocks there are men and women. All these living things have a time and then they are gone. To each his time is a lifetime and things are measured by this lifetime, things are longer and shorter depending on the lifetime. To the insect his brief time is a lifetime and one day or two days are long times. To the bird his time is longer. To the bird the life of an insect must be very short. The snake lives a longer time. And so it is. To men and women each of these other things has a short life. How is it then to the rocks, Tagliato? The rocks have looked upon many men and women and have seen them live and die as we see a dog live and die, or more, as we see a bird or an insect live in its small time. The rocks must think often that the reason for all these things is unimportant. The life of a man must be less to them than the life of a flea is to us. And each man takes on some of the knowledge of the rocks. Each man thinks that lesser things are of lesser importance. Each man thinks that the things that happened long ago are of less importance than the things that happened recently, or of even less importance than the things that have not yet happened. But men do not get to the final wisdom of the rocks, which know nothing of time, to which all things are equally meaningful and meaningless, whether they happened long ago or yesterday or will happen when the sun rises again."

Cochise seated himself. His eyes were burning. He spoke

with an even repetitiousness in his tone which gave his speech the cumulative effect of the beating of a drum.

"You have asked me whether a man may step apart from his own, whether a friendship may live between two men whose people war against each other. The answer is a double one and it is no answer at all, maybe. It is that it is possible and still not possible. It is possible because nothing that passes between people is important. Lift your eyes, Tagliato, and look around you. We are lost in time and lost in space and we are very small. What we do is of as much importance as what two ants arrange to do. How many men have sat here where we are sitting and what is left of them, and their arrangements and their thoughts? And yet, the other answer is right too, because a man is the limit of his kind. He can go no farther than his own manhood. It is only in knowing, in exchanging ideas and feelings, in counseling and receiving counsel, that a man may perhaps step beyond himself and gain the strength and wisdom of two men—which is a great move forward for a man, but which is still less than the strength and wisdom of the smallest and youngest stone you can see in that wall. A man moves toward his death, each day, each day, and his death is the final part of his life, the most important part, maybe, but with a friend at his side he moves with four eyes instead of two, with four legs and four arms, and, most importantly, with two hearts."

His voice took on a fire. An ascetic fervor dug lines into his face. Jeffords felt small and very young.

"There is nothing we do ourselves, Tagliato. I have found this out. Each man is driven. The things he thinks he does himself are done for him. Each man is like an arrow. The string is pulled back and at a certain moment it is released and the arrow goes in the direction it is pointed and although it seems to have a life it has no life and its movement comes from the string and its direction from him who pulls the string and presently the appearance of life vanishes and the arrow, which so shortly before has been flying through the air like a bird falls heavily to the ground and again is a piece of wood. Your people and my people kill each other, Tagliato. We are of that war. One day perhaps we shall try to kill each other." There was a ghost of a smile on his face. "If I die of a bullet I hope that it is your bullet. It is said that the bullet of a friend hurts more than the bullet of an enemy but I have never believed this. The life of a man is the most precious thing he owns, more valuable than a horse, maybe. It is better to give that life to a friend than to an enemy."

"I should not have asked," Jeffords said almost inaudibly.

"There are no questions that are better unasked," Cochise

answered quickly. "I am tired of what goes on inside my head. It is like a country I have seen too often. There are many things there that do not make me happy. Now I have your mind to look into. And you have mine. We must look into each other as though each of us were an unexplored land, filled with many new things. If we speak with a straight tongue your mind will be as though it were mine and mine as though it were yours."

When he finished Jeffords did not answer at once. He felt himself under the same compulsion he felt so strongly the first time. He did not know entirely whether Cochise had answered him but he wanted to believe he did. He lay flat on the rock and stared at the sky. He thought he had never felt such peace. The silence was without strain. The day lost itself. The sun lighted the east side of the Stronghold. The rocks caught the color and spread it so that there was a broad band of lambent flame stretching from one end of the canyon to the other. The trees became blurred in the endless refraction. "Do you think," he asked at last, "that the minds of other men may one day do the same?"

Cochise's manner changed abruptly. "I do not speak for other men," he said harshly.

Jeffords filled his pipe. He had asked the question almost aimlessly; now that it was answered he thought more on it.

"You have talent for silence," Cochise said. "That is more important than talent for speaking, maybe."

"People talk too much," Jeffords said, his teeth clamped on his pipe bit.

"Only those who speak only with their tongues."

After the evening meal the people gathered around the fires. Jeffords began to pick out faces he remembered from the other time. He met Nahilzay and when he looked into his eyes he felt his old warning flicker. In Nahilzay he read the first open animosity he had encountered in the tribe. The young warrior greeted him curtly and then walked away. Then Jeffords met Chee, a son of Mangas Coloradas, who was being raised by Cochise, and then a tall, lanky, incredibly ugly Indian named Teese, whose ugliness was matched only by his good nature. Teese was originally a kind of court jester for Mangas Coloradas and when Chee joined the Chiricahuas he followed the son of his dead chief. He soon established himself as the leading buffoon in the Chiricahua camp. His face was long and as flexible as a sponge. He attached himself to the person of Cochise and, carrying a long lance, with a single eagle feather drooping limply from it, he followed Cochise everywhere.

Upon meeting Jeffords, Teese reared as though the sight of the white man blinded him. He put his hands in front of his eyes as though he were shading them from the sun. Then, while the Indians laughed like children, he sprang back and forth like an ungainly dog, pretending the need to work up courage, and then he came close to Jeffords and touched his beard gingerly. He immediately pulled his fingers back and shook them in the air as though they were burned. The Indians roared. The pantomime was funny and Jeffords laughed with the rest. Jeffords picked up a water gourd and walked to Teese with a consoling expression on his face and poured cool water on the fingers Now the Indians shouted and looked upon Jeffords with new approval.

A great deal of tiswin was drunk and Jeffords discovered the brew was not unpleasant. Cochise said something to Tahzay and the youth disappeared, to return with a huge jug. Cochise offered it to Jeffords. He put it to his lips and then he felt sick. "What is this?" he gagged.

"Castor oil," Cochise said with satisfaction.

Jeffords picked up a gourd of tiswin and poured half of it into his throat. He refused more of the delicacy and watched the castor oil pass from mouth to mouth as the Indians drank it happily. "There are some things," Jeffords said to Cochise, "in which we will remain ever different. Castor oil, among us, is for ailing children."

After a good deal of tiswin was drunk the social dancing started. The women made a circle inside the men's circle and with their backs to the fire and their arms intertwined, they danced in stately rhythm, moving to and from the men. Following the rules the men pretended to ignore the women, whose dancing gradually became more and more animated, and who began to sing as they danced, accompanied by drums and guitars. The women suddenly broke their ranks and darted through the circle of seated men and roamed behind them. The men continued with their drinking, elaborately pretending nothing was happening. As the girls moved around they touched men lightly on the shoulders and then returned to their original places and reformed the circle, leaving space this time for the chosen men to fill in.

It was now a test for the men, for each man had to know who it was who tapped him. He must now rise and join the circle, going to the woman whose fingers brushed his shoulders. If he failed to go to the right woman it was considered a grievous insult and many family feuds had started from just such a failure. One thing only the men had to guide them: it was never their own wives who signaled to them; it was considered foolish to dance with your own wife.

Seated next to Cochise, a cheroot in his mouth, Jeffords had felt the fingers rest lightly for a moment on his neck. He rose

282

with the other men and walked around the circle of laughing, giggling girls, seeking out her face in the shadowy light and then he saw her glowing face and he moved into the open space at her right and he took her hand.

The men faced the fire. When the circle was completed the dance resumed, men and women facing opposite directions. It became wilder as the men, excited by the tiswin and the mark of favor shown by the women, stepped up the tempo and showed off their agility and skill. Jeffords, his hand holding hers, his other hand clutching the hand of another Indian girl, the tiswin rising to his head, his face breaking with sweat, thought suddenly of the formal *bailes* in Tucson and laughed out loud. She turned and looked at him, but when he turned his head toward her she looked away instantly. He looked at her profile in the flickering light. He thought again how Apaches must be a unique breed among Indians. There was nothing flat-nosed and Mongolian about them. Their noses were straight, the men's sharp and hawk-shaped, and the women with a purity of line that was almost Grecian.

As he jogged around he caught sight of Nahilzay, who had not been chosen, and who sat erect, his eyes blazing and his face fixed with hatred as he looked at Jeffords. Jeffords thought he would have to watch him; the narrow face and the close-set eyes were capable of anything.

The dancing continued. The widows and divorcees made love pacts. The young unmarried girls did not speak at all. The married women joked with their partners and flirted freely, because both sides knew the rules and there would be no misunderstanding. Young warriors who were as lions on the field of battle were shy and silent, although the selection by the young women indicated to them that future courtship would not be unfavored if they were so minded. When the dancing ended the time for story-telling began and the women retired to their own circle, outside the male circle, and the men resumed their seats and cooled off with fresh tiswin.

The dance-master ended the dancing officially, saying, "Let nobody walk off with each other now," as a warning to young people who made love pacts. To prevent them from wandering out to the brush the dance-master had stationed assistants at strategic places on the outer rim of the meeting ground. But not all lovers were kept from their destinations.

Cochise, his eyes dilated with drink, leaned over to Jeffords and asked, "Do you know of Coyote stories? You will hear them. Coyote is a great figure. He has a nature everybody understands. He is good at tricking other animals and people, too. And he is always getting fooled by those in whom he places too much trust. Coyote shows our pleasure in outwitting our enemies and he also shows how Indians may be fooled." Cochise placed his arm on Jeffords and smiled. "They are old, old stories."

It was Teese who told the first story. "Coyote tried to catch a turkey one day. Turkey was up a tree. Coyote tried to catch Turkey by chopping down the tree. Just as the tree was about to fall Turkey flew to another tree. Coyote chopped down the tree. Turkey flew to another tree. Finally Coyote was tired and collapsed and Turkey got away."

The women gave their shriek of applause and the men nodded gravely.

Then Nahilzay spoke. As he uttered his first words Jeffords knew that the story would in some way refer to him. "Coyote met a bumblebee one day," Nahilzay said raspingly. "Bumblebee had something in his hand. Coyote asked him, 'What do you have there, old man?' Bumblebee said, 'I don't want anybody to meddle with this.' Coyote pleaded with Bumblebee but Bumblebee said, 'This is not for you.' Coyote insisted and finally Bumblebee said, 'All right. But you cannot see it here. You must take it home and get your family to build you a new hut and cover the hut with skins so that nothing can get in or get out. Do not even leave an opening at the top. Then get inside and close the door and have rocks rolled up all around it so that you cannot get out and then open this package.' Coyote grabbed the package and raced home and did as he was told and when he was inside he opened the package and inside of it were many bumblebees and they started to sting him and he screamed for help but the bumblebees stung him to death."

During his recital Nahilzay kept his eyes on Jeffords. When he started to speak Cochise had the mouth of a jug of tiswin lifted; knowing the story, he slowly lowered it and listened quietly; when Nahilzay finished Cochise again lifted the gourd and his eyes were thoughtful.

"Coyote met a quail," Tahzay said in his pleasing voice. "Quail had all his family lined up in a straight row behind him. Coyote asked him, 'How did you ever get them in such a straight line? How pretty they look!' Quail said, 'I will tell you. This is what I did. I sharpened a stick and then I took a long rope and then I lined up my family. The mother was at the head and the children behind her. Then I pushed the stick through their hearts and pulled the rope through it. I did that to all of them and they walked that way for a while and then I took the rope out and now they stay in a straight line.' Coyote raced home and told his wife about it and ordered her to line up the family. Then he sharpened a stick and got a long rope and then he pierced the heart of his wife and after that the hearts of all his children and he drew the rope through

284

the holes he had made. When he finished he noticed his family was lying down and he said, 'Hey, it is not time to sleep yet, get up!' But when he looked closer at them he found they were dead."

The stories had been told many times before and each person listening followed the words of the narrator with his lips and could have told the story as well as he. The stories never lost their charm for them, however, and there were so many of them that there was always one that applied to some personal occurrence in each listener's life and at one time or another every Apache felt sure that one Coyote story was intended only for him.

Now Teese raised his hand. His face was screwed up in his enjoyment of the story he was about to tell. By now the young unmarried girls had gone to their wickiups. "Coyote found a white man taking care of goats," Teese said. "This man had a pretty wife and he lived a short distance from where he was watching his goats. Coyote said, 'My, those are pretty goats. Can I help you herd them?' The man shook his head and said, 'I have heard you are not to be trusted. You better go away!' But Coyote pleaded with the man and promised that he would take care of the goats and the white man, who was lazy, finally agreed and said, 'All right. But do not let them get in that mud over there. They will get all dirty.' So the white man went back to make love to his pretty wife. Coyote began to herd the goats. Finally he began to kill the goats and eat them. He cut off their heads and tails and stuck these into the mud and ate the rest. When he was finished he called the white man. When the white man stuck his head out of the door Coyote shouted, 'All the goats are stuck in the mud!' The white man ran over to the mud hole and Coyote said, 'I am sorry. I will help you get them out. We better use a shovel.' So Coyote ran back to the house and this is what he said to the pretty wife, 'Your husband said I must make love to you.' The wife said, 'He loves me too much for that.' 'All right,' Coyote said, 'I will prove it.' He opened the door and called to the white man, 'Your wife will not give me what you told me to tell her to give me.' The man shouted, 'Hurry, hurry, give it to him, give it to him quick!' Coyote turned to the wife and said, 'Well, you heard him, did you not?' And the wife said, 'All right,' and Coyote made love to her."

The men and women roared. Teese ran into the circle and did a few jig steps and then bowed and returned to his place.

"Coyote had some money," Chee said. "Just a few dollars, and he was walking along a road trying to figure out how to change those dollars into something more valuable. Then he saw some American prospectors. They had horses and mules and provisions and blankets and guns and plenty of ammunition. Coyote had a brilliant thought and he put his money up into the branches of a tree. When the Americans rode up they asked him what he was doing. 'I am watching this tree, it is very valuable,' Coyote said, 'Why is it valuable? What is in that tree?' the prospector asked. 'Money grows on this tree,' Coyote said. 'When I shake it money falls out.' The prospectors laughed at him so Coyote shook the tree a little and his dollars fell out. Now the men were very interested. 'Sell us that tree,' they said. 'No,' Coyote said, pretending not to want to. 'This is the only tree in the world that grows money.' The prospectors said, 'We will give you everything we have. Our horses and mules and everything else. We will just climb down and you can have everything.' Coyote still pretended not to want to and then he let the prospectors persuade him. 'All right,' he said finally, 'I will sell you the tree. There is only one thing. See those blue mountains over there? Well, you will have to wait until I get there. If you shake the tree before that nothing will come out and you will spoil it forever.' The prospectors agreed and Coyote jumped on one of the horses and rode away with everything. When he reached the blue-mountains the men shook the tree and only one dollar fell out. That was the last of the money that Coyote put in the tree."

Because it pointed up American avarice and the Indians identified themselves with Coyote this story was a great favorite. Now Nahilzay told the final story. His face was heavy with drinking and his eyes were inflamed.

"Coyote found some rabbits playing with their eyes under a high cliff," he said. "The rabbits tossed their eyes high into the air and then the eyes fell down and fell into their places again. 'That is a wonderful game,' Coyote said. 'Let me play it.' The rabbits said, 'Go away. You might lose your eyes.' But Coyote insisted and the rabbits took his eyes and threw them up into the air and they fell back into their places. 'That is enough for you. Now go away,' the rabbits said. But Coyote insisted, 'Let me play just once more.' So they threw his eyes up again and while the eyes were up in the air one of the rabbits said, 'Let the eyes stick to something and never come back.' And the eyes did not come back."

As the men left the fire Cochise said, "I have had a wickiup built for you alone, Tagliato. It is not far from mine."

"Nahilzay wishes to be an enemy," Jeffords said.

"You have no enemies while you are in this camp," Cochise said evenly.

"Let us fight it out and get it over with."

"You have no enemies in this camp," Cochise repeated. They walked to their dwellings. "He offered three horses and saddles to the parents of the girl," Cochise said.

Jeffords looked at him quickly.

286

"They were not accepted," Cochise said. "It was a handsome offering but they were not accepted."

Jeffords pursed his lips.

"She beckoned to you tonight, Tagliato."

"I understand."

"Nahilzay is full of fire. He has a head for fighting and for nothing else. But you have no enemies in my camp."

Jeffords entered the wickiup prepared for him. He pulled off his boots and lay down on the pallet. He lighted a cigar. He smoked it and thought of Nahilzay and his horses and he thought of the girl. He thought of how easily he had slipped into the complexities of life in the tribe.

6

He rose early in the morning. He walked to the stream and washed. The summer rains had been plentiful and there was a good flow of water. The water was very cold and splashed noisily against the little blue stones in the river bed and there was a new feeling in the air, as though it had never been breathed before, and the sycamores along the bank looked clean in their white skins and the branches curved over the stream and through them the sky looked very blue. He had slept well and he thought how good it was to wake in the open, to step from his sleep into a place with trees and water and the smell of the open. He thought how good it was to be alone when he first woke, to be able to get himself fully awakened alone. He disliked people in the morning more than any other time of the day and he thought walking into a dining room filled with people at breakfast time was unpleasant and wrong. As the day wore on he could get himself accustomed to people but in the morning he had no resistance. He took off his shirt and scooped up great handfuls of water and dumped them on his head. He rinsed his mouth and rubbed the cold water into his eyes. He listened to a squirrel chatter in an oak tree on the far bank. A second squirrel joined him. The voice of the newcomer was loud and domineering. Jeffords thought of Duffield.

When he finished washing he walked along the stream bank. The beauty of the canyon filled him. In the morning the east wall was shaded and it was the west wall that caught the light and the canyon seemed thrown in another direction. He thought of how truly Cochise fitted into his surroundings. He walked alone, silently, examining rocks, trees, shrubs. He found some manzanita still in blossom, although the flowerings were faded and white and had lost all their delicate pink color. He found bearspaw and greasewood and snakewood and saw the long slender spikes of the chilicothe plant. He tugged

287

on one stalk and cut his finger slightly as he knew he would. He thought of Tucson and the dusty streets and the noise and the people crowding everywhere and the constant talk, and he stood alone by the stream and breathed the clean mountain air. He wondered if there was a final right. What he was doing was right for him; he could not feel it so strongly if it were not.

He walked back to the camp and wandered among the wickiups. He looked with interest at the quiet steady work that was going on. Women were scraping skins, making gourds, sewing clothing, preparing food. Men were making arrows, new lances, refitting bow strings, cleaning guns. Even little children were working. The girls helped their mothers and the boys fashioned toy weapons.

Nobody noticed him. He felt calm and at ease.

When he returned to his own wickiup he found food. There were cold cakes made of mesquite beans and honey from the mescal and yucca stalks and a jelly made of algerita roots. There was fruit from the prickly-pear cactus. He sat down alone and ate everything that had been left for him. His appetite was enormous and the food was delicious.

Then he walked back to the river and stretched out and lighted his pipe. After a while he rose and started to walk along the bank in a direction opposite to the one he had taken earlier. He came to a curve in the stream and he saw her kneeling on a rock, washing. Her skirt was gathered high above her knees and was twisted and tucked in to keep it dry. Her legs were a golden color and they were wet and they shone in the sun. Her hair was drawn tight against her head and gathered together on the nape of her neck with the figure-of-eight device. He knew that the device proclaimed her marriageable status. Her hair was the color of the wings of a crow and as the sun rested on it there were deep blue shadows in it. Her full breasts filled her shirt as she leaned over the water and the tightly drawn skirt was taut on her curved flanks. He thought of a doe kneeling over water to drink. Then he felt ashamed at watching her unobserved and he turned to leave. His boot disturbed a pebble and it rolled down and splashed into the water and she looked up and saw him.

"Hello, red-bearded one," she said without surprise. Her voice was low and had the quality of a flute. He remembered thinking that the last time he had heard her speak he thought the richness of her voice had come from the ritual she was passing through.

"Are you washing?" he asked foolishly.

"Yes." She held up the wash gravely to show him.

"How are you called?"

"Sonseeahray."

"Morning Star," he said in English.

"What do you say?"

"I said your name in my own language."

"Say it again, redbeard."

"Morning Star."

She cocked her head slightly and her eyes danced. "Is it a pretty name in your language?"

"Yes."

She lowered her head and laughed. Her teeth were white against the even golden color of her skin. "It was a name given to me as a child."

"Do you still have your child's name?"

"When I was born there was a single star that could be seen, my mother told me. It was the morning star. There was one star and there was one me."

"It is a fitting name."

"And how are you called?"

"Tom."

She repeated it hesitantly. "Do I say it properly?"

"It never was said properly before."

She turned her head away and he felt she was withdrawing into herself. "I know that one does not speak so closely as quickly as I did," he said.

Her eyes sparkled. "Do you always speak so closely when you first know a girl?"

"I never did before."

"Why did you to me?" she asked guilelessly.

"I spoke what I felt. If it offended I am sorry."

She thought for a moment and then said, "It did not offend." She repeated his name again. He thought she made it sound like a musical note. "How do you speak our language so well?"

"I studied with an Apache boy."

"Why?"

"So that I could speak with Cochise."

"Why did you want to speak with Cochise?"

"I wanted him to stop his war on people who work for me."

"That is what they said. It did not seem possible."

"He stopped his war."

"You must have learned to speak the language very well." She smiled slightly. She started to rub the clothes with yucca suds. Then she looked up again and asked, "Why do you wear a beard?"

"I do not know."

"Among us it is considered foolish to have hair on the face."

"I know."

"Our men pick out the hairs one at a time." She giggled.

289

"Sometimes they hurt themselves but they go on, picking out each hair. Why do you wear hair on your face? Is it to hide something?"

"Maybe," he admitted.

"Is your face ugly under the hair?"

"I do not know. I think not too ugly."

"The hair is like a mask."

"Yes," he said. "That is it, maybe."

"It is like a mask the dancers wear."

He stroked his beard. "It never felt so strange on my face before now."

"Do you hide something?"

"I am not clever that way."

"One has to know you well to see you, I think. One has only your eyes. The rest of your face is always the same." She laughed again like a child. "And the color is so funny. It looks as though your face was on fire."

"I will cut it off, maybe."

She stopped laughing. "No," she said slowly. "Do not cut it off. This is the way I first knew you. I would have to find you again."

"I will leave it on."

"It might be hard to find you again." Her face reddened and she began to pound the clothes hard.

"You are very lovely," he said. He sat down beside her and filled his pipe. "Among ancient people there was a belief that beautiful young girls, half divine, came from the woods."

She became frightened. "You must not speak of supernatural things," she said. "It is unlucky."

"Such talk is not considered unlucky among us. There are many things I must learn."

"When you speak it is hard for me to believe that you are not one of us."

"Do I speak your language well?"

"Yes. It is only now and then that it sounds strange. And then the strangeness is only that of a different tribe. What do you do among your own people? It is said that with the Americans not all men are warriors."

He tried to explain what mail was and what he did with it. As he spoke she seemed to grow fearful. "Can all Americans speak to each other over long distances?"

"Almost all."

"It seems more than a human should be able to do. Does it not offend the *ghons?*"

"The Spirits are no more offended than by Apache smoke signals which also allow men to speak over great distances."

"Your *mail* must be like the writing on the rocks made by the ancient people."

"Yes. Little pictures are put on paper and whoever looks at the paper can understand what the pictures are saying."

She nodded her head slowly and then resumed her washing. He leaned back and smoked his pipe and watched her. She was as graceful as a young animal. Her eyes looked at him from time to time and they moved with the quickness and completeness of an animal. The whites of her eyes had a bluish tinge and the iris was dark and soft as velvet. Then she asked suddenly, "Why did you leave the ceremony after the first day?"

"You knew I left?"

"Nahilzay said it was because Americans think that Indian ways are childish and foolish."

He sat up. "It was not for that reason."

"Why did you leave?"

"I could see no more, nor listen more."

"Was it displeasing?"

"My eyes were filled and my ears were filled and my head was heavy with new thoughts. You must understand what I am saying. I felt I could stay no longer. Do you understand what I am trying to tell you?"

"I am not sure. I think I do, maybe."

"Only so much that is so different can be taken into a man's mind at one time," he said.

"Why did you take so long to return?"

"I returned as soon as I could."

"I thought you would come back sooner." She spoke quietly and with a child's innocence.

"Are you happy that I returned?"

"Yes, I must be happy."

"Must be."

"The things that a girl feels during the rite are the true things of her life," she said simply. "It was told to me by Tesalbestinay and she is the wife of Cochise and she is the wisest woman among us."

"What did you feel during the rite?"

"When you came into the dwelling I felt differently than I have ever felt when I saw a man," she said.

"How differently?"

"I do not know. With the others there has always been nothing. It was just as though a man was the same as a girl."

"And with me?"

She put the clothes down and looked away. Her eyes became pained. "I do not know," she said slowly.

"Please. It is important."

"It was funny, in a way. It was a tickling inside." She looked at him artlessly. "Is that not strange?"

He wanted to say her name but he could not. It was a lovely name, he thought, like something out of an old tale, but it also

291

was a self-conscious name for him to say and he was not free-speaking in these things. When she spoke to him he felt that he was finding a new purity of language, in which words went no further than themselves and had no associations and no implications. It was like the language that a child might use, literal and plain.

"Did it tickle you too?" she asked seriously.

"Yes," he said.

"Other girls have said they felt something like that but I never did before and I always thought they were making jokes."

"It was no joke." He turned on his side and looked at her. She was something that had emerged from the woods. If he reached out and touched it she would disappear. "Why did you return the horses to Nahilzay?"

Her face flushed. She dipped her finger in the stream and moved it idly back and forth. "You know of that?"

"Why did you return them?"

"I do not like him. His eyes are too close to his nose." She laughed nervously. "I will choose my own husband."

"Will not your parents choose him?"

"Apache parents do not choose husbands for their daughters," she said proudly. Then she asked, "Have you a wife?"

"No."

"Why not?"

"I do not know." Then he grinned. "American men choose their own wives."

"Is it true that Americans take only one wife?"

"Most of them."

"Are there some who take more?"

"Some take many wives, like Apaches."

"Are you of that kind?"

"No."

Her eyes flew across his face and then she lowered them again. "I do not believe in more than one wife for a man. One husband and one wife. I do not believe in sharing a husband with another."

"You have thought a great deal about it, have you not?"

"Most girls would rather be the second or third or fourth wife of some man. They say it would be less work. I do not believe that." She picked up her clothes suddenly and stood up. She was tall for an Apache girl, he thought, and as she stood there, very straight, like a sapling, he could see the curve of her breasts under her shirt and her thighs under her close-fitting skirt. He suddenly hated the figure-of-eight device in her hair. She looked down at him and he suddenly rose and faced her.

292

"Your face looks different to me. Do not girls among you pluck your eyebrows?"

"Yes."

"You have not."

"I do not like them that way." Her eyes twinkled. "You have hairs on your face. I do not want a naked face either." She reached out and touched his cheek lightly and then she walked quickly away. He looked at the place between the trees through which she disappeared and he thought the silence of the forest was beautiful to hear.

7

He found the men in the camp excited when he walked back. A rider had reported a great herd of deer on the plains toward the north end of Sulphur Spring Valley, a rare sight now, and the Indians immediately had organized a hunt. More than one hundred and fifty men had repaired to their wickiups to get their weapons and horses. Jeffords found Cochise and was asked whether he would like to join the hunt. He agreed willingly and said he would get his gun. Cochise shook his head. "No gun," he said. "Only arrows. Guns make too much noise. If we used guns there would be no game at all."

"I never shot an arrow in my life," Jeffords said.

"I will give you a bow and arrows," Cochise smiled. "You can begin learning now."

When Cochise gave him a long bow and quiver filled with arrows, Jeffords shook his head dubiously. "I could not hit the side of a mountain with these."

"Try a few shots," Cochise said.

Jeffords fitted an arrow clumsily on the bow and then he looked around for something to shoot at. A number of Indians collected to watch him. Teese, with a grimace, fastened a piece of red flannel to a tree a hundred feet away. Then he scurried off, holding his head. Jeffords aimed carefully and released the arrow. It described a high parabola and drifted far to the left of the red flannel. The Indians slapped their thighs in glee and Jeffords grinned. He tried again. The arrow came no closer to the target.

"Perhaps the American should start an arm's length from the target," Nahilzay said with noisy sarcasm. Jeffords looked up. Nahilzay was regarding him with amused contempt. Jeffords tried again. With his fourth arrow he managed to hit the tree from which the flannel was dangling. "I think I will just go along for the ride," he said to Cochise.

Nahilzay walked up to where Jeffords stood. Then, so swiftly that the movement of his right arm could hardly be seen, he reached over his shoulder and took an arrow from the quiver, fitted it to the bow, loosed it, and before the arrow had struck dead in the center of the flannel, he had a second on its way, and then a third and fourth and a fifth. There was no pause in his actions and he moved with beautiful grace and when he was finished there were five arrows pinning the flannel against the tree.

By now the women were standing around. Jeffords saw Son-seeahray and saw distress on her face. Nahilzay walked indolently to the tree and extracted the arrows. The women cried, "Yieaaah, Yieaaah," and the men nodded gravely and then looked at Jeffords and he read an important question on their faces.

There was a queer tension in the air. Jeffords understood that it had worked out so that he was on trial. What started out to be funny, his clumsy, inexperienced attempts to shoot arrows, had been challenged in a serious way by Nahilzay. The next move was up to him. Nahilzay, his arrows returned to their quiver, was walking back toward him, his long, narrow face drawn in a sneer. The Indians waited. Even Cochise made no move. Jeffords knew that he had quite suddenly and unexpectedly come to a point in his relationship with the tribe, and that what he did now, or failed to do, would from then on be the basis on which he would be judged.

He went to his wickiup and buckled on his cartridge belt. He picked up his shotgun. He returned to the Indians. He walked out to the center of the circle of people. He took a silver dollar from his pocket and rubbed it on both sides against his pants until it shone. Then he tossed it up into the air once or twice and the sunlight reflected brightly on it. Then he hurled it into the air again and with almost the same movement pulled his revolver from its holster and fired and the coin rang silverly and when it fell to the ground a child ran to it and picked it up. It was twisted out of shape. The child looked at it curiously and then brought it to Jeffords. Jeffords, without glancing at the coin, tossed it to Nahilzay who caught it involuntarily, and then, recovering himself, threw it on the ground.

Teese ran over to Jeffords and hugged him. Jeffords offered him a cigar. Teese thanked him volubly and Jeffords struck a match and held it to the end of the cigar. "Now walk down to the tree," Jeffords said. Teese puffed out a mouthful of smoke and looked at Jeffords with a puzzled expression. "As a favor to me," Jeffords said. Teese walked slowly to the tree, still not understanding. "Turn sideways and leave the cigar in your mouth," Jeffords said.

Now Teese comprehended and he put up his long arms in protest and contorted his face painfully around the cigar. Cochise said something sternly and Teese stopped clowning. He stood so his profile faced Jeffords and the long cigar stuck out from his face and then Jeffords dropped his hand to the butt of his gun and without taking the revolver from its holster he fired and the cigar clipped off in the middle and fell away leaving a small shattered stump in Teese's mouth.

The women screamed and slapped their hands together and the men seemed to relax; it was as though they had been afraid Jeffords could not meet the challenge. Then Jeffords looked up into the sky and presently he saw a hawk circling lazily and when the hawk came within range he lifted the shotgun and fired and the bird made another half circle and Jeffords held his breath and then the hawk plummeted to the ground.

While the people were still watching the downward course of the dead hawk Jeffords returned to his wickiup and put down his guns. He returned and picked up the bow and quiver and walked to Nahilzay. The Indian stiffened as he approached him and the people leaned forward slightly. "Perhaps you will teach me to use this," Jeffords said evenly.

Nahilzay's eyes were shot with hatred. "Each man to his own, white man."

Jeffords picked up the twisted silver dollar. "Would you like to keep this? To keep your memory fresh?"

The two men faced each other silently and then Nahilzay strode off without answer. "Get on your horses," Cochise called out. "We leave for the hunt."

There was no sign of either approval or disapproval on Cochise's face. The other Indians walked to their horses. Jeffords climbed on his own. He felt he had passed his test.

The men rode down the two miles of the canyon and entered Sulphur Spring Valley. At the threshold of the valley the scout who had brought the first information about the deer pointed the direction to be taken. The men started again and rode for several miles and then, at a signal from Cochise, broke into two parties, half the men in each, and the first group, led by Cochise, rode about a quarter of a mile ahead of the other.

They spread out so that each rider was fifty yards from the man on either side of him, and the two distended lines of horsemen, riding abreast, one in front of the other, continued to advance until the herd of deer was seen a half a mile distant. The first line of men raced ahead, the ends of the line moving faster than the center, making the line into a huge U, and then sweeping around the deer in a great circle, the two ends finally meeting and closing on the far side of the deer. The second line of riders closed in a circle outside the first circle, so that when they were finished the deer were surrounded by two circles, one within the other, the deer in the center. The Indians had ridden silently but once the second circle was closed they began to scream and the deer milled around frantically in panic. The riders closed in and the space between each man compressed. No animal could pass out of the inner circle without coming within range of one frenzied hunter or another, and if, by some miracle, the animal succeeded in getting through the first line, men waiting in the outer circle picked it off with ease.

The Indians shrieked ecstatically as they fired arrow after arrow. The animals tumbled in scores, some of them with three or four or more of the long, heavy hunting shafts buried in them; the hunting arrows were heavier and more weightedly tipped than battle arrows and the impact of one of them was as great as that of a rifle ball. Jeffords, caught in the excitement, succeeded by luck in hitting two of the deer. When the hunt was ended there were more than one hundred dead animals lying on the grassy floor of the valley and the men collected, dripping with sweat, and congratulated each other.

Cochise left a score of men to gather the animals together and guard them and the hunters started back for the Stronghold. Cleaning the animals and bringing them into camp was women's work.

The men talked and sang happily as they rode back. There would be plenty of fresh meat for many nights to come. They began to tell stories of other hunts and of this one, and boasted of their skill. Tahzay told a story that illustrated the hunting etiquette observed by the Chiricahuas. When a Chiricahua killed an animal and a less successful man came up to him, the fortunate huntsman was required to offer his kill to the other man, asking only "what you don't need leave for me." Since the hide was the most important part of the animal the man who made the kill had to offer it to his partner, if the partner wanted it. This courtesy was so rigidly adhered to that a man who killed an animal while in the company of another man was said, in the Apache phrase, to "kill it for his friend."

This was the story Tahzay told. Two men were out hunting together. Both were excellent shots and they came upon a big deer, so close, that neither one could have missed it if he tried. "Each of these men," said Tahzay, "tried to make the other one shoot the deer so he could have the skin. They made many excuses of all kinds. One man said, 'I have shot many for you. You kill this deer. I need the hide.' While they were arguing the deer ran away and neither one got it."

The hunters laughed loudly. Tahzay looked at his father for approval. Cochise nodded slightly and Tahzay smiled happily. He could not overcome his awe for his father and he was proud when Cochise was pleased at anything he said.

296

"How did you like the hunt?" Cochise asked Jeffords.

"It was good."

"We will go together one day."

"I will get plenty of hides," Jeffords laughed.

"We will put on deer masks."

"Deer masks?"

"We will join the deer. Ho, they are surprised when they find two of the deer among them are men."

"You mean you can mingle with the deer?"

"You will see, Tagliato. There are many things I will teach you."

"I believe you," Jeffords said sincerely.

"I will teach you to use the bow and arrow. You need no teaching in the use of your own weapons." This was the first reference Cochise had made to the incident. "Nahilzay is a good man in war. There is none braver. His head is not good for quiet."

"I am sorry that he regards me as enemy," Jeffords said soberly.

"Tagliato."

"Yes?"

"When you are among us you are as one of us. Nahilzay is another arm in battle and he is loyal. But no man among us has to have his manhood pushed against and remain silent. Do you understand? No man is required to be less than the man he is. Manliness is the proudest thing a man owns. That manliness, if he is a full man, includes wisdom and understanding as well. It is difficult to be vengeful if you understand. That is not always true for one who leads his people because he must then substitute the understanding for his people for the understanding for himself. But if one does not have this responsibility he may make judgments entirely on the basis of himself and with that understanding and with his own degree of courage, a man makes his decisions."

"There is no need to go on," Jeffords said.

"Good." After a while Cochise said, "There are always two persons in a man, one who acts and one who watches. It is not what one does before others that is important, but what he does before himself."

"I do not kill easily."

"Because you have shown how easy it is for you to kill. What you did today was necessary and I am happy that you did it. You served a warning. It was done in the open. Now you have nothing to prove. May it be that it will pass over peacefully. I have gained a friend. I do not want to lose him. I do not want to lose my war lieutenant, either."

Cochise lapsed into silence and his face was grave. As he rode by his side Jeffords realized that he had been given permission to kill Nahilzay if it were necessary without fearing reprisal.

The women hastened out with pack mules and several hours later began to straggle back with the game. Jeffords watched Tesalbestinay and Nalikadeya with interest. He had the curious thought that Tesalbestinay reminded him somehow of Mrs. Wilson and he smiled to himself and wondered how either woman would react to the suggestion. Nalikadeya was pregnant and she moved slowly and proudly. Even among Apaches, he thought, each woman thinks she is carrying the first baby ever to be brought into the world.

Tesalbestinay quickly skinned their allotment of game and gave the skins to Nalikadeya. Then Tesalbestinay expertly cut off what meat would be consumed that night and jerked the rest of it. She cut the thick parts into thin strips and hung them in the sun to dry. After the strips were dried she pounded them with stones and when they were soft and very thin she buried them in a cool cache. She discarded the hearts, because it was considered bad to eat heart. She gave the brains to Nalikadeya.

Nalikadeya scraped off the remaining flesh on the skins with a sharpened deer bone and then put the skins in a basin shaped from a stiffened hide.

"How long does it soak there?" Jeffords asked.

"For three days. Not longer or it would spoil." Now she procured some skins which had already been soaked and which had been pegged into the ground and stretched in the sun. She brought these skins to another leather basin. Into this basin she put the brains given to her by Tesalbestinay and she worked the brains in hot water until they were malleable. She put the sun-dried skins into the solution and worked them until they were soft. When they were almost dry she removed them and by holding one end on the ground with her feet, she pulled and stretched them.

Jeffords offered to help her but she refused with a smile, and then Tesalbestinay looked up and said seriously, although there was a hint of laughter in her eyes, "Occupy yourself with something else, Tagliato. Take the bow and arrow and practice. Maybe in a little while you can go out as a novice."

Jeffords laughed and scratched his beard. Tesalbestinay laughed with him, and then she stopped. "Be careful," she said. "Arrows make no sound." She got up and walked over to him. "You have made a change here," she said. "I have given thanks for it. He drinks with a different mouth since you have come here." She paused. "For a long time he has had Ghost sickness. Sometimes I thought it would break out of his head. He has no thoughts I do not know. He tried to do a very great thing in the beginning and he was not allowed to go on with it. I thought it was dead inside of him and only now do I think that one day it may again come alive."

"I have thought of this, too," he said.

"My brother was Mangas Coloradas," she said proudly. "There is no reason for me to love your kind. But wisdom does not need love. What he was trying to do before was right. With you he will try to do it again, maybe."

"It will take a very long time," he said softly.

"It will take patience. But it has started, maybe, and you have done that. He has stopped dying the other way and now dies no more than others."

"To try to change him is to try to reshape a steel blade."

"It will not be a change," she said earnestly. "He was that way before. It will be bringing him to himself again. Do not try to hurry it. It would be worse than anything to try too soon and to end thus the chance for all time. You love him, Tagliato. I can see that. I love you for it. But do not hurry. There are many things, many persons, all of them involved. Go slowly and learn everything and when the time comes, even though it is a long while from now, you will be able to do it."

"I hope so," he said.

"You came here for a purpose," she said. "He believes that all things are planned. One day you can make him understand that peace with your people also is planned, and when he permits himself to believe that again, he will welcome it."

In the morning he sought out Cochise and asked him where he might find Sonseeahray.

"How is it between you and her?" Cochise asked.

"In what way?"

"There are many widows here, and other women whose men have walked away from them. They have knowledge of men."

"It is not that way," Jeffords replied.

"Good. You know how it is with young girls here?"

"I said it is not that way."

Cochise directed him to her family dwelling and he found her working on hides. Her eyes lighted when she saw him and the corners of her mouth lowered. "You are leaving again," she said.

"Let us walk to the stream."

She put down the skin and followed him. "When will you return?"

"As soon as I can." He took her hand and it was trembling. "It will not be so long this time."

"It will be long enough," she said unhappily.

299

"No longer than for me."

"You do not just speak?"

"No," he said gently. "There is truth between us." He sat down before the flowing water. "I would like to tell you how it is with me. How it is to be here, among all of you, with you. I am not good with words in my own language and less so in yours. I know what I would like to say but it would come out wrong."

"Words can be used by anyone," she said.

"I will say this: I feel as though I am leaving my own and going forth to strangers."

"You are not different from us," she said fervently. "I was afraid you would be very different. Come back quickly. I am alone without you now."

He lifted her hand and kissed her palm.

"What is that that you are doing?" she asked nervously. "I felt the feather tickling me again when your lips were on my hand, stronger than ever before."

Her lips were parted and slightly moist. He kissed her on the lips. They remained parted against his own. He stroked her hair and kissed her again without response.

"I am frightened," she said. "There is a fire within me. What is it that you do with your lips?"

"I am saying goodbye," he whispered. "Stay here until I am gone and when I come back to your camp I will find you here and it will be as though I have never gone."

She touched his lips with her fingers. "I do not feel the feather now," she said wonderingly. She lifted her face and touched his lips with her own again. He put his arms around her and held her tightly. She shuddered against him like a frightened animal. "I feel it now," she said.

Chapter Fifteen

The morning after Jeffords returned again to Tucson, he and St. John walked to work through streets filled with soldiers.

"Ever since they moved the military headquarters here from Prescott I keep thinking we are living in some kind of an Army camp," Jeffords said. "There are half a dozen soldiers for every civilian."

"And each soldier looks like a bright shining piece of gold to the Ring," St. John said. "I wonder how those people would survive if we really stopped having Indian trouble and they removed the military. I think maybe they'd import some more Indians from somewhere."

"It's in the nature of a government to play sucker," Jeffords said.

"Cynical and true," St. John nodded. "But this goes a little further than anything I've ever heard of. They are selling grain to the quartermaster at exactly five times what anybody else can buy it on the open market. The paymaster is like a Santa Claus. When he passes through there is gold. After he's gone we go back to script. I think if the Indians ever actually made peace Tucson would go bankrupt."

"Don't worry about that," Jeffords said. "That crew would never permit an Indian peace."

A rancher trotted down the dusty street. He waved to Jeffords and Jeffords lifted his hand. "Look at his saddle. I can count three Indian scalps. It's one of the amusing things about this crazy place. Of all Indians Apaches don't scalp. Out here it is the Americans who do the scalping."

"How did things go this time?" St. John asked.

"All right."

They entered their office. Jeffords sat down and bit off the end of a cigar. "How did they go at this end?"

"Quietly. Too quietly."

Jeffords looked up. "How do you mean, too quietly?"

"You know this town. People are being killed right and left but the mail riders are going through. Some people don't like it."

"I was waiting for that to start," Jeffords said.

A week later the town rocked with the news of the latest raid led by Cochise. Fort Buchanan, burned at the beginning of the Civil War, had been recently rebuilt. Cochise had waited patiently until the fort was reoccupied and fully garrisoned. And then he attacked the fort, drove out the soldiers, burned the buildings again, and escaped with all the supplies. After this feat, which soon was talked about from one end of the territory to the other, Cochise was first called the Red Napoleon, and although white men hated to dignify him with that title, the name stayed.

Wherever Jeffords went he found himself the center of discussions about the Apaches. His opinion was asked; he was questioned by civilians and officers. When he entered a saloon he was surrounded immediately. At mealtimes in the Scat Fly questions were hurled at him from all parts of the room. Men stopped him in the street and came into his office. The attitudes varied. Some regarded him as a brave man. Others looked upon him suspiciously and talked darkly about his relations with Cochise.

He was naturally disinclined to play the part of public figure, and, additionally, he was confused as to how he should move

301

next on his own plan. He began to avoid places where people gathered. He spent more and more time locked in his office, drinking alone, deep in clouds of smoke, trying to figure out what to do.

His goal was manifest. Sometime, in some way, he would try to end the war between Cochise and the United States. That was what it amounted to now, he thought, a full-scale war, as deadly and bitter, although on smaller pattern, as any war the United States had entered. Campaigns against Cochise now were being planned by staff officers exactly as they had made plans in the Civil War just ended. And Cochise demonstrated himself increasingly as a scientist in desert and mountain fighting. He met companies of soldiers wherever they were sent out, and he had the genius to force the fight at his own time and his own place, and while he lost men in battle he was also almost invariably successful.

This war must be brought to a close, he thought. He was not a professional patriot; he had been too close, too often, with the men who represented his country and he did not think highly of many of them. But he knew, although his nature would not put this thought into an orderly sentence, that he had a duty, as an American, to capitalize on his unique friendship with Cochise.

How he would do it was another matter. It had to be with honor for Cochise, first of all. He would do nothing to betray him. Since he would be underwriting the peace as far as Cochise was concerned, he had to trust fully the representative of the government. Cochise could not be turned over to some of the men who controlled Tucson, or even Arizona. The spokesmen of the territory were calling for utter extermination of the Apaches. No session of the territorial legislature had yet been held without issuing proclamations to that effect. At that very moment Governor McCormick was in San Francisco pleading with military officials to send more soldiers to the territory for the Indian wars, and Goodwin, the former governor, now a delegate in Washington, was asking for the same thing in the federal capital. The leaders in Arizona had a faithless record in their handling of the Indians and if Cochise were surrendered to them no amount of pledges might save him.

No, it would have to be a treaty with honor on both sides. And Jeffords had no doubt that whatever promises Cochise made would be kept. The American representative could do no less and even if some of the lesser authorities in Arizona might be trusted the orders they received from Washington would, in the end, be what counted. As for Cochise, he would take a long time to persuade, but once persuaded, he would keep his word.

It would take a long time. It would take care. It would require a miraculous juncture of the proper people and the proper time. And until it would be worked, he would have to keep his plans to himself. Premature revelation might ruin the project. He wanted nobody's interference and he had to do it his own way and if he failed no one would be wiser. He was not made to act in public. In the end he might be able to do what nobody else had been able to do.

The mail riders continued to bear charmed lives. Their orders were to get the mail through and keep out of any trouble they saw. And they might have been invisible, or creatures of another planet. Everywhere around them white men and Indians fought and they passed through untouched. And, as St. John had said, the citizens who were at first grateful soon altered their attitude. They could not understand why an Apache would give protection for nothing. Rumors started that Jeffords was secretly supplying Cochise with weapons, ammunition, liquor. The rumors spread although, with the simple economic conditions that obtained in Tucson at that time, the charge could very easily have been either proved or disproved. The gossipers did not explain how a man could get a shipment of weapons in any large quantity in that isolated community without somebody actually knowing about it.

From feeling an honest admiration for his feat of riding into the Indian camp, the citizens changed in their confusion and looked upon Jeffords with distrust and suspicion. The members of the notorious Tucson Ring who were making fortunes selling supplies to the Army at fabulous prices nurtured and encouraged these rumors. The possibility that the citizens might come to believe an Indian possessed honor kept them awake nights. Such beliefs, the Ring shuddered to think, might have got people thinking along the wrong lines, might even have got them to think perhaps a peace could be made.

No one brought his suspicions to Jeffords direct. His handiness with his guns was too well known and the accuracy of his shooting was already something of a legend. But they got to his ears anyway. His first thought was to quit the job and tell the good citizens of Tucson to go to hell. He exploded one afternoon in his office, and when he finished cursing St. John got out his bottle and poured him a drink. "Get rid of it all," he said. "It will do you good. You've been walking around here capped up for weeks."

"I'm not making a dime out of this job," Jeffords said in cold fury. "All over this damned country there is gold and silver waiting for a man to come and pick it up. Why am I putting up with this nonsense?"

"You are getting the mails through."

Jeffords snorted. "So people can write letters telling how I'm turning renegade?"

"It doesn't matter what they write. You have been able to accomplish what no man in Arizona has been able to do before you. You have saved lives and you are doing your job."

"Oh, Christ." He poured another drink.

"You are working for the United States Government," St. John said earnestly. "You are keeping this part of your country in communication with the rest of the country. Without you we become isolated again. Men get killed. Mail is destroyed. We are fighting a kind of war here. It is our own kind of war. It belongs to us, in a very special way." He leaned forward in his intensity.

"If this is what happens when they think I saw Cochise just once, what in God's name would they say if they knew I had gone to see him again, and probably will again?"

"No one must ever know that you continue to visit Cochise. They can suspect what they please but they must never know for sure."

"My seeing Cochise is my own damned business."

"If it interferes with your getting the mail through it is not your business. When you first took this job it was your business. You could have quit any time you wanted to. But then you got yourself into something. You went up to see Cochise and there you stopped being your own boss. Just so long as you and you alone can keep Cochise from attacking mail riders you are not responsible to yourself. You are responsible to the United States, and the United States is a little bigger than some of its representatives here." St. John relaxed. "You know it all better than I am telling it to you."

Jeffords smiled faintly. "You are too god-damned clever, St. John." His blue eyes were very bright and he decided he wanted to tell St. John the whole story. "It goes further than you think," he said. It was unnatural for him to confide in this manner and he spoke slowly, and when he was finished St. John's face was filled with wonder.

"And you let me go on about your duty," he said. He got up and began to pace up and down the office. "My God, what that will do to this country out here. If Cochise stops fighting the rest will be simple. The other Indians will stop too. They follow his lead. He is a symbol of their resistance. With him at peace this whole country will become peaceful."

"It's a long road," Jeffords said.

"It may take years. Five years. Ten years. But what are ten years to the future of this part of our country. It would be worth waiting five times that to bring Arizona into its own."

"For some of the characters who are here now?" Jeffords asked sarcastically.

"No," St. John said, "for ordinary Americans. Not the gun-toting hombres, not the tough boys and the killers—not that some of them aren't all right, you know that as well as I do; this country would never have been settled, we never would have spread out from the East if it weren't for some of the pioneers like the pioneers in Arizona—but I mean the ordinary citizens. The little farmers and business men. The ones who wouldn't know one end of a gun from the other. This thing started with the mails but it will be bigger than the mails. It will be as big as this whole territory."

"I haven't told anybody else about this," Jeffords said. "I don't intend to."

"It has to be kept quiet or it will get back to Cochise and he may not understand it."

"I'm no damned Judas sheep," Jeffords said, "not even for the government. I won't lift a finger until I'm sure that the right man is sitting opposite Cochise. They are not sending that breed of man from Washington these days."

"Have you thought of writing to Washington?"

"Through channels? With every crooked Indian Agent out here in a position to add his own opinions and make a liar out of me before the letter leaves the territory?"

"You could write direct."

"Maybe, some day. I'm not ready for that yet. I have no assurance Cochise will listen to reason yet. The thing I have to do is just sit and wait and try to work it out slowly." He bit off the end of a cigar and lighted it. "You might as well know everything," he said. "I met an Indian girl up there."

St. John did not answer immediately. Then he said, "You've got to make that peace then, haven't you?"

Jeffords looked at him with gratitude. "That's how you would answer me," he said softly. Then, he went on, "You know how it's been with Terry. This is different."

"You know you can't marry this girl," St. John said quietly. "Why not?"

"The legislature has passed a law forbidding marriages between white men and Indian women."

"The hell with the law. We can go somewhere else. East."

"And your big plan?"

"It keeps getting more complicated, doesn't it?" Jeffords shook his head.

"Are you sure about this?"

"What do you mean?"

"This girl is different, strange. Are you sure? You've known Terry for a long time. You are too used to her."

305

"I'm not a schoolboy, Silas."

"No." St. John smiled. "Only remember that your project is the most important thing. It is more important than any personal thing you want to do."

"I can marry her in an Indian ceremony," Jeffords said.

"You can do that," St. John agreed.

"Maybe it won't hold water among white people. But they believe in it and that's the important thing."

"And that, Tom, will have to be the greatest secret of all. They have a name for that. It's not a pleasant name. It would make you mad. There would be killing. You can't risk it. You can't risk anything until you do what you have to do."

"You make it sound like living in an eggshell."

"What are you going to tell Terry?"

"The truth, what else?" Jeffords said bluntly.

"Anything but the truth. That would be the worst thing you could do, to tell this to a woman who is in love with you. It would be over Arizona within a day."

"I'm not in the habit of lying."

"No. Only you will have to lie now. You will have to loose yourself from Terry without telling her anything about this Indian girl." He paused. "Unless you don't intend to loose yourself from Terry. An Apache marriage is not recognized here. You don't have to say anything at all to Terry, if you don't want to."

Jeffords raised his eyes and looked at St. John. His eyes became very blue and turned cold and he said, "You don't exactly realize what you are saying."

"I know exactly what I am saying," St. John said. "And you've answered me."

Jeffords continued to look at him. "Of course," he said. "You would know better."

2

A week later a mail rider came into town with an incredible story to tell. He had started out from Bowie and a few miles from the fort he had come upon an Indian party attacking a wagon train. Despite Jeffords' orders, the rider had entered the conflict. He was captured by the Indians and bound with a lariat and then tied to a tree.

"I figured it was curtains," he said. "I could feel the fire on my feet. They left me there for three hours. They went back to their fight on the wagon train and I watched them until they killed everybody in the train. They stripped it of all the supplies and cut the horses loose and started fires in the wagons. Then they came back to me. A tall Indian, he looked like the boss, untied me. I never saw an Indian with a face like his. I

306

felt his damned eyes were cutting holes in me. He put me back on my horse and gave me my pouch and then slapped the horse on the tail and sent me on my way." He dumped the mailbag. "I got to get a drink. Tied up after I started shooting at them and they let me go. I even think maybe I killed one of them. And they didn't do nothing."

He started for the door. St. John tried to stop him, but Jeffords told him to go on.

"He will make trouble," St. John said.

"We can't keep him locked up forever. He's going to talk sometime. Might as well get it over with."

Within fifteen minutes there were murmurings outside the mail office. Jeffords walked outside. There were half a hundred men gathered, talking angrily. "Anything wrong, gentlemen?" Jeffords asked pleasantly. The talking stopped and the men looked at each other, waiting for someone to act as spokesman. "Your mail isn't ready yet," Jeffords continued evenly. "It will be an hour yet."

"How come the Indians didn't shoot your rider?" a man yelled.

"Yeah, what the hell is going on between you and old Cochise?" someone else called out.

The crowd started to talk again.

"What have you got against the rider?" Jeffords asked. "Would you rather he was killed?"

Will Oury walked forward slowly. Jeffords took out a fresh cigar and carefully bit off the end. "Anything I can do for you, Will?" he asked softly.

"Yeah. People would like to know why old Cochise and you are suddenly such great friends."

"Would they, Will?" Jeffords struck a match and lit his cigar.

"Nobody around here is fretting because your rider wasn't killed. Nobody wants the rider nor any other white man killed. People only want a straight answer what's between you and that red bastard."

Oury stood indolently, his thumbs stuck into his belt, his long, big fingers almost touching his guns. Jeffords felt his own hands fall on his revolvers. A tall, red-faced youth, his mouth stained with tobacco juice, pushed his way forward. "We don't favor nobody who calls an Apache his friend," he said.

Jeffords raised his head slightly. "My job is to see that the mail goes through. The mail is getting through. Nobody is getting hurt by it. There were twenty-two riders killed before I took over here and when I first started. There hasn't been a man shot since I went up and talked to Cochise. That was all right with everybody. What's the trouble now?"

The young man curled his lips and spat juice at Jeffords' feet. Jeffords pushed his cigar out of his mouth with his tongue. The man glared at him. "As Oury says, *Captain* Jeffords, we ain't complaining about riders not getting shot. But there is something that stinks to high heaven about you making pals with an Apache. This town don't like renegades."

The crowd moved back a little. "What did you say, mister?" Jeffords whispered.

The man opened his mouth to chew and left it open. After several seconds his lips twitched slightly.

"I asked you what you said," Jeffords repeated. His voice was so low that the men halfway back in the crowd could see only the movements of his lips.

The man tried to grin. "My tongue ran away," he said.

Jeffords sighed softly. His wrists were cramped. He took his hands away from his sides and flexed his fingers. His forehead was beaded with sweat. He moved his head slightly and the young man blinked his eyes and walked away. Jeffords wet his lips. His head suddenly ached.

Duffield shouldered his way through the crowd. "What in the name of jumping hell is going on here?" he roared. He pushed men right and left and walked until he was alongside Jeffords. "I asked what the hell is going on here?" He looked furiously at the crowd. "I been hearing talk around here I don't like. It's been killing talk and why the hell Jeffords ain't been doing some killing I don't know. I been hearing crazy talk about him selling out to Indians. I say that's a damned lie! I say that's a god-damned lie! He couldn't pass along a chile bean without my knowing it, and I say it's a lie. And I'm god-damned sick and tired about hearing talk about it. Tom Jeffords don't need no assistance from me, so far as I can make out. He's the last man in town I want to have to shoot against. And everybody in this damned dust hole knows I can shoot his ears off without half opening my eyes. But I'm saying this. From now on talk against Jeffords is talk against me. The next hombre who makes noises like an old woman will have to answer to me as well as to him. Anybody who's got anything to say let him say it right now, or put his damned tail between his legs and get the hell out of here. This is a United States Government office and there is work to be done."

The men broke up and walked away. All but Oury. "Jeffords."

"Yes, Will?"

"We have known each other a spell."

"Yes."

"We ain't lost no love between us."

"What are you trying to say, Will?"

Oury put his two hands out and held onto the railing in front of the mail office. "Don't turn on your killing voice. I'm just saying I didn't bring this crowd here and I didn't shove that crazy kid on you." Jeffords lifted his chin slightly. "I do my own shooting. I don't send out a boy to do a man's work."

Jeffords nodded. "Thanks, Will."

"Another thing. That talk. I don't hold with it. You know how I feel about Indians. In my book the only good ones are dead ones. I trust them when they have a bullet in them where it counts, and only when I put it there. Only there's this. I don't hold with this renegade talk. None of it. Not any part of it."

Jeffords sagged a little.

"I'm not your kind of man, Jeffords. You're not my kind. But I don't think you're the other kind either." He turned slowly and walked away. Jeffords watched his big figure move down the block. Duffield started to speak and then he clamped his mouth shut tight.

3

During the meal that evening Jeffords ate in silence. He felt Terry watching him. When he finished he walked out onto the patio and waited for her. He filled his pipe. The smoke tasted harsh. He had given his old pipe to Cochise. Presently she came out and sat down, and then he said gently, "Go ahead and get it off your mind, Carrot."

"What's happened to you and to me?"

It might as well be now, he thought, clean and final and now. "We've sort of drifted."

"We have drifted, Tom. You've known it, too."

"People grow along, Terry," he said.

"You mean that now that you are back here and have seen me again and have gotten to know me better you don't want me."

He couldn't say it right away.

"You don't want me, do you, Tom?" she repeated clearly.

"I guess not," he got out.

"Why?"

"I don't know why," he said harshly.

"You've changed. I haven't changed."

"I've changed then."

"You've changed ever since you went to see that Indian."

"Maybe you think I've turned renegade, too."

"I don't know what to think. I wanted to be so proud of you."

"Instead you have to listen to people talk about my selling guns and whiskey to Apaches."

"Tom," she said, "let's go away from here. You and me. We can go to California. Or back East. Anywhere. This place isn't good for us. It's doing something to you. I used to think of you being so clean. . . ."

". . . And now?"

She sat up and hardened her face. "There is something unwholesome going on with you. It's not right for a white man to mix with Indians. Something happens. It's happening to you."

"Are you finished?"

"Let us go away."

"I can't go away."

"Please, Tom," she pleaded. She took his hand and lay her cheek against it. "We can make it the way it was in the beginning. We can have the fun we used to. Being together. It's this place, it isn't us."

"You can't make things happen by just wanting them."

She moved away. "Then you really do not want me?"

"Do I have to say it again?"

Her eyes looked as though they were ready for tears but there were no tears. "It needs two. Don't get angry because you think I am embarrassing you." She straightened her skirt. "I think I shall go away for a little while. I've been working here more than five years without a vacation. I think I'll take a trip to San Francisco." Her voice was normal. "Everybody who has been there tells me that it is a wonderful city. Lots of stores and restaurants."

He stood up and hammered out his pipe.

"Don't look so sad," she said cheerfully. "You can't make yourself feel what you don't feel. Any more than you can unmake yourself."

"Carrot." He touched her cheek.

She pulled away from him violently. "Please don't touch me," she said. She hurried into the building.

4

Klosen, father to Sonseeahray, lumbered into his wickiup and sat down with a wheeze. He was a short, fat old man. His name meant "hair-rope" and had been given to him many years before as a compliment. At that time, when he was young and muscular, he had lassoed an enemy Indian and had dragged him to death. It was many years since he had thrown a lariat or had even ridden on a horse but he was still called Klosen.

"Everywhere I go there is talking," he grumbled. The fatty sacks under his eyes quivered. "What is there between you and this American? Wife, we must speak to this girl. She walks away with the white man. Everywhere people are talking."

His wife, Melana, was a tall stately woman and it was from her that Sonseeahray took her golden shapeliness and her small, well-formed hands and feet. Although Melana was not a young woman there was still attached to her a grace and beauty, like the faint odor of a long-pressed flower. "What has he said to you?" she asked.

"Nothing," Sonseeahray said, flushing.

Klosen made a sound of disgust. "I am an old man. Your mother is an old lady. I can no longer hunt or fight and provide for my family. I have expected you to find a husband who would care for us in our old age." He straightened out his fat rheumatic legs with a groan. "I have not had good luck with my children. My eldest daughter married a Mescalero man. Her husband stayed with his own people, although that is contrary to all the customs. Her husband is rich and they have many horses and they do not help us out at all. My son, of course, is living with the family of his wife, as he should, and it is all he can do in these times to provide for them. Then, as though by a miracle, my youngest daughter is returned to me and by another miracle she carried no man's brand on her. And what happens? Nahilzay, one of the greatest hunters and warriors in the tribe, who is called right hand by Cochise himself, makes an offer for marriage and she causes us to reject it." He shook his head and sighed dolorously. "Now he is insulted, as he should be, and he is our enemy and no man can foresee what will happen next. And to make it worse my daughter consorts with a white man."

"Klosen!" Melana said sharply.

"All right, all right," Klosen said petulantly, waving his hand. "I did not mean exactly that. I know she has not been in the brush with this white man. But it is still a scandal. Everybody talks. When I walk around everybody looks at me in sympathy." He looked at his daughter belligerently. "Who is going to make a living for us? Who is this man? Is he rich? Is he a great hunter? Will he live here with us as a son should and provide for us?"

"He has not spoken of marriage," Sonseeahray said unhappily.

"Oh," Klosen snorted. "He has not spoken of marriage. And you refused Nahilzay!"

"Let the girl be," Melana said. She put her arm around Sonseeahray.

"I am still the head of my family," Klosen said. "A man

has to think of his old age. I do not want to starve to death."

"You are many pounds away from starving," Melana said. "You could live off your fat for many harvests."

"I am an old man. I can no longer hunt. We have been living like beggars on what Cochise sends to us."

"He has been very generous."

"It is undignified. A man who raises a daughter has a right to expect to be taken care of with dignity in his old age." He picked up a gourd of tiswin and lifted it to his lips.

"You drink too much," Melana said. "You are short-winded enough."

"I will drink as much as I please!" Klosen said angrily. "What are things coming to? Now I cannot drink! Things are changing too much. In the old days a man could choose a good husband for his daughter and there would be the end of it. Nowadays a girl must be in love with her husband. What kind of nonsense is that?"

"You were chosen as my husband because you were strong and active," Melana said. "Look at you now. You are so fat one cannot tell where your face ends and your neck begins."

"Such talk is not dignified in front of our daughter," Klosen protested.

"Our daughter has had a strange life," Melana said gently. "For a long time we thought of her as one who was not here." She used the Apache euphemism referring to the dead. "Then she came back, as though newly born. It is plain something different in the way of a life has been designed for her. One cannot change things."

"I saw Nahilzay this morning," Klosen said sulkily. "When he came upon me he was so ashamed he turned and walked away. He feels he is disgraced before the whole tribe by the return of his horses. Such fine horses they were, too, so young and healthy. And from such a fine man. He is a public figure."

Melana looked lovingly upon her daughter. "You must listen to your father because he is your father and he has a right to speak. But there are things beyond ordinary understanding sometimes. We are grateful to have you back. You must follow your path." Then she asked, "Do you love this man?"

"Yes," Sonseeahray said.

"Then we will wait and see."

"Love," Klosen said with vast disgust.

"Yes, love," Melana said. "Have you never heard of it?"

"Marriage should be an arrangement. It is the duty of a father to see that a good arrangement is made."

"Do not worry," Melana said with gentle scorn. "You will

312

not hunger. It is said Cochise loves the white man more than any other, even Nahilzay."

"That is so," Klosen said. "I had not thought of it."

Melana went to a large reed basket. She took from it some deer-skin garments. "I have made these for you," she said to her daughter. "The nights soon will be cold."

The clothing was very beautifully made and decorated. Sonseeahray took them and held them close to her. "You are good to me," she said.

"You are so beautiful," Melana said. "When I look at you it takes me back to when I was your age."

Klosen rumbled, "She is not so beautiful as you were, wife."

"Ah, you are chewing rocks," Melana said, blushing.

"It is true. None was more beautiful."

Melana turned her head away shyly. She was still able to do this.

The girl went to an isolated place on the stream and slipped out of her blouse and skirt and stepped into the water. She did this without concern. No Apache youth would ever look at a girl bathing. She slid into the water and felt the cool flow on her skin. The days were still warm. The nights were beginning to cool, as her mother said. It soon would be the season called Thick with Fruit.

She lay against a rock and the water cooled her blood. She had not allowed herself to think about Jeffords asking to marry her, but now she thought of being his wife. She looked at her body and was happy that it was beautiful. She looked at her hands and feet and was happy that they were well shaped. She looked at her breasts, cupping them in her hands, and she was happy they were round and firm and did not hang and that the nipples were small. She looked at her waist and was happy it was slender. She put her hands under her hips and was happy they were not broad. She lifted her legs from the water and was happy they were round. She looked at her thighs and saw they were soft and not fat and she was happy. She thought of her body as something to give to him and she was almost impersonal in her survey and she thanked Yusn that what she had to give him was good and desirable and she hoped he would think it was beautiful.

She washed herself and stood up, glistening, the water making her body new and shining in the bright sun, and she lifted her arms upward and shivered and then she rubbed her hands on her sides and she was happy to be living. She stepped from the water and stood on a rock until the sun dried her and then she put on the new clothing her mother had made for

313

her and the soft leather felt luxurious against her. She put on her high moccasins and then, on a sudden impulse, went to the wickiup of Tesalbestinay. She stood in front of the dwelling and when her ritual mother came out she smiled to her, and Tesalbestinay said, "There is sunlight in your eyes."

"May one speak to her mother?" Sonseeahray asked.

"Yes."

She knelt before the elder woman. "My mother knows what speaks in my heart."

"It speaks loudly."

"My father thinks it is a bad thing."

"He thinks only of his stomach."

Sonseeahray looked at her with her eyes filled with grief. "Is it a bad thing, my mother?"

"Nothing is a bad thing in itself," Tesalbestinay said. "Some things do not judge themselves by rules. A man and a woman meet each other and at the moment of meeting cease to be strangers."

"It was so," the girl breathed.

The gaunt face of Tesalbestinay was filled with a tender light. She looked at the wickiup which Cochise shared with Nalikadeya. "When it is that way it does not change, maybe," she said. "When a man and a woman get that between them they stop being alone for the first time. They stop being themselves. They make something new between them and that belongs to both of them from then on. And whatever happens the thing they made stays with them and the other things are of no importance."

"It was so with you," Sonseeahray said.

"It has been a long time but when he speaks to me it is still the same between us. I have no beauty but it is still the same. It will be hard with you. We can teach him the rules. How to avoid your mother, how to use polite speech with your relatives, those things can be taught to him. He already knows many of our ways. But it will be hard because he is of a strange people and his mind is not as ours."

"I can learn his ways." Her eyes were shining.

"You will both throw away your own ways and make new ways. That is the only thing to do. The new thing you will make will have part of you in it and part of him, as though it were a child. You will give to each other. It is only by giving that you can make it worth anything. It is easy to take and it may seem at first that it is more pleasant to take but the real thing is to give. It is only when there is a big empty hole in you that it is worth anything. If he takes something from you and leaves a hole that you can feel, then it means something."

Her face was radiant. "I know what you mean, my mother.

I feel this hole in me now. There no longer is all of me when he is not here."

"When it has truth it does not take time. You cannot learn it. It comes to you and you have it."

Sonseeahray stood up. "Do you think he will find me good to look at in my new clothes? Look at me. Am I something that will please him?"

5

"I think I knew the moment you entered the rancheria," she said. "It was as though you sent a signal to my heart."

"I have been doing that."

"It was only a little while ago that I felt it," she said. "It was so funny. I was working and then the feather started to tickle me again and I knew that you were here. You belong here. When you left it seemed something was missing, as though someone removed a tree."

"That is because I am big," he teased.

"You are big," she agreed gravely. "Only Cochise is as big."

"Is he here?"

"No." The corners of her mouth lowered.

"Do not explain," he said instantly. "I will hear of it in Tucson."

"You are truly friends."

"Yes."

"When he does what he is doing now, it means nothing?"

"Nothing to our friendship."

"There is talk. Some think you are here to spy on us."

He laughed. "In Tucson they think I am Cochise's spy."

"Cochise called his warriors together. He said he heard about the talk. He said he wanted it ended. He said you were no spy. He asked what you could spy on. He said that the white men knew the Chiricahuas are in the Stronghold, one or the other. He said the white men knew all about the Strongholds because when the Chiricahuas were away from here the white men came here sometimes and looked around and burned the empty wickiups. Then he asked how you could betray him and there was no answer. Then one man said maybe you were here to kill him and he said that if that was what you were here for you could have done it long ago and after that there was nothing anyone could say."

"Who said I might want to kill him?"

"It does not matter. No one believed him."

"Nahilzay?"

"I think he is a little crazy these days."

"I understand his craziness," he said. "If you returned my horses I would be a little crazy, too."

"It is bad when love is on one side," she said. Then she looked at him suddenly and her eyes got wet and her lips parted tremulously. "Are you going to ask my parents for me?"

"Yes."

"Sometimes Apache boys joke that way. They think it is funny."

"I am not joking. Will you return the horses?"

"No, not even if they are not good horses. My father would be angry if they were bad horses but I would make him keep them."

"I will send good horses." He grimaced. "It is like buying something in the market."

"The gifts to the parents do not mean much. It is usually arranged between the man and the woman before the gifts are sent." She smiled. "Nahilzay sent his gifts without arrangement. He was a fool. I told him I would not take him for husband. He sent the gifts anyway. He thought my father would not dare return them because he is a great warrior."

"We do not do it that way."

"How is it done among you?"

"Oh, the man and the woman see much of each other and then he asks if she will marry him and if she says yes he makes arrangements."

"Are not the parents of the girl consulted?"

"Yes."

"Then wherein lies the difference?"

"We don't send horses."

"Are no gifts given?"

"Yes, many things."

"Things of value?" When he nodded she said triumphantly, "There, a horse is the thing of greatest value to us. There is no difference at all."

He had long since abandoned the argument but he continued to listen to her voice. "Then they go to a church to be married."

He used the English word for church since there was no Apache equivalent. She repeated the strange word after him and then asked him to explain its meaning. "It is a dwelling where Americans go to worship their Spirit. There are shamans who are wise in religious ceremonies and one of these shamans makes a ceremony."

"Why must they go into a place?" she asked puzzled. "Do you confine your Spirit to a single place?"

"No. It is a special place, like your ceremonial dwelling."

"We believe Yusn is everywhere and cannot be put into one place. He would not like us to make a building and keep him in it. He is in the trees, in each tree, and in each blade of grass and in each rock. He is in the rain and the thunder and he shines with the sun. At night he sleeps and White Painted Lady helps him. She keeps one eye open, only one, because the stars help her to see. She tries to keep that eye open all the time but she gets sleepy too and her eye gets more and more closed and finally she dozes off and only the stars are awake and when she sleeps they look sharper than ever, and then she wakes again, slowly, and her eye opens more and more and finally it is fully opened again."

He closed his eyes and listened to her voice.

"I have not thanked you for wanting me," she said.

He looked at her in surprise. "Thanked me?"

"I hoped you would want me and I have not shown enough how happy it makes me, maybe," she said. "It makes me very happy and I will be a good wife to you."

He took her hand and held it tightly. "I will try to be a good husband to you," he said.

"There is no place here like your church," she said. "Our Spirit is different from yours, maybe. If it will make you happy to be married your way I will do it."

"No," he said. "There are other things to talk about. The details of our marriage can be settled. But there are other things. You have to know how it is going to be. I will not be able to make my home here with you always. I have work to do. I will come here as much as I can but there will be times when I cannot be here."

"Apaches are always going away," she laughed. "Sometimes for three moons or more." She looked impish. "If you do not see too much of me at one time you won't get tired of me so soon, maybe."

"Tired of you."

"It will be even better with us," she went on. "When Apache men go away it is to fight. Women do not know whether they will see them alive again. I will always know you will come back."

"What must I do first? How soon can we be married?"

"You must have one to carry your burden," she said.

"I do not understand."

"Some one must be go-between, to come to my parents for you."

"I do not ask them myself?" he asked in some relief.

"No. It must be another, a good friend."

"Cochise?"

"It would be good if Cochise would do it," she said excitedly. "The more of a public figure the go-between is the more difficult it is for the parents to refuse. It would be insulting to him. My parents would not like to insult Cochise."

"They would like to refuse a go-between from me?"

"They would rather have an Indian ask for me," she said matter-of-factly.

"Nahilzay?"

"They wanted me to marry Nahilzay."

He whistled. "Cochise it is then."

She looked startled. "Do not make that sound with your lips. It is dangerous. Sometimes in the night you can hear that sound and nothing can be seen and it is a Ghost doing it. You get scared and then you get sick and have to put ashes on your face and throw other ashes in the direction of the sound and put still other ashes under your head when you sleep. I wish you had not done that." Her eyes moved nervously.

"Ignorance will be forgiven," he said, stroking her hand. "How many horses shall I send? Three, four, six?"

"Just three," she said quickly.

"Just three?" he laughed. "I want everybody to know how much I think of you."

"Just three. If you send more it will be in bad taste. People will say my parents did not want me to marry you but had to give their permission because you sent such a rich present they could not refuse. With three horses it will be just as though you were one of us and then they will all know that I wanted it and was not just sold for horses."

"Sweetheart."

"I feel more than your sweetheart. I feel as though I am your wife. We have been sweethearts for a very short time."

"Is it too soon for you?"

"No, I want to be your wife."

"I will ask Cochise as soon as he returns."

Her eyes went far away. "During all the years I was with the White Mountain people I wondered about being a wife. There were young warriors there who wanted me. I thought I would accept one of them, maybe. I thought I would always be with those people and it would be better to have a husband. But I never accepted one. I do not know why. I knew the things a wife must do for a husband and there was no man I wanted to do them with. The men all were strangers, in a bad way. I never met a man there without feeling there was something between us that we could not get through. I thought then it was because the White Mountain people were not my people. But when I came back here it was the same way with the Chiricahua men. I thought about it and I felt that I was haunted in some way. I thought that I was neither White Mountain nor Chiricahua and that I would always be a stranger. And then you came to me." She brought her eyes to him. "And then you went away so quickly."

"I think I have been looking, too," he said. "Something inside of me must have been frightened."

"I love to listen to you speak my language. How do sweethearts among the Americans talk? Do they say special things?"

"Yes."

"What things?" Then she put her small hand over his mouth. "I do not want to hear them."

"I do not know them to tell to you," he said softly.

"Let us make up our own things, that were never said before by anyone," she said. The splendor in her eyes blinded him. "We have two languages. We will be able to find new things to say."

6

The raid into Mexico had been successful and the Indians had taken more than two hundred sheep and they returned in good spirits. They moved swiftly over the country, running the sheep with them. They had taken the strongest sheep and had lashed them by their horns, in couples, and then had made a mobile parallel sheep fence out of them, spacing the bound sheep about thirty feet apart, herding the remaining animals between them. Warriors on foot ran alongside the outer edges of these lashed sheep and in that manner the entire herd was kept moving rapidly.

One group of men rode ahead and led the way. The main body rode in the rear to watch for pursuers. It was nightfall, and since early morning when the raid had taken place, the Indians had traveled almost sixty miles. The runners were almost as swift as men on horses and when they tired they changed off with riders.

The pursuit had petered out long before. At twilight, in a secluded canyon, some of the sheep were slaughtered and the meat roasted. The skins were stripped and some of the men quickly made them into comfortable robes. After a quick meal the men moved on again.

The men were happy and talked about the welcome their wives would give to them when they brought in their huge haul. There would be meat for everybody, new robes, new blankets. They talked about the raid and the surprise of the Mexicans and complimented each other on their courage.

Of them all Cochise alone was depressed. He took no part in the good-natured chaffing and joking. He rode by himself, his head sunk low, and he thought of the face of the Mexican he had killed in hand-to-hand combat, with a knife, and in that face he had seen the face of the man he had caused to be buried and devoured by ants, and his head felt tired and filled with rocks, as though the Ghost of the tortured man was in there, jumping back and forth.

He had not felt him for a long time, not since Jeffords had

319

come to him, and had filled, in a strange way, his need for a friend and a confidant. It used to be that the Ghost of the tortured man had come almost every night, and that the more he drank to rid himself of its presence, the more he felt it. He had tortured many men, before and after, and yet that one alone stayed with him, and he closed his eyes painfully and again saw his face, lying like a beheaded skull, and he could see the crazed eyes and hear the agonized screams and he listened again to the curse the man laid on him, and he could see the ants, tiny and without number, crawling, tearing out tiny pieces of flesh, pulling at the soft skin under the eyes.

It got bad again as he rode, deaf and blind to his surroundings, and he felt the old horror. There was nothing alive that he feared and death was something that he almost courted, challenged, ignored; but this was something that was beyond all that.

He had done all the things Nochalo prescribed. All the skill of the shaman's ceremony had proved futile. The memory of that maddened face would not leave him. Sometimes, in violence, he could push it out of his head, but in the times of silence it returned.

He thought about the raid. He went over it slowly, step by step, to determine whether mistakes had been made. Mistakes cost lives of his dwindling tribe and although he knew better than any other Indian what would happen in the end he proposed to lose his men as stingily as possible.

The sheep had been grazing just outside the Mexican village. A small company of Mexican soldiers had been on temporary bivouac in the village. Cochise had planned on the presence of the military giving the villagers a feeling of false security and he had not been wrong. The people were careless, thinking Indians would never dare attack while the soldiers were there. Cochise had sent a part of his force under Nahilzay to maneuver to the south of the village. He sent them at night so that when the first light of day came the villagers had found the Indians, some forty in number, riding up from the south, as though they were a complete unit. Cochise and the rest of his warriors, numbering almost one hundred and fifty, had remained hidden to the north.

When the soldiers saw Nahilzay's party they went out to meet them. Nahilzay retreated slowly and skillfully, fighting, withdrawing, luring the soldiers farther and farther from the village, and then Cochise sent another force of fifty men in a wide arc around the village to fall upon the soldiers from the rear. Skinyea led this group and his men and Nahilzay's men came together in a sudden and terrible squeeze with the soldiers between them, and at the same time Cochise attacked the unprotected village.

320

The Apaches cut down the Mexicans like stalks of corn. Cochise led the fighting on the village and Pionsenay and Tahzay rounded up the sheep and drove them off.

The expedition was conducted with the care and precision that was the mark of Cochise's warfare. There was no hesitation when the fight started. Each Indian knew what he was supposed to do, and did it at the right time. They screamed in their blood-curdling manner, but the screams were mainly for effect; under them the operations were accurate and deliberate.

Nahilzay and Skinyea knew exactly how long they had to engage the soldiers. At the proper moment they scattered, reformed, and rode north, in order, keeping the soldiers on the south of them, keeping themselves between the soldiers and the village. When the soldiers got close enough to see the horde of Indians around the village they fled, as Cochise had known they would. The Indians reassembled and went off with incredible celerity. There were but two Apaches killed.

Cochise questioned each of his lieutenants and analyzed their operations and decided that Skinyea and Nahilzay should have had a few more men for their part of the job. The analysis, for a time, drove away his gloom, but later the memories returned with a thud and he felt the old ache and his lips drew back against it.

A rider rushed up with the news that a party of white men, eleven men and two wagons, were camped in a valley to the north. The lieutenants gathered around him. "Do we attack them?" Nahilzay asked. There was a strained, questioning look on his face.

"Mexicans are good," Cochise said abruptly. "White-eyes are better." The ache would go away now, he thought.

He detached a score of his men and sent the rest on a detour, arranging where to meet them the following day. With Nahilzay at his side they rode north until they came to the valley. In the dark they could make out the Americans, grouped around a fire.

The Indians lay quietly through the night and Cochise tasted in advance the pleasure of the kill. At dawn he led the attack. Three of the Americans were killed in the first volley. Five others died in succeeding attacks. The other three were bound to the wheels of their wagons, head down.

Brush was piled under their heads. Cochise knelt and watched. The Indians worked without instructions at an old game. The three men struggled at their bonds. Their blood filled their faces. They chewed at their gags.

Nahilzay brought a torch to one of the piles of brush.

"Stop," Cochise said.

Nahilzay paused. He turned slowly the flaming torch in his

hand. He looked carefully at Cochise. The other Indians became silent.

Cochise rose. "Unbind them." Nahilzay did not move. "Unbind them," Cochise repeated.

Nahilzay put down the torch. He faced Cochise in silence for several seconds and then he unbound the white men. They got to their feet.

"Take everything you can carry," Cochise said to his men. His voice was flat and toneless. He stared at the three Americans. When the Indians collected everything they wanted, he said, in the same voice, "Mount your horses." Then he jumped on his own horse and led his men away.

The rest of the journey to the camp was made in silence. Cochise rejoined the main body of his warriors at the appointed rendezvous and word quickly spread of his unprecedented gesture of mercy to the three Americans. Several times one or another of his lieutenants rode up to speak to him, but at the sight of his face they rode away again without a word. Nahilzay, who knew better than any other man the cause of his leader's action, alone kept away from him. ·He too detached himself from the other men and his head was filled with bitterness and rage.

The singing pain was there again as the Indians entered the Stronghold. The women came out shrieking and Cochise did not hear them. He ignored the almost hysterical people who danced around him and went to his wickiup. He threw himself on his pallet and held his hands over his ears. The noise in his head dizzied him.

He did not know when Tesalbestinay followed him into the wickiup, and stood there watching him. He did not know she found Jeffords and said to him, "It needs some time. For now, return to her."

7

Cochise lay in his wickiup and the day changed itself. He did not stir for more than ten hours. Then he sent Tahzay to order a sweat bath made for him and he again lay on his pallet. When Jeffords entered the wickiup he sat up, exhausted, and held out his arms. His face was haggard and the lines on it were cut deeply, like furrows burned with acid. "When did you come?"

"It is two days now."

Cochise rose and walked outside. In the daylight his face looked more tormented than ever. His lips were dry and his eyes were shot with blood. "I have ordered a sweat bath. Share it with me."

Inside the bath house Cochise stretched out and relaxed. His lean, powerful body rested heavily on a slab. There was a new wound across his chest, memento of the last raid. Cochise touched it lightly. "It could have been an important one," he said. He looked at his body. "The marks are old friends," he said. "Each one is a message. It is like the writing on the rocks that the ancient people made." He touched the newest one again. "Just a little closer and this might have been one of the important ones. It could have started the long journey and I would know the answer now." He pulled the steamy air into his lungs. "One thinks too much about death," he said. "I think death is regarded as having more importance than it truly has. We die each day and when death comes at last it is always too late."

The sweat-bath boss threw fresh water on the hot stones and the rocks hissed noisily. The steam filled the wickiup and Jeffords could not see Cochise, and his voice, when it came through the fog of steam, seemed to come from a long distance.

"An old woman once said I would not live to be old and that I would not die in battle," the voice said. "I have waited long for the bullet which would make her into a liar."

The men lay in the clouds of steam for almost an hour. Then Cochise said, "Does it feel good to you?"

"Yes," Jeffords said.

"It does not make you weak?"

"Just a little."

"A little is good. The steam goes through you like a hot wind. It purifies."

"Cochise."

"Yes, Tagliato."

"Do you wish to talk about it?"

"No. It is going away. Come, we have had enough."

They left the steam hut. They were dripping with sweat. They walked to the stream and plunged into it. The water felt like liquid ice. When they stepped out of the stream Cochise seemed to have recovered himself. He looked like a son to the man Jeffords had seen in the wickiup.

"I have a favor to ask," Jeffords said. "I want you to carry my burden."

"Good. To whom?"

"You know to whom," Jeffords said.

"I will dress and go now."

"Not right now. I have no presents."

"I will give you horses."

"That is not the same thing," Jeffords protested. "I wish to give what is mine."

"I give them to you. They are almost yours. They come from friends of yours."

Jeffords pulled at his beard. "I would rather bring my own."

"You are acting like a child," Cochise said with approval. "That is a good sign. It is no good if it does not make you into a child again."

"Take the horses," Jeffords said in resignation.

Cochise put his hands upon the shoulders of his friend. His eyes searched into him. "I am now going to speak, Tagliato," he said with great seriousness, "as though you were one of my own warriors. I would say, 'There are young women in my tribe who already have a brand upon them. They know all the things necessary to make a man happy and it is not necessary to marry one. Speak and you can have one or two or even three or more of these women and when you tire of them you have no responsibility toward them.' I would say, 'This girl is new. She is innocent. This girl can be made to suffer.' "

"And if you asked that," Jeffords replied, "then I in turn would answer you, 'It is not wanting a woman. There are white women for that. This girl is to be my wife. From now on what makes her suffer makes me suffer as well.' "

"*Enju*," Cochise said. He went to his wickiup and returned a short time later in ceremonial dress, lacking only face paint. "I go now to carry your burden," he said gravely.

Jeffords sat down and lighted a cigar. He tried to smoke it but he was too nervous and he smoked it too rapidly and it burned his tongue. He threw it away and his hands were wet. He rubbed them on his shirt. He wondered what he would do if her parents refused. It seemed hours that he sat there. It must have been at least thirty minutes. He wondered why Cochise took so long. Maybe he had an argument on his hands. Then he heard footsteps and Cochise walked into his wickiup. His face was long and gloomy. Jeffords jumped up. "They refused," he said. Cochise sat down sadly. "I will take her away from here," Jeffords said loudly. "She will come with me."

Then Cochise burst into a loud laugh. He stood up and slapped Jeffords on the back. "They did not refuse," he said. Jeffords looked at him wide-eyed. "It was a joke," Cochise laughed. "It is always a good joke."

Jeffords grabbed his wrists. "Tell me straight."

"It is all arranged," Cochise said. He started to laugh again.

"Was it hard to persuade them?" Jeffords asked timidly. He felt himself get a little weak and he sat down.

"They were not crazy about the idea," Cochise admitted. "Klosen said he wanted a son-in-law who could take care of him in his old age. I told him that henceforth when you were not here it would be as though I were his son-in-law. Just regarding food, you understand. I told him he would not go hungry.

I even told him I would practice avoidance with Melana if it made him feel better."

"You are a friend, Cochise," Jeffords said.

"I will make a good Indian out of you."

"What is this avoidance?"

"You must never look at the face of your mother-in-law. It is the way it has to be. Do you know the polite speech of our language?"

"I do not think so."

"It is almost another language. You must learn it. It is a sign of respect to use the polite speech to the relatives of your wife. You will be on a special standing with them and must do certain things and not do other things. You must never become familiar with them as you would with other men, for instance."

"When can our wedding take place?"

"When the new moon is full."

"That will be almost ten days," Jeffords computed.

"The waiting will do you good."

"Why must we wait so long?"

"The girl's mother picked the day. We leave those things where they belong. There are many things to be done. The girl and her mother must build a wickiup for you near the family wickiup. Then there must be another wickiup built far into the canyon."

"For what?"

"For you, Tagliato, and for your new wife. There you will spend the first ten days of your marriage. You will be alone. The place will be distant and you will not be disturbed. It will be stocked with food, so you will have nothing to do except to make your wife know how much she is your wife."

"What must I do in the meantime?"

"Nothing. It is better not to see her. Compose yourself. Rid your mind of bad thoughts. Come to her as pure as you can. That is the way it is done among us."

"I will go back to Tucson tomorrow and finish some of my work so I can stay away from there when I come back."

"Good," Cochise nodded. "That is a good way."

When he was among the Indians later he knew that word had gone around. The people looked at him slyly, and one or two of the warriors whom he had got to know better than the others made humorous remarks as he passed them. The familiar attitudes, so typical in any society when a man is about to get married, warmed Jeffords' heart. It was the same, the same as it would have been in Tucson, or back in Chautauqua, or anywhere else. The differences were all minor, he thought, and only on the surface, and were differences in presentation and not in kind; they could be resolved, he thought, and the

325

basic similarity, the sameness, could take over. The language, the customs, the habits, all these things could be understood mutually, and once understood, there would be no need for hatred. Hatred was impossible when there was understanding, and for each people, among itself, the deep things were the same.

8

After dinner of roast mutton he sat and smoked a pipe with Cochise. The Indian appeared to have rid himself of whatever thoughts had filled him upon his return from the raid. He was pleasant and courteous and, as Tesalbestinay watched him, her face softened with pleasure. When he was with Jeffords, she thought he was more the Cochise of the old days than at any other time. She thanked Yusn for sending the white man to Cochise and she prayed that he would remain with him long and keep him from drifting out into the dark places in his mind.

Jeffords finally went into his wickiup and lay down. He thought of the fragility that would bind his marriage and he thought that it would be that fragility that would support it. There would be nothing conventional to hold them together and it all rested solely on him. He closed his eyes and he could see her quite clearly.

He realized that he was awake and had been awake for some time and he realized that he was taut and warned. His mind quickly traced the last moments, carefully, and then fastened on what it was, the faintest sound of footfalls, and then, as he understood it, he heard it again. Without thought, moving automatically now, he shifted slightly on his pallet, edging himself off to one side, and then there was a darkness, darker than the night and he smelled something stale and there was a soft thud and he saw the glint of something and then he stretched out and grabbed the wrist and forced back the knife. He felt the wrist, slightly greasy, slip in his grasp, and he pushed himself upward and tried to get the man down. He knew who it was as though it were bright daylight and he could see his face. They rolled back and forth and Jeffords clung desperately to the wrist. Then the man brought up his knee and it crashed into Jeffords' belly and he felt nauseated. He groped with his left hand until he found the man's throat and he began to press. The man twisted and tried to pull away and Jeffords kept his hand against the throat, like a steel bar, pressing it back, the ground bracing him, and then he heaved again and he was on top of the man and he had his arms stretched out flat against the ground and he got his knees on

326

his arms, just below the shoulders, and then he raised his big right fist and brought it down like a sledge on the face that was upturned under him and he heard the bones break in his nose and the man made his first sound, a sharp exhaling frustrated sob and then he did not move any more.

Jeffords waited. He stood up warily. He lit his torch. Nahilzay was out cold. His nose was bleeding and was pushed over to one side of his face. He was breathing noisily, little flecks of blood splattering out. In his right hand he still held his long knife. On the pallet, where Jeffords had slept, was a deep slash.

He picked up a gourd of water and drank deeply. He held up the torch and looked around. One side of the wickiup was caved down from the force of the men struggling against it. He reached down and took the knife from Nahilzay's hand and tossed it away. He took another drink and then poured the rest of the water on the Indian's face.

Nahilzay stirred and opened his eyes. The opening of his eyes became the beginning of one unbroken motion that brought him to his feet. He wiped the blood that dripped from his battered nose. His eyes glittered with hate.

There was another sound. Cochise entered the wickiup. He looked at Nahilzay. He looked at the knife. He looked at the rent in the pallet. He turned and walked out of the wickiup. A moment later he reentered, carrying his shotgun.

Nahilzay made no attempt to move. His mouth was a tight, thin line and he held himself in rigid pride. His eyes sought no mercy.

Cochise looked at him almost tenderly. Nahilzay slowly walked out of the wickiup. He did not look at either Cochise or Jeffords. He held his head stiffly and his arms were straight and stiff at his sides. Cochise moved to follow him, not yet having spoken, and Jeffords said, quietly, "No."

Cochise jerked his head around. "This is not your affair."

"You are not going to shoot him."

"Do you give orders to me?" Cochise said angrily.

"No one shoots in my behalf."

"Keep your silence," Cochise said. "Do not interfere."

Jeffords understood the torment that was giving Cochise his manner. He put his hand on his friend's shoulder. "This *is* my affair. This man tried to kill me, not you. Whatever the vengeance is, it is mine."

"His trying to kill you is your affair. If it happened elsewhere it would be something between you. But his trying to kill you is not the important thing. What is more important is that he attempted to kill one to whom I had given safety in my tribe. He must die, not for attempting to kill you, but for turning me into liar."

Through this talk Nahilzay stood unmoving. He folded his arms across his chest and listened with no concern, as though he had no connection with the conversation.

"I am no child, Cochise," Jeffords said.

"In this place it is I who give orders," Cochise replied harshly. He turned to Nahilzay and Jeffords might not have been there. "There has been none like you with me in battle," Cochise said. "Your life and mine were often mixed. It is ended." Then, as though discussing a minor thing, "You should not have betrayed my word."

He walked past Nahilzay, out of the dwelling. Nahilzay followed. Then Jeffords went after them.

Dawn was bringing its clear light. There was a chill and a silence. Cochise walked across a clearing toward a place where the men shot arrows in contests. Nahilzay followed a dozen paces behind him. Jeffords strode up to Cochise. "Listen to me," he said sternly. "My honor is involved in this, too. You think only of yourself. I am not a woman nor a child who needs to be protected. What do you think will be thought of me among your people when it is known that Cochise himself has to be my stepmother?"

Cochise pondered and then said, "Among us there are laws. This man has violated the greatest of these laws, my word. The punishment lies with me. There is no talk of vengeance. This is just punishment."

"No matter how you explain it this is my business and I will settle it my own way," Jeffords said stubbornly. "This man has challenged me. All right. I accept his challenge. You have no right to order it otherwise."

Cochise looked troubled. "How will you duel? He is less than you are with the gun. You are far less than he with an arrow."

"He tried to kill me with a knife," Jeffords retorted. "A knife is good enough for either of us."

Cochise looked at the two men whom he loved more than any others. Nahilzay appeared not to have heard a word that was spoken. He stood docilely and waited for whatever would happen.

At last Cochise sighed sadly. "I have no right to deny you, Tagliato," he said. "But I say this: Nahilzay no longer is as a son to me. You will fight, you two, but if Nahilzay is victor he is banished from his people. You will be given a chance for your life, Nahilzay, but if you are successful you leave here and if I see you again I myself will kill you, as I should kill you now."

He turned again to Jeffords. "You say your honor is involved. If you say it, it is enough. This man should be placed

328

against a tree and shot. That is our way. But if you insist on giving him a chance to kill you I cannot stop you."

There were several other Indians now standing around silently. Word passed quickly and soon more than a hundred men and women collected in the whitening morning. Cochise sent Tahzay to his wickiup and the youth returned with two knives. The blades were more than eight inches long. The handles were thick and made of wood, with thongs twisted around to make a grip.

Cochise examined the two knives and then threw them point down into the ground. They quivered for a moment. Teese handed Cochise his lance. With the sharp iron end of the lance Cochise drew a large circle on the ground, some fifteen feet in diameter. The knives were in the center.

Nahilzay stepped into the circle, his heels on the line Cochise had drawn. Jeffords removed his shirt and walked to the line on the opposite side of the circle. Cochise held his lance extended and looked first at Jeffords and then at Nahilzay. Then, his face cold and dark, he lowered the lance and stepped back.

Nahilzay and Jeffords looked at each other carefully. They moved slightly from side to side to get the feel of the earth. They were matched. Nahilzay was slenderer, but his chest was the deep barrel of an Apache fighting man. His arms were long and sinewy. As he moved the fluid muscles in his thighs and legs rippled under his skin.

Jeffords was as lean and spare as the Indian. His arms were not as long and his muscles, if not as pliant, were equally developed.

Suddenly, swift and light as a cat, Nahilzay darted forward and picked up one of the knives. As he moved away his left foot flicked out and he attempted to kick the other knife away. But as he had moved in the beginning Jeffords moved as well and the heel kicked into empty space and the other knife was secure in Jeffords' hand.

The two men moved back to the rim of the circle and studied each other. Nahilzay's movements were filled with grace. His feet, in their soft moccasins, padded almost daintily on the earth. Jeffords, in heavy boots, moved less gracefully, but almost as swiftly.

Then, without any crouch to give him spring, Nahilzay leaped against Jeffords, a light-quick leap that gathered its momentum from nowhere. The knife flashed like a twinkle in the morning light and Jeffords twisted only in time and saw the blade slide past him, missing him by less than two inches. Now he whirled and with his left hand he struck Nahilzay down and with his right tried to get the knife into the Indian's body. Nahilzay twisted as he fell and darted under his arm and in a moment was again on the farther rim of the circle.

Jeffords knew he could not match the easy swiftness of the Indian. He felt he had greater strength and he would have to use that strength against speed. He could not leap like a frog across the circle. He would have to accept each attack and, after Nahilzay committed himself, try to turn the attack away and get his knife in afterwards.

Indians gathered in greater numbers. None made a sound. There was no sound except the breathing of the men in the ring and the sounds of their movements.

Again Nahilzay leaped and in midleap he pulled his magnificent body down and changed his course from midair to below Jeffords' waist and he came in, almost diving, his knife arm half coiled. Jeffords thrust out with his left hand and cracked Nahilzay hard on his neck, as a man kills a rabbit, and then, kicking out suddenly, struck Nahilzay's right wrist. The wrist, numbed, loosed the fingers on the knife. The blade fell to the earth. Nahilzay reached for it. Jeffords stepped on it. Nahilzay jumped back, unarmed, and then he stood and waited. He folded his arms across his chest and looked contemptuously at Jeffords.

There was a low sigh among the Indians. By Indian law it was Jeffords' right to walk over to Nahilzay and plunge his knife into him. Jeffords put the point of his right boot under the blade and kicked it toward Nahilzay. The Indian bent down and picked it up and in the same move again leaped at Jeffords.

This time Jeffords was waiting. He had timed the Indian's incredible leaps and this time he held himself unmoving until just the last space of time and then he shifted slightly and as Nahilzay passed he shot out his left arm and wrapped it around the Indian's waist, pinning Nahilzay's two arms against his sides and then he twisted him around until Nahilzay almost faced him, his tight mouth only a few inches from his own, and he lifted his right arm and brought it down hard and he felt the blade enter Nahilzay's back and he pushed down until the hilt stopped it from going farther.

For a moment Nahilzay gave no sign of any kind. Holding him Jeffords could feel the powerful resistance in his torso, still feel the attempt to lift his right arm under his grip. The Indian's eyes were bright and glittering and then Nahilzay slacked and his body became loose and the eyes clouded and a film crossed them and then Jeffords opened his arms and released him and the Indian slid down along his body and fell softly on the earth.

There was a long breath from the Indians, as though the sound had come from a single mouth. Cochise walked into the circle and knelt before Nahilzay. Then he stood up. "The duel was fair," he said. His voice spread out to the people. "It is over and finished. There will be nothing of this to remain in the heart of any man." He looked down again at Nahilzay. He pulled the knife from the back of the dead man. He picked up the knife that had fallen from Nahilzay's hand. He handed the two knives to Teese. "Destroy these," he said.

Chapter Sixteen

The wedding ceremonies, feasting, and attendant celebration lasted four nights. To show his love for Jeffords Cochise had provided the most elaborate affair the people could remember, and throughout the rites, dances, contests, and other games he remained at the side of his friend.

For her wedding Sonseeahray wore a costume of fresh, light-colored deerskin, with long strands dangling from the sleeves and skirt. At the end of the strands were small silver cone-shaped amulets which tinkled against each other like tiny bells as she moved. On the skin, across her bosom, was painted a symbol of White Painted Lady, the moon, and near it was a single star. Around her neck was a heavy necklace of turquoise and her arms were covered with silver bracelets set with turquoise and other stones.

Jeffords wore Indian costume, a present from Cochise, who had directed his wives to decorate it with all the symbols of strength and fortune normally reserved for the dress of the chief himself. Jeffords felt comfortable in the costume; it was not unlike the deerskin garb he had frequently worn as a scout. His red beard alone caused comment and merriment. Cochise upon seeing him dressed said dryly, "There is no need to put the symbol of the sun on your shirt, Tagliato. The hair on your face is brighter than any paint and larger than the sun itself!"

When he first dressed and prepared himself Jeffords felt a sudden strange uneasiness. He wondered if he were not attempting something that was beyond the possibility of success. When he saw her for the first time his qualms left him. She was radiant. Her eyes had a luster that was almost feverish. He felt his blood as she walked to him.

For three nights they sat side by side, forbidden by custom to speak to each other, and on the fourth night Nochalo appeared, dressed for the final ceremony, and there was an immediate cessation of all speech and song. The shaman was painted and he carried many charms. Jeffords, slowly learning the complicated religious practices and beliefs of the Apaches, was able to interpret some of the devices he bore.

Nochalo raised a long wand in his right hand. He moved the wand in a stately arc and then motioned to Jeffords and Sonseeahray to come to him in the center of the circle of people. Jeffords took her hand and brought her to her feet. Her hand in his trembled so violently it was as though he was holding a small bird within his fingers. He led her to the shaman and there they both knelt.

Nochalo took Jeffords' right hand and Sonseeahray's left hand. Then he made a small incision under the first joint of the index finger on Jeffords' hand and another incision at the same place on the same finger of Sonseeahray's hand. He pressed the two cut places together and quickly bound the fingers with a twisted thong.

As their blood mixed Nochalo sang,

> *"Now for you there is no rain,*
> *For one is shelter to the other.*
> *Now for you there is no sun,*
> *For one is shelter to the other.*
> *Now for you nothing is hard or bad,*
> *For the hardness and badness is taken by one for the other.*
> *Now for you there is no night,*
> *For one is light to the other.*
> *Now for you there is no cold,*
> *For one is warmth to the other.*
> *Now for you the snow has ended always,*
> *For one is protection for the other.*
> *It is that way, from now on, from now on.*
> *Now it is good and there is always food,*
> *And now there is always drink,*
> *And now there is always comfort.*
> *Now there is no loneliness,*
> *Now, forever, forever, there is no loneliness."*

Then Nochalo sprinkled pollen on both their bowed heads and he said, "There are two bodies but now there is but one blood in both of them and you are the same person."

Nochalo walked away and Cochise came rapidly to Jeffords and said softly, "Go."

Jeffords and Sonseeahray slipped away and no one turned to watch them go. At the edge of the camp there were two white horses and they mounted them and rode away.

They rode for almost an hour until they came to the far end of the canyon and then they turned their horses' heads up the sloping trail that was before them and rode for a little while longer. Finally they came to a flat platform that jutted out

332

over the canyon. On the rock platform was a newly constructed wickiup. Silver bells were fastened to the sides of the door and when the air stirred the bells moved lightly with it.

They dismounted and entered the dwelling. The inside was filled with desert flowers.

"Listen to the bells," she said. "It is as though they are singing in my heart."

2

When he woke in the morning she was not there. He sat up and threw off the bearskin blanket and rushed from the dwelling. The sun was high. She was nowhere to be seen. There was a fire started. He called to her. There was no answer. Nervous thoughts tumbled through his head. He called to her again. In a moment she burst from the forest. She wore only a short skirt. Her hair was wet.

"Where have you been?" he asked. When he looked at her he hurt.

"Swimming."

"Why did you not wake me?"

Her eyes crinkled. "You were sleeping with a smile on your face. I could not wake you."

He took her head between his hands. "It was bad to wake and not find you at my side. I thought I was ending a long dream." He stroked her streaming hair. "Why did you not wait for me to go swimming?"

"Together?" she asked, startled.

"Yes."

"A man and a woman do not swim together."

"Why not?"

"No one does," she said. "No one ever does."

"Would you not like to?"

She lowered her eyes. "Would it please you, husband?"

"Only if it would please you, too."

"Is that what is done between American men and women?"

"There is special clothing for it."

"We have no special clothing," she said ingenuously.

He cupped her chin and kissed her. She moved her lips against his. "Do I do it right?" she asked. "I like to touch our lips."

"Yes," he said. He kissed her again. "You do it right."

In the daylight he could see that the flat rock made a sort of terrace halfway up the wall of the canyon. From where they stood they could see the wisps of smoke rising from the rancheria below them. They could not see the wickiups, hidden among the trees on the canyon floor.

"Everything is here," she said happily. She pointed

around. There were containers with mescal cakes, sacks of ripe acorns, cakes made of juniper berries to be eaten with water, roasted pinyon nuts, mesquite cakes and mesquite powder to disolve in water for a beverage, powder made of sumac berries for another kind of beverage, dried mustard seed, roasted yucca fruit, paste made from yucca, a fruit tray covered with the fruit from the prickly-pear cactus and the fruit from the sahuaro.

All the necessities for preparing food had been provided. There was a new food strainer made from bear grass, spoons made of yucca leaves, liquid containers from the hard interior of the sahuaro. There was a metate, water gourds, fire drills.

In front of the wickiup was a crescent-shaped cooking enclosure, four feet high, which also served as a windbreak for the wickiup. A little to one side was a *ramada* made of oak and covered with willow branches, under which food could be kept cool.

"Did you make all this?" he asked wonderingly.

"Not alone," she said. "Oh, it was fun. I helped to make the things and bring the food up from below and every once in a while I seemed to understand anew why I was doing it and I thought I could not go on. My heart would start to beat so fast I thought it would come out of my body."

"Are you happy?"

"Happy?" she repeated. "I have often been happy. I was happy when I was with the White Mountain people. Then when I was returned to my parents I thought then that I was happy. When I had the rite I thought that I finally found what it was to be happy. Now I do not know what to think. Each time I think I have reached the end of the feeling and then something more comes." She looked up at him, half frightened. "A girl should not talk of these things, maybe. They say it is not modest. But last night after we came here it seemed that such good feeling could not go on. It seemed that surely one must die. It seemed that one could not have that and then not have it. I thought when I was having it that way that I could never live again and be happy not having it, but then afterward there was something just as good, not the same, but just as good, and then this morning I did not want the other feeling at all. I woke and looked at you and touched you and felt your face and listened to you breathe and there was nothing I wanted different. I think I would not have liked it if you had wakened then. It was as it should be. Then I left you and there was another good feeling because it hurt to leave you and while it was hurting I could say to myself, I do not have to do this, I can remain here with him, only it was a good kind of hurting, walking away from

334

you and thinking, soon I will be going the other way, back to
him, and the thought gave me that feeling of my heart coming through my skin again, and then I went to the stream,
there is a deep place up there and it is almost a pool, and
when I got into the water it felt different against me because my body was different. I looked at myself and it was
almost as though I looked at a stranger. I kept thinking what
you did to my body and I loved my body very much because
it had given you happiness." She walked away from him.
He saw she was blushing. "It is not modest to talk that way.
You asked me if I were happy," she said defensively.

"There is no modesty between us," he said.

"A girl should not talk that way. My parents would be scan-
dalized."

"No," he said. "Do not think that way. Everything can be
said. Nochalo said it last night, we are two bodies and one
blood. It is as though I were another girl or you were another
man. As though you were my father or I was your mother.
Everything can be said, the good and the bad, the beautiful
and the unlovely. That is the way it is. There must be nothing
secret between us, no words that we cannot listen to from each
other, nothing we cannot do with each other."

"I do not want you to think I ever said bad things before."

"Listen to me," he commanded. "Each time something is
held back it makes a little part of a wall. Each little thing,
no matter how small, adds to that wall. And then you will
find you are on one side of the wall and I am on the other
and there will be no way of crossing it. Until now we have
each lived within ourselves, alone, and now we must share
everything together. We must not grow alone in any way now,
only together."

"Yes," she said at last, "like two streams that have wandered by themselves now coming together. Oh, do you feel
the things I do?"

"Yes. I cannot say them. I cannot say them in my own
language and I can say them less in yours."

"Are they not good feelings?"

He went to her. "Each person thinks he or she alone has
these feelings, as though the feelings were created each time.
And each person is right. No one feels the same things. They
go by the same names, but they are different, just as faces are
different."

She broke away from him suddenly and turned her back.
When she turned around he saw that she had cried a little.
"I am not being a good wife to you. You must be hungry."

"I have forgotten about food."

"You must eat," she said seriously. "My mother said a
husband judges his wife by the way she prepares his food. I

335

do not want you to think I have no skill as a wife." She hastened to the cooking enclosure. "Go to the stream and swim. When you return everything will be ready."

"Come with me."

"No. Not yet. If we went we might not come back for a long time."

"We wouldn't, all right," he said in English.

"What did you say?"

"I agreed with you."

"You see? Now go. The water is cold but it is good." She lifted a long stirring stick and pointed. "The water is over there. It is not far."

He went to the stream. It widened at a place and the water was several feet deep. He plunged into it and felt the icy chill over him. He stepped out after a while and stood naked in the sun. He felt more like a living man than he had ever felt before. When he returned the food was ready. There were cakes, gruel, and cold roasted meat. He started to eat. Then he asked, "Are you not eating?"

She shook her head and bit her lip. "I cannot eat."

"I will not eat either."

"No," she said. "Please, to please me. I cannot."

"Why are you crying?" He put down his plate.

"No. Please," she said. "I do not know. Maybe when one feels happy it shows in the opposite way."

He moved toward her. "No," she repeated. "Please, please, do not move. Just go on eating. Please." She wiped her eyes. The tears seemed like diamond dust on her face. "It is taking a little time. All this has happened. I have not had time to understand it. Please, do not come near yet. Just go on eating and let me sit here and look at you."

He tried to eat. The food which had tasted so good at first now could not be swallowed. He put the plate down again and crossed over to her.

"I am glad you came," she said. "I did not want to spoil your eating, but I am glad you came." She shivered against him. "Just let me stay this way for a little while. I will try to get over this as quickly as I can. I know now how a bird must feel the first time it flies. I know now how a little dog must feel when its eyes open and it sees for the first time. It is very beautiful but it is big, too, and it is frightening." She lay her head against him. "You will not grow tired of me?"

"No."

"This has been so much that even if there were nothing else it would be enough, but you will not grow tired of me and go back to your people?"

"Never to leave you, sweetheart."

336

"My father said that a white man could never be happy always with an Indian wife."

"I am not a white man. You are not an Indian. There is nothing outside to which we belong, no people, nothing, only each other."

"You must tell me that often," she whispered. "You must not let me forget that."

He picked her up and carried her into the dwelling.

"Not in the day," she said. Then she said, "Just hold me tightly for a little while. I would like to get inside of you. If I were inside of you I would never again feel fear, maybe."

Then she said, and there was no fright now in her voice, "Where do all the feathers come from? Oh, where do they come from?"

3

He stood in the deep part of the stream, the cold water reaching his waist, his head and beard covered with soap suds.

"Do not look," she said.

"I cannot look. I would get soap in my eyes. Come in."

"Turn your head. Do not look until the water covers my hips."

"I have soap in my eyes," he shouted. "I cannot see anything!"

She was naked behind a tree. She looked at his body above the water. She thought it was very white, up to his wrists and his neck. She suddenly felt ashamed of the golden color of her skin. She slipped past the tree and darted into the water behind him. The water line reached just below her breasts. She put her arms around him from behind and held him as though she were losing him. The suds got on her face and in her hair. He sat down in the water, pulling her down with him and then they both emerged, laughing and coughing.

She was greatly embarrassed. She looked around as though she thought someone might be watching her.

"Would you like me to wash your back?" he asked.

"If it would please you," she said timidly.

"It would please me very much." He worked the suds around her back and under her armpits and then around her breasts.

"Does my back come around to the front now?" she asked demurely.

He kissed her between her breasts. "It is like a wave through me," he said. He crushed her hard and kissed her again. "How much I love you."

"With the skins so different," she said.

"What skins?"

She held her arm next to his.

"What difference does that make?" he demanded. He lifted her chin and looked into her eyes. "What are you thinking?"

"You are so white," she said piteously.

He lifted her out of the water and carried her to the bank. He put her down gently on a bed of pine needles. "Would you rather have an Indian for a husband? Would you like to take one of Cochise's men? Are you tired of me already?"

She put her hand over his mouth. "It is not for me that I speak and you know it. It is for you." She touched his beard lightly with her fingertips. "Would you not like me to be white as you?"

He looked at her golden body lying on the green pine. Her skin was the color of honey. He felt his blood again and he was too choked to talk. He kissed her gently on each breast, and then he said, "The smallest change, the very smallest change, would be sinful."

"You say that to make me feel good."

"There could be no change," he said reverently. "Not the tiniest thing, not in your face, not in your eyes, not in your body. And not in your skin. It is as though the sun were shining only where you are lying."

"You do not lie to me?"

"The color in you is sunlight. Look, look at my hands. Where the sun has been on them they are darker than any part of you, much darker. The sun has entered into all of you, just as it has touched my two hands. It has passed into all of you and finding you lovely it has stayed in you and lives there. It is in your color all the time and sometimes it comes into your eyes and sometimes it lights inside your face."

"The thing that is in me is love," she said. She lifted her hand. "Listen, it comes from my fingers. Can you hear it, husband?"

"Yes."

She placed her hand over her heart. "Put your head there. It is being said there too. Can you hear it?" She pressed his face against her breast. "I told you we would make our own language."

4

The time passed, the days and nights mixing, one passing into the other. She never ended delighting him. He noticed how clean she was, about herself and the little dwelling, how she kept it swept out, how she arranged the food and utensils neatly and kept them covered. She mixed the basic foods they had in many different ways, so that the distinctive flavors blended and he never tired of it.

He practiced regularly with the bow and arrow and one day managed to kill a deer. He cleaned it and brought a large part of it to her and watched, in fascination, as she skinned it, cut it up, roasted some of it and dried the rest, and then set to work on the hide, making a deerskin blanket softer than any velvet he had ever touched. He could not marvel enough at her quiet and swift efficiency, at the way she managed to do several things at once and still be ready always for anything he suggested.

They ate and they swam and they walked through the forest. They lay in the sun and listened to the songs of the birds, who were without fear, who sat on her wrist and took nuts from her fingers. The birds seemed to accept her as another living thing in the woods and he understood perfectly.

And in the nights they sat by their small fire and smelled the burning wood and after the fire died they covered themselves with their hide robes and lay on their backs and looked at the sky and they asked each other many questions.

One night dry lightning flashed across the sky. She got on her knees and crossed her hands against her breast and said,

> "Go along without anger,
> Be kind as you pass above us,
> Do not put fear into our minds,
> Lightning, please make no trouble."

When she lay down she was trembling. He questioned her and she whispered how potent Lightning was. "There are different accounts, but many of the old people say that Lightning is the father of Child of the Water," she said. "It is said that White Painted Lady lay down during a great storm and that Lightning struck her four times and that it was this that caused the birth of Child of the Water, who was conceived without a father. Later Lightning thought that Child of the Water was his son but he was not sure and he tested him in many ways giving him difficult things to do, and when he was assured that Child of the Water was his son he gave him great power and Child of the Water was able to kill a Giant who was preventing the People of the Woods from getting enough food to eat."

As he listened to her stories he thought that somewhere in the long past there was some connection between the Chiricahua mythology and the Biblical teachings. It may have derived from the early Spanish missionaries, although when he questioned her he gathered that the Apache mythos was older than the coming of the *conquistadores*. It may have come from another place entirely, a place where the Apaches originated. Twisted, changed to suit their own life and customs, the story of the birth of Child of the Water, the great culture hero, was always ascribed to some magical means—and always immaculately—either by Lightning, or, as some versions had it, during a fearful storm.

"One night," she related, "in the very old days, White Painted Lady was saying some prayers. A Spirit came to her and said, 'Take off your clothes and get down on your back. The rain will make a child for you. When that child is born you must call him Child of the Water. Let the water fall into you here.' " She pointed to her vagina. "Then the water fell, four times, and that is how Child of the Water was born."

There was really no basic difference in the varieties of the legend, since Lightning and storm and water were all part of the same thing. There was another legend about a flood that destroyed the world and she told him there was a mountain not far away where one could still see the marks of the water at its highest point. He questioned her about the story of the killing of the Giant and it was similar to the story of David and Goliath. There was one odd feature of it: the Giant was killed by shooting an arrow into the heel of his foot, the only vulnerable part of his body, and that aspect of it reminded him of the story of Achilles.

The stories she told him gave him an odd comfort. He was not a religious man but somehow he found an indefinable security in these distant similarities, implying an earlier linkage. Then he thought that if he felt that way she surely would too, and he tried to remember what he knew of Biblical stories and told them to her, and as she too began to understand that there might somewhere have been a common source for both of them she drank assurance from his words and questioned him even more painstakingly than he did her.

It gave her a grave and quiet ecstasy finally to believe they were not in the beginning as strange and as separate from each other as she had thought.

Then one morning she showed him a small piece of wood on which were a series of small notches. She counted ten of the notches and then counted them again, to make certain.

"Why cannot we stay longer?" he pleaded.

"We cannot remain more than ten days," she said. "That is how it is."

On this she was firm and they started back for the rancheria and he knew that there would be other good things but that it would never be quite the same again anywhere.

340

Chapter Seventeen

By an act of the Fourth Legislature of the Territory of Arizona and in the face of loud charges of fraud, the capital of the territory was moved from Prescott to Tucson in 1867. Now both military and civil headquarters were centered in the Old Pueblo. Tucson was not only the military headquarters but the chief depot for Camps Lowell, Cameron, Wallen, Bowie, and Grant.

Stores for these outposts were bought locally in Tucson or were shipped there from Yuma and thence redistributed. Freight rates soared upward due to distances involved and the constant Indian depredations.

Tucson grew more and more into a unique and segregated community. Paper money of the United States depreciated to half its face value. Prices rose uncontrolled as the merchants of the Ring held the community in its grasp and compensated for scarcity by inflation. To their purposes the Indians served almost as silent partners, keeping the supply of food low.

An Indian reservation, one of the first in the territory proper, was established on the Colorado River about forty miles north of Yuma, and Jeffords watched its progress with great interest because he knew that the success or failure of the reserve would influence all the Indians in one way or the other, and he knew that Cochise would have frequent and accurate reports on conditions there.

The reservation was a disastrous failure.

One of the smaller branches of the Apache nation had made a peace treaty with the white men in 1863 and had tried to uphold it from then on. They had kept their part of the agreement and, for their pains, were slaughtered wherever they showed themselves outside of their forests near Prescott.

When the new reservation was formed these Apaches elected to undertake a tribal move, from Prescott to the Colorado, to find the peace they could not find on their own land. On this hegira across Arizona old men and women died like flies. When the remainder of the tribe reached the reserve they were put to work, and although, like all Apaches, they had little knowledge of tools and labor, they soon constructed a huge irrigation ditch.

They found no peace. The Superintendent of Indian Affairs for the Pacific Coast proceeded to double-cross his own Agent on the reservation and then the Indians. Food and money allotted by Washington for the maintenance of the reserve disappeared. The Indians were hungry and without clothes.

They pleaded with the Agent and he in turn pleaded with the Superintendent. Nothing happened. The elders of the tribe, who had respect for the Agent, gave him funds to buy horses for them so they could hunt for food. The Agent was promptly arrested by the Superintendent on a charge of outfitting Indians for the warpath—by purchasing horses for them. The Indians got the Agent free and he escaped.

And then one night the Apache warriors left the reservation. They left their wives and children behind them and went on the warpath.

It was not until almost five years later that these same Indians surrendered again. They gave up to General George Crook, the greatest military scourge of the Indians in Arizona, who in the end brought a measure of peace to the territory. It was Crook, who had no love for the Indians, who said that his experiences had taught him that the Indians never broke a treaty they made—and the white man never kept one.

During the months that followed, Jeffords divided his time between Tucson and whatever place Cochise established his camp. His manner of life and his own nature caused him to be regarded by his own kind as a strange man, a mysterious man. It was known that he had friendly relations with the Indians and yet no one knew how close these relations were.

The stories about him were without number. It was reported that he had been seen among the Indians on their raids. Some persons continued to believe he supplied the Apaches with arms, although no one could prove it.

He kept the mail running efficiently and safely and the citizens of Tucson finally accepted him as an unknown among them. He welcomed the judgment. He encouraged the coolness he felt around him. He wanted no confidences and he gave none and he asked only to be left alone. And he felt that his true home was among the Indians.

He maintained his close friendship with St. John and told him of many of the things he had done and St. John kept his silence. Duffield stopped asking questions, saying to St. John one day, "I don't give a damn what he does with the Indians. I know he isn't selling them guns. And he's keeping the mail running—that's all I care about."

St. John who continued in Jeffords' confidence and who, through him, led a vicarious existence of his own among the Apaches, knew that Jeffords supplied Cochise with nothing to pursue his implacable war. Jeffords always brought gifts when he visited the camp, tobacco for Cochise and Klosen, flannel, calico, cotton, blankets, needles, thread, butcher knives, shirts, food of different kinds. And in his gifts there was always something special for his wife.

She was never out of his mind. He could always pause in what he was doing, anywhere, and close his eyes and see her. His enforced absences from her increased his moodiness and made him withdraw even more into himself.

He became, in his thinking, almost more Indian than white man. He understood the problems of the Indians as clearly as he did his own. He became closer to Cochise as the months passed and listened to him and advised him, and he developed a profound respect for the deep, complicated nature of the Indian. He found that when Cochise was not under the spell of one of his frequent depressions, he could lift his mind to brilliant heights. He found him witty, kind, and possessed of an incomparable understanding. When Jeffords was not in the Indian rancheria Cochise watched over Sonseeahray as though she were his own daughter and he loved her second only to Jeffords.

In their many talks the tactics of Cochise's war never were mentioned. Specific raids made by Cochise's warriors were never discussed. But the large strategy of the war Cochise had committed himself and his people to did not fall into this instinctive taboo. As he grew more and more to be trusted and loved by Cochise, Jeffords slowly, bit by bit, attempted to convince Cochise of the futility of his position, of the ultimate inevitability of his defeat. The force of his argument was largely spent from the start. Cochise readily admitted he must in the end lose all, but argued, in his place, that there was no substitute for his war, that the Americans had made it impossible for Indians to live in an honorable and dignified peace, and that death was better than servitude.

The debacle at the River Reservation on the Colorado was a terrible handicap to Jeffords' efforts. When he searched his own mind he had to admit that rather than see the Chiricahuas betrayed in that manner he would prefer to see them continue as they were.

2

Nalikadeya had a difficult time in delivering her second son to Cochise. She was in labor for more than eighteen hours. Several midwives in the tribe came to assist her. When her pains continued and the child failed to come forth, a special shaman who had knowledge of the ceremony of childbirth was summoned and he began to sing his holy song and at the same time worked gently over her abdomen.

Nalikadeya knelt with her legs separated before a post of wood, clinging to the post for steadiness, and the midwives

343

bathed her loins with water containing special herbs. To hasten the birth they gave Nalikadeya yucca leaves swallowed with salt and finally one of the midwives bore down on the distended abdomen and the child was delivered at last. Nalikadeya's face was glassy and wet and yet she did not cry in her pain.

The child was large and healthy and the gathered women waited and, when he did not cry immediately, they proclaimed that he would grow into a strong, healthy man.

Cochise, who had been taken for a long walk into the hills by some of the other men, since fathers never stayed around while their wives were giving birth, hastened back to his wickiup when the good word was brought to him. Tesalbestinay had already rubbed a mixture of grease and red ochre over the infant's body to prevent the skin from inflaming, and another woman had gathered the afterbirth and had wrapped it securely to prevent animals from getting to it, and had put it into a juniper bush, so that the annual fruition of the bush might work its beneficent life-giving qualities on the child.

Despite the delay and pain of the birth, Nalikadeya was on her feet the next day. She tied a rope around her belly to keep her stomach from dropping and resumed her normal duties. Within a few months the infant's neck was strong enough to support its head and it was placed in the reed cradle and carried around on Nalikadeya's back.

The ears of the child were pierced, so that his hearing would be improved, and tiny turquoise earrings were hung from the tiny ears.

For this ceremony Sonseeahray had sewn a new buckskin jacket for the infant. On the shirt she had affixed quail heads, arrow points, quartz crystals, shell beads, and pine twigs, to ward off bad luck and disease. Under her instructions, Jeffords made a necklace charm, fitted with cholla to keep the child healthy, with corn for good luck, and with spots of red paint to make the child strong.

During the rite there was much drinking and eating. The Indians sang and danced, but Cochise took no part in the merriment. He appeared to be unwell and he sat alone and watched the festivities with a dull and heavy eye. Jeffords watched him for several hours and then he joined him, asking, "What is troubling you?"

Cochise struck his belly. "Pain."

"Too much tiswin?"

"No. There are knives in there." Cochise's mouth was twisted. He pointed to the fire. "What do you see there?" he asked hoarsely.

"Nothing. Just the fire."

"No," Cochise said. "There is a face." His voice was so tortured Jeffords looked at him in astonishment. He reached out and rested his hand upon his arm.

"Do you have bad memories, Cochise?" he asked quietly.

"Not memories, Tagliato. A memory." There was an uncanny fear in his eyes. "Do you believe in a Ghost?"

"A bad memory can become like a Ghost," Jeffords said.

"I have a Ghost. It lives with me. It was only a Mexican. I do not know what I did that was wrong afterward. But the Ghost is with me. The face is there now, in the fire."

"Tell me about it, Cochise."

"It was nothing. I have done it often. I ordered him buried and covered with ants. There was something in his face. I have never forgotten it. I saw him last night in a dream. The door to my wickiup opened and he came in. I wanted to get up and fight him but I could not. I could just say, 'Ah, ah, ah.' I said, 'What do you want? Go away.' He stayed a long time and then I woke and I was wet all over with sweat."

There was a time when Jeffords might have laughed. He had stopped mocking many things. "Cannot Nochalo help you?"

"He made many ceremonies. He has a knowledge of Ghost-sickness. But he cannot help me. Sometimes it is in my head. It rocks there as though my head were filled with stones. Sometimes I have the feeling of knives in my stomach. When I swallow food the food gets teeth."

"This is not just one man, maybe," Jeffords said.

"I see only him."

"You think it is his face alone. His face is made of many faces. The faces are all the things you would like to forget."

"There is nothing to forget," Cochise said harshly. "I have done what I have had to do."

"Listen, Cochise. It is your whole life of hatred that is haunting you."

"The path was made for me. I followed it." His face became stony.

"You do not believe that yourself. It was not so before. You were happier then. There is a long line of dead faces."

"I did not start this war."

"That is true. It was caused by a fool. But you know that it is a bad war. There will always be more white enemies. No matter how many you kill there will be more. There are more white men than all the Indians combined. They are like grain. They are without number. You can kill them every day and every night but in the end there will be more."

"You speak of your own people as 'they,' Tagliato."

"I think with you."

"I am not defeated."

"No, you are not. You are a greater warrior than they are.

But in the end they will defeat you, as you have said. And now, while you still are victorious in battle, you are becoming defeated inside of yourself. I speak as your brother, Cochise. I speak only because I love you. You are losing your war. You have less warriors now than you had six moons ago. Each harvest the ranks of the Chiricahuas become thinner. Your women share husbands because there are not enough men to go around. And you, yourself, are filled with Ghost-sickness so that you cannot find pleasure in the ceremony for your own child."

"What else can be done?" Cochise asked, shifting unhappily. "What else is offered to us? Are we offered a just peace? Are there honest men to treat with? There is nothing but treachery. Indian leaders who bring their tribes to the white men live to see them slaughtered like sheep."

There was no answer to this.

"What are we offered? A reservation? What is a reservation? A large jail, where Indians starve and go cold. Look around, Tagliato. Show me a reservation where the Indians are treated justly, where they can live in dignity as befits men."

"The fault lies not with the reservations but with the men who administer them," Jeffords replied. "The way things are, each Agent is the supreme boss. But if there was a good Agent it might be a good thing. Until there is a peace between each white man and each Indian, until they can walk among each other as brothers, it is necessary to keep the Indian separated from the white man, lest one bad white man or one bad Indian undo all the work that good Indians and good white men have accomplished."

"Why not put the white men on reservations, Tagliato, and find honorable Indians to be their Agents?" Cochise asked mockingly. "This is our country." He smiled painfully and said, "No, Tagliato, I have my own burden to carry. I would rather see my people dead than deliver them to white soldiers. You are a true brother. I listen to you as I listen to myself. There is no answer. We will not conquer. But we will die like men." He stared into the fire. "I will not die of hunger because white men do not give me food. The Chiricahuas are not beggars. We need no one to give us food. We will take what we need to live and if we get killed, well, a man can do worse than die in battle. I will not die of a bullet in my back while I sleep. Mangas Coloradas lived to be an old man to die that way. It would have been better for him to have died fighting, a gun in his hand, a bullet in his chest." He shook his head. "A bullet hurts more when it enters from the back. When it enters from the front it is almost without pain."

The celebrants had departed and it was quiet. Jeffords stood up and hit his pipe on the palm of his hand.

"It would be good if all men spoke with a straight tongue, Tagliato," Cochise said, as though in revery. "Why is it that men do not speak without lying?"

"I do not know."

"A man should never lie."

"No, he should not. But a great many do."

"That is true. But they need not do it. If a man asks you or me a question we do not wish to answer we simply say, 'I do not want to talk about that.' "

Jeffords walked away. He entered his wickiup and sat down wearily. Sonseeahray pulled off his boots and then he undressed and lay next to her. There were no impossible questions to be answered with her.

3

When the rider left, Jeffords poured himself a drink and slowly drained the glass. "There is an answer somewhere," he said. "I can't believe there is just one alternative, war or imprisonment on a reservation. He was dead right and he knew he was right. Supposing I could get him to sit down and talk peace. Who could I bring him to? Who is there in this whole damned territory he could trust as far as he could throw a bronc?"

"You could write to Washington," St. John said, as he had said before.

"Washington! And who in Washington ever heard of me? What could I say? 'Cochise, the Chiricahua Apache, is a personal friend of mine. If you send an honest man out here maybe I could arrange to have the two of them sit down and chew a little fat.' What would happen? Six months from now the letter would finally get where I sent it. A year from now, maybe, that thief who is running things out on the coast would get instructions to get in touch with that Jeffords guy. No, he wouldn't either. He'd be told to send a flunkey. And if I convinced him that Cochise was not a wild animal, then what? A few square miles on the River Reservation?"

"Our governor is very proud of the River Reservation," St. John said. "He recently sent a note to Congress telling it that the River Reservation is an example of how we handle our red charges in this part of the country."

"St. John, this whole business stinks," Jeffords fumed. "We are supposed to be a country of free and equal men. We just fought a war to get rid of slavery. We're a democracy. It says so in the books. The great American democracy. We are a country of endless horizons, according to the books, where a man can go as far as he is able to. Look at us out here. We talk about an Indian problem. This isn't an Indian problem.

347

It is an American problem. It's not the Indians at all who are being tested, it's us. What good are we as a people—what good will we ever be—if we can't find a reasonable answer to all this? What have we learned? What do we know? What kind of men have we running our affairs? We fought four wars in less than a hundred years and what have we learned? We haven't even learned that we are not just a country, but an empire. We are an empire. This is a colony out here. It's the same as though there were thousands of miles of water around us instead of desert. And what lousy colonizers we are turning out to be! And what hypocrites. The country was in an uproar about the way Maximilian was treating the Mexicans. Juarez was a hero. And how did Maximilian act in any way worse than we are acting out here? If any European nation came out to Arizona and handled the Indians the way we are handling them there would be a fifth war."

"You've struck on a truth," St. John agreed soberly. "We don't have trained colonizers. We have West Point and Annapolis to make soldiers and sailors but we have no place to make administrators to handle the affairs of the alien people we have conquered, whose lands we are occupying. They seem to think in Washington that anybody can run an Indian Agency, including the nearest Army officer. Just why a man who is trained to lead men in the field is considered automatically competent to serve as civilian governor for a foreign people is something I have never understood."

"God help us if we are ever called upon to handle a job any bigger than this one," Jeffords said violently.

"We are not a temperate people," St. John went on. "We are a nation of formulated likes and dislikes. We develop a crowd attitude. The crowd attitude in Arizona is hatred for Indians. There are men here who are normal and rational in almost everything they do—but mention Indians and they go crazy. They just hate Indians. They think of Indians as they do of rattlesnakes. There are no degrees of Indians. Outside of the few tribes that gave in from the start and are like tame animals in a zoo, all Indians are bad."

Jeffords poured another drink. "The burden is on us," he said slowly. "We are supposed to be the civilized ones. We are the ones who have to prove ourselves to the Indians, not them to us. They are here. They have always been here. We are the newcomers. If we are better than they are we have to prove it. We have to talk sense and have to keep our word. It's a pretty rotten situation when a bunch of wild Indians do not trust the word of the Government of the United States." He leaned back and put his feet on the desk. He lifted the half-empty whiskey glass and looked at the amber fluid. "You know, Silas," he mused, "we ought to send some of our best citizens up to watch these so-called wild Apaches operate among themselves. Do you think we are a democratic people? There isn't a man up there who wouldn't die willingly for Cochise, but still, before any decisions of importance are made, they hold a council. I've sat in on them. Each man gets a chance to speak. There are no insults, no endless rhetoric, no personal axes to grind. Just a bunch of men expressing their opinions—and knowing that they are planning and figuring for the good of the tribe. Everything is for the good of the tribe. The tribe is like some spiritual body. Personal desires don't count. There are no laws handed down. Cochise seldom issues a decree. Everybody there knows exactly what he can do and what he cannot do, governed by the traditions and natural laws that have lasted since the beginning, I guess. During the fighting Cochise gives orders, to meet the situations as they arise, but in ordinary life there is no need for that. Custom, tradition, the country, the weather, everything, all have combined to establish certain immutable laws, and each Indian governs himself by them. And personal violations are regarded as violations against the whole people. Anything that harms a single person is considered as harming the whole body of them. They have made a perfect adjustment to their social and economic life, and to the land they live on.

"Do you think we are charitable? You ought to see them. Nobody goes hungry—if there is anything at all to eat. There is no private hoarding, no cheating. Whatever they have is divided equally. Everybody gets the same protection, whether there is a man with a gun in the family or not. Why, those Apaches would expect the sky to fall on them if they let their old people go hungry or cold. There are no slums in the Apache rancheria—and there are no railroad tracks either. There's no caste system, and no aristocrats and no commoners. Look at the way civilization developed in Europe and look at them. For centuries, in Europe, there has been the idea of hereditary ruling classes and heriditary commoners. Where do you find that idea among the Indians? Nowhere, and tell me why. How did the people in one part of the world just naturally develop the king idea and the people of another just never did? We can't understand it, not even us, the democratic Americans. So we try to change it. We talk about Indian kings and Indian princesses. There never was an Indian princess. There never was an Indian king or emperor. Cochise's children are no better than other children and if Tahzay, the oldest one, doesn't show he can handle the job, he won't be elected to succeed Cochise at all. He'll probably be given the chance, but if he falls down, out he goes. Montezuma was called an emperor because that was the only English word that could be applied to him. He never was anything of the kind. He was chosen to be a military leader specifically to deal with the Spaniards. If he had defeated them he would have gone back to his old job—some minor chief. But we cannot understand that. Despite our boasts we just cannot conceive of any people being inherently democratic. We have to invent conditions that never existed to satisfy our own conceptions of how things should have been.

"I wonder by what standards we have arrogated to ourselves the right to call Indians savages. We could learn from them. We could learn some very complicated things and some very simple things. But we are not learning. We are growing up into being a big boy among the nations of the world now and we ought to be learning all the time. We are moving out into a tough world, a little late. Other people have had a head start. We ought to be working like hell learning how to catch so when the play is tossed to us some day we won't fumble it. But we are not learning a thing, not a god-damned thing at all." He stood up. "Let's get out of here. I've talked too much."

4

They walked toward the Congress Hall. The streets were crowded. Soldiers ogled Mexican girls. Mexicans were sleeping on the plaza. There were drunks on the streets, although it was not much past noon. There was noise of all kinds, horses' hooves, the blacksmith's clanging, children shouting, rumble of military wagons, singing and a piano playing in one of the saloons.

As they walked St. John's thoughts went back to the Jeffords he had first encountered at Mesilla, and he thought of how he had matured and developed since then. Some men act upon each other like chemicals, he thought. That was how Jeffords and Cochise affected each other. Without each other they would have been different men. He did not know Cochise these days; the Indian was older and less malleable, probably, but the change must be in him, too. Somehow Jeffords had reached out and had touched something deep in the Indian, or they would not be to each other what they were. He thought how strange it was that Jeffords, an educated American, a man of experience, a man who had traveled widely through his own country, needed an Indian to lift him out of himself, to give him balance, a new wisdom, an understanding, and, possibly, a certain greatness. Jeffords had a greatness, he thought, and he got it from Cochise, and if Jeffords had it, there must be others who had the same thing and maybe the kind of people who were filling and running the territory did not matter at all.

The Congress Hall was more than usually crowded. There

was an epidemic of malaria sweeping the town and most men believed alcohol was the best preventive. Jeffords walked to a small clearance at the bar, looking neither to the right nor left. He knew that, as always, there would be eyes on him and covert whispering. St. John, walking behind him, saw the drinkers look at him, some curiously, some angrily, some with half-hidden respect.

A little later there was a commotion at the door. A man lurched toward the bar. Jeffords glanced at him and at first thought he was drunk, and then he saw he wasn't drunk at all.

The man was followed by several other men from the town. They were cursing loudly. The first man reached the bar and asked for whiskey. He finished three drinks rapidly. The men who followed him were talking to other people in the saloon. "Tell me what happened, Deke," somebody called out.

The man called Deke finished a fourth drink before he spoke. He was a rancher, from Sonoita. He was working in the field. The Indians came. They killed his wife and two children and set fire to his house. The first thing he knew about it was when he saw the smoke from the house. By the time he got there the Indians were gone. He got on his horse and went after them. He didn't care much about staying alive but he wanted to take an Indian with him. He never caught up with them.

He talked as though his mouth were a hollow cave. His words came out almost with an echo. He looked around vaguely. He was not focusing yet. "What do I do now?" he asked nobody in particular.

A heavy man with a two-day beard stubble on his face banged a hamlike fist on the bar. He was Les Hawkins, a rancher near Pantano, whose place had been raided by Cochise's Apaches some two weeks before and whose cattle had been stolen. He pushed some people aside until he reached Jeffords. He pointed at Jeffords and shouted, "Why don't you ask him?"

Deke, in a daze, sidled up to Jeffords. "What do I do now, mister?" He wiped his face vaguely. "Can you tell me?"

"He can tell you," Hawkins said. "He knows all about Indians."

The drinkers began to move back. Jeffords looked steadily at Hawkins. He spoke to Deke but he never stopped looking at Hawkins. "The Indians who raided your place ought to be caught and killed," he said.

Hawkins roared. "Jesus! Listen to him. 'The Indians ought to be caught and killed.' Go ahead, Deke, ask him whether he wants to help kill them."

"The Indians ought to be killed," Jeffords repeated evenly.

351

"Then some of the white men who made them that way in the first place ought to be killed, too. Then we could start all over again."

"What white men made them what way?" Hawkins asked nastily. "What the hell you trying to say, Jeffords?"

"I think you've been drinking too much," Jeffords said softly.

"That's my business," Hawkins said. "I drink like a white man."

Jeffords cocked his head.

"I do everything like a white man," Hawkins said.

"You might quit talking," Jeffords said.

Hawkins' hand went to his holster and Jeffords fired. Hawkins' right arm hung limp.

"That wasn't a miss," Jeffords said. He looked around. "This thing isn't Deke and the dozen Indians who killed his wife and kids. Those Indians ought to be strung up, same as anybody who kills without cause. Only there will be more of it." He tried to think of what to say to them. It was beyond saying at a bar. He suddenly thought of the time he worked a boat on the Mississippi. He remembered how the river overflowed, regularly, and how the people built their puny dikes and how nobody tried to find the cause, just went on building dikes that got destroyed. "Is there anybody here who ever tried to figure out why Indians started killing in the first place?" He looked from face to face. He saw admiration in their eyes; they were only thinking about how he outshot Hawkins. It was no use. He walked out of the saloon.

When St. John found him in his office he was slumped in his chair and his eyes were like lead. "What can you do?" he asked him. "Where can you make a start? The damage is done, the real damage. Cochise has a lot of fighting men. Ponce is one of them. Say it was Ponce who pulled the raid on Hawkins. How the hell can Hawkins be made to understand Ponce? How can Ponce be brought to understand Les Hawkins was an all-right guy? Deke's wife and kids probably never hurt an Indian in their lives. How long would it take to make Deke understand why Indians do what they do?" He dug the heels of his hands into his head. "It's happened all over the world. It probably started with the beginning of the world. It's going on everywhere, all people, all countries. Who the hell is going to explain to Deke? It might have been Ponce. I know Ponce. I've sat and talked with him. I've drunk with him and I've gambled with him and I've played games with him. They had a racing contest up there one day. My wife won among the girls and Ponce beat the men. They competed with each other. Ponce beat my wife by only a few feet. Then we all sat down and had a big meal. Ponce is a nice kid. He has a sense of humor. He laughs. He's fair. He's generous. He gave me a lance for my wedding. He made it himself. He's a nice kid and yet he can go out and kill off white women and children the same way a rancher can slaughter beef."

"Hawkins is decent when he isn't in his cups," St. John said.

"They're both getting pushed," Jeffords said. "Ponce and Hawkins, both of them." He took out his revolver and removed the shell. He blew through the barrel. "I might have had to kill Hawkins," he said slowly. "Because Ponce helped kill Deke's family." He jammed the gun back into its holster. "It's like being lost in a forest."

5

When he entered the Scat Fly, Mrs. Wilson came up to him. Since Terry had left she had regarded Jeffords with a great coolness. "There is a letter for you, Captain Jeffords," she said. She handed him a letter with a San Francisco postmark. It must have arrived while one of his clerks was distributing the mail, he thought. He held the letter in his hand and then he saw that Mrs. Wilson wanted to speak to him and he didn't want to listen to her. He thanked her hastily and went to his room.

He never could think of Terry without remembering the day he found her in the ambush. He thought of how fond he was of her, and how it might have worked out differently. The letter was dated November 24, 1868, and he read:

I guess you are just never going to write to me (I gave my address to Aunt Abigail and if you wanted it you could have obtained it from her) so the only thing to do is to write first, even though that is not considered lady-like. But then I always was the first to write, wasn't I, Tom, even in the old days, and even then you never answered all my letters. I hope you will answer this one.

It seems so long since I saw you and the rest of the people in Tucson. Things have happened (not big things, but all the little things that go to change a person) and Tucson seems so far away. And yet, I think that if I just closed my eyes and made a wish and then opened them I would find myself back there, and all this time I have been away would be just a dream.

It isn't that I haven't been having fun. I have. But I think there is too much of the desert rat in me. I think you put it there. (Remember when you told me about the smell of the sage?) San Francisco is a wonderful city. It's like no place I have ever seen, but then I haven't seen much, have I? Anyway it is full of hills, not our kind of hills—far apart and all spread out—but hills pressed closely together, all squeezed in, and when you get to the top of one of them you look out into the water and there are always gulls flying around and ships in the bay and there is a salty smell. It's beautiful, in its own way, and sometimes when I stand alone on one of the hills I get something of the same feeling I used to get on one of our hills. Not the same, but something of it.

I've met some lovely people here, friends of people in Tucson, and they've been wonderful to me. I've received three proposals of marriage but I haven't said yes yet. They are really very nice young men, too. One of them has a large sailing boat and we go out into the ocean.

I thought at first that I would get some kind of position here but the opportunities for a lady to work are not many. A friend of Aunt Abigail has a hotel here and I thought I would try to manage the restaurant but it was not the same as the Scat Fly and I didn't like it at all. I keep telling Aunt Abigail I ought to be working but she said I worked hard enough all those years I was with her and for me to enjoy myself.

So I've started going to art galleries and I've seen a few of the old California missions down south and I even started taking lessons in Spanish. When you see me again you will be surprised at how much I know that I didn't know when I left Tucson.

And when are you going to see me again, Tom? Don't you want me yet? Is this the way it's going to be forever? I think of you so much and sometimes I get so lonely that I think I'm going to leave right away. Only I don't. Why don't you send for me?

What are you doing? Aunt Abigail tells me you are still running the mails and that you are stranger than ever and that people don't understand you any more and that you disappear for weeks at a time and nobody knows where you go, although there are all kinds of rumors. She says that if everybody wasn't afraid of you and that if you didn't keep the mails going so perfectly she doesn't know what would happen to you.

She says you are not married yet and that you are not even seeing any girl in town. That's the best news she ever told me.

Will you write? Will you write soon? I'm hungry for news from you. Just a little note—or a long letter if you can. Anything. And take care of yourself, Tom, please take care of yourself.

He put the letter down. He was a little surprised at how much emotion he felt reading it. Funny redhead. What could he write to her? That Aunt Abigail didn't know what she was talking about and that he was married to an Indian girl whom he loved dearly and that his disappearances were only visits that he was paying, as a husband, to his wife? He could see her lying on the deck of a sailing boat with her red hair blowing in the wind.

6

When he did not know where the camp was he rode out to the valley and sent up signals and when he got his answer from some distant mesa he went to her. He would go along for days, doing his work, eating and sleeping, and in the night, drinking alone, avoiding everyone but St. John, and then it would be too much and he would have to go to her. He would have to find her and be with her and listen to her and watch her and talk to her. He had to find her body, that he now knew so well, and listen to her sounds and make her forget her own loneliness. When he came to her everything that was cloudy and twisted in his head went away from him and he found peace again.

She was always changing. Sometimes she was like a small child and she delighted him with the things she said, filling him so full he thought his skin could not contain him. Then she was altogether a woman, as complete and as complex as a woman could be, passionate and eager, strong as he was, sometimes so violent that he fell back drained and aching with the hollow pain of his love for her. Sometimes she seemed much older than he was, full of odd, ancient ideas and fancies. Sometimes she was almost like another man; they walked and hunted together and it was not correct to say she loved to be with him in the forests. She was the forests. She was everything he saw and listened to and smelled. She was the same as the birds and the wild animals they found. She was the waters of the stream and she was the earth.

She learned laboriously to speak his language, the love phrases first, and then in the depth and extent of her passion with him she forgot the alien expressions and reverted to her own tongue and cried and sobbed strange things. She was studious and eager in her quests to find that which he loved best when they were together and it was not long before he forgot that he had ever known a woman before her.

At the beginning, when he returned from his times in Tucson, he was hurt by what seemed to be her lack of enthusiasm when she first greeted him. Then he understood, after a while, that it was not the nature of the Indians to show distress when their men departed, nor to feel the need to express their happiness openly upon their return. It was bad taste to show tenderness in public and as taciturn as he was he found the Indians even more controlled, and he understood them. He picked up the customs and he tried to make them his. He found how acutely the Apaches sensed what was fitting and what was not. He tried to make himself more of an Indian than the Indians themselves; he wanted the strange marriage to be fully accepted by the tribe so that when he was not with her she would have security.

When he journeyed to her from Tucson he told her everything he did during the time he was away. As she listened gravely he found himself remembering unimportant little things he thought would amuse her and in some way bridge their periods of separation. He pictured his world as being filled with persons and events of only minor importance; he wanted her to know, as he knew, that his home and his life were with her.

And she was as full of gossip when he came to her as he was. He listened to all the things she told him with great soberness, and he tried hard to remember all the difficult Indian names so he would know whom she was talking about. He learned the rigid, stiff polite usage of the language and used it to her relatives and many of them accepted the compliment and used the polite speech to him. This mark of mutual respect made her happy and it made him happy to do it.

One night they entered their wickiup and she slipped out of her clothes and he felt the quickness in him. He could never get over his feeling that there was something of an untamed animal in her. He pulled her down to him, and then, later, when she was lying next to him, still crying, he asked her if they might not, one day, revisit the place where they spent their ten-day honeymoon.

"That can never be, my darling," she said.

"Why not?"

"We can never go there again."

"Why not? Would you not like to?"

"We must not even think about it or talk about it," she said. "That is the way we do it. We never go back there. It would be bad luck."

He knew better now than to argue against these inflexible codes.

"You must never even think about it again," she said. "Not even to yourself."

"How can I forget that time?"

"Just a little," she said. "You can think about it a little. But you must never speak of it again."

356

He stroked her body. "I thought about you all day yesterday. I think I hate Tucson now."

"Did you? I never stop thinking about you when you are not here. I think I just go to sleep when you are away and wake up when you come back. My mother always says I will hurt myself one day, walking around in my sleep." Then she said, "Are there girls in Tucson who are prettier than I am?"

"No."

"No American girls who are prettier?"

"No. No Mexican girls and no Indian girls either."

"I think of all the girls who can look at you down there and then I feel bad."

"How about all these handsome young braves who are with you all the time?"

"Ah," she said in disgust.

"That is how I feel," he said. "Ah."

"Would your friends laugh at you if they knew you were married to an Indian girl?"

"I would like to take you down there with me. I would like to walk around with you everywhere and show you to everybody and say, 'This is my wife.' I think they would think you were almost as beautiful as I do."

"Am I beautiful?"

"Yes. And I would be so proud of you. You would walk so straight with your head up and your eyes shining and a smile on your face and people would stop and look at you and they would look ugly to each other."

"I am so much in love with you," she said. "Sometimes I think it is over me, like a decoration."

"One day we can go among my people, maybe," he said. "Not in Tucson, although one day we might be able to do it there, too, when things are different, and the white people understand the Indians. Or somewhere else, maybe. This is a large country. We could go many places and see many things and always be together."

"No," she said, touching his face.

"Do you not want us to be together all the time?"

"Oh, yes. But only here."

"Why only here?"

"Because we belong here. This is our home. This is our place. It would not be so good anywhere else."

He kissed her in the soft part of her neck.

"It is good here," she whispered into his ear, holding his head very tightly. "Everything loves us here. There is nothing between us here, nothing. Remember how you said we would be just one thing, you and I? That is how we are here. But it would not be the same anywhere else."

"Sometimes you make me feel like a child."

"You go where you have to go and I will stay here and I will always be waiting for you."

"I go no farther than Tucson," he said. "And even that seems a great distance."

"Even if you took another wife, I would still wait here for you. Even if you took another wife you would come back to me. That is how it is."

"What are you saying?"

"You might want to take an American wife."

"Do not say it."

"Only do not take an Indian wife. I think I could understand if you had to take a wife among your people, but do not make me live with another Indian wife."

"I am not going to take any other wife," he said. "Sometimes I think you are too much wife all by yourself."

"I do not joke."

"I do not joke either." He pulled her against him. "Why would I need another wife?" he asked.

"If we could not do our things?" she asked timidly.

"And why could we not do our things?" he asked. Then he suddenly remembered that Indian men did not make love to their wives from the moment they were sure of pregnancy until the child was weaned, something like three years afterward. He lifted her chin and tried to see her face in the dark. "Sweetheart," he said.

"You tremble," she said. "I am not sure. We can do our things now." He kissed her eyes and tasted the salt of her tears. "Is it what you wish?" she asked, almost fearfully.

"Yes," he said.

"You hurt me," she said. "It is good. You can still hurt me that way. I am not sure yet and you can hurt me." Then she said, "I will try not to be sure as long as I can."

7

A tall, massive, full-bearded man arrived on May 29, 1869, to take over command at Fort Bowie in Apache Pass. His name was Colonel Reuben F. Bernard, and he was the same man who, as a sergeant, had protested the decisions made by Bascom. After being acquitted at the court-martial, Bernard returned to the field and was commissioned during the Civil War. He fought bravely, and frequently spectacularly, during the war and against Indians after it, and he rose rapidly in rank. He was sent to Bowie, which had become something of a bad-sounding joke in the way of forts, to see what he could do against Cochise, who had by then broken enough military reputations to staff an army.

It was the first time Bernard had been in Apache Pass since

the Bascom affair. It was the first time he ever saw Fort Bowie. When he arrived the Chiricahua Indians, as usual, were scattered around in the hills on all sides of Bowie, hooting and insulting the soldiers.

Bernard went to work immediately. He ignored the important debate of the moment—whether it was better to have a great many forts in Arizona, thinly garrisoned, or only a few forts, heavily garrisoned—which was being argued on reams of paper from one end of the territory to the other, and set about to get his soldiers interested in Indian fighting.

He found morale was on the bottom. Officers hated territorial assignment. Soldiers feared the Indians and feared the Cochise Apaches beyond all others. Mules and horses, sold to the military by unscrupulous racketeers, were so bad that even the Indians hesitated to steal them.

Bernard, a blunt, honest soldier, fought with civilians, who constantly heckled the Army for its lack of success, fought with his superiors, fought with Washington. By working tirelessly and patiently he managed to collect some decent mounts and pack animals, and with these, he started a series of exhaustive training campaigns to harden his troops. When they finally were ready he went out after Cochise.

He had no illusions about the treatment handed the Indians by the white man. "All they know of whites is their evil deeds," he wrote to his superiors in outlining his plans. "One of the worst Indians now on this continent is Cochise. This Indian was always at peace with the whites until he and his family were invited to dine with an officer of the Army, who had his company ready to arrest him for the purpose of keeping him as a hostage for the return of a boy stolen by the Pinals. . . . This Indian was at peace until betrayed and wounded by white men. He is one of the most intelligent hostile Indians on this continent."

With great skill Bernard taught his troops how to travel by night and attack swiftly in the night. He ordered all male adult Apaches killed without warning. When he opened his campaign Cochise had fourteen raiding parties scattered throughout southern Arizona, New Mexico, and northern Mexico. Cochise sent out couriers to alert the parties and meanwhile conducted a series of skillful maneuvers, fighting, withdrawing, moving elsewhere.

Chapter Eighteen

The alarm was brought by a vidette. He reported a party of mounted soldiers approaching the rancheria on an open hill near the Guadalupe Mountains, not far from the line dividing the territories of Arizona and New Mexico, just north of the Mexican border.

The women were out gathering mescal and mustard seed when the warning came. They gathered their burden baskets quickly, slung the leather bands around their foreheads and hurried back from the fields to the camp. The men were already burning the wickiups and collecting their belongings. Then the first volley of bullets came from the soldiers.

Tesalbestinay took charge of the household goods. Nalikadeya adjusted her cradle on her back. Sonseeahray made a bundle of the Indian clothes belonging to Jeffords and slipped them into a parfleche and lifted the clumsy bundle on her back.

Ponce was in command at the camp. He deployed his men rapidly and ordered the women to retire over the hill into a canyon beyond. He sent half of his men in a wide flanking maneuver around the enemy's right, a trick taught to him by Cochise, to move the point of combat away from the camp and give the women greater opportunity to get away.

The soldiers had also received special instructions from Bernard. Instead of turning to fight off the counter-attack from the right, or withdrawing to prevent encirclement, they split their own forces, turning half of them on the flank attack and the other half moving forward.

The women struggled up the hill. Tesalbestinay seemed made of iron. She pulled and clawed her way up the steep incline. Sonseeahray was at her side.

"Give me something of yours," Sonseeahray said. "I have but one thing to carry."

"You carry enough in your belly," Tesalbestinay panted.

Sonseeahray moved the parfleche higher on her back. She was heavy and uncomfortable. "Where is Nalikadeya?"

"With us. Save your breath. Do not injure yourself."

Sonseeahray looked around. "Where is she?" The women paused. They looked down the hill. Nalikadeya was prone on the earth, clinging to a rock. She tried to regain her footing. Sonseeahray dropped her heavy bundle and ran down to her. She knelt and asked, "Are you hurt?"

"I fell," Nalikadeya said.

There was a yell of rage below them. The soldiers had pushed their way through to the clearing of the camp. The clearing was filled with smoke from the burning wickiups.

Sonseeahray lifted the cradle from Nalikadeya's back so she could regain her feet. Then, when Nalikadeya was balanced, she lowered the basket carefully, and pushed her. "Hurry," she said. Then a bullet struck her in the back and she fell on her face.

360

There was no pain. It was as though someone had slapped her heavily on the back. She tried to stand up. Her mouth filled and overflowed and she wiped her lips and her hand was covered with blood.

She fell again. Her cheek scratched on the hot hard ground. She thought how unhappy he would be.

Below the soldiers milled around the smoking camp. They found themselves at a great disadvantage. They could see nothing in the blinding smoke. The Indians knew every inch of the rancheria. They stopped fighting a pitched battle and began to fight as individuals. The soldiers retreated.

Ponce ordered his men up the hill to join the women. He sent others to get the horses. He hurried up the hill, his eyes tearing from the smoke. He stumbled over Sonseeahray.

He bent down and saw the red stain on her back. He lifted her and put her over his shoulder and he continued up the hill.

The women were gathered in the shelter of the far slope of the incline. Ponce lowered her gently to the earth. Tesalbestinay, wiping the sweat from her forehead, stopped the movement of her hand and then fell on her knees next to the girl. She emptied a water skin on her face and Sonseeahray opened her eyes.

"Do not let him be angry with me, my mother," she said.

"No."

"It is not fair," Sonseeahray said. "It was so good." Blood was spilling down each side of her mouth. She looked at Tesalbestinay and smiled like a tired child. "It was so good," she said.

Tesalbestinay held her in her arms and watched her die. A fly lighted on a thin line of blood below the girl's mouth and Tesalbestinay brushed it off.

Chapter Nineteen

The Apache boy Juan came into the mail office. Jeffords looked up and smiled pleasantly. "There is a man to see you, outside the walls," Juan said in Apache.

Jeffords buckled on his guns. "I'll be right back," he said to St. John. He went outside and got on his horse. He offered a seat to Juan but the boy said he would run. Juan led him to a small ravine to the southeast of the town. "He is there," he pointed.

Jeffords rode down the ravine. Halfway down an Indian stepped from behind a boulder. "Ponce," Jeffords said. "What is wrong?"

"Your wife has been killed," Ponce said.

In a little while Jeffords asked, "Where is she?"

"She was brought to the Stronghold."

"Are you mounted?" Jeffords asked.

"Yes."

"Come," Jeffords said.

They came to the East Stronghold. Cochise walked to him. His face was covered with black paint.

"Where is she?" Jeffords asked.

Cochise led him to a grassy hillock on the south side of the canyon. In the center of the hillock under a small oak tree there was a rise on the earth of a new grave. The rise was covered with stones to keep away wolves and coyotes.

Cochise left him. He sat down at the side of the grave and picked up a stone and dropped it and he looked at the grave and tried to know that she was there.

He sat there through the afternoon and through the evening and through the night, picking up little stones and dropping them, and when the sun rose the next morning he was still sitting there, staring at the grave. He knew the stones were adequate for their purpose and he was happy they were no larger and did not weigh too heavily on her.

In the afternoon he came down to the camp and Tesalbestinay told him how his wife was killed.

"Do not hold yourself in," Cochise said to him. "Even a man may cry."

Jeffords went to his wickiup and sat there alone. He stared at the familiar things. Then he lay down and closed his eyes.

In the morning he rode up the canyon to the place where he spent his first ten days with his bride. There was nothing there but the burned ashes of the wickiup and the blackened remains of their cooking fire.

He walked around. He went to the pool and looked at the water. He walked through the forest. He returned to the rock platform and sat there through the night and in the morning he went back to the grave. Then he rode alone out of the Stronghold.

BLOOD BROTHERS

———◆———

Chapter Twenty

Jeffords wandered for many months. He tried to go East but
he could not make himself do it. He could not remain in Arizona either. He drifted over to New Mexico and moved aimlessly from place to place. He wondered where his feelings
were. He felt nothing.

He tried to abandon his own identity. He shaved his beard.
When he saw his clean-shaven face it was good. It was like
looking at a stranger. He moved through Sonora and then
Chihuahua and back to New Mexico.

After a while he tried prospecting again. It wasn't any good
being alone in the hills. He had to be alone but he could not
bear to be alone by himself.

He decided he would go East. He got ready. Then, at the
last minute, he couldn't do it. Whatever he had that were his
substitutes for roots were in the Southwest. He had to stay
there.

He tried finally to think. He remembered something St. John
said to him when he returned from the Stronghold and quit
his job. St. John had said, "And you cannot blame anyone, not
the soldier who fired the shot, nor the officer in command of
the platoon, nor even the man on top, giving the orders. Nobody. Maybe that is what is going to be the hardest thing for
you—trying to hate a situation." It was true. He could not
blame anyone. It was like trying to hate rain for causing a
flood, or lightning for starting a fire.

She was dead for him in a strange way. He had never seen
her dead. They told him she was under a pile of rocks but all
he could remember was the last morning he saw her, beginning
to show the child she was carrying.

In the early spring of 1870 he was sitting in a saloon in Mesilla. An Army captain walked up to him. "Mind if I join you in a drink, Captain Jeffords?" the captain said.

"Sit down."

"My name is Farnsworth." He was a tall, gray-eyed man.

"You know my name."

"I enquired about you."

"Why?"

"I need a scout."

"Indians?" Jeffords asked.

"Yes."

Jeffords swallowed his drink. This would make the full cycle.

"My last two scouts were killed," Farnsworth said.

Jeffords poured another drink and swallowed it. "Why not?" he said.

2

The aimless drifting of Jeffords through the Southwest had been watched effectively, if distantly, by Cochise, whose men by now were everywhere. The Apache leader received regular reports on the man whom he loved as a brother, and whose sorrow was his sorrow, more so since Sonseeahray had been killed while attempting to help Nalikadeya. The powerful hand of Cochise lay like a remote shield over Jeffords, guarding his safety wherever he went. When Cochise heard that Jeffords had removed his beard, he smiled sadly to Ponce, saying, "He tries to change his face."

"He who saw him said it makes him into a different man," Ponce said.

"It is not that easy. He tries to find another body to live in, but it is not that easy. The beard will not be there but the eyes will be the same."

When he told Tesalbestinay she asked, "How much longer can he run? A man can run so far before he discovers he cannot run away from himself."

"A man cannot run away. It always gets bigger behind his back. He will return here. He has much of her in him now. When he loses some of it he will return for more."

Within a short while after Jeffords joined Farnsworth's troop as scout the news was brought to Cochise by Tahzay. The youth was astonished to see his father nod his head in satisfaction. "The news is good," he said.

"Good news? That he is leading soldiers against us?"

"It is the beginning of recovery. He finds himself again."

"He is your enemy now," Tahzay said, bewildered.

364

"He and I are not enemies. He is returning to life."

Tahzay shook his head. "What if he leads troops here?"

"We will fight them."

"You and Jeffords shooting at each other?"

Cochise nodded, his eyes alight with compassion. "Why not, my son?" he asked. "It would not matter. The important thing is that he no longer runs away. That is the worst thing. That is worse than dying."

"Why does he join soldiers, men who killed his wife?" Tahzay asked.

"There are many things you must try to understand," Cochise said. "One day you will sit in my place and your understanding must go beyond you, and enter into all things. Why does Tagliato join soldiers? They are his people. When one is hurt he goes to his own kind. Try always to look under what a man does, to see the reason for his so doing. If that man is a friend, then the reason for his action is more important than the action. If he is your enemy you must act against his action, but if you understand him it will give you added strength."

It was two days later that Jeffords rode up to the East Stronghold. Cochise mounted his horse and rode down the canyon to meet him. When the men reached each other they sat awhile and looked at each other. It was almost a year since they had been together.

Cochise studied the clean-shaven face. He thought the beardlessness made him appear younger. Then he looked at his eyes.

"How are you, Cochise?" Jeffords asked.

"Nothing has changed."

They rode toward the camp. Jeffords lifted his chin. "The smell of an Indian camp," he said. "It is an old smell. I think I would know the air in your Stronghold if I came upon it with my eyes closed." They entered the camp. "The wickiups in the same place," Jeffords said. "The faces the same."

"Not all the faces, Tagliato."

"Not all the faces. Not during a war. And it is the missing faces you see most plainly."

When they reached the place where Cochise dwelt, Jeffords said, "Three wickiups?"

"I have taken a third wife," Cochise said. "It made Tesalbestinay happy."

"Happy?"

"Before there were two. That made the two equal. Now there are three. She feels her position is better now." Cochise looked at him gravely and then he embraced him. "My eyes are grateful for the sight of you."

"It has been a long time. When I tell you why I came you will not be so glad to see me, maybe."

"It does not matter why you came. You are here."

Tesalbestinay came out of the wickiup. When she saw Jeffords she frowned at first and then her eyes widened and she rushed to him and threw her arms around him. "Why have you waited so long?" she asked. "Are you hungry?" He nodded. "Good." She hurried away and gave orders rapidly to Nalikadeya and the young Indian girl who was the third wife to Cochise. As Jeffords watched he grinned to himself. Cochise had been right. The third wife had in some way lessened the status of Nalikadeya.

"She has them under control, Tagliato," Cochise sighed. Then he shook his head. "I can call you that no longer. Your face looks like a tree in the winter time."

"I want to tell you why I am here, Cochise," Jeffords said seriously.

Cochise gazed at him calmly.

"I have agreed to serve as scout for the military. I could not start without telling you."

Cochise's face was without expression.

"I came here first," Jeffords said. "If I return I become an enemy of your people. I know more about guiding soldiers to Apache rancheria than most men. I will be a valuable man to the military and a great danger to you."

He stopped speaking and stared away. "I am alone in your camp," he said. "I am your prisoner."

"It is a long time since you spoke the Apache language," Cochise said mildly. "You are forgetting how to speak it. It is very difficult for me to understand you."

Jeffords chuckled softly. "You understand me. You understand everything."

"We talked of this before, a long time ago. We knew it might be so one day."

"And now it is that day," Jeffords said.

"Tell me," Cochise said, his eyes shining. "Are we still the same, you and I, one to the other?"

"Yes, Cochise."

"Two times you have come here alone. The first time made me love you like a brother. Do you think that this time will do less? Listen to me. When I saw you last you were dead inside. You left here and it was as though I saw you dead at my feet. Now you have come to life. You have a purpose. That is the important thing, you have a purpose. What does it matter what the purpose is? We fight each other. All right. But we fight each other, still as brothers. And you have a purpose again. I told you when I loved you less that your bullet would not hurt as much as another's."

Jeffords waited until he could speak. "Things should have been different. What we could have done together."

"No one does anything," Cochise said. "We think we do things. But we do not. We merely sit and watch things get done. Sometimes we even think we can change things, but we cannot. Everything has been decided. All we do is sit and watch it happen."

"Do you believe that truly, Cochise?"

"There is a path for everyone. Each man has his path and the paths of all men merge and make a larger path. Maybe we can move a little from side to side, but it is always within our path. The path must be followed. I saw the path of my people long ago. It is a path leading to the edge of a cliff. We all walk the same path and soon we will have to go over the cliff. Some sooner, some later. It does not matter."

Jeffords nodded, feeling again the potent mysticism.

"You have seen us run sheep. On the outside we make moving fences where the strongest ones go. Between the moving fences the others go. They run around in all directions, but they are always going in one direction, the direction we make them go. We are not different from those sheep."

"That is how the fighting is," Jeffords said. "Men moving like sheep against each other. The reasons are forgotten now but the fighting goes on."

"Men fight," Cochise said very simply. "Men will always fight. If there were no white men here we would fight other Indians. Or Mexicans. If there were no Indians here your soldiers would find someone else to fight. Everything that lives fights. From the smallest to the largest. That is how it is intended. Each thing lives on what is weaker than himself. By destroying another living thing he makes his own place in the forest safer."

"The forest is big enough for everyone, maybe."

"Each always wants just the place the other is standing."

"And the end?"

Cochise gestured widely with his hands. "The weak always lose. For a long time we were the strong. Now we are the weak. We will lose. We will die. Slowly, on reservations, or swiftly, in battle. But we will die. Then it will be your turn. You will no longer have us to conquer so you will fight others. You have tried, Jeffords, to tell me of this earth. You have told me there are great waters and other lands and other people who speak strange languages. There will always be fighting among all of you. Maybe you will defeat them, maybe they will defeat you. It does not matter. There will be fighting. Everywhere, all around in everything with life, there is always fighting. It is coming to the time of our end, and then, maybe it will come to the time of your end. No matter how strong men are there always are men who are stronger." Again he embraced his friend. "It was good of you to come here. We still speak to each other with a straight tongue. Listen to me again. I knew of your decision, before you came here. We still stand higher to each other than our people stand to each other."

"That is true, Cochise," Jeffords said.

"And now we shall become brothers."

"We are brothers, Cochise."

"We shall mix our blood and become brothers."

"Now? When I leave you to become your enemy?"

"Now, when you are closer to me than my own sons."

"You are a great man, Cochise," Jeffords said. "You are a very great man."

"It is our brotherhood," Cochise said quietly. "It makes a man greater than himself."

In the night Nochalo prepared the ceremony. Only the closest leaders among the Chiricahuas were ordered to attend. Cochise and Jeffords knelt, facing each other, and the chosen warriors sat in a small circle around them. Then Nochalo stepped inside the circle and he lay before him two small beaten silver goblets, covered with intricate markings.

There was no sound. For this ceremony, alone of all the sacred rites, there were no singers, no musicians.

"What a man is," Nochalo announced, "is in his blood." He lighted a small fire and placed a knife blade in it. "The quality of a man, the things of his body, the things of his head, the things of his heart, the things of his soul, are in his blood."

He held the right wrists of each of the two men in his hands. "In each drop of blood there is all of a man. There is everything he thinks and everything he feels. A man is made of his blood, which is got from his father, which his father got from his father, which he gives to his son, which his son gives to his son."

He released his grip on the wrists and took the heated blade from the fire. He waved it to the directions and then he plunged it into the earth.

"The blood is the man," he repeated, "and the earth is his mother."

He took the still-hot knife from the earth and he cut open the flesh in Cochise's right arm eight inches above his wrist and he held the arm over the silver goblet and let blood flow into it.

He took Jeffords' right arm and cut open his flesh eight inches above the wrist and held the arm over the other goblet and let blood flow into it.

Then Nochalo placed their right arms together so that the

368

incisions covered each other and the flowing blood com-
mingled. He held the arms together for several minutes and
then he released them and said, "Drink."

They each picked up the cup which had the blood of the
other and drank.

In the night when the camp slept Jeffords went to her grave.
He could feel nothing. He could not believe there was anything
of her under the small stones.

When he left the next day, he said, "When I come back here
alone I come as friend. If I come with others, I am an enemy."

"We no longer are friends, Sheekasay," Cochise said, using
the Apache word, brother, for the first time. "We now are
brothers."

3

Army commanders continued to arrive in Arizona and the
routine was inevitable and identical. They came, promising
great things, were hailed as saviors by the citizens, fought un-
successfully against the Indians for periods ranging from a few
to several months, and then departed, the objects of bitter and
violent attacks from all sides. One of these military commanders, General E. O. C. Ord, who became commander of the department of California, was startled to learn that Indians were
not safe on government reservations in Arizona. They were not
safe, he discovered, even when they joined forces with the
white men and fought against their own kind. They were slain
for their endeavors and he wrote, in amazement, the white men
who killed them were "not proceeded against by the civil authorities in the country."

"Reservations," he said, "to be at all safe from such attacks in that country must be forbidden ground to all white
men, save the troops sent there to watch the Indians and officers of the Indian Bureau."

On April 15, 1870, the new department of Arizona was
created and soon afterward General George Stoneman, Civil
War hero, was put in command, and Stoneman found himself ground between two stones. Awakening interest in and
sympathy for the Indians among people in the East caused him
to be criticized every time he campaigned against Apaches;
on the other hand, Stoneman found himself reviled more violently than any other commander of his rank by the citizens of
Arizona for not going ahead more ruthlessly on a policy of
exterminating every Indian.

Two reservations were established in the territory—and

were abandoned when soldiers fought with the Indians on reserve grounds.

There were other matters to harass the military. The government decided to economize on expenditures for the Army. Posts were abandoned. Troops were withdrawn. Soldiers deserted, taking their horses and guns, which could be sold on the black market for three hundred dollars. Since the reward for turning in deserters was only twenty dollars, few were surrendered.

During these months Jeffords worked indefatigably as a scout for Farnsworth. He never led troops to one or the other of the Strongholds because he knew better than anyone else how impregnable those fortresses were. He scouted New Mexico and Arizona. He had no other interests. He sought no man's friendship. He did not seek death, but he never avoided it. He was indifferent and without spirit and seemed to move in a silent world of his own.

On several occasions he encountered members of Cochise's band. Only once did he personally fight against Cochise himself. In a close, man-to-man encounter in the southwestern part of New Mexico he recognized Cochise. The battle lasted through an afternoon and into the night and then abruptly ended. In the morning Jeffords went through the ranks of the fallen Apaches. He did not find Cochise.

In February of 1871, Eskiminzin, chief of the Arivaipa Apaches, appeared with his tribe at Camp Grant, in the fertile Arivaipa Canyon and said he wanted to make peace with the white men. Lieutenant Royal Whitman, in command of the post, told him he had no authority to promise them a reservation, but permitted them to remain while he sought, through proper channels, to obtain such permission. The Indians moved in and lived at peace. Whitman respected them and treated them with great fairness. He received no answer to his request for permission to establish a formal reservation, and wrote to his superior in Tucson. "I have a wonderful family out here in the desert. These Arivaipa Apaches, especially their chief, Eskiminzin, have won me completely. The men, though poorly clothed and ignorant, refuse to lie or steal. The women work like slaves to clothe their babies and themselves and, although untaught, hold their virtue above price. They need help to show them the way to higher civilization and I will give them this help as long as they are permitted to stay."

In April Indians drove off a number of horses and cattle from San Xavier and killed a man. Citizens of Tucson and San Xavier, led by Will Oury and Jesus Elias, charged the culprits were members of Eskiminzin's band. Crowds gathered

370

in the two towns and public meetings were held. Oury and Elias demanded that the Camp Grant Apaches be destroyed.

Military authorities, from General Stoneman down, investigated and were assured by Whitman that the Arivaipa Apaches had not left Grant. The military refused to attack the reservation. Oury proposed a citizens' posse to do what the Army refused to do. The citizens were enthusiastic, but only four Americans besides Oury and Elias volunteered.

Oury was not fazed. He engaged forty-eight Mexicans and one hundred Papagos, all of them traditional enemies of Apaches, and on the night of April 27, they departed secretly for Camp Grant. They were given a wagonload of arms, ammunition, and supplies by the Adjutant General of the Territory of Arizona.

In the early hours of April 30, while the Indians slept, Elias and Oury led the attack on the camp. Oury ordered that clubs and knives be used at first so that no one would be aroused unnecessarily.

The Americans and the Mexicans and the Papago Indians went to work silently. The war clubs were raised and brought down. For a while there was no sound but the thudding of the clubs on sleeping skulls. Then women began to scream. Arivaipa men woke up. They were brained as they tried to get to their feet, rubbing sleep from their eyes. They fled to the hills. Then the attackers set fire to the wickiups.

On the charred reservation at Camp Grant the next day there were one hundred and eight bodies. Eight of these were men. The rest were women and children.

When Oury returned to Tucson he announced, "The red devils have been killed or captured or driven off. Not a man in our party has been hurt to mar the full measure of our triumph. We may return to our homes with the satisfaction of work well done."

The story of the outrage spread over the country. President Grant dispatched a letter to the governor of Arizona in which he threatened to place the territory under martial law unless the perpetrators of the massacre were brought to trial before a civil court. Of the Oury party, one hundred and four men were indicted. They were tried before a federal judge and jury in Tucson. The jury deliberated twenty minutes and declared the defendants not guilty.

Cochise said to his people, "I have chosen in the past to lead my people to die like warriors instead of dying of starvation on reservations. Now it seems that starvation is too slow. Indians on reservations now must die faster. Some of us have grown tired of our long war against the white-eyes. I have grown tired, too. Eskiminzin was tired and his people were tired and now only the dead are not tired."

371

Word of the outrage reached Jeffords in Silver City, New Mexico, and he thought, Cochise, my brother, who among us now dares to call you savage?

The Camp Grant Massacre, as the Oury-Elias affair came to be known, turned the attention of the country on Apache troubles in Arizona, transforming a local affair into a national problem. Religious leaders, humanitarians, and editorial writers protested so vehemently President Grant created a Permanent Board of Peace Commissions in Washington, with a mission to formulate a policy of "justice and understanding" in the official treatment of Indians. Grant gave various religious groups the power to supervise reserves, satisfying those who demanded humane treatment for the Indians; at the same time, he sent General George Crook, renowned for his victorious campaigns against the Sioux Indians, out to Arizona to replace Stoneman and to soothe the outraged feelings of the citizens of Arizona who still were clamoring for total annihilation of the red savages. Thus nobody could complain.

Crook took up his new command in June of 1871. Three months later Vincent Colyer, a Quaker and a member of the Peace Commission, also came to Arizona and New Mexico. Both men were in natural and instinctive ideological conflict. Colyer puttered about, filled with compassionate zeal and little else, made promises, talked to Indians, rectified a few grievances, and won a few Indians to reservations, where they were treated as fairly as Colyer could arrange. His peaceful enterprises caused him to be vilified by the citizens; his life was threatened, and he finally returned to Washington bitterly disappointed. His chief failure was his utter inability to make the remotest contact with Cochise, recognized in Washington as the nucleus of Apache resistance in the Southwest.

In February of 1872 President Grant sent another man to the Southwest to try to find Cochise and make peace. This man was General Oliver Otis Howard, a great hero of the Civil War, in which he lost his right arm, and a military commander who was known as the Christian Soldier. Intensely religious, a crusader, tall, white-bearded, with a soft and gentle manner, General Howard inspired 'n all who met him one of two emotions: reverence or mockery. He himself was convinced he was persecuted everywhere because of his holy zeal.

He also had something else: the rank of a major general, by virtue of which he outranked Crook, a brigadier, who was nominal military leader in the territory. It seems that Colyer had complained to the President that Crook did not co-operate.

Having sent Howard out to see what he could do, Grant turned around and approved the War Department's instructions to Crook to proceed with his plans for a bloody campaign against all Indians who continued to show hostility.

It took Howard four months to discover he could do very little. He followed Colyer's route, made a few more changes, tried vainly to get someone to bring Cochise in to see him, and finally, in the summer of 1872, returned to Washington with a batch of Indians to exhibit them in the East before church leaders.

4

Captain Farnsworth and Jeffords rode at the head of the company of cavalrymen returning to garrison headquarters in Tulerosa in the western part of New Mexico. The soldiers had been out on a routine scout, rather less successful than the average. The conflicting orders from Washington, alternating adjurations to regard the Indians as suffering innocents with commands to go out and kill them at sight, confused and bewildered soldiers and officers.

Farnsworth shifted tiredly on his saddle and said to Jeffords, "I am told General Howard is out here again."

"He just left," Jeffords said.

"I know, but he is here again."

"With some more copies of the Good Book?" Jeffords asked sarcastically.

Farnsworth laughed. "He is in a very difficult part of the country to promote missionary work," he admitted.

"It's a lot of damned hypocrisy," Jeffords said.

"Don't you believe in the teachings of the Bible, Captain Jeffords?" Farnsworth asked with a smile.

"The Bible is printed in English," Jeffords said shortly. "Anybody can quote from it who knows how to read the language."

"General Howard is said to believe what he quotes."

"Sure," Jeffords said. "That's all the Indians need now. A few well-chosen lines. That ought to make up for everything."

The troop entered the camp. "How about joining me in a drink, Captain Jeffords?" Farnsworth asked.

Jeffords nodded. He moistened his dry lips. Farnsworth turned the troop over to a junior officer and he and his scout entered a large tent that served as an officers' club. A few minutes later General Howard entered the tent.

The officers sprang to attention. Howard acknowledged the gesture and then looked around the tent. He saw Jeffords and he walked up to him. "I am General Howard," he said quietly. "Is this Mr. Jeffords?"

"That is my name," Jeffords replied.

"Can you take me to the camp of the Indian Cochise?"

Jeffords' blue eyes became very clear as they rested full on Howard. The officers in the tent became silent as they listened. Howard waited calmly for an answer, an expression of profound sincerity on his patriarch's face. "Who sent you here, sir?" Jeffords asked.

"The President of the United States."

"Everybody is responsible to the President."

"I am responsible to him directly, Mr. Jeffords. I have come here as a personal representative of President Grant explicitly authorized to treat with Cochise."

"What powers do you have, General?"

"I have full powers, Mr. Jeffords," Howard said.

"And who sent you to me?"

"Colonel Nathaniel Pope, Superintendent of Indian Affairs in New Mexico, said you were the one man in the Southwest who could arrange for me to see the Chiricahua Cochise."

A strange look came over Jeffords' face. "Will you go there with me without soldiers, General?"

"Yes, Mr. Jeffords, if necessary."

Farnsworth protested. "You will never get out alive, sir." The other officers chorused their agreement. "I insist, sir, that you take a strong military escort with you," Farnsworth said.

Jeffords and Howard continued to measure each other. They might have been alone in the tent. "It is immaterial to me whether you go or not," Jeffords said quietly. His eyes were unwavering. "But if you are going there with soldiers you will need more than two hundred and fifty of them and in that case it will be war." He leaned forward slightly. "If you go with me alone I think you can make peace with him." He felt a distant, almost forgotten excitement in him.

"I will go alone with you, sir, as you suggest," Howard said. He raised his hand as the officers again protested. "Furthermore, Mr. Jeffords will be in complete command." He turned back to Jeffords. "I am under your orders, sir."

"Yes," Jeffords said, almost to himself. "Yes."

"Would you care to accompany me to my quarters so that we might make our plans, Mr. Jeffords?"

"Yes, sir," Jeffords said.

When they entered Howard's tent the general excused himself and picked up a small, worn Bible. He read from it silently for a few moments, and Jeffords removed his hat and stood

374

silently, curiously impressed. When Howard finished with a brief prayer, he put down the book and looked up. "What are your plans, Mr. Jeffords?" he asked in a vigorous voice.

"I will get started immediately. There is an Indian named Chee. He is the son of Mangas Coloradas. He is not far from here. I will find him. You must try to make a friend of him. Cochise has never forgotten how Mangas Coloradas was murdered in cold blood by orders of an American general. There is another young chief named Ponce. His father was a great friend of Cochise. We will find him and take him, too."

"Everything will be done as you wish, Mr. Jeffords. There is only one thing. I promised some Mimbres Apaches that I would try to do something for them at the Canada Alamosa. I can do it now or when we return."

"Do that first, sir," Jeffords said. "If you promised something to the Indians do it first and keep your word. I will go along with you."

Howard held out his left hand. "I shall pray for the success of our mission," he said.

When he reached his own tent Jeffords lay down on his cot. He told himself not to be hopeful. He told himself nothing had been accomplished yet. He told himself Cochise might refuse to talk to Howard.

And yet he could not rid himself of the feeling that perhaps the time had now come. And he thought of his wife for the first time in many nights and he felt very close to her.

5

Howard finished his business at Canada Alamosa and on September 20, 1870, the party departed. The group included Howard, Jeffords, a Spanish-American interpreter named Jake May, two packers leading the load horses, Captain J. A. Sladen, aide-de-camp to Howard, and Chee.

On the first day out of Canada Alamosa, crossing the tributaries of the Rio Grande, Jeffords picked up the fresh track of unshod horses. "The rider has ridden to the brow of that hill," Jeffords said. "He saw us and turned back. We'll follow."

They rode until they came to a steep descent leading down to an abrupt gorge. The Rio Conchinillo Negro flowed at the base. Jeffords pointed. On the side of the river was an Indian camp. "There is Ponce," Jeffords said. He spurred his horse and rode to his old friend. Ponce embraced him and Jeffords spoke to him rapidly. Then he returned to Howard. "He says that he would come with us except for two things. He wants to know who will take care of his little band. And he says he doesn't have a good enough horse." He winked at the general.

"We can satisfy him," Howard said.

The band was taken to a nearby hamlet and there Howard ordered the people supplied with a thirty days' ration of food on the word of Ponce that they would remain at the hamlet and not go off on any raids. Then Howard presented Ponce with his own spare horse.

The next morning Ponce appeared, ready to accompany them. He was on foot. "Where is your horse?" Howard asked.

"I gave it to my wife," Ponce said innocently.

Howard had no other horse. "We will share my horse," he said. Ponce nodded happily. The group started again. From the start Ponce either rode behind Howard on his horse or else one or the other walked. Jeffords missed none of these incidents. He thought that the more he saw of Howard the more he felt that at last a different kind of man had come to the Southwest.

The 23rd day of September was spent at Fort Bayard, in New Mexico, and stores were replenished. Then the group started out for Silver City, the next stop on their journey.

The procession had a frightening effect upon the residents of Silver City. Upon seeing the two Apaches, Chee and Ponce, miners barred their doors and took down rifles. By the time the men reached the town itself a mob was waiting for them. Angry miners demanded that Howard turn Chee and Ponce over to them to hang. Howard sternly ordered the mob to disperse and rode out alone and faced them. There were several minutes of tension and then the men slowly broke up and walked away. Chee and Ponce remained with Howard through the night and the next morning the group left without trouble.

Ten miles from town they encountered a prospecting party. One of the prospectors recently had lost a brother to the Apaches. When he saw the two Indians he lifted his rifle and pointed it at Chee. "I'll get one of you bastards," he said.

Howard stepped between the prospector and Chee. "You will have to kill me first, sir," he said.

The prospector slowly lowered his rifle. He cursed and rode away. Chee put his arm on Howard's shoulder and held it there for a moment.

"You have a friend who will never forget you," Jeffords said.

In the camp that night Howard finished his usual reading of the Bible, and then asked Jeffords, "If Cochise agrees to make peace will he live up to his word?"

"If he gives his word he will keep it."

"Is there anything I should know before I talk to him, Mr. Jeffords?"

Jeffords took out his pipe. He stuffed it slowly. "Only one thing, General," he said slowly. "Do not make any promises you cannot keep. If you promise him ten things, and give him only nine he well remember you as the man who failed to give him the tenth thing. It would be far better to promise only nine things, or six or three, and deliver every one of them. I do not know how well you know Apaches, General, but they keep their word, to the last letter. As far as I know Cochise has never violated his sworn word. If you do as well there may be a peace."

"I believe I have a reputation for some honor, Mr. Jeffords."

"Reputations don't mean anything," Jeffords said. "But I believe in you. For some reason I believed in you when I first saw you. That is why I am taking you to see Cochise."

"You have known him for a long time?"

"Yes."

"And you have great respect for him?"

"Yes, General, I have great respect for him."

"And you do not have very much respect for some of the men who represent our government out here?"

"No, General," Jeffords said. He smoked in silence.

"Mistakes have been made," Howard said. "I would like to have some of your ideas, Mr. Jeffords." When Jeffords did not reply, he said, "Treatment of the Indians cannot be improved without the good will and cooperation of those white men who know the Indians best. If there is anything you can tell me, Mr. Jeffords, I should be greatly obliged. We who come out here from almost a different world do not know very much about the difficulties that exist here and we can accomplish our purpose only by knowledge."

Jeffords stared into the fire. There were some things to be said. He looked suddenly at Howard. The old man was in repose, his face lighted with a serenity that seemed his alone. "We are getting too big for our own good," Jeffords said. "We are moving all over this country and wherever we move we push people around. Always pushing people around. We buy and sell land that never belonged to us in the first place and when we move in we push." He pulled on his pipe. He was not saying it right, he thought, and he wanted to say it right to this old man.

"Yes, Mr. Jeffords," Howard said gently. "Please go on."

"We don't know anything. Men come out here and give orders and try to run things and they don't know anything. They don't try to find out anything. They think the Indians are like all the rest of the wild life out here. They don't try to find out anything about them. They don't try to understand that the Indians are like a foreign nation, or nations. They don't try to find out what makes them tick, what they think, what they believe in. They don't even try to learn the language. They wouldn't think of trying to hitch mules to a team without breaking them in first and Indians are human beings. They were here a long time and they have a lot they believe in and we came along and started pushing them around and they are mad as hell. Sure, they're mad as hell. Why not? Who are we to come along and try to make them over our way? What's so good about our way? What kind of an example are we setting for them? When we first came to this part of the country the Indians tried to understand us. We never returned the compliment. They thought we were something special. There is an Indian legend about the coming of white men from the East. We were special, all right."

He pulled a lighted piece of wood from the fire and held it over his pipe. Howard looked intently at his lean face, brightening and then darkening again. "We forgot our Christian birthright," Howard said.

"Was that it, General?" Jeffords asked, smiling thinly. "Maybe that was it. It's been so long since I've seen anything resembling a Christian birthright I wouldn't know. I've found one thing, General. The Apaches practice their religion with more sincerity than most Christian Americans."

"I believe that, Mr. Jeffords," Howard said soberly.

"We're getting to be a big country now," Jeffords went on. "We have to start growing up. We've been fighting since we've been in this country and we'll fight some more. Soon as the kids who fought the Civil War grow up and forget about it their kids will be old enough for a new war. We're going to take over all of this country, from coast to coast and from Canada to Mexico. We'll have to fight big wars some day. We're part of the world. Maybe we'll have to run some other country. I hope I won't be around to see that day. Because we don't know a damned thing about running anybody. We don't even try to learn. Some of the men who have come out to Arizona have been kicked out of every civilized place in the country. They're the ones who are trying to run things. The Army is a laugh. Man for man the Apache is worth three soldiers, the way the soldiers are trained and equipped. Cochise is smarter than anybody that went into the field against him. And as far as trying to understand anybody else, the officers are the worst of all."

"How would you have it, Mr. Jeffords?"

"How would I have it? Before a man is sent out to command a fort in Indian country he ought to be made to study the language of the Indians he's going to have to handle. He ought to be made to study the history and the religion and

378

the customs and the traditions of the people he is going to work with. I know Cochise. He has more pride than a troop of cavalrymen. He's proud and he's honest and he's a damned king among his own people. We never tried to understand that. Most of the people out here look at him as a red savage, better off dead. Well, there's been millions of dollars lost and thousands of people killed because we didn't figure out Cochise—and others like him—for the man he is. Now you have to come out here, a personal ambassador from the President of the United States, to try to straighten things out. A second lieutenant with horse sense could have done that twelve years ago. Just as a second lieutenant started it."

"I think that we do not disagree, Mr. Jeffords," Howard said. "Perhaps we interpret it differently. My answer is that in our haste and lust to conquer this new country we have forgotten the teachings of Jesus Christ and we had to pay for our forgetfulness."

"The Apache Indians are the most religious people I've ever known."

"Their beliefs are equally holy before God."

Jeffords stood up. "If you really believe that, General, maybe you're the man I've been seeking for years."

When he lay down to sleep he looked at Howard. The general was praying by candlelight. His lips moved as he read from his small Bible. Jeffords looked at the calm, quiet, serene head, the white beard soft and hazy in the flickering light.

The men rode for days. Howard and Jeffords held long conversations, and Jeffords expressed himself freely. Howard was a listening man. Chee and Ponce gave him their friendship.

Once Jeffords showed him the prints of many horses. "Those belong to Cochise Apaches," he said. "No other Indians shoe their horses with deerskins tied above the fetlocks. It won't be very long now."

The men wound around among the sandhills and through the waste places of southwestern New Mexico until they came within sight of the Peloncillo Mountains. Chee rode ahead of the others and made eight fires in a large circle. Howard questioned Ponce, who replied in Spanish, "Peace, smoke of peace." A little later Chee barked like a coyote and was answered by a similar sound from the mountainside. He scurried up the slope and another Apache appeared as though out of the earth. Ponce led the group on until they reached a spring, and there they found Chee and the Apache who had greeted him on the hill, with several Indians of both sexes and all ages.

"One of Cochise's smaller bands," Jeffords said.

"Is he close?"

"I don't think so. He has rancherias scattered everywhere. I'll see." He rode up to the Indians who recognized him and greeted him with excitement. He saw Skinyea and embraced him. Skinyea pointed to Jeffords' beard, which he had grown again, and started to laugh.

"It is you again, Tagliato," he said.

"I was getting cold," Jeffords replied. He spoke at length to Skinyea and then returned to Howard. "Cochise is still a hundred miles away." Howard said nothing. Jeffords waited for him to suggest that Cochise be brought to him. "Do you want to go on?"

"Yes, of course," Howard said.

"I think you will have to get rid of some of your men. I told you you would have to come alone."

"Can Captain Sladen remain with me?"

"I think so, General, but no one else."

Howard dismissed the rest of his men and sent them on to Fort Bowie.

The next morning Howard, Sladen, and Jeffords set out with Chee and Ponce. They entered the Chiricahua Mountains and went up a steep ascent on a trail so blind Howard and Sladen could make nothing of it. Sladen, a young officer who had an almost reverential awe for Howard, said, "General, aren't you doing wrong? Don't you think you are taking too much risk? Eight of us could have made some resistance, but now there are only five of us, and two of them Indians at that."

"The risk is great indeed," Howard said gravely. "But I have thought the matter over carefully and am determined to proceed." Howard pondered sending Sladen back. He thought it was one thing to risk his own life, but another to commit a friend to the same risk. His face became sober and then, after a while, he lifted his head and said, "Captain Sladen, whosoever will save his life shall lose it, but whosoever shall lose his life for my sake, the same shall save it."

When Jeffords heard these words he looked up astonished. He wondered fleetingly whether Howard was joking but when he saw the rapt expression on the old man's face he realized it was not a joke. Howard was speaking seriously and he believed himself and Sladen believed him, too.

That day the men rode forty miles over the Chiricahua range. The heat was intense. The sun scorched everything that lived and the rocks radiated heat like an oven. Of all the riders Howard, the oldest of them, minded the heat least. In full uniform, his right sleeve neatly folded and pinned together, he rode with a martial pride, uncomplaining, and Jef-

380

fords began to think he was a remarkable man. The Indians led the party from one water hole to another, only to find each one dry.

"There is a big spring on the west side of the mountain," Chee said. "We will have plenty of water tonight." Just before sunset he rode off. He returned a short while afterward. "No *agua*."

The men pushed on. They separated slightly and searched in passing ravines, in deep gullies, for signs of water. At twilight they came to some high, perpendicular rocks. Jeffords lifted his hand and cocked his head. "Listen," he said.

"Water," Sladen shouted. "I can hear it."

The water was trickling from a spring into a hollow basin on the bottom of the rock.

Before turning in for the night, Jeffords said, "You see one of the problems in this country, General. When you have to fight for water it is hard to fight anything else."

The next day the sky was cloudless and the heat continued. The men rode across Sulphur Spring Valley. Jeffords pointed ahead to a range of mountains that bounded the west side of the valley. "Those are the Dragoons," he said. "It is in those mountains that Cochise has his Strongholds."

In the late afternoon the men reached the old stage station in the valley. They decided to rest there. A small guard of soldiers was stationed at the depot. The soldiers were startled to find a general turning up in the desert.

"Can you give us something to eat?" Howard asked.

"I've got something better than that," one of the soldiers replied. "I have some whiskey, sir."

"We don't want whiskey."

"Why not, sir?" the soldier asked in astonishment. "It's good whiskey."

The guard shared their rations of bread and bacon and then Howard said he would take a nap. He noticed that Chee was edging away from three dogs who were snarling at the Indians. "Come and sleep with me, Chee," Howard said gently.

Chee ran over to him and looked at the bearskin which covered him. "Bear no good," he said. Howard threw away the skin and pulled his overcoat over him. Chee lay alongside of the general and Howard covered both of them and they slept. Jeffords gazed at the general and the naked Indian, sleeping side by side, and then he told the soldier he would accept his offer of a drink.

Shortly after midnight Jeffords woke Howard and they started out again. They moved in a southwesterly direction toward the outer slopes of the Dragoons. They made a dry camp and rested until dawn and then without pausing for breakfast started out again through Middle March Pass in the Dragoons. They came to a cool, swiftly flowing mountain stream and Jeffords ordered a pause.

"That water looks wonderful," Sladen said. "It must come down from one of the Strongholds."

"Yes," Jeffords said.

The men and animals rested through the day. Chee disappeared soon after they made camp. Ponce made circular fires, numbering five, from time to time. When the men were eating supper two Indian boys came down from the western hills. "They're coming from the Stronghold," Jeffords told Howard. "I think you won't have long to wait."

Without saying a word the two boys seated themselves and began to eat the food that was laid out. When they had filled themselves, they pointed to a gap behind them and said Chee wanted everyone to come up to one of the rancherias. The men started out again, winding around the foothills to the west. It was the old familiar road to Jeffords. He rode in silence, recognizing every foot of the way, each rock, each tree, each curve of the trail. Then, before his eyes there appeared the wickiups of the Stronghold, each one of them so known to him. The Indians were waiting and, as they saw him and recognized him, they shouted his name and he waved to them.

Chee appeared and said that Cochise was in the other Stronghold. Jeffords led the men to the stream and there, under a sycamore tree, which Jeffords remembered from a long time before, they made their camp. Howard spread out his blanket. "Will I have time for a little rest, Mr. Jeffords?"

"Yes, General," Jeffords said. His thoughts were far off. "Rest comfortably. I will call you."

"Thank you, Mr. Jeffords." He took out his Bible and read from it by the light of a small candle. Then he lay down on his blanket. Jeffords squatted on the side of the stream and stared into the rippling water. "Will it be peace, Mr. Jeffords?"

"I don't know."

As Howard made himself comfortable several little Indian children walked up to him and stared at him curiously. Then one lay down at his feet on the blanket. When he did not tell him to go, several others followed. Howard shifted so that his head was among the children. They snuggled against him, like puppies. "This does not mean war, Mr. Jeffords," Howard said softly. And then he slept.

In the morning the men sat around after breakfast. Howard asked Jeffords where Cochise was, and Jeffords replied that he did not know.

"Does he know that we are here?"

"He has known exactly where we have been for days," Jeffords smiled.

382

"What shall we do now?"

"We'll pack as though we were going to leave," Jeffords said.

The men started to collect their gear. Suddenly Ponce leaped to his feet and shouted, "Someone is coming!"

There appeared, riding down the ravine, a single horseman. He was painted in black and vermilion. "That isn't Cochise. That's his brother, Juan," Jeffords said.

Juan rode up to Jeffords, jumped from his horse, and put his arms around him. He spoke to Jeffords, and then Jeffords said to Howard, "He will be here in a few minutes. He will come on horseback and will have behind him the ugliest Indian you ever saw, by the name of Teese, carrying a lance."

Five minutes later Cochise came down the ravine.

He rode up to Jeffords. He dismounted and then turned his back on Howard and put his arms around his friend. His eyes were sparkling. "Sheekasay," he said emotionally. "It lightens my heart to see you again."

"My brother," Jeffords said. He held tightly to the man he loved more than any other man in the world.

Cochise held him at arm's length and looked at him. He laughed out loud when he saw the beard. "I never believed it would make me so happy to see hairs on a man's face. You no longer hide from yourself. It is almost as before."

"Almost, my brother."

"It makes everybody here happy to see you."

Cochise turned slowly and with great dignity until he faced Howard. The warmth and the smile left his face and his features composed themselves in their normal austere mold and his lips compressed tightly.

"This is the man," Jeffords said to Howard.

Howard held out his left hand and Cochise took it. *"Buenos días, Señor,"* he said.

Cochise then sat himself on a folded blanket prepared by Ponce. Jeffords seated himself at his right and Howard and Sladen and the other Indians arranged themselves in a small circle. Then Cochise asked Jeffords, "Are these good people?"

"I think so," Jeffords replied.

"How long have you known them, Sheekasay?"

"For almost thirty days."

"Can they be trusted?"

"I think so. I believe so."

"Will they do as they say they will?"

"I do not know," Jeffords said quietly. "I think they will. I cannot be sure but I think they will. I will see that they do not promise too much."

"Enju," Cochise said. "It is enough that *you* brought them to me."

Then he turned to Chee and Ponce and questioned them exhaustively. As they spoke, Cochise nodded approvingly. Cochise then spoke and Jeffords translated for him. "He says will the general explain the object of his visit."

"The President of the United States sent me to make peace between Cochise and the white people."

When Jeffords translated this, Cochise said evenly, "Nobody wants peace more than I do."

General Howard exhaled slowly and then said with great emphasis, "Then, as I have full power, we can make peace."

Cochise turned his eyes on the old soldier. Howard felt that every pore on his face was open, that the black eyes which were fixed upon him were probing into his most secret being. Without removing his eyes, Cochise began to speak. He spoke for more than an hour, slowly and deliberately, pausing often so that Jeffords could make his words over into English. As always, when he turned his mind over to the treacheries visited upon his race, he could not maintain his ordinary phlegm. His voice rose and fell harshly and he gestured violently with his hands. The cords on his neck were taut and his eyes lashed the white-bearded face like a whip.

Howard listened to him without interposing a word. Himself a religious mystic, he was profoundly affected by the fanatic fervor of the Apache. He had come prepared to treat with almost any kind of Indian, and he found himself confronted with a naked force that seemed almost to transcend the man who contained it. He was a man older than the Indian and yet as he succumbed to the blazing intensity of his personality he felt, as Jeffords had felt often before, that he was untutored and young. He knew, as Cochise finished his long, bitter monologue, that he had to convince this man of his own sincerity; he felt from his own deep Christianity that to meet this fundamental truth with anything less would be a sin.

"I know of these things," he said. "There are two kinds of people in the United States. One is friendly to the Indians. The other is hostile to them. The friends of the Indians now are in power and General Grant is the leader of these good Americans."

"And later," Cochise said quickly, "if the bad white people come into power. Then what happens to us?"

"If the Indians prove that they are friends they will have nothing to fear." As Cochise's lips curled slightly, he continued, "Believe me, O Cochise, we are not a bad people. We have been stupid and unthinking, but we are not bad. You have seen the worst of us, perhaps. Americans leave their own tribes when they do wrong things and go to distant places, just as Indians do. There are good Americans who came to this land from a distant land just to escape from bad governments

384

and bad rulers. These people understand what it is to be persecuted, for their religion, for their political beliefs, for many things. These good Americans can learn to look upon the Indians as brothers and to live by their sides in peace."

There was nothing in what he said, in the words, in each shading of emphasis, in each tone and nuance, that was not caught and analyzed and tested in the mind of the Indian.

"I would like to persuade you to bring your people to a fertile land on the Rio Grande," Howard went on. "I would like to bring all the Apaches there and give them as much land as they need to support themselves and live in peace and dignity."

Now there was a subtle shift in Cochise's attitude. He had pleaded his case and now he was settling down to bargaining. "I have been there," he said. "I like the country. Rather than not have peace I will go and take such of my people as I can, but that move will break up my tribe. Why not give me Apache Pass? Give me that and I will protect all the roads. I will see that nobody's property is taken by Indians."

"Perhaps we could do that," Howard yielded. "But it would be vastly to the interest of the Chiricahuas to go to Alamosa. Five rivers are near there, the Rio Grande, the Alamosa, the Negro, the Palomas, and the Puerco. In their valleys are fine planting grounds and good grazing for thousands of cattle. Plenty of mescal plants are there and there is good hunting in the mountains."

With the experienced tactics of the born negotiator, Cochise changed the subject abruptly. "How long will you stay?"

"I came from Washington to meet you and make peace," Howard said, a little bewildered. "I will stay as long as necessary." He was startled by the question, considering that his life and that of Sladen's were obviously at the disposal of Cochise.

Cochise said to Jeffords, "I am going to send him to Bowie and see how much of a friend of the Indians he is." Then he said to Howard blandly, "My people are out making a living. If they come across any whites they will kill them, and it may be that some of my people will be killed. If my people are killed I will take care of them and if my people kill any whites I do not want to be held accountable for them for they are out making a living. I want you to go to Bowie tonight. I will send for my people but I do not want the soldiers firing upon them as they come in."

"I will send Captain Sladen to Fort Bowie to notify the garrison and to telegraph to other posts," Howard said.

"The soldiers may not obey Captain Sladen," Cochise said evenly. "They will obey you. I want you to go. Jeffords and Captain Sladen can stay here." He smiled slightly. "Our young women will care for the young captain."

Howard put his hand over his eyes. His face was weary. He

said to Jeffords, "I am very tired. I don't know how to get to Bowie from here."

"I think you ought to do as he says," Jeffords replied. "He wants to know how much to trust you. The Indians will show you a new route to Bowie. You can make Sulphur Spring, about twelve miles from here, direct, sleep there, go to Bowie tomorrow, and return in about three days."

Howard sighed heavily. "If you think it will be useful, Mr. Jeffords, I am ready to go."

Jeffords felt sudden compassion for the old man. "I think it will," he said sincerely.

Howard indicated he would accede to Cochise's request. "I will call my people," the Apache said. "It will take about ten days to get them together." He stood up and walked away. Later he returned. Women brought food and drink.

"We were once a large people covering these mountains," Cochise said. "We lived well." He paused. "One day my best friend was seized by an officer of the white men and treacherously killed."

"There are many white men who are bad," Howard said. "There are differences among us, as there are in your people."

"The worst place of all is Apache Pass. There, six Indians, one my brother, were murdered. Their bodies were hung up. Now Americans and Mexicans kill an Apache at sight. I have retaliated with all my might. My people have killed Americans and Indians and have taken their property. Their losses have been greater than mine. I have killed ten white men for every Indian slain, but I know the whites are many and the Indians are few. There are fewer Apaches every day." His black eyes were filled with gloom. Then he said suddenly, "Why shut me up on a reservation? We will make peace. We will keep it faithfully. But let us go around as free Americans do. Let us go wherever we please."

Howard's voice, when he replied, was filled with distress. "Hear me out, O Cochise," he said. "This country is large. It does not belong entirely to the Indians although the Indians were here first. All of the children of God have an interest here. Until there is trust, complete trust, on both sides, something we cannot order or establish over night, there must be control. To keep peace we must fix boundaries. A peace such as you propose would not last a week. Suppose that some rough prospectors should fire upon you and kill a portion of your band, or suppose some of your wild men should take the life of a citizen, the peace then would be hopelessly broken." He shook his head sadly, "No, believe me, a reservation is not a prison. It is as much for protection of the Indian as it is anything else. There you will be safe and secure and your families can rest and your young men will not be troubled and your children will not be endangered. I know how many bad Americans have mistreated Indians on reservations before, but I pledge you my own word, and to me my word is a holy thing, that what I promise I will give to you, and that if we make a peace, you and I, it will not ever be broken by the white man. Let us put the whole history of our warfare behind us. Let us start out from the beginning, with no bad memories. There were mistakes and outrages on both sides. Let us close the book on them and forevermore walk as brothers. And if we are honorable and truthful with each other, one day there need be no reservations. White men and Indians will have come to trust each other and all may walk freely without fear."

Cochise meditated on the words. Then he said to Jeffords, "I think he speaks with a straight tongue, Sheekasay. How do you think?"

"I think so, too," Jeffords said.

Howard rose. He straightened his uniform and squared his tired shoulders. As he stood erect, stiff, proud, there was a genuine quality of nobility about him. "I will go to Fort Bowie now," he said. "I will give the necessary orders. Who among you will come with me?"

Chee stepped forward instantly. "I will go."

Howard put his arm around Chee's shoulder. "Good, my friend, come with me. We ride together again."

The general and the son of Mangas Coloradas mounted their horses. Cochise and Jeffords walked by their sides until they came to the west mouth of the Stronghold. There Howard dismounted and Cochise led him up a small hill. They leaned against a huge rock and looked around them. Below them lay Arizona.

"My home," Cochise said.

Chapter Twenty-one

The day after General Howard departed for Fort Bowie a small band of Chiricahuas rode into the Stronghold and reported they had encountered five white men and had killed them. Cochise summoned Jeffords and Sladen. "I do not think the troops can follow the trail of my Indians," he said, "but if they do they will be here tonight and we will have a fight."

Jeffords told Sladen of the new turn of affairs. "If the troops find this place they will be beaten. If you want to leave you better go right away. An Indian will take you to General Howard."

"What are you going to do, Captain Jeffords?" the young officer asked.

"I'm going to stay here. But you're an officer of the Army. It might complicate matters if soldiers found you here."

"If you are going to stay, I'll stay, too," Sladen said firmly.

"All right," Jeffords said. He started to walk away. He paused and said, "Keep your eyes open, Captain. You may learn something as a military man."

With great interest Sladen watched Cochise go about his preparations for defense. The Chiricahua leader moved the camp up among higher rocks. Then he placed warriors everywhere, taking advantage of every natural protection the canyon afforded. Cochise gave his orders tersely and without hesitation. He arranged the women behind the men, so they could move farther into the canyon, into safety, if the soldiers arrived. Sladen saw how simple it would be for the Indians to destroy any small force rash enough to attempt to climb into the canyon and attack them. And, at the same time, he saw how Cochise had established the new camp at the foot of a rough path, practicable only for leading horses and mules to the summit of the mountain, in the remote event that the soldiers should make a successful attack.

Jeffords and Sladen spread blankets on the ground and lay down on them. Cochise joined them. "It looks as though a long trail has come to its end, Sheekasay," he said. "I know what you are thinking. You are thinking that if the trail ended sooner it would have been better. It could not be that way. The arrow must fly its full course. That is how it must be. If this is a peace it could have been so sooner."

Jeffords filled his pipe and did not answer.

"I have faith in this man because of you," Cochise said.

"I may be wrong, my brother."

"No. Since it came through you it must be good. It would not have been made so that you became my brother only to bring treachery among us. I have told you none of us acts, we only watch. Your general speaks much of his god. The Indian has a god, too. Maybe the two gods arranged this."

Jeffords smiled. "Maybe, Cochise."

"It is more important that you have tried to do good among us," Cochise continued. "If it proves bad, still it also proves what I said long ago. We are above our own people, Sheekasay." Then the hard, lined face softened and in the opaque eyes there was a sudden tenderness. "I am selfish, Sheekasay," Cochise said. "I talk only of my things. I know where your heart is and where you want to go. Forgive me."

Jeffords got up and walked away. He smoked his pipe until there was nothing but ash and then in the bright light of the desert night he walked to her grave. He knelt before it and looked at the earth, the curved rise now slowly sinking until soon there would be nothing of it. He could still not feel anything of her there. He could not come, in his mind, to believe that whatever was left now, whatever bones, whatever anything else, belonged to her. He returned to his blanket and lay down beside Sladen. The captain was asleep. Jeffords lay on his back and thought that there was more of her left in the air he was breathing.

2

General Howard got back to the camp the following afternoon. He had ridden all night, had accomplished his mission with great speed, and had returned without resting. The troops, against whom Cochise had made his defense, never appeared.

Cochise, Jeffords, and Sladen, from a lookout point, had watched for a long time and saw the two figures of Howard and Chee hours before they arrived in the Stronghold. As Howard came up the long approach, they descended and met him. Sladen rapidly told him of the expected attack by the troops which never materialized and spoke excitedly about the deployment Cochise had made of his forces.

Howard entered the camp and looked around with a trained eye. He said to Cochise, "No general in the United States Army could have made a better disposition of his men to resist an attack from an enemy force."

"I have learned these things a hard way," Cochise replied dryly.

He then led the white men to the West Stronghold. There Howard gazed in awe. "I thought that your other camp offered a perfect place for defense," he said. "It is nothing to what you have here. God did not intend for you to be defeated in battle."

"Your God or mine?" Cochise asked.

"There is but one God," Howard replied sternly. "All creatures are His children."

"That is something God may know," Cochise said. "His children know it not."

The Chiricahuas celebrated the return of Howard with a dance of welcome. Jeffords and Sladen first went to a great mound of stones and, upon the uppermost tip, planted a white flag. The women shrieked their approval and began to chant, repeating a long Apache word endlessly.

"What are they saying?" Howard asked Jeffords.

"The flag of peace I love."

Howard knelt and bowed his head. When he rose his face was marked with a radiant hope.

Cochise provided a comfortable dwelling for Howard and Sladen, and gave them an old Apache woman to serve as cook and housekeeper. When the general and his aide had rested and cleaned themselves, they joined the people in their celebration. The women immediately besought them to dance.

"Go ahead," Jeffords said. "Everything you do now will be of significance."

"It is an easy thing to do, to dance with these people, Mr. Jeffords," Howard said. "They are good."

The two officers joined the dancing circle. The men and women were in their traditional positions. One girl held on to Howard's left hand and another grasped his empty right sleeve. They danced back and forth and Howard kicked out his legs like any young buck. Sladen found himself between two attractive Indian girls and he smiled from ear to ear as he bounded to and from the fire. Jeffords and Cochise, sitting side by side, looked on and when Jeffords could watch no longer he walked away and Cochise followed him with eyes that were scalded with pain.

After the dancing there was the usual feast. Roasted pieces of meat were passed out and Cochise whispered to Jeffords, "This is good meat for you and me, Sheekasay. How about them?"

"Let them eat," Jeffords said.

Sladen and Howard ate voraciously. Sladen gnawed all the meat from a bone and tossed the bone away. He belched. He wiped his greasy mouth. He shook his head with satisfaction. "What kind of meat was that, Captain Jeffords? Venison of some kind?"

"Did you like it?"

"It was delicious. I think I'll have another piece."

Jeffords' eyes twinkled. "Do you remember that paint pony grazing in the corral?"

"Yes."

"You've eaten part of him, Captain Sladen."

3

Daily the warriors returned in small groups, singly, in twos and threes. Howard, filled with a calm serenity, prayed frequently and soon it was whispered among the people that he was some kind of holy man, something like a shaman. He walked around the camp, his kindliness trailing him like a

390

strange effluvium. Men who were possessed, men whose natures gave them a one-mindedness, always impressed the Apache Indians, who saw in them some relationship with the Spirits. They saw this in Howard, sensing it the way a dog senses love or fear in a human. The Indians, called savage, were in closer kinship with the religiosity of the white stranger than were his own kind. He watched the women at their work and the children at their play and he always had several of the younger children following him, a white-bearded, one-armed Pied Piper. He kept a detailed diary and when he sat to fill its pages the children clustered around him like flies. One afternoon he taught Nachise to write his name. The children were fascinated and he had to listen to each of their names and write them down. This almost caused a crisis in the camp since the adults became frightened; putting down a name on paper was thought in some way to bind the soul of the person. Jeffords explained what Howard was doing and the excitement subsided. To compensate, Howard attempted to learn a few Apache words and the children became hysterical over the pronunciation.

Studying him, Jeffords felt that he reminded him of someone else, and it was only on the fourth day that he realized who. There was something about Howard that brought St. John to his mind, and of course it was the lack of arm in each case. But it was more than that, as though the affliction had gone deeper than the flesh, had affected the inner being of each man, removing each in the same way from the pale of other men.

When all the sub-chiefs and warriors finally were gathered in the Stronghold, Cochise assembled them for council, and asked Howard, Jeffords, and Sladen to join them. By this time Cochise trusted Howard entirely. If the old general had planned every action, every gesture, since his arrival at the camp he could not have comported himself in a way surer to win Cochise's respect. His coming alone to the camp made the Indian respect his courage. The fact that Howard was ingenuous and sincere, that his friendliness and attraction to the children was genuine, had quieted the last suspicions of the Apache and he joined with Jeffords in feeling that at last, after the years, here was a white man with honesty and with the power to put his honesty to purpose.

Before the warriors Cochise recited the proposals made by the American envoy, and then, turning to Howard, said, "We must be allowed to remain in our own country. These mountains have been our home for as long as there is any memory in our people. We will not be moved elsewhere."

Howard bowed to the inevitable. "It will be as you say."

The leading warriors spoke in turn. Howard could not understand what they were saying, but he realized that opinions were varied. Some of the men appeared to welcome the offer; others as bitterly opposed it. Cochise sat without expression and listened each man out, making no attempt to argue or to reason with him.

In the evening the Indians moved to a high plateau a quarter of a mile from where the first council took place. This time they went without the white men. "What are they doing there?" Howard asked Jeffords.

"They're having a prayer meeting." Jeffords' eyes, blue and unwinking, looked at Howard.

"A prayer meeting?"

"They are up there consulting their Spirit, General," Jeffords said. "They are telling him what you have offered and are waiting a sign."

"May I go and join them?" Howard asked.

"No, General Howard. That is something between the Indians and their own Maker. They'll come down and tell us whether they want to make a peace or not."

"Then there is nothing to do but wait," Howard said. "I too can tell my Maker what has been offered. In His wisdom and beneficence He surely is on our side."

"I'm glad that you don't think what they are doing is funny, General," Jeffords said in a quiet voice.

Howard looked at him gently, as though he were a child who had said a foolish thing. "What could be funny about a man asking God for guidance, Captain Jeffords?"

Then he removed his hat and knelt and Jeffords did a strange and wholly unprecedented thing. He knelt beside the old man and bowed his own head and although he had no words to say he too asked that the verdict be peace.

The three white men then sat in a long unbroken silence. From off in the distance they heard the muffled sound of many voices. The women moaned in unison, as though imitating the rising and the falling of the wind, and then the men's voices joined them and together they rose higher and higher, filling the canyon.

Sladen stared ahead of him. Howard read from his Bible. Jeffords smoked and listened and lost himself in his thoughts.

Then Tahzay appeared, his long hair hanging in braids down his back, his face streaked with paint. He was a sudden, violent appearance, but when he spoke his voice was gentle. "You will all come and join us," he said.

The three men followed him. When they reached the plateau they saw the men seated in a circle, and around them, in

392

a larger circle, were the women. Tahzay pointed to a space in the women's circle and the three men sat down.

The singing was ended. Cochise spoke. He spoke with his arms uplifted and his head turned upward. He told of the offer made by the representative of the President of the United States. Howard heard his name repeated frequently as Cochise, through his recital, continuously emphasized that Howard had been brought to the tribe by Jeffords, to whom he never referred by name, but always by the Apache words, Tagliato or Sheekasay.

When he finished the warriors spoke, one at a time, and then Cochise spoke again. He stretched himself to his fullest height. Then he walked over to Howard and in a very clear voice, he said, "Hereafter the white man and the Indian are to drink of the same water, eat of the same bread, and be at peace."

When Jeffords translated these words to Howard the general lifted his own face and said, "I thank Thee, oh my God, for having given my mission success."

4

On a map which Sladen took from a leather envelope, Howard drew an outline of the new Chiricahua Reservation. The line, beginning at Dragoon Springs, near Dragoon Pass, ran northeasterly, touching the north base of the Chiricahua Mountains, continuing to a point on the summit of the Peloncillo Mountains, thence southeasterly along that range to the Mexican boundary, thence westerly along the boundary for fifty-five miles, and thence northerly, following substantially the western base of the Dragoon Mountains to the place of the beginning.

Cochise, with his old knowledge of maps, obtained years before from Major Steen, followed the boundary delineation with great satisfaction. Then he said, "There is one more condition."

"What is that?" Howard asked.

"Captain Jeffords must be Indian Agent."

Jeffords started to translate and then he stopped. "What!"

"What is he saying?" Howard asked.

"Yes," Jeffords said to Cochise. "What are you saying?"

"Captain Jeffords must be Indian Agent," Cochise repeated smoothly.

"What is he saying?" Howard asked again nervously.

"He says that I must be Indian Agent," Jeffords said in a measured voice.

"Excellent. I cannot conceive of a better choice," Howard said.

"Nothing doing," Jeffords said. Then, in Apache, "No, Cochise, not for me."

"We will make peace," Cochise said, as though Jeffords had not spoken. "All cattle and horses that we have taken from the whites will be returned. The Indians will live at peace—but Captain Jeffords must be our Agent."

"I do not want the job," Jeffords said.

"Then the peace talk is ended," Cochise said with finality.

"What did he say, Mr. Jeffords?" Howard asked. When Jeffords did not answer him, he repeated the question in an alarmed voice. Jeffords was staring at Cochise. "Mr. Jeffords, I have asked you what he has said," Howard cried.

"He says that the peace talk is ended," Jeffords said, still staring at Cochise. "I want no part of this job, General. I've seen too damned much of this business. I'm not a politician and I know how these agents have to operate. Fighting off the Army, the civilians, the officials from the territory, Washington. No, General, I've done my job. I brought you here to see Cochise and now I'm through."

"Unless you consent to act as Indian Agent I cannot make peace, Mr. Jeffords. You must understand what your refusal means."

Jeffords still was looking at his old friend. Cochise was without expression, but Jeffords saw a faint, a very faint, glint of amusement in his eyes. "Nothing doing," he said.

"Mr. Jeffords, we have gone beyond the point where we can permit any obstacle to stop us in our work. Make your terms. I will grant them. We cannot reach this point and then fail."

"All right," Jeffords said. "I'll take the job. But I've got to be absolute boss. I must have complete control and authority over the Indians. No soldier, no civilian, no official of any kind will be allowed on the reservation without my permission. And I refuse absolutely to be responsible to any superintendent in this territory. I want my authority direct from Washington, with nothing in between."

"There is no Indian Agent in the United States with that authority, Mr. Jeffords," Howard protested.

"You can take it or leave it, General, and I'd rather you left it. I do not want the job."

"You have it," Howard said quietly. "In the name of the President of the United States, by the authority granted to me by the Secretary of the Interior, I appoint you Indian Agent for the Chiricahua Reservation, under the conditions you have specified."

Jeffords, like a machine, his head whirling, translated the

words. Cochise strode over to him and embraced him. "It is as I have said, Sheekasay. We are above our people."

"How long have you planned this?" Jeffords demanded.

"It is better that you stay with us. You are more Indian than I am. You are better off with us. We will watch out for you so you will not get hurt. Besides, there will be no more fighting. I want somebody to talk to."

THE FIFTH BOOK

THE FINAL TIME

———◆———

Chapter Twenty-two

And now it seemed that the silence was louder than the
noise. Now the fight was ended and the last bullet was fired
from the last rifle. The stillness had in it its own sound and in
the clamorous quiet men waited, still waited, their fingers still
resting on the triggers, their eyes alert and suspicious. The
stillness crept like a heavy cloud, into the Santa Cruz, into
the San Pedro, into the lovely Sonoita. The countryside
screamed its silence. The men waited but there was nothing
to wait for. The fighting was ended.

The Agency for the Chiricahua Reservation was established
in the abandoned stage station at Sulphur Spring. In a way,
as Jeffords came to understand later, the Agency building
symbolized his job. It set the tone. The stage depot was an old
adobe structure. The mud walls, dried and flaky, were pocked
and cracked. There were no windows in the building. There
was no door. There was no furniture inside. Everywhere there
was an air of decay and abandonment.

This was an unusual situation. The Department of Interior,
which was in charge of. Indian reservations, had long before
learned that Indians were exceedingly literal minded and that
they judged large intangibles, like The Government and The
Power of The Army, by the concrete evidence on hand, without permitting their minds to proceed further and become impressed by implications. For this reason Indian Agencies were
normally quite sturdy and occasionally quite elaborate affairs,
designed to establish quickly and strongly in the Indian mind
that the government was an efficient and potent thing.

But the Chiricahua Agency looked like a squatter's shack.
It was a broken-down, old, crumbling building, a dreary,

396

dirty place the Indians had ridden by, to and from raids, for more than fifteen years.

Jeffords set to work grimly. He had never pretended with the Indians so he had nothing of the all-important face to lose. Cochise gave him a dozen young Indians for helpers and they managed to clean up and restore the depot so that it was habitable. In the midst of their work, the first assignment of government beef reached the Agency. There was no corral for the animals.

Cochise summoned his lieutenant and gave strict orders that none of the animals was to be stolen. He went further. He assigned several young Indians to the task of guarding the beef. They had never guarded beef before. They rode back and forth on their ponies, bewildered at their strange job.

Before a packing case that served him for a desk, Jeffords looked upon the unusual sight. "Would you have thought," he asked Cochise, "that one day your warriors would be peaceful cattlemen?" He stuffed his pipe. "I have been making plans," he went on. "All this beef is to be given to your people. I have been reading how it is done on other Agencies. It is a very complicated process and I do not intend to issue rations as it is done elsewhere. Families are given rations and a certain amount of beef is given to each family, depending on the size of the family. The Indians have to call for it and are counted off. It seems to me that that makes a great deal of unnecessary work. I am not going to have a roll call on this reservation. If Indians want to be bad they can always manage to be present for roll call—and at the same time be somewhere else, maybe. It is enough for me if you say your warriors are on the reservation. That will make a great many people angry but this place is not going to be a prison. There will be no reading of names. Here is the beef. You know how many persons you have in your tribe. We will divide all the beef evenly. Appoint men to be in charge of small groups and let these men be responsible for issuing the beef to their own groups. Does that satisfy you?"

"Yes, Sheekasay."

"We have to make this work, Cochise," Jeffords said earnestly. "There are many persons, your enemies and my enemies, who are waiting only for us to fail. They are just waiting for you to go on the warpath again. You know I did not want this job. But now I have it and I am going to make it work."

"You are Agent," Cochise said quietly. "Give your orders. They immediately become law among my people."

"I do not want just to give orders," Jeffords said. "We have been together too much, you and I, for me to hand out orders. I want to talk things over with you and come to agreements with you. Whatever orders are given will come from both of us."

"I am getting old, Sheekasay. I have given orders for a long time. It will be good to sit back and listen to someone else proclaim the law." His face was imperturbable as he went on, "Sheekasay, your white brothers in Tucson do not think much of your peace?"

Jeffords looked startled. "How do you know that, Cochise? You have not been away from here and your people have not left the reservation. How do you know what they say in Tucson?"

Cochise smiled and put his hand on Jeffords' arm. "You do not, after all these many harvests, question how I learn things?"

"No, I guess not. You are right."

"Do not the Americans want the Chiricahuas peaceful?"

"Many do," Jeffords said. "But those who do, some of them, do not trust the peace. Others do not want peace. Others say that General Howard gave the Chiricahuas too much land."

"*Gave* the Chiricahuas too much land?" Cochise repeated. "Who gave the land to General Howard to give to the Chiricahuas?"

"Others say that you are simply accepting government hospitality for the winter and that as soon as spring comes you will again go on the warpath."

"Have you noticed, Sheekasay, how a man who lives by lies always knows that other men live the same way?"

"There are even some who say it is not a legal peace because you did not sign your name to a formal treaty," Jeffords said.

"That is a compliment," Cochise said. "I have never heard of an Indian who was stopped from doing what he wanted to do because he made a mark on a piece of white man's paper."

"I do not worry about these things," Jeffords said. "They all seem to me to be challenges. They only make it so much more necessary that we do not fail."

"Sheekasay," Cochise said. "*We* will not fail. We have already succeeded. It does not matter what will happen. We are a success."

"There is another thing I want to ask you," Jeffords said. "How do you feel?"

"An Indian has no feeling."

"Are the pains still with you?"

"Sometimes."

"Will you let me get a doctor for you?"

"A white doctor? For me?" Cochise laughed shortly. "I am growing very tired, Sheekasay. I am too tired to have work done on me by a white doctor. For what ails me, Nochalo

398

can serve. If it is intended that I shall be in pain, so be it. You have said my pains were from my conscience. Now my conscience is feeling good these days. Let us see if the pains go away."

"I spoke to a doctor," Jeffords said. "I described your trouble to him. He is not a very good doctor, maybe, but he is the best we have around here. I told him you had bad pains in your stomach and there were times you could not hold food. He said you must be careful of what you eat. He said you ought to drink milk."

"Milk?" Cochise said scornfully. "Am I then a child? From whose nipples shall I suck milk?"

"I told him you would not. He gave me some medicine. He said to swallow some of it when the pain got too bad." He picked up a bottle containing yellow liquid and handed it to Cochise.

"White man's medicine," the Indian said, "is bad medicine for an Indian."

"This is good medicine."

"Ah."

"That is my first order," Jeffords said. "The Chiricahua leader must take this medicine when he is in pain."

Cochise picked up the bottle. "Yes, my brother."

"Another thing. The doctor said you must not drink so much whiskey and tiswin."

Now Cochise roared in fury. "No whiskey? No tiswin? But milk! For the Chiricahua chief! Does the doctor think because I have made peace with the Americans I have turned into a stupid old man?"

"I received word today we are to have a visitor," Jeffords grinned. "Governor Safford wishes to see you."

"I have become something to be seen," Cochise said. "Like an animal in a cage."

"A tamed lion," Jeffords agreed.

"Is he an important man?"

"He is the chief of Arizona."

"I will see him," Cochise said. He rose. "Goodbye, *Agent Jeffords*," he said smoothly.

Jeffords laughed and was about to tell him to go to the devil but he remembered in time that Apaches do not take remarks like that in a joke. So he waved his hand and watched Cochise mount his horse and saw the wave of pain that crossed his face as he swung into the saddle. The pain set the features of the Apache into an iron mold and he rode away, erect and with the seat of an emperor. It was hard to believe that Cochise was in torment half the time. He watched him ride off. It was impossible to think of him aging. He had the permanency of his own rocks, Jeffords thought. He was a part of the country, like the mountains, and when he would die the world would come to an end.

Jeffords put his feet on the packing box and lit a cigar and looked around him. He never thought he would end up as an Indian Agent. He, a damned Agent, like any one of a hundred Indian nursemaids. Not quite the same, however. He was boss as no one else was boss. He had stipulated it would have to be his way and it was. When he had announced he was going to let the Indians on his reserve keep their arms the howl must have been heard clear to Washington. Then when the Indians returned every living animal stolen from white men the howls changed to gasps of astonishment. The Agency seemed to be marked, from the start, he thought, and, as usual, things were different for him than they were for anybody else. And it had to work. It wasn't just Jeffords and it wasn't Cochise and it wasn't Howard either.

The Indians didn't need Christianity, he thought. Unless, by Christianity one meant fair dealing. He thought the distribution of the Indian tribes to the different religious sects was foolish. Because men believed sincerely in Christ, or at least in their own interpretation of Christ and His teachings, was no sign they could handle Indians. That was something else. That took knowing Indians. And whatever else these traveling men of God did know they did not know Indians.

He was not in the least interested in making Christians out of Chiricahua Apache Indians, who had an arguable religion of their own. He was interested only in proving what he had believed, what he had stood for, stood for so long as he had known them. That was, if they were treated decently they would return decency.

It was a poker game, in a way. His hand had been called, after all these years. He had to lay it down. He had been called by Oury, or maybe it was Elias, or Les Hawkins. They would love to see a bluff called.

2

When the aged, weary General Howard entered the town of Tucson he found he was a villain. He had left the Old Pueblo some weeks earlier, a sort of hero, with people cheering him in the streets and calling out words of encouragement. Word of the treaty had been sent on ahead of him, on the new telegraph line from Bowie to Tucson, and when he returned the citizens had had ample time to digest the terms of the treaty and they had already decided Howard was a senile scoundrel.

As the white-bearded general rode through the town the same people who had offered encouragement now turned their backs on him as he passed down the streets. People less polite shouted insults. Little boys ran after him, hooting.

The greeting was far different from what Howard had expected. He rode along, stiff and bewildered, with Sladen at his side, and listened to the gibes of the people with amazement. He rode to his quarters and spent several hours in deep prayer and meditation, and Sladen went out to find out why the opinion of the people had so radically changed. "What is the matter, Captain?" he asked when his aide returned.

"I don't entirely know, sir," Sladen said. "The people resent the peace we made with Cochise."

"Resent the peace?" Howard was aghast.

"There is quite a commotion here. The newspaper has been running some very bitter editorials. They say that we gave in completely to Cochise, that he gave nothing, that his word cannot be trusted, that within a few months he will be back at his old tricks." Sladen's face was filled with pain. He could see his words lacerated the old man. "They say that we should have arrested Cochise when we had him in our hands."

"Arrested him? When we came honorably to deal with him?"

"To say nothing of the manifest impossibility of arresting him under the circumstances under which we met."

Howard rose. He lifted his hand. His face had the wrath of an Old Testament prophet. "If he had entered a military establishment alone and surrounded by five hundred soldiers, he would have been permitted to leave in safety," he said, "even though he had refused to make a peace. I do not give my word, only to violate it."

"It seems that people here do not believe a man has to keep his word with an Indian."

"Captain Sladen," Howard said wrathfully, "the roots of the hostility of people here to the Indians go deeper than we know. They are a godless people. They have forgotten the basic principles of Christ. They live and die in violence. In their godlessness they cannot accept the fact that Christian mercy and forbearance have brought peace to this bloody land. My religious beliefs are well known. It is not the first time they have been used against me." He picked up his Bible. "It does not matter. The peace is accomplished. My conscience is clear. I have served my country to the best of my ability and strength and I have served Jesus Christ as well. The Indians are His children, just as we are, and He will not condemn me for bringing an end to bloodshed."

He fell upon his knees. Later he rose again and sat down heavily. "We leave here tomorrow," he said. "I will not be unhappy to see Arizona behind me."

3

In the middle of December Jeffords left the Agency and went to Tucson, the first visit he had made to the town since he left the mail service. He rode slowly through the countryside and he felt the peace and quiet that was in the air. He saw farmers working peacefully behind their ploughs, their rifles put away. He saw new ranches that were springing up everywhere. He saw children playing in the fields, as though the fields were in Pennsylvania or Connecticut or Virginia. He saw wash on the lines and horses grazing and sheep grubbing for food, unattended or with a single herdsman and his dog. He passed people riding along confidently without fear of attack. He saw prospectors moving to the hills.

It was good to see and it was good to know that he had had a part in it, even though somewhere within him there was an intangible feeling of sadness. It was something like the feeling he had when the war ended. It was the realization that a time had ended, that a new time was here, that the new days would be better, but that they could never be the same. He felt old and a little tired and he could not but think how it might have been if the peace had come two years earlier. She might be alive, he thought. It was crazy to regret and think back but she would be alive, and when he thought of her the old hurt twisted in him. It was like the rest of his life. He had helped make the peace when he had lost whatever value it might have had for him. Well, not exactly whatever value. It was a good thing for all of them, the good ones and the bad ones. It was too damned bad the bad ones benefited equally with the others, but the peace was not really for them. The old crew was passing on. There would be newcomers and there were small children and the peace was for them. For the men and women now there it was just a breather, a hiatus, before they went on to whatever came next. The adult Apaches would not change any more than the Ourys and the Eliases. They would keep the peace because they pledged their word but when they died they would be the same inside. They would never be farmers and they would never be ranchers and they would never take on the ways of the conquerors. Each would die by himself and when he died a little piece of the Chiricahua Apaches would die with him. And when they were all dead, maybe the children would be shaped by the peace. The Ourys and Eliases would not change, either. They would go on, hating Indians, protesting, grumbling, finding everything the Indians did wrong, but they too would die before too long and maybe the white men who came after them, maybe they too would be shaped by the peace. There

402

was really no peace now, he thought, no matter how it was called. There was just an armistice. The true peace would not come until later, when it was born, automatically in each individual heart.

He found his pulse quickening when he entered the Old Pueblo. It was the same, he thought, as though he had left it yesterday, as though he were returning to his office after being with her, the taste of her still on him. He thought sadly how he was losing her face; he could hear her voice always but he was losing her face. It was the same lazy hot town, the Mexicans sleeping in the streets, the sun beating down like fire, even in December the noise and movement of the Americans contrasting, as always, to the somnolence of the Mexicans. He saw some new stores, new buildings, a couple of hotels now, new saloons. He recognized no single face and yet it seemed all the faces were familiar.

He pulled up at the mail office. There was a new sign, in larger letters. He entered the building. St. John was at his desk, writing as he always was writing. There was a quiet talking among the other employees. St. John looked up, quietly and courteously, as always, and then he leaped to his feet and ran across the room. "Tom! God, it's good to see you again!"

"Hello, Silas."

"Let me look at you. You're a sight to see. Lord, it's good to see you." He took his hand and held it tightly. Then, in another voice, "You look fine, Tom."

"You look good, too, Silas."

"How are you, Tom?"

"All right."

"It's two years, isn't it?"

"Yes." Jeffords sat down. "It feels longer than that."

"And you did it."

"For better or worse."

"I know. Well, at least you are given full credit for your part."

"Well, well," Jeffords said mockingly. "I hear they're after Safford now."

"It's almost funny, isn't it, Tom?"

Governor Safford had paid a visit to Cochise and a few days afterward had written an account of his experience in the Tucson *Citizen*. His report was a highly favorable one, so much so that the people who had put him in office were shocked. Safford had gone so far as to predict that Cochise might keep his word, which was almost blasphemous. He had written at some length about a strange occurrence that took place during his visit. Jeffords had originally notified Cochise that he would bring the governor on a certain day. On that day, it happened that some new band of Indians appeared on the reserve and asked to be admitted. Jeffords was delayed arranging for their acceptance, and when he and Safford started out for Cochise's camp they were twenty-four hours late. On the way they came upon Cochise, riding in their direction, at the head of his band of warriors, all of them heavily decked in war paint and all of them armed for battle. Safford was greatly frightened, but when Cochise saw Jeffords he jumped from his horse and embraced him in relief. He told him that he had been concerned over the delay and had thought that Jeffords had run into trouble with the new band of Indians which had arrived the day before. He had armed his men and had gone out to kill every member of the newly arrived Indians, if Jeffords had been harmed. Safford was so overcome by this sign of friendship that he devoted a considerable portion of his article to it, and together with the other complimentary things he said about the reservation this had provoked the kind of vilification that only the citizens of Arizona were capable of at that time.

"You must be parched," St. John said. "Let's go get a drink. I'll take the day off. This calls for a celebration."

"There don't seem to be many changes around here," Jeffords said as they walked to the Congress Hall.

"Tucson is getting larger. It isn't changing."

They entered the saloon. Jeffords was recognized immediately. Men gathered around him. The bartender greeted him loudly by name and pushed a bottle over to him. "On the house, Captain Jeffords," he grinned.

"I don't get it," Jeffords said to St. John. "They tore General Howard to little pieces. Why are they so damned glad to see me?"

"They think Howard sold them out. But they figure that your contribution was all right. Besides you're a local boy. They're proud of you."

"How's the old Indian fixer?" a man called out.

"Have a drink with me, Cap."

"Why don't you bring old Cochise down with you?"

"How did you do it, Jeffords?"

"He's just come down from a long ride, men," St. John said. "How about letting him wet his whistle."

The men walked away good-naturedly. "Maybe not all of them think the peace is so lousy," Jeffords said.

"They don't. You know this town. It's not different from other towns. The newspaper doesn't speak for them. And the spokesmen don't speak for them. Not everybody here is a damned fool. And, as usual, the less a fool a man is the quieter he keeps. There are a lot of people who said prayers for the first time in years when they got word of what you did up there."

404

Jeffords swallowed his whiskey. He poured another glass. He looked into the mirror across the bar. He had not realized how gray he was. He saw a tired man looking back at him.

"How long can you stay?" St. John asked.

"A few days. I have an assistant up there. You know Freddie Hughes."

"And how is it going, Tom?"

"All right. For now."

"For now?"

"I'm going to have trouble." He lifted his glass to his lips. "I'm having a time getting supplies. I think they don't approve of my ideas of running a reservation. We got some beef, but so far no corn, no blankets, and no calico or any other kind of cloth."

"Red tape."

"No, it's not that. When they set up their pet reservations they always start off with enough stuff to outfit ten tribes. It peters off after a while if the Agent is a crook and keeps the allotment, but it usually starts out like a flood. I've got some ideas—you might call them unique ideas—and I guess that I'll have to pay for them. Besides, the way I hear it, the Indian Bureau is a little worked up because Howard was able to come out here and do what none of the local generals were ever able to do. And he's given me too much authority, according to them. The other Agents don't like it."

"How are the Indians taking it?"

"You know Cochise. He's kept his word to the letter. He has the Indians right on the line. Some of them don't like it. But his word is law. And he does what I ask him to do, and no questions. I don't know how it will be if they continue to hold up my supplies, but right now it's working fairly well."

"There's talk that the Chiricahuas are devoting themselves to Mexico now that they are at peace with the Americans."

"Sure they are," Jeffords said. "They will for a while. Cochise or no Cochise, you don't change the nature of an Indian overnight, or anybody's nature. The Mexicans are worse enemies to the Chiricahuas than the Americans ever were. They can't understand why we object to them raiding in Mexico. They say it's none of our business."

St. John toyed with his glass. He lifted his eyes questioningly. "There's talk that General Howard gave them the right to maraud in Mexico."

"That's a damned lie. Howard told them we were at peace with Mexico and that raids there would be looked on in the same light as raids in Arizona. Cochise is working like hell. He's given strict orders to keep out of Mexico. But some of the Indians are like bronchos. They need gentling. It will take time. This Geronimo is making a big appeal to some of the younger men. I can't do everything at once. I've got to sell them the idea that we are on the level, that they all will be treated fair and square on the reservation, that they will get the food and clothing promised to them, that there is no need to run off and raid in Mexico. Then, slowly, maybe, I can wean them. Not overnight, but gradually." He swallowed another drink. "The reservation is a big place. It runs sixty miles by sixty miles, maybe more. That's thirty-six hundred square miles. That's a lot of miles. The country is some of the wildest in the territory. There are other Indians on it besides the Chiricahuas. Indians from other tribes raid in Mexico and cross the line and trade with Cochise's Apaches. It's pretty complicated and it will take one hell of a long time but Cochise is working at it and I'm working at it and some of the younger chiefs are on our side." He breathed heavily. "I once thought things would change overnight once Cochise made peace, but a lot of things are just beginning, and it needs patience. Miracles don't happen."

"How is Cochise?"

"Sick."

"What do you mean?"

"He's sick. I don't know how sick. He won't let an American doctor work on him. He's too much Apache for that."

"What's the matter with him?"

"Some internal trouble. He gets spasms of pain. His food hurts when he swallows it."

"You don't think he's going to die?"

"I don't know. I'm no doctor. But he seems sick, as much as you can see. He doesn't let it show. He has a face like brass. He keeps quiet about it. Indian quiet. I hope it's nothing serious. But if anything happens to him it will fall on Tahzay to take over. I'm glad Tahzay is on my side."

"What about Nachise?"

"I'm not so sure of him. He's been jealous about Tahzay for a long time. Younger son and older son sort of stuff. But Tahzay is all right."

A heavy-set man with thick glasses touched Jeffords on the shoulder. "Pardon me, Captain Jeffords. I'm from the Tucson *Citizen*. I wonder if I could talk to you for a few minutes."

"A reporter?"

"Yes, Captain Jeffords."

Jeffords looked at St. John. "I'll be damned." The reporter asked a number of questions about the reservation and Jeffords answered him. Other men gathered around and nodded solemnly as Jeffords spoke. His words were accepted with an almost painful respect, and when the reporter finished and thanked him, Jeffords drank another glass of whiskey and said, "Let's get out of here. I don't like this public figure business. I'm not used to it."

On the way out Tevis stopped Jeffords. "You probably don't remember me," he said. "I'm Jim Tevis. I used to know Cochise. How is he?"

"He's fine," Jeffords said.

"I used to know Cochise," Tevis repeated slowly. "I felt good when I heard he quit fighting. I think you did a good thing, Captain Jeffords."

"Thanks," Jeffords said.

"Say hello to him for me, will you?"

"I will. And thanks again."

Outside the Congress Hall, St. John suddenly stopped. "I almost forgot," he said. "Terry's back."

"Is she?"

"Come on over to the Scat Fly. Don't tell her you've been in town this long without my letting you know about her. She'd shoot me."

"Wait a minute," Jeffords said. He rubbed his beard. "When did she get back?"

"A few weeks ago."

"What is she doing?"

"Working at the Scat Fly. The same as before." St. John grinned. "And she's not married and she is as beautiful as ever, maybe more."

"What does she know?"

"About you? Nothing."

"Let me try to think for a moment." After awhile he said, "There is no use seeing her."

"Why not? Look, Tom. You can't just not see her. You'll be coming down to Tucson now. You'll run into her, one way or another. Besides there is no reason to avoid her. She has been terribly anxious to see you. She asked me to take her out to the Agency. I was going to." He put his hand on Jeffords' shoulder. "Come along. You'll find it quite easy."

"Do you think so?"

"She's a grown woman now, Tom. She's twenty-five. She's different. Traveling has changed her. She wanted to write to you at the Agency, but she decided not to. She said you never answered her letters."

4

She was self-possessed and very cool. "Why, hello, Tom." She held out her hand.

"Hello, Terry."

"How nice it is to see you."

He nodded. "It's good to see you."

"Let me look at you. You've changed. Your hair is gray. You look older, Tom."

"I am older."

"I mean a different kind of older. I guess it's your responsibilities now."

"Probably."

"Sit down, won't you? You must tell me all about yourself. I'm sure you have been doing lots of interesting things since we last saw each other."

They were in the office. He sat down. She held her hands gracefully in her lap. She held her head very high and she had a trained, courteous expression on her face. There was a new polish, something rather hard and a little brittle. "Everybody is talking about your splendid achievement in getting that Indian—Cochise, is it?—to agree to stop his war."

He filled his pipe. He began to feel relieved.

"You must feel very proud, Tom. You always did have faith in the Indians, didn't you? Some of the men around here said General, what's his name, Howard, practically gave Cochise a lien on the United States Government and that the old savage is only holing up until spring, but you don't believe that, do you?"

"No."

"I knew you wouldn't." Her voice was gracious. "You must have had your usual faith in Cochise or else you would not have taken on the rather thankless task of Agent, would you?"

"Let's stop talking about Indians," he said. "Tell me about yourself."

She held up her hands. "Why, Tom," she said with well-bred astonishment, "I thought Indians were all you cared about."

He could have asked her to quit and she would, he knew. But it was what she was waiting for. And that would change the tone. He thought it was better to leave it as it was. "Tell me about San Francisco."

"I told you a great deal about San Francisco in several letters I wrote to you," she said in a friendly way. "Perhaps you never received the letters. You never answered them, you know, and I thought perhaps they never reached you."

"They reached me."

"Then you just didn't answer them. I told myself you could not be rude enough just not to answer, but that was what it was."

He knew she was trying to work him to the point where he would stop her. He could get up and shake her and then kiss her and the brittleness would be gone and it would be the way it was before. "I've been moving around. Not much time for letter writing. But you look fine. Pretty as ever. New style hair-do."

408

"That's the way they dressed it in San Francisco." There was a trace of disappointment in her voice. "I don't know what I'll do down here. There is nobody in Tucson who knows how to dress hair."

"Maybe when you get some desert dust in it again you won't have to worry. Climate here does things to a woman's hair."

"Perhaps so."

"How long do you intend to stay on?"

"For good," she said quietly.

"I thought you liked San Francisco."

"I liked it." She got up and walked to the window and turned her back to him. "I've got too much desert in my veins." Then she turned and smiled brilliantly. She sat down again and they looked politely at each other. She seemed to be waiting for something. It wouldn't be any good at all, he thought. He had nothing to offer her, even less than before.

"Do you think you could find a place for me to sleep here?" he asked. "Or had I better look around for a hotel room?"

She closed her eyes for the briefest moment and the hard brightness left her face and she looked like a child and he wanted to go to her; he wanted to put his arms around her. When she opened her eyes again her features composed themselves, and she said, "Surely we have a place for you here. Aunt Abigail would never forgive you if you stayed anywhere else in Tucson. How long do *you* intend to stay on?"

"Just a day or so. I have to get back to the Agency."

"The Indians again. Then you won't be here for Christmas?"

"I don't think so."

"Well, you wait here. I'll see about your room. I think your old one is occupied but we'll find something just as good, I'm sure."

She rose gracefully and walked out of the room. He looked at her arched back and the way she held her head. Funny redhead, he thought, and she had never married, not even the man with the sailing boat.

There were some old faces at the dinner table that night and many new ones. When Duffield entered the room and saw Jeffords he gave a great shout and slapped him on the back. "By God, Jeffords, it's good to see you. Even though you walked out and left me flat."

"How are you, Duffield?"

"All right, all right, couldn't be better. This town is getting a little too civilized for me. I think I got to move on to Prescott or some other place where they don't bother a man so damned much." He laughed loudly. "It's getting so damned namby-pamby around here a man is afraid to carry a gun."

Everybody in the room started to laugh. There was some joke. "What do you mean?" Jeffords asked.

"What do I mean?" Duffield bellowed. "Someone tell him what I mean. I got you to thank for it partly, Jeffords."

"Me?"

"Sure, ain't you the one who helped make the peace around here? This town is getting full of law and order and hombres like you are responsible."

"Duffield has had some trouble with the law," St. John explained.

"I gather as much," Jeffords said.

"Trouble, brother, trouble," Duffield said. "You ain't never seen the kind of trouble I get into. Tell him about it, St. John."

"Well," St. John began, "we have a new chief justice here, Judge Titus. He comes from Philadelphia and he is full of brotherly love for everybody except Milt Duffield."

"Brother, and that's the truth," Duffield roared.

"Judge Titus got the notion that our Milt was one of the town reprobates. He didn't like the way he goes around shooting at things. There are now laws about carrying concealed weapons and displaying them, and so on. Nobody pays much attention to them, but they're on the books. Judge Titus and Milt got to be sort of mortal enemies and the old judge decided that he would hang a concealed-weapon charge on Milt. He just bided his time until one night when the Mexicans were having a *baile* and everybody was supposed to leave their hardware home. The *baile* was held in the Congress Hall and we were all sitting in a little back room and just for the hell of it some one asked Milt how many guns he had on him. Old Milt was dressed up for the *baile* and you wouldn't think he was carrying a thing, no bulges anywhere. Well, he started to unload. The tools of his trade, you might say. He began to remove shooting pieces, mostly derringers, from the armholes of his waistcoat, his hip pockets, his boots, from behind his neck, from out of his sleeves. When he was finished he had twelve guns and one knife on the table."

"Twelve guns!" Jeffords laughed.

"Yes, sir," Duffield said proudly. "Twelve of them and hid so good that a lady dancing with me never could feel a thing."

"Well," St. John continued, "Judge Titus felt he had Duffield at last. Next day he had him arrested for carrying concealed weapons. He held a regular court, jury and all, and then he called Charlie Brown, you know, the owner of the saloon, for chief prosecution witness. Brown stood up before the judge and jury and Judge Titus said, 'Mr. Brown, please show the jury how Mr. Duffield drew his weapons.' And old Charlie, he said, 'Well, Judge, he drawed just like this,' and

410

Charlie pulled out a six-shooter, fully cocked, from his hip pocket!"

Duffield roared and pounded the table. "My God!" he shouted. "That killed the case. Judge Titus had to throw the case out of court. Hell, I thought Titus would bust a gut when Charlie started to wave his six-gun around. 'Just like this, Judge.'"

Duffield shoveled great quantities of food in his mouth, pausing to laugh to himself every few minutes. Mrs. Wilson, who had greeted Jeffords with her normal brusqueness, watched Jeffords like a hawk and when he finished refilled his plate. On the third refill Jeffords protested. "I haven't had food like this for a long time, ma'am," he said. "My stomach has got unused to this kind of eating."

"You ought to come here more often," she said sharply. "You wouldn't look as skinny as a rail."

"I sure ought," Jeffords agreed. "And I believe I will."

Terry had eaten in silence; now she lifted her beautiful head and looked around the table brightly. "I am sure that Tom has some interesting things to tell all of us," she said with a brilliant smile. Her eyes were doing a forced dance.

"Sure thing, Jeffords," Duffield said, holding up a long knife, the blade laden with food. "Tell us about the Indians. We ain't heard the story of that powwow yet."

Jeffords drank his coffee. He began to feel the old discomfort.

"Go on," Duffield said. "Give out."

"Yes, Tom," Terry said, the fixed smile still on her face. "Tell us how you accomplished your miracle."

Jeffords bit off the end of a cheroot. He sniffed at it. He lit it carefully. "It just worked out right," he said at last. "Cochise decided that he could trust Howard and that was all there was to it."

Duffield looked at him soberly. "You did a good job, Tom," he said. "Me, I ain't one for quiet. But Indian peace is good for this place. Guess folks got a lot to thank you for." He pushed away his plate. "They say the Indians are raising a lot of hell in Mexico. Not that I give a hoot in hell what goes on in Mexico." Suddenly he raised his head and looked around the room. "Hey, Johnny, tell old Cap what happened to you in Mexico."

Jeffords, glad to change the subject, said immediately, "What happened?"

A short, grizzled man at a nearby table started to laugh.

"That's Johnny Hart," Duffield explained. "By way of being a prospector. Not that he ever found anything, but he's full of hope, ain't you, Johnny?"

"I'll strike. I was grubbing around Mexico in Sonora, and I

411

wasn't finding anything. Them Mexicans got all the good stuff staked out for themselves, but I was poking around anyway. One night I was awakened from my sleep by a bunch of Mex soldiers. Them greasers had me handcuffed while I was sleeping. I said, 'What the hell is this?' They told me I was needed as a *voluntario*. I said, 'I ain't volunteered for nothing.' But they marched me over to the headquarters of a Mexican division and told me I was a volunteer Mexican soldier working for General Pesquiera. I told them I was a danged American citizen and wasn't no greaser soldier working for no greaser general, but that didn't cut no ice. They told me all I had to do was cheer. 'Cheer for what?' I asked. 'For our noble constitution and General Pesquiera,' they said. So I figured, what the hell. It wasn't a bad life. I wasn't doing no good prospecting. We only marched a little now and then and didn't do no fighting. The country was filled with chickens and eggs and goats and nothing was too good for the men protecting the constitution and General Pesquiera. Well, things went along fine until one day we got into a little town and I started to shout. As usual I shouted, 'Viva General Pesquiera! Viva General Pesquiera!' and then the first sergeant came over and hit me in the face. I asked him what the hell was the matter and he said, 'You crazy fool, don't you know enough to cheer for General Candara?' "

The men in the room roared. Jeffords looked puzzled.

"Johnny found out that Pesquiera had sold out the whole division to Candara the day before for a dollar six bits a head while Johnny was out foraging," Duffield explained.

"How the hell was I to know?" Johnny asked plaintively. "I figured then that greaser politics was too complicated for me so I got out first chance I had."

"That's a crazy country, all right," Duffield chuckled. "You heard about Sam Wisser, didn't you, Jeffords?" When Jeffords shook his head, Duffield said, "Well, old Sam is another miner. He was traveling around down below the border with a pal. This pal was a sick man, or at least he thought he was sick. He carried around a big bag filled with every kind of medicine known to man. He had just about a hundred bottles and boxes, I guess. Well, this pal finally kicked off in Mexico and old Sam buried him and when he poked around what he left he found this valise with the medicines. Old Sam wasn't doing no good finding silver nor gold so he set himself up as a traveling doctor. And he had to travel. He treated people all over Mexico. He had enough medicine to open up a hospital and he had patients everywhere. Of course he had to keep moving because most of his patients died after he gave them medicine. He got rid of all the stuff and now he's here in Tucson retired and happy." Duffield stuck a black cigar into his mouth. "People won't let him alone. The Mexicans still come around and ask him for medicine. He would like to stick a sign, *Medico,* on his door only there's so damned much law in this town now he's afraid to take a chance."

The stories went on. Jeffords felt the warmth and friendliness in the room and he understood that the stories were a sort of welcome, the way the men had of telling him they were glad he was back. They were being told for him, to bring him into the fold again, and he listened to them and he felt it was good to be there.

Later he went out onto the terrace with Terry. She sat down slowly, gracefully, as a lady in San Francisco might seat herself in a drawing room. She gathered her skirts around her and looked at him pleasantly. He stretched out in a chair and filled his pipe. "Just like old times," she said. She had the drawing-room tone in her voice, he thought.

"Yes. The place seems familiar."

"It is very pleasant, isn't it, Tom?"

"Yes, Terry."

"How does it feel to be back?"

"Good. And you?"

"It feels wonderful, Tom. Tucson will always be my home. I enjoyed it so much in San Francisco, but I never felt at home."

"That's a big town, they tell me."

"It's big, but it's very friendly. There is always so much going on, dances, parties."

"Did you have fun?"

"Oh, yes. The young men seemed to think I was quite pleasing."

"I'll bet they did."

She turned away her head. Her profile was very beautiful. Her hair was caught in a low chignon and gleamed in the clear light. "I used to tell them about the desert," she said. "How it looked in the spring. They all seemed to think that the desert was a barren place. It was difficult for me to convince them otherwise. I don't think they ever really believed me. I told them how the desert blossomed in the spring, how it smelled so fresh and clean, how it stretched for miles without end, how there seemed to be room for everything, for the biggest mountains, how a person could breathe—they just listened to me, but they didn't believe." She kept her face turned away. "They ought not to call this a desert." Her voice was low. "It is really a garden. A strange and peculiar garden, but a garden. And when it gets into your blood it never leaves it. The ocean is grand and the smell of the sea air is grand and the foggy nights and the little lights you see

413

from the hills—they are very beautiful. But there is only one place for a desert rat and that is on the desert."

"Yes, Terry," he said gently.

"When I got back here I tore off some sage and buried my face in it and I started to cry. Wasn't that foolish, Tom?"

"No."

"It was foolish," she insisted, biting her lip. "But I think that a smell can carry you back faster through your memory than anything else. When I smelled that sage I just closed my eyes and no time had elapsed, no time at all." She turned and looked full at him. There was a tear under each eye.

He felt himself going weak and he stood up suddenly and tamped out his pipe. "I think I'll turn in." His voice surprised him. His tongue was thick and his words came out in a hoarse blur. "I had a long day."

She stood up instantly. She smiled politely again. The two tears slipped hurriedly down her face as though hastening to escape. "I don't know what I must be thinking of," she said, "keeping you up this way. You must be very tired."

"I'll see you in the morning, Terry."

He went into the house. She covered her face with her hands. When he came down in the morning she was not there and he did not see her again before he left.

Chapter Twenty-three

The government appeared to ignore the newly established Chiricahua Apache Reservation during the first winter of its existence. After the initial consignment of beef, no supplies of any kind were sent to it. The Indians remained quietly on the reserve and waited patiently for the food and clothing that was due them, but nothing came.

In January Jeffords went to Bowie to find out why he was not getting the normal consignments he was entitled to. He had worked tirelessly to keep the nomadic bands content on the reservation. His influence, supported by the stanch loyalty of Cochise, was more powerful than that of any Agent in the Territory, but he felt the restiveness of his charges, without food, without occupation of any kind, unable to hunt. He would have had trouble on several occasions had it not been for the iron hand of Cochise, who now sat regularly at his side in the Agency building, implementing with his own un-questioned authority every directive Jeffords issued.

Jeffords had written to his superiors twice, requesting that the ordinary supplies, the things sent to Indian reservations as a matter of course, be sent to him. Nothing arrived. Despite this conspicuous inattention, Jeffords refused to believe that the Indian Bureau was attempting to undermine the Chiricahua peace, and so, in January, he went down to Bowie to make a personal plea.

He was brought to Major Winter, commandant of the fort. Winter received him in a genial, friendly manner. A great friend and admirer of General Howard, Winter had been party to the feast at the fort which celebrated the peace pact.

Winter had an open, amicable face. He invited Jeffords to speak his mind and he listened attentively, but as he spoke the Agent was aware that there was something else in the air. Winter, despite his apparent lack of guile, was not treating openly with him. He was courteous, considerate, and a gentleman, but as Jeffords laid the facts before him he felt that there was some barrier between them.

"I don't understand, Major," Jeffords said. "You know that when Indians are put on reservations these days, supplies come automatically. We're not starving Indians any more, as I understand it."

"That is true, Captain Jeffords," Winter agreed.

"Then what is holding up my supplies? The people in Washington must know that of all the Indians out here the Cochise Apaches are the least amenable to reservation restraint. They must know the years of war that preceded this peace. They must understand that it would be difficult enough to keep them in line if everything else was perfect. How do they expect me to keep the Chiricahuas on the reservation if they won't send me food and clothing? Washington knows by now that even Indians have to eat."

Winter nodded equably. "How are the Indians behaving, Captain Jeffords?" he asked casually.

"They are behaving damned well," Jeffords said. "You know that better than anyone else, Major. There hasn't been a single report of Indian trouble anywhere in the Chiricahua country since Cochise made his pact with General Howard." Jeffords looked at him keenly. "It is odd that you ask me that, Major. You are the military commandant here and you know how quiet it's been."

"That's very true," Winter said. "Things have been most quiet here."

"Then what is the trouble? I know that other Agencies have been getting their supplies—since we've been established. It's not just red tape."

"It's so quiet," Winter mused, almost to himself, "my soldiers have little to do."

415

"Would you rather have them out with General Crook? He's having a time of it and probably could use every man you could spare."

Winter appeared to be struck by a sudden thought. "Captain Jeffords, why don't you let my soldiers help police your reserve?"

"Help me in what way? There is no trouble there."

"Not yet," Winter persisted. "But you never know with Indians. You might have an outbreak at any time and then perhaps it would be too late to get military assistance."

"There won't be any outbreak. Cochise has given me his word."

"And he appears to be an honorable Indian," Winter agreed very quickly. "But wouldn't it be wise to have troops there, just in case?"

"When I took this job, Major, I took it on condition that no soldier would set foot on my reservation. That was part of the pact. I gave my word on that score to Cochise. The Chiricahuas will police themselves. Soldiers on a reservation mean trouble, soon or later. We haven't had any trouble yet and I don't anticipate any so long as I get the supplies that are due me."

Winter sighed softly. He watched a fly buzz noisily around the room. "Well, then, Captain Jeffords, I am afraid there is very little I can do for you." His face closed. It was as though a door had shut.

Jeffords leaned forward. His lips thinned. "Are you trying to tell me I'm being cut off from supplies because I won't permit soldiers to patrol on my reservation?"

"Not at all," Winter said. His mouth moved but his face stayed closed. "Do not jump at conclusions. I merely suggested if you altered your method of governing a reservation so that it would fall into a more orthodox category, well then, perhaps things, other things, would follow in more orthodox fashion."

"I think I understand, Major," Jeffords said. "The brass can't tolerate Indians behaving themselves without soldiers standing over them with guns. It throws the whole military conception of controlling Indians."

"I did not say that, Captain Jeffords."

"There is no war around just now, is there, Major? Indians are about the only excuse for officers holding commands these days?" Winter refused to rise. "No soldiers, no supplies." Jeffords smiled grimly. "All right, Major. If that's the way it's going to be I'll get those damned supplies my own way. But supplies or no supplies there isn't going to be a single soldier put his foot on the Chiricahua Reservation while I'm Agent there." He smiled again, a softer smile. "And you know, Major, what happens if I walk out."

Winter rose to his feet. His face was arranged in pleasantness, but his eyes were cold. "As you will, Captain Jeffords," he said. "I was merely trying to be helpful."

"I'm sorry I took up your time, Major."

"By the way, I received a letter from General Howard. He wants to know how the Agency is coming along."

"Tell him it's coming along fine," Jeffords said.

2

In February the food gave out on the reserve. There were still no new supplies delivered to the reservation and no signs that any were coming. Jeffords went out on his own. He went to the nearby ranches and bought beef, signing for the purchases in his official capacity as Indian Agent. He bought material for clothing, blankets, corn, medicine, in Tucson. In some quarters he met a hesitancy to deliver the goods to him over his official signature. He promised to pay out of his own pocket if the government defaulted.

Using Indians as cowboys he rounded up his beef. He borrowed freight wagons from some of the Tucson merchants to haul the other stores to the Agency. He was surprised to find that many of the merchants were genuinely interested in helping him keep peace on his reserve. The good will and cooperation renewed his energy. He had to make it work.

When all the supplies were at the Agency he discovered that some four hundred members of a distant branch of the Chiricahua tribe had settled on the land. After consulting with Cochise he accepted them, and then he distributed his beef and cloth equally. The distribution was made as before. There was no lining up, no rationing check-off. A count was simply made of every living person on the reservation, and the supplies were divided up. When the issuance was over he retired to his office and prepared a long memorandum to Washington, listing the indebtedness he had incurred and protesting in strong terms against the crookedness of the official policy toward his Agency. Cochise joined him and sat in his chair. "You have been ashamed, Sheekasay," the Indian said.

"I have been, Cochise," Jeffords said.

"You have been ashamed for your government," Cochise said. His lined face relaxed. "You must never be ashamed before me. Before the others, but not before me."

"It has been rotten."

"Governments never keep their word," Cochise said indifferently. "They are like all bodies that govern. They promise much and deliver little."

"Every single thing that General Howard and I promised to the Chiricahua Indians has been delivered," Jeffords said quickly.

"Yes, my brother," Cochise agreed. "You have kept your word. Nothing that has been promised has not been given. But your government is clever. It is possible to keep a promise and still break it."

"You are right, as usual, Cochise."

"The government keeps its word. We have our land. There are no soldiers. You are our Agent. But there are no supplies. What happens? The wild Indians are supposed to break out. Then the government shakes its head and sheds fake tears and points to the impossibility of making good Americans out of Indians."

Jeffords looked long and silently at his friend. "Does all this make you laugh sometimes, Cochise?"

"The Americans are civilized," Cochise said.

In the third week of March Jeffords received a severe reprimand from the Superintendent of Indian Affairs for the Territory of Arizona for his revolutionary methods of obtaining supplies. He read the letter and then crumpled it savagely between his hands. He was not supposed to be responsible at all to the territorial superintendent; he had sent his memorandum to Washington direct. Apparently the official in Washington had notified the superintendent and had told him to censure the Chiricahua Agent. This was in direct violation of the terms agreed to by Howard. Jeffords wrote an angry reply to the territorial superintendent and reminded him that under the terms of the Chiricahua pact he was not under the supervision of the Territorial Agency.

He received no answer to his letter, but then, suddenly, in April, he received a large consignment of subsistence supplies. The consignment came unexpectedly and when the wagons came in Jeffords and Cochise ran outside the office and the Agent shouted with joy. Cochise's eyes sparkled and he said, "You have won, maybe." Then they looked at the consignment and found that it consisted of a vast quantity of wheat. There was no corn.

Wheat was useless to the Indians. They knew of nothing to do with it. Corn was their mainstay. Corn was needed to ward off the usual epidemics of fevers and dietary troubles. No Agency was ever supplied with wheat. Meanwhile here was wheat.

When Cochise looked at the grain his face hardened again. Jeffords said harshly, "We are not beaten yet." He made his former rounds again, and swiftly managed to trade off the

418

wheat for corn before it spoiled. The corn was distributed to the Indians.

And now it was spring. Now was the time when the Chiricahua Apaches, for years beyond recall, started out on their great annual raids. It was the time the Indian haters had waited patiently for, the time they had predicted would mark the end of the peace.

"Sheekasay," Cochise said shrewdly. "If it was intended that my people should break from the reservation at this time, the sending of the wheat instead of corn would be a clever thing, would it not?"

The thought was too diabolical. "I cannot believe that," Jeffords said.

"Still, wheat would have infuriated the wild Apaches, would it not? If they were not sure whether to break out or not it would make their decision for them."

"They must not," Jeffords said quietly.

"They will stay," Cochise said.

The Indians remained peacefully on the reservation. They had visitors. A large band of White Mountain Apaches, filled with the spring elation, visited them and held formal counsel with Cochise. They sought the aid of the Chiricahua Apaches in a new plan of warfare against General Crook. Cochise, in a violent scene, ordered them from the reserve.

"We will not join you," he said in a deadly voice. His eyes were like a black fire. "And it goes further. My warriors will fight with the white soldiers in any warfare against you. This reservation will be a battleground between our peoples if you come here again."

The White Mountain Indians left quickly and soon were engaged in war with Crook. And Jeffords wondered how he could make his people know the kind of man Cochise was.

Throughout the summer of 1873 nothing further was done for the Chiricahua Apaches. The usual practices of establishing schools, hospitals, trading stores, were omitted. There was no reservation doctor. There were no agricultural teachers. From their most ancient days the Chiricahuas, alone of all the different tribes in the great Apache nation, had never tilled the soil. They knew nothing of farming; additionally, the location of the reservation was not conducive to agriculture. Jeffords sent out protests by the score, but everywhere he met with a solid blank wall. The only replies he received were official criticisms for not making farmers out of his charges.

And yet through that summer, their first on the reservation, the Indians kept their peace, with a fortitude and patience that

419

caused Jeffords to develop a hatred for the intangible forces that had lined themselves up against him. He could see, with painful cruelty, how successful his job could be, how basically successful it was, despite all the odds against it. Time and again he wanted to throw up the job, to release the Indians from their pledge. But he fought on doggedly and he found that Cochise, almost more than he, was determined to prevent the failure that was expected, almost waited for. The indomitable mind of the Indian fought not to keep his people prisoner; he was resolved, in his own implacable manner, that Jeffords personally should not fail.

There was not a whole peace. Small groups of Chiricahua warriors went into Mexico from time to time and raided there. Cochise struck hard at this practice, and many of his men were exiled from the reserve by his orders for this practice, and went over the border to join the swelling ranks of Geronimo. Slowly and surely he was bringing the practice to an end; the intractables were being forced out.

And nowhere in southern Arizona, scarcely nine months before a graveyard for Indian and white man both, was there a single recorded incident of Indian attack.

By August the manifest loyalty and honesty in the relations between Jeffords and the Indians finally convinced some of the higher officials in Washington. The Acting Commissioner sent out a consignment of food—still withholding any clothing—and additionally, although with great reluctance, agreed to pay the $6200 worth of debts Jeffords had contracted in getting supplies for the Indians six months earlier.

3

The attempt, whether deliberate or not, to provoke discontent and rebellion on the reservation through failure to send adequate supplies, had failed. A new trouble began. Inspectors visited the reservation, and soon after they left, Jeffords was ordered suddenly to remove the tribe from the Sulphur Spring Valley to the San Simon Valley. The excuse given for the order was that the soil in the San Simon was more suitable for agriculture, and Jeffords was ordered, further, to get the Chiricahuas to till the land and support themselves as much as they could.

When the news of the impending removal reached Cochise he went to Jeffords. Cochise, who seemed to have aged beyond his years, was worried. "Is it true," he asked, "that you must move my people to the San Simon?"

"Those are my orders, Cochise."

"It is not good for the Chiricahuas to live there. We are a mountain people. The land is low in the San Simon and there are fevers there. When the Chiricahua Apaches go to the San Simon and stay too long they become filled with fever Ghosts."

"We will have to try it, Cochise," Jeffords said quietly.

Cochise sat down. His face was old and tired. "I think it is a good thing that I sicken and grow old, Sheekasay," he said. "The things that are happening are not good."

"There are difficulties, Cochise," Jeffords said earnestly. "It is up to us to overcome them." He spoke with a confidence he no longer felt.

"Tell me, my brother. Do you think our peace has been a success?"

"No," Jeffords said.

"Look at my people. Do you think they were made to live this way, on charity, like women?" He shook his head. "No. This is wrong. You are good to us. You try to make the medicine taste good. But it is bad medicine. We are a nation of fighters. We are like wild animals in the forest. We have lived violently and died violently. Now we are to be tamed. We live like women. We wait for our food to be given to us and when it is not given in time we go hungry. Look, look at my people! They are without clothing. They are without blankets. We sit, like rabbits, and wait until the white man gets ready to feed us." As Jeffords started to speak, he raised his hand. "I am not going to make changes, Sheekasay," he said in a very gentle voice. "I have given my word, and I do not betray you. We remain at peace, as long as the terms of peace are not violated by your government. But I am not happy. My people are not happy. We are not farmers. We are not valley people. We are people of the mountains. That is our name. Now we must go to where the fever lives and many of us will die and the others will try to use the tools of a farmer." He looked at Jeffords. "And I have brought this upon my people. It was I who made them this way."

Jeffords looked at his stricken face. Was it worth it to break such a man, he asked himself. "Cochise," he said, "I love you more than any man. Listen to me. Some of the things that happened could have been foretold. Others could not. There are bad men in my government but in the end the badness must lose to the goodness. In the end it will be good. It will not be good for grown men and women, maybe. The change is hard. You cannot take a mountain lion and teach him to pull a wagon. But you can train the lion's cub, maybe, and if not the cub, the cub of the cub. It will work out. You will not live to see it, maybe, nor I, but it will work out. The children who are not yet born among you will one day be grateful to you for your wisdom. Through you the Chiricahua people will live on, with the white man, as brothers. In the time that

421

will come the hatreds will be forgotten and the Indian and the white man will share this country. And when that time comes yours will be a great name people will speak. That is what we are working for, you and I, and we must not forget it, not for ourselves, but for the children your children will bring into life."

The face of Cochise was old and almost shriveled and it was as though he had not heard. His face was Indian, in a way Jeffords had never seen before. Without answering he rose and walked slowly from the building and Jeffords saw that his straight back was bent and his broad shoulders were sagged and he was broken.

4

At the end of August Jeffords made his first annual formal report to the Commissioner of Indian Affairs in Washington, and he again asked that supplies be sent to the Indians. He pointed out that the Indians had kept their part of the pact with literal scrupulousness. "Wayfarers can now be seen on our highways traveling alone and unarmed," he wrote. "Farmers and miners are pursuing their labors with as much unconcern as to safety as their brothers of the East, and confidence in the good faith of these Indians on the part of the settlers appears to be universal. For their honesty," he continued angrily, "the Indians had received nothing. A few blankets and a little manta and calico were furnished by General Howard to the first parties that came in to make peace and nothing has been furnished since," he wrote. "Their condition is deplorable. Many of them may be seen with nothing but a piece of corn or flour sack tied around them to hide their persons. It is now nearly a year since I first brought in these people and I think nothing will go further to show their sincerity in their peace than to know that they have waited this long to have the promises of the government fulfilled."

He might as well tear up the report and scatter it to the desert wind, he thought. He might as well burn it as soon as he finished it. The letter would go, with scores of other letters, and the clerks would look at it and it would be just a piece of paper with complaints, one of many pieces of paper with complaints, and it would be printed neatly in the book the department got up each year for the President and that would be the end of it.

He finished the report and signed it. He was writing in an un-understood language to a foreign people. Nowhere, at no time, he thought viciously, was there a colonial policy as inept as this. In its worst days Imperial Spain dealt with its colonies with more sense. What kind of country are we developing, he wondered. Lives could be wasted in fruitless war. Money could be tossed around in millions to maintain armies. But when the victory was won the pennies were counted. What was the reason for this consummate idiocy? Whose fault was it? There were good and honest men in Washington, men with wisdom and experience, and they could not see what stood before their eyes with painful simplicity.

He had to stop thinking about it, he thought. He got too mad. The impulse was to throw back the job he never wanted in the first place, to tell the bureaucrats, the men with the soft faces and the white hands, to go to hell, God damn it, to go to hell, and then to tell the Indians to get the hell out, to go out on the country again, to find their food and their clothing in their own way.

You could talk to a man, he thought. You could explain and argue and show, but who on God's earth could talk to a bureau? Who could explain to a Department? What could you do against files, reports, letters, levels, channels?

How could you make a building in Washington, more than two thousand miles away, understand the look of a starving people?

The tribe moved to the San Simon. They moved with the dull apathy with which they now did everything. They packed silently and moved, like cattle, without protest. They were all breaking, he thought. They had all lost something. They had been killers before, but they also had been alive. They had been a people and now they had become animals, without hope and without spirit.

He could stand it no longer and he saddled his horse and rode to Tucson. He had to get away from their faces for a little while.

5

As they had been indignant before about Indian atrocities, the leaders of Tucson now were as indignant about their submissiveness. They looked upon the restraint of the wild Apaches, upon their refusal to be drawn into a violation of their word, upon their adherence to their own honor, as a personal insult. The Indians were making liars out of them and the Ring was seething.

There were no more atrocities and they could not manufacture any. In other parts of Arizona rebellious groups broke reservation from time to time, only to be hunted down by the relentless Crook, but there was no trouble from the Chiricahuas and this was almost too much to endure. It destroyed all their concepts, it imperiled the basic tenets upon which their civilization was drawn.

They looked everywhere and they finally discovered the plight of their Mexican brothers. Ranchers, miners, leading citizens, men who had hitherto treated the Mexicans like dirt, now began to wail about the horrendous atrocities the Chiricahuas were visiting upon the little people below the border. It was always the Chiricahuas. Every Mexican who was killed, every horse or mule that was stolen below the border, was blamed on the Cochise Apaches.

Public meetings were held again. Circulars were disseminated. The Mexican became the hero of the hour, the beloved little brother to the south, the heroic peon who was making a last stand against the frightful incursions of the red savages. The people of Tucson felt secure for themselves. It was almost a year since the Chiricahuas had struck at them. The days when the name of Cochise made them shiver were gone. The sight of Apaches on horses no longer made them run. Now they felt their great hearts bursting for their good neighbors across the border. They petitioned the government, the Army, the territorial legislature, to punish the Cochise Apaches for their crimes in Mexico.

This vast sympathy, these copious tears, never extended to the Mexicans who lived in Arizona and who were still despised as an inferior race. It was only that somehow when the invisible line that divided the two countries was crossed the people took on something new and noble.

This new turn of affairs puzzled and delighted Governor Pesquiera, of Sonora, a Mexican gentleman who had obtained his position in the same manner that other Mexican officials did at that time, through graft, violence, bribery, and bloodshed. The governor found an unexpectedly sympathetic audience in the Americans. It was something he did not understand, but then he never understood the crazy gringos.

The Tucson *Citizen* began to publish long editorials listing the Indian depredations, supplied by Pesquiera. The newspaper reported the crimes word for word as the Mexican governor sent them up, as though he were an infallible and unquestioned source, something no one had ever, oddly enough, believed before. Pesquiera, finally understanding what was about, blamed the Chiricahua Apaches for everything, although, from the description of the raids, it was difficult to ascertain how Pesquiera, or anybody else, was able so accurately to determine the culprits. He said, invariably, that the trails led to the "Chiricahua or Cochise reserve." All this meant, in truth, was that the Indians, whoever they were, had left Sonora and had crossed the line into southern Arizona, but it was enough.

When he arrived in Tucson, Jeffords went to see St. John who was always able to listen to him and to soothe him. St. John was finishing up some work and Jeffords picked up a copy of the *Citizen* and started to read it. As he read his face flushed and he felt his gorge rise.

Months had passed, the newspaper stated, since "Cochise and his Indians were treated with by General Howard and such divine assistance as he uses in emergencies, and since that time there have been almost constant wails coming up from Sonora in consequence of the butchery of Mexican men, women and children and thefts of their stock and destruction of their crops and other property. It is not denied by those in authority that the Indians rationed on the Chiricahua reserve have made a business of raiding into Mexico. Cochise told General Vandever [the Government Inspector] that he had taken steps to prevent this raiding and denied the right of the Government under the agreement—by divine aid—by and with General Howard, to use troops to stop it."

Jeffords exploded. "The lying bastards!" Cochise had told Inspector William Vandever nothing of the kind. He had admitted that some of his warriors were implicated in the raids, and said that he and Jeffords were doing everything they could to stop it. It was Jeffords who had refused to permit soldiers on his reserve.

St. John looked up. His thin face was worried. "Take it easy, Tom," he said. "There is more to come. I wanted to talk to you first."

"Agent Jeffords," the editorial continued, "told the proprietor of this paper, in April last, that he did not care how many Mexicans his people (as he paternally called them) killed in Mexico; that for acts of treachery with those Indians, the Mexicans deserved killing, etc., etc."

It was Jeffords' first experience of this kind with the press. He was finding out for the first time how words could be removed from their context, changed ever so slightly, so that an entirely new interpretation would result. He read on, his fury climbing, his hands gripping the newspaper like a pair of vises. "As heretofore," the editorial concluded, "it is now with reluctance that we refer to this Cochise business, but the constant wails and complaints which weekly come to us from Sonora, so well authenticated as to causes, compel us as a journalist to notice them, and in doing it, our opinions will find expression."

Jeffords read the last part aloud. Then he threw the paper away from him violently. "Just what the hell does he know about 'causes'?" he demanded.

St. John walked over to him. "You forget journalistic omniscience," he said dryly. "Ownership of a newspaper and the mechanical facilities to put little lines of type in print seem to automatically make a man all knowing." He picked up the newspaper. "You might as well know all of it. You'll be hearing enough of it around here."

Jeffords took back the paper and continued to read.

"When General Howard hunted up Cochise and let him dictate the terms upon which he would consent to cease murdering people and stealing from them in the United States, the *Citizen* took decided grounds against the wisdom of the performance. Deny it he may, we were advised by a commissioned officer of the Army at the time of his arrival from that noted peacemaking in the Dragoon Mountains, that General Howard expected an ovation by the people of Tucson for his work and illy concealed his chagrin and disappointment when he found the people here, with hardly an exception, felt he had performed no service of goodness or bravery worth any demonstration other than that of disgust. They felt and knew that if left wholly to General Crook, Cochise as well as other Apaches would soon be brought to a condition of peace that could be trusted by citizens and would be respected by Apaches."

"Just like Crook is doing now," Jeffords said. "He has his hands more than full with the Indians who are still at war."

He finished the article in silence. He threw the paper away. He bit off the end of a cigar. "Crying their damned crocodile tears about the poor defenseless Mexicans," he said. "They don't spit on the best part of a Mexican around here. They think Mexicans are worth less than good mules in this town and they always have." He got up abruptly and started for the door. His face was suddenly dangerous.

"Where are you going?" St. John asked.

"I think I'm going to have a little talk with the man who wrote that piece," Jeffords said.

St. John walked swiftly to the door. "That won't help you. What will it prove? That you can shoot faster than he can? What will that prove? That you and Cochise are a bunch of murderers? That's what he's saying now." He smiled. "It can't be accomplished overnight, Tom. It needs patience. Look at me. I'm a great believer in patience." He looked at his empty sleeve. "I had to learn all over again. Maybe that's why I feel for Howard. Between the two of us we have a pair of good arms."

"I'll admit that Howard's sanctimonious piety sticks in a man's craw after he's heard too much of it," Jeffords said, "but the man believes it. He's no hypocrite. And if he wants to believe it, if he wants to live in what he calls a Christian way, why the hell must these muckrakers smear him for it?"

"Cochise."

"That's right. Anything to knife Cochise."

"Let's change the subject," St. John said. "I understand you had to move to San Simon?"

"Yes. To a swampland."

"How did it go?"

"Apaches are used to moving. They loaded their mules and burned their wickiups and moved. To a marshland. The place is damp and unhealthy. The Chiricahuas have lived in the mountains for centuries. Now they've been stuck under water. Sometimes I wonder if the government is just trying to kill them off."

"You don't think that?"

"I don't know. We say 'Government.' With a capital 'G.' That's an impressive word. 'The Government of the United States.' It sounds beautiful. A sort of splendid, holy, bright package. Big and vague and something filled with ideals. But that government gets itself translated into a lot of little, jealous, quarreling men. Politicians. Christ, I despise politicians! When you say the Government of the United States what you mean is a group of little men in derby hats. This is November. We moved in September. Until then we had two people in the tribe die of natural causes. Since then more than a dozen have died of fever. Maybe they are trying to kill them off. I don't know." He threw away his half-smoked cigar.

6

When he left the building he was still seething. He went to a saloon, avoiding the Congress Hall, and had several drinks, and then he knew he wanted to see Terry. He paid for his drinks and went over to the Scat Fly. She wasn't there. He waited for her.

"Let's get out of town for a little while," he said when she returned.

"Yes, Tom."

She didn't ask questions. They rode out of the town. There was no place he could go. The Indians didn't have it any longer and the town never had it. He rode silently at her side and he was grateful for her silence. It had to be somewhere, he thought. A man could not be wholly lost.

She pulled the air into her lungs. "Our smell," she said. "I still want to identify things that belong just to you and to me. The desert always seems to smell different to me when you are with me. I think the smell of old memories must be mixed with the sage."

There must be some place, he thought. "Funny redhead."
"It's gone now, isn't it, Tom?" she said after a long while.
"Yes."

"The tone we made. When I first came back here we made a tone. We both spoke in that tone. We could never talk to each other because of that tone. Now it's gone."

The tone *was* gone, he thought. He had clung to it through all these months and now it had slipped through his fingers as stilly as though he had been holding on to fog.

"There were always the Indians," she said, as though struck with a new thought. "I suppose there have been many things that girls all over the world have found cause to be jealous of but no one has had anything quite as I have. It seems almost ridiculous, doesn't it? To be jealous of a tribe of Indians."

"Not a tribe," he said.

"Not a whole tribe?" she asked.

He got off his horse and helped her down. "Let's sit down, Terry," he said. She sat down and he thought he had to tell her. He walked back and forth. "There is a great deal to tell you."

"I know, Tom. I have been waiting for a long time to listen to you."

"I can't tell you at once. It's long and some of the things aren't out of my mind yet and I can't talk of them."

"I'll wait," she said. "It seems I must always wait."

He looked at her. Her lips were parted slightly. Her eyes seemed to go on forever. "I was in love with an Indian girl," he said. "We were married."

"White men can't marry Indians," she said, panic-stricken.

"We were married in an Indian ceremony. In the Dragoons. She is dead. She was killed in an attack on an Indian rancheria. She's buried up there."

It came out quite easily, as though he were talking about something that happened to someone else.

"Thank you for telling me, Tom," she said at last. Her voice came from where her eyes started. "I am still beholden to you." She rose suddenly and turned her head away from him. He did not go near her. "It must have done awful things to you," she said, her face still turned away from him. "It makes so many other things clear." When he did not answer her still she turned slowly to him. Her face was quite white and he saw the rippling of the pulse in her throat. Her voice, when she spoke again, was low, and almost husky, and he had the strange awareness that her voice had always been low and that he noticed it now for the first time. "Did you love her very much, Tom?" she asked.

"Yes, Terry."

"So much that you did not care how it worked out, or if it

worked out, so much that you only knew that it was the only thing that could be?"

"Yes."

Her hands found each other and clung. Her face was now a deadly white and her hair flared like a final flame. "It is a fine feeling, isn't it, Tom? It makes up for everything else, does it not?"

He wanted to reach out and touch her and yet he knew that he could not touch her, it still was not time.

"I am glad you know," she said clearly. "I am glad you have had it." Then suddenly her eyes overflowed. She moved quickly away from his hands and seemed to close in on herself. "It is another bond, Tom."

He could not speak.

"You have had it, too," she said wonderingly. He moved as though to speak and she put a gloved hand over his mouth. "Please do not tell me any more now, Tom," she said. "I don't have a large mind and I can take only a little at a time. Don't tell me any more. Let me think about it and when I've got it so it doesn't hurt so much you can tell me more."

She bit her lip. Her eyes swam in a dark recessive hurt. "Later on I shall want to know what she looked like, what her name was, how she spoke, everything, everything you can tell me. I have to know her. Can you understand me?"

"I've always understood you."

"I have to know her," she repeated with a painful urgency. "I have to know all about her. I think I can make her something we have had together." Then she said, "It's been a long time, Tom, and now it shall never be everything."

He rubbed his face tiredly. "It won't be much of anything," he said. "There isn't very much of that left."

"How idiotic it is," she said. "Whatever little is left is still the most important thing to me. It will take time. You must tell me everything and I must listen and then we shall see what there is left to make anything out of. Whatever it is," she said slowly, as though revealing a secret, "that is for us, for you and for me."

She pulled off her gloves and put her hands against her face. Then she looked up. "We had better start back," she said. She didn't move. "It is good we started when I was very young," she said. She flicked at a yucca bush with her riding crop. "You have made me wait so very long, it's good I had an early start." Then she stopped and looked at him as though she saw him for the first time that day. Her face flooded with blood and she raised her hand, holding the crop. "God damn it to hell!" she said. She stood there unmoving, her hand raised to strike him. "God damn it to hell, and God damn you!"

When he took her arms his fingers dug into her flesh. He held her, as though trying to bring his fingers together, through her arms. She winced and twisted her head and then he pulled her toward him and he kissed her. Her lips were like ice. Her face was filled with a terror and then she shuddered violently and slumped against him and she kissed him. Then she pulled way.

"It's like a curse," she said. "After all these years it's like a curse. Spoiling everything else, spoiling everyone else. It's something that drowned in my blood so long ago I don't remember when it wasn't there." She lifted her face proudly. Her skin was very white and her eyes were wide and shining. "I love you," she said. "I love you so damned much."

She waited a long time and then she said, "You can't say it." She moved slowly away from him. Her head was twisted as though her neck ached her. "And you never will. You never will, you know. And that's how it will be."

She fled to her horse and climbed into the saddle. "Will you come to see me soon?" she asked quietly.

"Yes, Terry."

"Don't make it too long."

"No."

"It has to be often. I've waited too long." Her hands, on the reins, shook. "It is terrible to need someone as much as I need you." She dug her spurs into the horse.

Chapter Twenty-four

The air in the San Simon hovered like a gray nimbus. It quieted movement and seemed to shroud life in a limp vapor.

"Well?" Jeffords asked.

General Everett nodded. "I think it is as you have represented, Mr. Jeffords," he said. He sniffed noisily. "There appears to be a high prevalence of fever here."

Jeffords' eyes flicked. "Can we move?"

"I believe I can approve a removal on the basis of health for the Indians," the inspector from Washington agreed.

Jeffords sighed softly. "Thank you, General," he said.

"I want you to know, Mr. Jeffords, that there are many things in the manner in which you conduct your affairs here that I heartily disapprove. You do things in a most irregular fashion, most irregular." He took out a large white handkerchief and blew his nose loudly.

"They seem to work for us," Jeffords said.

"That is not the point," Everett replied testily. "In order to have an Indian policy there must be consistency. Standard practices, uniform methods, must be employed everywhere. You ignore everything that experienced men have adjudged proper in the administration of an Agency. You refuse to have roll call. There is no ration keeping. You forbid soldiers to patrol your reserve. These conditions obtain nowhere else in the country."

"There is no need for roll call," Jeffords said. "If Indians want to break loose they never are stopped by having to appear once a week to answer to their names. There is no need for keeping rations. I don't get enough food to give my people full rations and I've never gotten a yard of material for clothing since this reserve was established well over a year ago. As for soldiers, soldiers are supposed to keep order, but I've found they cause nothing but trouble. I've never had any trouble— not a single case, at no time—since this reservation was established. If these Indians are proving themselves capable of self-protection and self-rule, if they are proving daily that their word of honor is sufficient, why must we call them liars and put soldiers on the reservation to show we mean it?"

Everett smiled faintly. "You are a very persuasive man, Mr. Jeffords. Were you not formerly a lawyer?"

"The hell with sarcasm," Jeffords said.

Everett laughed openly. "Come now, Mr. Jeffords, don't be so sensitive. I have heard you were a difficult man with whom to do business, but there is no need to flare up with me." His eyes twinkled. "Why don't you relax? We can do it gracefully. We have the Indians collected. Let us reestablish the reserve on more conventional lines. If we handle it delicately and swiftly the Indians will find it inconvenient to protest."

"You mean to suddenly surround them with soldiers and guns?" Jeffords asked bluntly.

"There is no necessity to lose your temper, Mr. Jeffords. After all, they are merely Indians. They do not know what is best for them. We do. Oh, I know how a man feels about his word. Giving one's word is serious business. But there is no need to carry it to extremes. The end justifies the means, Mr. Jeffords. Empires have been built on that principle. We can arrange this to suit ourselves, keeping the welfare of the Indians in mind at all times, you understand, and in the end things will be much more satisfactory."

"While I remain as Agent there will be no soldiers on my reservation," Jeffords said stilly. "If you want to overrule me, please accept my resignation."

The inspector lifted his hands sadly. "Very well, Mr. Jeffords, you may continue as Agent here. Please try to understand, however, that you are likely to find recalcitrance returned with a similar attitude."

"Is it all right to remove the tribe to some other place?"

"Yes, certainly, I have said so. Where would you suggest?"

"Where we came from."

"The land in the Sulphur Spring Valley is not arable."

"And the Chiricahua Apaches are not farmers."

"They will be, Mr. Jeffords."

"Is it the intention of the department to establish a school to teach them?"

"I am afraid you will have to await the decision of the department on that score."

Jeffords nodded. "All right. How about Pinery Canyon? It's in the Chiricahua Mountains. It's high enough to be healthful and there is some good bottom land for the Apache farmers."

"Pinery Canyon will do very well," Everett said blandly.

"Are you going to try to get me some supplies?"

"I am afraid the contents of my report must be considered confidential until it reaches you through the ordinary channels, Mr. Jeffords. I can tell you this: you are categorically forbidden to make any further unauthorized purchases in your capacity as Agent. The sutler's store of Tully and Ochoa at Fort Bowie has been instructed not to issue any merchandise on Agency credit."

Jeffords took two cigars from his pocket. He gave one to the inspector and then lit it. He held the match to his own cigar. "There are more ways than one to skin a cat, aren't there, Inspector?" he asked genially.

2

Again the Indians collected their belongings and again the tribe moved, this time to Pinery Canyon. Here the land was more to their liking. They left twenty-three graves in the San Simon to mark their stay there. The altitude was more suitable for them in Pinery Canyon and the surroundings were more to their needs, but it also was colder there and as the winter of 1873–1874 closed in on them they found their old enemy, Ghost Face, more unwelcome than ever.

The Indian Office continued to provide insufficient goods for the tribe. Food stocks diminished rapidly. There still was no clothing. A few blankets arrived, enough for one person out of ten, and that was all.

The Indians huddled in their new camp in the bitter cold. An epidemic of influenza struck the tribe and there were several deaths. What food there was, was given to the children and to the old and weak. Jeffords, Cochise, Tahzay, and some of the other leaders moved from dwelling to dwelling, fighting against the smoldering resentment. Jeffords wondered how much longer it could last. He was convinced the Indians had a patience and faith that was almost beyond human comprehension, but there must be an end to it somewhere. A group of warriors gathered around Skinyea and protested that they could go on no longer. Skinyea, chosen as their spokesman, went to Cochise and Jeffords.

"There is no hunting," he said. "The animals are gone. There is no food given to us. There is no clothing. Yet we are forbidden to go out and make a living as we did in the old days. We are forbidden to take what we need from the white man, who has more than he needs. That is not just. It is not right that one man should have more than he can use while another goes hungry. In ordinary times the cold and hungry man tries to make a living for his family and he gets what he needs or else he is killed and in either case he no longer is cold nor hungry. But we cannot do this. We are told the white man is our brother and we must love him. But our brother is warm and well fed and we starve."

Skinyea looked at the sick and failing Cochise. "You have given your word that your people shall be at peace. There is no one who wishes to make a liar out of you. But your people are close to death. Your word is a valuable thing but the lives of your people are valuable, too. When a man goes to Mexico to make a living he is punished. He is forbidden to make a living here in Arizona. How is he to live? The rocks cannot be eaten. The cold is not a blanket."

Cochise nodded somberly. In the year and a half he had been on the reservation he had aged as though each month were a year. His hair was almost white and his face was thin and his cheeks sank against his teeth. His eyes, which had been like shafts of darkened fire, were now covered with a dull glaze and were sunk deep in their sockets. He now was unable to eat anything without experiencing violent pain and his food seemed to give him no nourishment. He refused absolutely to let a doctor treat him, and Jeffords knew that he was right; the death that was closing in on him was from no physical cause. The fires were being put out, slowly, little by little, and there was no medicine for that.

He still held his people to him, through loyalty and through memories, but his domination no longer was automatic and casual. Now when he was forced to pit his will and his reason against opposition it took violent effort. He had to gather from within his tired and racked body all the strength he could, to reach a point where he could again act a leader. And when he finished with these efforts he was left weak and drained.

Jeffords left the Agency. He had a small amount of gold from his prospecting days, and with it he bought food and clothing and brought it to the tribe. It was not very much but it got the Indians through the winter, and through those months they still waited patiently and remained on the reservation and Arizona was still peaceful in the land of the Chiricahuas.

All of Jeffords' protests were ignored. No clothing was issued. No food was sent to him. He realized he was being penalized for his stubbornness, but he also knew that if he permitted soldiers to enter the reservation the Apaches would consider the peace pact nullified by the government, and feel free to act accordingly.

The soldiers at Fort Bowie, which was the nearest military establishment to the reserve, who were simple and plain men with no concern for high policy, became almost friendly with the Apaches. They were impressed with the manner in which the Indians maintained their pledge and when they visited the post the soldiers gave them food when they could spare it, and old clothing and shoes. An instinctive understanding appeared to develop between the Apaches and the soldiers, and Jeffords, who watched this with great interest, thought that it might be well indeed if these soldiers could be permitted to move into the reserve without being crippled by directives from superiors. It would never work, he knew, because the brass would never let it work, but it was reassuring in a strange way, to know that it could work.

The tiswin which used to give Cochise release from emotional agonies did not serve to give him the same value for the physical pains which were constantly with him. He visited the officers' club at Bowie and became friendly with some of the younger officers and drank great quantities of whiskey, which alone seemed to cover the blaze that tore through him.

His alcoholic capacities became legendary, but no matter how much he drank he always left the post at sundown, and he ordered his people to do the same. He knew too well how easily trouble started in the night when men were drunk and he wanted no accidents.

One day when Cochise was in Pinery Canyon a Mexican named Juan Luna came up from Fronteras with two ten-mule wagonloads of beans and corn he wanted to sell to Tully and Ochoa's sutler's store at Bowie. For protection he brought with him twenty frightened Mexican soldiers led by a colonel of Mexican infantry. They were given space to camp near the fort and then Luna asked to see Cochise to make a commercial pact with him so he could cross the line regularly to trade at the sutler's store.

A courier was sent to Cochise. The Apache leader was recovering from a violent attack and was lying half-conscious on his pallet when the messenger arrived. Over the bitter protests of Tesalbestinay, Cochise got up and dressed in ceremonial raiment. He mounted a horse, although the effort brought sweat to his face, and accompanied by Chee, who would not leave him, he rode to the fort. With an incredible effort he pulled himself together as he approached the camp and he cast his features into their old indomitable rigidity. He held his head high and his wasted face was proud and unyielding.

When Jeffords saw him enter the camp he closed his eyes for a moment, and then he stepped into the background and listened. Cochise remained on his horse, looking down with the scorn of an emperor at the ragged soldiers and the trembling colonel. Luna approached him ingratiatingly and made his offer and, when he had finished, Cochise looked at him with contempt and said, "You come here to ask to make a treaty with me to cross my reservation with your wagons and goods. You forget what the Mexicans did to my people long ago when we were at peace with the Americans. You would get my people down into your country, get them drunk on mescal and furnish them with powder and lead, and tell them to come up and get the big mules from the Americans. And when they would steal mules and bring them back to your country, your people would get them drunk on mescal and cheat them out of the mules."

He spoke in a harsh, unmusical Spanish. His own words seemed to give him an inner strength and, as Jeffords watched with misery in his heart, the old Indian seemed to fill out and his speech took on a fire and his eyes flashed with an ancient power.

"Now you are asking for a treaty for safe-conduct across my reservation to sell to Tully and Ochoa," Cochise continued, spattering his words like shot from a gun. "Tully and Ochoa are friends of mine, and anyone who wants to bring their produce and trade with them is entirely welcome. But I want to warn you that you shall never cross the American line again with an escort of soldiers."

He said the word "soldiers" with infinite scorn and he looked carefully at each man as though he were something that had crawled into the daylight from under a stone. The American soldiers and some officers had collected by now and as they listened to the pain-racked Indian they were moved by a strange respect. Most of them had known Cochise only as the affable Indian who visited Fort Bowie after the peace was made and this appearance of the Cochise from a fabulous past was something they would never again forget. And as for Jeffords he kept as far back as possible. He wanted to lose himself in the crowd. He thought he could not endure to witness the wastage of the man he had known in his days of greatness and as he watched him and listened to him he was filled with a sick sadness.

"You have twenty soldiers and what do they amount to?" Cochise asked in a ringing voice. "I can take five of my men and wipe your soldiers off the earth and capture you. I have made a treaty with the United States and I am living up to that treaty so that no one need to fear to cross my reservation, for he will be safe."

Chee fingered his rifle nervously. As Cochise delivered his scornful denunciation the young Indian became more and more distraught. His eyes dilated and he shivered in rage.

"I want you to know," Cochise said, "that I consider it an insult for you to come here and ask for protection when I am not fighting Mexicans."

Chee could contain himself no longer. He could no longer listen to the words of Cochise. He raised his rifle with a wild cry and pointed it at Luna. The Mexican trader screamed and fell to his knees. Cochise lifted his hand. He did not look at Chee. Chee turned his eyes from the Mexican to his leader, his face working with a furious hysteria. Cochise kept his fingers erect. Then Chee dropped his rifle and lay his face on the neck of his horse and burst into tears.

And Jeffords knew he could watch no more. The salt was in his eyes and his throat choked him and he turned and walked swiftly away.

3

Little Eagles arrived timidly as always and somehow, as always, Ghost Face fled, and the hard land changed its sex and became soft and girlish and the rocks and the sand yielded green and there was a downy fuzz everywhere, and in the grace and loveliness Cochise appeared to recover and Jeffords had a wild dream that perhaps whatever it was that was ailing him might have succumbed to the power of his body and his mind. The warmer weather brought relief to all the Indians and then some food arrived; and there was something of a revival of the old feasting and dancing. Cochise moved about with relative ease and his razored features filled out and his eyes took on some of their old coruscation.

He was seen everywhere among his people, as though he were renewing his old relations with them. He was followed by his dog, a large black and white animal, and he wore always his striking red blanket which had his name woven into it.

There was a story behind the blanket, which had been presented to Cochise by Colonel Henry C. Hooker, one of the great pioneer ranchers in the Southwest. Some years before, when Cochise was still at war, Colonel Hooker had driven a large coach into Dragoon Pass, near the East Stronghold, and had found himself surrounded by Indians. The colonel, a bold and gallant man, pretended to show no alarm. He drove into the camp and climbed down. The Indians brought him food and tended his animals, and then Cochise appeared. The Indian told him that he knew who he was and could have captured or killed him on many occasions, but that he spared him because Hooker brought cattle into the country and Cochise did not want to cut off a major source of his food supply. He thanked Hooker for the high quality of his beef and assured him that he would continue to help himself when he needed food, and then he permitted the astonished colonel to depart safely. Soon afterward Hooker had the magnificent blanket woven to his order and sent it to Cochise.

During these months in the early part of 1874, Jeffords visited Tucson several times, and spent a great part of his visits with Terry. With her he now found a peace and comfort that he had thought he never again would experience. It was nothing that touched his memories of his wife; that part of his life was sealed off. It belonged to someone else, not himself, and it happened some long time before, almost another time. It never faded and it never became lost; it was as though it had become frozen into a dreamed permanence. What he felt with Terry was almost a complement.

Then, one day in late April, Jeffords received word that Cochise had fallen unconscious in his camp and had been carried into his wickiup. Jeffords picked up a doctor from Fort Bowie and went to him immediately. He found Cochise had recovered consciousness but was unable to rise from his pallet.

Cochise nodded feebly and then refused to permit the doctor to examine him. Jeffords was stern and unyielding and ordered Cochise to submit himself to an examination. The Indian, with an odd expression, agreed, and the doctor knelt beside him and Jeffords went out of the wickiup and strolled through the camp.

He greeted his old friends and paused from time to time to talk to them. They seemed to be a different people, he thought, from the Chiricahua Apaches he once had known. How long ago was that? The reservation life did not agree with these nomads. It was not just the miserliness of the government. The food, the living conditions, everything might have been better and yet they would not thrive. Not the adults, anyway. They were being destroyed on all sides, he thought: their freedom, precious as the air they breathed, had been removed from them, and they had not been repaid with even the normal physical reward for such a deprivation.

They looked betrayed. It was as though something they did not understand were being done to them. They were following blindly, still, most of them, but they were bewildered. They wandered apathetically around their camp, aimlessly, without hope or ambition; the old purposeful, commanding, arrogant air of the warriors was gone; the women, though they busied themselves as always, did so in desultory fashion, moving almost automatically, without spirit or application.

He told himself he was seeing the worst of it. It was the generation who were set in their ways, who remembered vividly the old days, who had to suffer most. They had to come to terms with his country, he thought, and the violence of the change made this listlessness inevitable. The wisdom and value of the change would not become clear until the next generation, or possibly the generation after that. That was how it was and that was how it had to be, he thought, but it was awful to see now. The abruptness and harshness of the change might have been lessened with a little more understanding and cooperation from his superiors, but that was not to be had. And meanwhile it was this way and the people were dying and what they had inside of them, whatever it was, whatever strength and value and integrity they had as a people, that was dead already.

He walked back to Cochise's lodges and there he found the doctor had not yet finished. He sat down outside and filled his pipe and he pondered on how it was Cochise, the greatest leader the people had ever had, who had led his people to their present condition, and himself, who had loved and understood the Apaches perhaps better than any white man, who had been responsible.

He looked up. Tesalbestinay stood before him. She too had aged with a terrible inevitability, but as he looked at her he thought that somehow, because of the suddenness and swiftness of Cochise's own failing, she seemed to have suffered less than he did. In the last eighteen months, he thought, Cochise had caught up with her and now they were together again, as they had been in the beginning.

Jeffords and the Indian woman looked at each other fondly. She smiled gently at him and handed him a gourd filled with cool water. He drank from it. "How has he been?" he asked.

"I do not know. He does not talk. I know he has been in pain but he does not talk and he does not let me talk. He drinks too much but if that is the only way he can forget his pain it is all right." There was a trace of a smile on her dry lips. "This is the third manner of his drinking. First he drank in a healthy way, to feel good. Then he drank in a bad way to hide himself from himself. Now he drinks to blind the pain so it will not find him so easily."

Jeffords nodded somberly. He felt heavy and oppressed.

"But he is still a man," Tesalbestinay said fiercely. "His wrist bears the teeth marks of his third wife, put there in jealousy because he has come to me alone again."

438

"You have been a very good wife to him."

She waved her hand. "He was the man for me."

"Yes, Tesalbestinay."

"He took other wives but that was all right. He needed from them what I could not give him. But he was the man for me. He was my husband the way he never was theirs."

"He still is."

"He does not live long."

"How do you know?"

"Is there anything of him that I do not know?" she asked wanly. "He is sick. He is sick in his body, but he is more sick in his heart. He thinks he has led his people to a wall and there is nothing to do. He knows it is wrong to fight and yet peace has brought him nothing. He is tired and he thinks he is no longer fit to lead his people and I think he is not sorry to die, maybe."

"The peace is a good thing," Jeffords said. "It will take time, but in the end it will be good." He looked up at her pleadingly, as though asking her to agree with him.

"Do you think so? Do you really think so?"

"It must work out," he said. "If two peoples cannot come to each other in honesty and decency and find a way to live with each other then there is no need to live in this world. There is so much blood on everybody's hands and it will take time for the blood to wash away. When there are men on both sides who have clean hands the trouble will disappear."

"Maybe," she said. She looked away. Her face was almost beautiful. "Anyway we have been good to each other, he and I. That is something."

He nodded.

"You know of that, do you not, Tagliato?"

His face jerked up suddenly. He knew of the superstitious abhorrence the Apaches felt in referring to the dead. "We have seen things," he said.

"I am happy my time of seeing is coming to a close," she said. "The things I see now are not so good."

The surgeon from the fort stepped from the wickiup. She walked away and Jeffords pulled himself to his feet. "What did you find?"

"Not much," he said. "Frankly, Jeffords, this is a little out of my line. I can fix up a gunshot wound or amputate an arm but I am not too familiar with internal ailments. He has something wrong inside of him. I don't know what it is. It might be cancer. It might be his gall bladder. I think the lining of his stomach must be worn out, what with the kind of food and drink these Indians have. He probably has ulcers. But I can't tell for sure what he has. What he needs is to be taken to a

439

hospital somewhere and kept under constant watch by doctors who know about these things. He ought to have a special diet. He needs rest and other things he is not getting."

"That isn't all, is it, Doctor?" Jeffords said quietly.

"No, it isn't. He doesn't want to live."

Jeffords nodded.

"There's not much I can do for him," the doctor said. "I left some medicine. It will help the pain a little. If he gets any worse, call me again."

"Thanks, Doctor," Jeffords said.

"I didn't do anything, Jeffords." The doctor shook his head. "I wish I could, but I didn't do anything."

Jeffords entered the wickiup. Cochise lifted his head and smiled. His face was as tight as that of a skeleton. His bones cut ridges against his cheeks. His neck seemed to be a coil of twisted wires.

Jeffords embraced him and felt the bones under his hands.

"Well, Sheekasay," Cochise said. "Your doctor looked at me. What did he say to you?"

"You are in a serious condition."

"Good," Cochise grunted. "I am glad you still do not lie to me. How long will I live?"

"I do not know. He did not know."

"Whenever it comes," Cochise said indifferently.

Jeffords opened a dispatch case. "I have some papers here. There is news."

"More of your government reports?" Cochise asked with faint contempt.

"You remember Inspector Everett who was here a few months ago? He made his report and they just sent a copy of it to me."

"What did he say?"

"Nothing very good. He said the reservation would always be a center for outlaws and renegades, a source of trouble with Mexico and a place where the Indians could never learn how to become good farmers and support themselves. He recommended that the Chiricahuas be removed to New Mexico."

Cochise raised himself on his elbows. His breath came fast and his lips curled. "They will never move us," he said. "This is our home. These hills and these valleys belong to the Chiricahuas. It was so promised by General Howard."

Jeffords lowered Cochise back onto the pallet. "Do not worry about it. Commissioner Smith said he thought Everett's proposal was impossible," he said soothingly.

"Why impossible?" Cochise asked arrogantly. "Impossible because your government has given its word and will not break it? Or impossible because Smith knows that the Chiricahuas could not be forced to move?"

440

"I do not know, my brother," Jeffords said, smiling. "Just impossible."

"What else have you to tell me?"

"Pesquiera has been complaining again."

Cochise snorted. "He always complains. I should have killed him long ago."

Jeffords grinned. "But this time he received an answer, and a good and proper answer, from Commissioner Smith, direct from Washington."

"What did Smith say?"

"It is a long official letter, sent by Smith, in his official capacity as Commissioner of Indian Affairs, to Pesquiera. It is too long to read all of it to you. But it is enough to tell you that Smith starts out by saying Pesquiera is mistaken when he charges your warriors received arms from Howard."

"Hah," Cochise said contemptuously. "When have we received arms from anybody? Or clothing or blankets?"

"Pesquiera said your Indians, dressed in white man's clothing, caused Mexicans to think they were civilized Indians, and that the Indians, when they came close to the Mexicans, killed them."

"How does Pesquiera know? Do the dead Mexicans sit up and speak to him?"

"Anyway," Jeffords went on, laughing, "Smith denies all this happens. He says Howard told you we were at peace with Mexico and that any attacks on Mexicans would be regarded by our government as attacks on Americans. Now listen to this. I will translate it from English as I read. 'That Cochise properly understood this agreement is evident from the fact that he has since frequently restrained members of his band who desired to raid in Mexico, and has driven off his reservation other Indians who had come with booty, evidently from Sonora, desiring to trade with his own band. At the time of the conference with General Howard, Cochise called attention to the fact that there were some fifty marauding Indian men completely outlawed who had abandoned other friendly and reservation Indians who were in no way connected with them, nor subject to his control, and for their conduct he could not answer, but would, at any time, on request, join the United States forces in their pursuit and capture.' "

As Jeffords read the document, Cochise slowly sat up. His face was filled with a fierce pleasure and when he spoke his voice appeared to have refound its strength. "Commissioner Smith wrote that?" he asked.

"Yes, Cochise, just as I have read it to you."

"Do you think, then, Sheekasay, that they finally believe we are honest in our peace?"

"You listened to the contents of the letter."

441

"They believe that I speak with a straight tongue," the Indian said. The bony muscles in his jaw worked against his thin cheeks. He threw off his blanket and struggled to his feet.

"Where are you going?" Jeffords asked.

"Let us go to the fort. I want some whiskey."

"Whiskey! You are a sick man."

"Good. I need medicine." Cochise was on his feet. He shook himself slightly and then walked back and forth limbering his stiff legs. "Well, Sheekasay, what are you waiting for?"

"Do you feel strong enough to go down to the fort?" Jeffords looked dubious.

"I feel good. I feel very good." He put his arms around Jeffords. "You will read the letter to me again. That is the important thing. That is the most important thing of all. I must be remembered as one who spoke the truth. We will go to the fort. There you will read the letter to me again."

When he walked out of the wickiup his step was light and springy. Tesalbestinay looked up startled. He touched her lightly on the cheek and she blushed like a girl. The dog yapped and Cochise knelt and scratched it and the dog's tail wiggled deliriously. Cochise called for his horse and he jumped gracefully into the saddle. He filled his lungs with the warm sweet air and then, without waiting for Jeffords, he rode off.

4

Jeffords sat in his shabby office and looked around with a quiet smile. The appearance of the Agency had not improved. Jeffords had finally got the consent of his superiors to build a new Agency and then discovered the local contractors were ready to hold up the government in erecting the building as they were holding up the government in everything else. He refused to agree to the graft-boosted prices they set and was trying to get a new building put up with the help of the Indians. It was a slow job.

He heard the sound of horses and he looked out. Then he jumped to his feet and went to the door. Terry and St. John dismounted. It was the first time either had come to the Agency. His lean, weary face lighted as he looked at her. "How are you two strangers?" he asked. "This is a wonderful surprise.'

"Strangers because you make it so," she said. He kissed her. "We were worried about you."

"Were you? Come inside. You both must be thirsty. You didn't come all the way from Tucson, did you?"

"No," St. John said. "We were visiting a ranch near here. The owner saw this little lady in Tucson and invited her out. She agreed to come—if properly chaperoned, and I was elected."

442

"I agreed when I discovered he wasn't far from here," Terry said.

"Well, come into the desert monastery," Jeffords waved his hand toward the Agency. "A poor thing but our very own."

"It needs a woman's touch," Terry said. "A few curtains. And a door and a window here and there wouldn't hurt either."

"The building probably will outlast us," Jeffords said wryly.

"More talk about removal?" St. John enquired. He noticed that Jeffords looked tired and depressed.

"Come inside. It's too damned hot to talk in the sun."

They went into the building. Terry looked at the small ugly room with its battered homemade furniture. She felt her throat constrict for a moment and she turned her head.

"Pretty awful, isn't it?" Jeffords asked cheerfully.

"Is this the windmill you tilt against?" she asked wistfully.

Jeffords poured a couple of drinks for St. John and himself and had one of the Indian boys go to his quarters and get an orange drink for Terry. The drink was brought into the office by an old Indian woman who was keeping house for Jeffords and at the sight of the housekeeper Terry stiffened and bit her lip.

"What is this new trouble?" St. John asked.

"The same old thing," Jeffords said. He tried to speak lightly. "Lieutenant Colonel Dudley, the Superintendent of Indian Affairs from New Mexico, was sent here to speak to Cochise. He tried to persuade him to agree to the removal of the tribe to New Mexico."

"That would mean trouble, wouldn't it, darling?" Terry asked.

"I've warned them. I've written so many letters I'm out of words. If the government violates Howard's pledge the Indians will feel free to walk off."

"What did Dudley say?" St. John asked.

"In a way it was a rather remarkable visit," Jeffords said. He picked up a piece of paper. "I have a copy of his report here. Listen to this: 'I learned that Cochise was lying very ill in the Dragoon Mountains, about forty miles distant, and that it was feared he might die.' This was when Dudley got to Bowie. He goes on: 'To hear fear expressed that the greatest and most war-like Apache might die, sounded strange enough, but when I ascertained that the great chief retained in peace the wonderful power and influence he exercised in war, that he regarded his promises made to General Howard sacred, and not to be violated upon any pretext whatever, I knew that it would be a calamity to the frontier to lose him from the ranks of living men.'"

He put down the paper and looked at Terry and St. John.

There was nothing said for several moments and then Terry rose abruptly and walked to the door.

"Did you read that to Cochise?" St. John asked softly.

"Not yet."

"I can understand what those few words must mean to you. They were worth everything, weren't they?"

"It was a remarkable visit," Jeffords repeated. "Dudley had a photograph showing him together with General Howard. He gave the photograph to Cochise. Cochise kept looking at it and looking at Dudley and there was nothing too good for Dudley after that."

"How do you know he will recommend a removal?" St. John asked.

Jeffords' smile was twisted. He picked up the paper again. He read, " 'My opinion is, that these Indians should be removed, at the earliest practicable moment, to the Hot Springs Reservation.' "

Terry turned suddenly. "You have done everything that a man could do," she said fiercely. "Oh, God, they are such fools." Then she walked quickly to his side. "But how can it be helped? Look at how long it has taken for us to understand."

He looked at her. She had never seen his eyes look so blue. "What are you saying?"

"You were right and we were wrong," she said. "No matter what happens you have nothing to reproach yourself for."

"Reproach myself?" He shook his head. "I'm just tired, Carrot. I think a man can stand for just so much cheating and then he gets tired."

"Take a look around the Agency, Silas," she said. When he was gone she fell to her knees and took Jeffords' hand. "It's almost time to stop fighting, my darling. Not even you can hold out forever against the United States."

"Terry."

"You need me now," she said in a small voice. "You need me almost as much as I've always needed you."

"Yes."

"You do need me, my darling," she said. "You're so tired."

"I've got to hang around until Cochise is dead. I hope he dies soon. It is almost a joke. His honor! His damned, foolish, antiquated honor! He talks and lives his honor as though this were still the age of chivalry. His ridiculous, idiotic, obsolete honor!"

"The two of you," she whispered. "The two sides to the coin. His honor and your honor." She put her face on his lap and kissed his hand. "It has taken a great many years but I have finally caught up. Do you understand me?"

He stroked her cheek. "Terry, Terry," he said in a voice that was barely audible.

444

"I'm not sorry for how I acted," she said. "I could not have been any other way. You know how it has been for me, about you. But I understand now. I understand what you have been trying to do and I know how large it is. Please may I tell you how much in love with you I am, and how very proud of you I am?" She looked up at him. Her eyes were wet. "Let me tell it to you. You are quite a great man, my darling, and I love you so much, and I understand now."

He lifted her from her knees and then he kissed her.

"There is nothing now, nothing at all," she said. "Thirteen years. It's been a very long time."

"Such a sweet face," he said. "Such a beautiful sweet red-headed face."

"Yours, Tom," she said. "And now I understand. Can we start with that? We shall start with that." She closed her eyes. "Once I would have thought that was not much," she said.

Chapter Twenty-five

For several weeks it appeared almost as though Cochise had recovered entirely. Of the Dudley report, Jeffords told him only of the part which spoke of the sacredness of Cochise's word, and the information acted like a tonic.

The two men began to ride into the hills daily. They seldom spoke. They rode silently, through the places Cochise had lived in and fought in, through the places he remembered from his childhood. They went to the canyons in the Dragoons and into the depths of the Chiricahuas, to the secret places which later came to be called by the Indians the Spiritland of Cochise. Cochise devoured his country as though it were food. He drank in his memories as though they were strong liquor. He found forgotten campsites, old hunting grounds, places of terrible beauty and unworldly isolation. He touched trees and stroked huge boulders and when he spoke it was only to say the names of the shrubs and the plants.

And as he rode and listened and watched, a silent shadow at the side of his friend, Jeffords understood, as though for the first time in his life, that the story of the Apache Indians belonged to the Apache earth. The story was part of the mountains and the deserts and the sudden gaping canyons and the river beds that were almost always dry, of the great clear hurtful openness, of the boiling sun and the quick blinding rains, of the heat that was like death and the cold that was death, and, in the night, of the whitened sky and the sounds of the living things that walked and ran and crawled and flew in their own loneliness.

It was a story, he knew now, that emerged slowly, piece by piece, as though from the origins, as though the earth belonging to the People of the Woods released it with a paced inevitability; and then, because it came as it did, and from where it did, it had turned into legend as it occurred with no pause, no waiting, no interval of time. Each incident had become fixed, ancient, the moment it took place; while happening, it also happened sometime long ago. The things that were done and the words that were spoken were done and spoken without spontaneity as though because of natural law they had to be done and spoken that way. And because all of these things were crystallized into legend by the lean sharp air with no hiatus, some of them were instantly disbelieved as though they were myths and romances repeated by old men who had heard them from older men.

While they happened, in the moment of being done, they were long done, because the place where they occurred itself belonged to another age, a timed and timeless age, and the story itself became part of that time and not of the time in which it ran its ordered course. To everything that was said and done the country, the earth, added its own meaning and it all would have been different if it had happened anywhere else, although it might have happened in some other time, and in that same place, and have been the same.

There was nothing in moderation. Everything was in the extreme. The heights and the depths and the heat and the cold and the sun and the rain and the natural richness and poverty, all were pushed to their ultimate, to their finalities, and the living things were shaped and forced by this largeness so that they too became their final size. A man could do nothing in a little way because at any time he could lift his eyes and see the hills and the endless, endless desert and the canyons that went down vertically into another world.

So, he mused, the good and the bad things were the human limits of good and bad. There, among the beginnings, each man was, at once, larger and smaller than himself.

And the smell of mesquite and sage and the color of the desert in the spring and the paleness of the nights and the blaze of the days, and the mountains, the bare convulsive mountains, made a winey mixture with the smell of sweat and blood in the high acrid air and the sounds were long in the spaces and a man could see farther miles than his eyes had ever been able to see before.

They stood in the Chiricahua Mountains on a high mesa that might have been a platform overlooking the earth. Co-

446

chise raised his long bony arm and pointed to the northwest. "What do you see there, Sheekasay?" he asked.

"The two peaks? Dos Cabezas?"

"Dos Cabezas—two heads. You and I, Sheekasay, two heads."

Jeffords looked at the distant twin peaks that strode the range and lifted their jagged heads to the sky.

"There are not many like us," Cochise said. "We are over there, alone." Then he said in a very low voice, "Dos Cabezas."

When he returned that night to his people he removed his camp to the East Stronghold and there awaited his death.

2

On the morning of June 7, Chee rode into the Agency and told Jeffords Cochise had become worse. Jeffords procured two fresh horses and the men left for the Stronghold. Cochise was prostrate. Jeffords looked at his face and he saw death. He saw more than death. He saw the welcome of death.

"I think it is coming now," Cochise said. "It has started toward me several times but I think it is coming now."

"I will go to Fort Bowie for the doctor."

"There is no need for that. It is better to have time to talk." He tried to sit up. Jeffords lifted him gently and propped him with a folded blanket. Cochise moistened his parched lips. "I am not sorry to die."

"Yes, my brother."

"A man has a time to live. He must not outlive his time. Then he becomes foolish and whatever he has done in his good days is forgotten and it is remembered only that he was a foolish man when he died. My time is over. It is better that I die."

Jeffords looked at his emaciated face and said nothing.

"Where did I make my great mistake, Sheekasay?" Cochise continued. "Somehow it has gone wrong. What should I have done that I did not do?" Then he lifted his hand weakly. "There is no answer to that yet. There are more important things. It was said to me that I shall be forgiven." His eyes flashed for a moment. "Forgiven by whom? I can forgive, Sheekasay, but I have not talent to be forgiven." He stopped talking and his breath came in thin waves. "I want you to take care of my people. You are as a father to them. We have been one soul, you and I, and when you speak it will be as though I were speaking. There are things still to be learned. My people must have a friend who is true to them and who is loyal. You must take care of them as though they were small children."

"I am only one and they are many," Jeffords said. "They will not do what I ask them to do unless they want to."

Cochise called for his son Tahzay and then he ordered him to bring in his chief lieutenants. He lay back and closed his eyes, breathing unevenly, and then the men entered the wicki-up. There were the old faces, Tahzay and Nachise, Skinyea, Pionsenay, Teese, Chee, Ponce, Nochalo, and others. They came in quietly and stood at the foot of the pallet and present-ly Cochise opened his eyes again.

He looked from one man to the other, and as his eyes rested upon each face, he uttered his name, quietly and slowly and with consummate love, as though pronouncing a benediction. "We have met in many councils," he said. "Before some of you were men I met with your fathers. Now we are met in a last council. I am going to die. I will no longer be with you. Listen carefully to what I say to you now.

"I appoint my son, Tahzay, to follow me as chief of the Chiricahua Apaches. He is not so well known among our peo-ple as I was and he will need all of you to help him. Tahzay is fit to be your leader. He is young but he is wise and if he is given to live and receives the help of all of you he will be a good leader. Before me, swear that you will be loyal to my son."

As though by one voice, one mouth, the men said, "I swear."

"Now listen to me more. Tagliato has been a friend to me for many harvests. He is more than friend. We have exchanged our blood. We are brothers and my blood is in his body. He has never spoken to me with a crooked tongue and he has been a father to all of our people. When he speaks henceforth it is as though I speak. My body is his body and my heart is his heart and my soul is his soul. When I am dead he is the living Cochise and you will listen to him and obey him as you would obey me." His eyes again swept across their faces. "Swear it."

Each man said, with no hesitation, "I swear it."

Cochise nodded. He was quiet for a long while, and then he said, "There must be no more war. I have pledged my honor and I have kept my pledge. The white man has kept his pledge. Not as faithfully as I have, but it has not been broken. It must not be broken by the Indians." He pulled himself together and then sat up suddenly without support. His eyes blazed on each of the men standing before him and he said, slowly, with great intensity, "There must never be war again against the white man."

Then he said, "Embrace me, Tahzay."

His son fell upon his knees and held his father tightly. When he rose, Cochise said, "Embrace me, Nachise."

And then each man in his turn, as his name was pronounced, knelt for the last time before Cochise and held him in his arms and rested his cheek against the cheek of his leader.

Then Cochise said, "Lift me and place me upon my horse."

448

Tahzay moved as though to protest but Jeffords silenced him with a glance and the two men lifted Cochise and carried him from the wickiup. Outside the people were gathered and Jeffords placed him in his saddle and put his feet into the stirrups. Then Cochise shrugged and Jeffords walked away. The chief stiffened in his saddle and looked at his people. His eyes roamed across the Stronghold. His body was strong and his head was proud on his shoulders and his face was austere and was already gone from them.

He sat for a full minute and then the sweat streamed over his face and he loosened. Jeffords ran over to him and caught him in his arms.

"Death should have come to me," Cochise said bitterly. "It was a good place."

Jeffords carried him back to his pallet. No one followed them into the dwelling. Cochise took his hand and held it tightly. "My shotgun is to be yours," he said. It was a great honor. Weapons always were buried with the dead. "Tell me, Sheekasay, do you think we have won out?"

"Not yet."

"But we will win?"

"Yes, my brother. Not you and not me. But in the end we will win."

"You believe that?"

"Yes, with my heart."

"Good. Then maybe it was right." He smiled. "We won between ourselves. If it can be done with us, it can be done with others. Although there are not many like us. There was no difference between us. No matter how it ends no one can take our own victory from us."

"I am going down to Bowie," Jeffords said. "A doctor still may be able to help you."

"Sheekasay?"

"Yes?"

"Do you think you will ever see me alive again?"

Jeffords closed his eyes. "No. I do not think I will. I think that by tomorrow you will be dead."

Cochise nodded. "I think so, too. Not long after the sun rises tomorrow." Then he looked at Jeffords with strange eyes. "Do you think we will ever meet again?"

"I do not know. What do you think?"

"I have been thinking a good deal about it while I have been sick here, Sheekasay. I believe we will." His face was exalted. "Good friends will meet again, up there."

"Where?" Jeffords whispered.

"That I do not know—somewhere. Up there, I think, beyond that hill."

He pointed to a peak in the Dragoons on which the blue summer sky rested. And then he slept.

Jeffords took a fresh horse and started for Fort Bowie. He got there before dawn and started back immediately with the post surgeon.

In the morning Cochise asked to see Tesalbestinay. When she left the wickiup a half hour later Nalikadeya and his third wife went to him, and then he asked Tahzay and Nachise to carry him up a slope of the Stronghold to a hill on the west side where he could once more see the sun rise on the eastern ranges.

He looked long and silently at the great valley to the east, flooded with the light of the early day, and then he closed his eyes and he died.

When Jeffords reached the camp he thanked the surgeon and sent him back to the fort. He entered the wickiup and was left alone with the dead Cochise. In a corner the dog whimpered.

The chief had been dressed in his war raiment. His face was painted and his war feathers were in his hair and he was wrapped in his red blanket. In death his face was imperious and godlike.

When he stepped outside the wickiup he felt himself blinded by the sun. Tahzay and Skinyea came up to him.

"There is a cave in the Stronghold wall," Tahzay said. "It is very deep. We tied a stone to a lariat and lowered it. Then we tied another lariat to the first and then a third and still we did not touch bottom. But there will be many who will look for the body of Cochise. White men have things to break open rock as though it were water. Will he be safe?"

"Let it be said he was buried in the broad meadow at the mouth of the Stronghold," Jeffords said.

"That is easy," Tahzay said. "But then men may look for his grave there. When they do not find it they will look elsewhere."

Jeffords thought, and then he said, "We will bury him in the cave. Then, afterwards, gather all your warriors on their horses. Have them ride for a long time, back and forth across the meadow, so that no piece of earth remains unturned. Then I will say that he was buried there and that his warriors galloped over his grave to hide it."

That, he thought, was the first lie between them.

In the late afternoon, while the women cried like wounded animals and the men stood silent, their faces painted raven-black, Cochise was placed upon his horse and Tahzay climbed up behind him and held him.

Jeffords held the reins of the horse and with the Indians following in a long file, brought the horse up a steep incline in the

Stronghold to an isolated place amid great rocks and gaping chasms.

There Cochise was taken from his horse and placed gently on the ground.

Tahzay drew a knife and in a single stroke cut open the horse's throat and while the animal still quivered pushed him into the vast depths of a fissure in the cliff. Then Tahzay picked up the dog and with the knife still red with the blood of the horse, stabbed him in the heart, and then dropped the dead dog after the horse. Then, one by one, the weapons of Cochise were dropped into the cave, his lances, his bows, his quivers filled with arrows, his rifles and his old powder horns.

Then Jeffords and Tahzay picked up the body of Cochise and held it upright over the opening and then they released it.

For four hours the men stood with their lips sealed in silence and the women lay with their cheeks on the ground and poured tears into the earth.

When the tribespeople moved down from the burial place Jeffords and Tesalbestinay remained. They knelt and stared into the black hole in the rock and when Jeffords rose finally and left her she covered her head with a blanket and still did not move.

Back in the campsite Jeffords got on his horse and started back for the Agency. He paused at the wide meadow and watched the men gallop back and forth, screaming finally in their grief, and he listened to the wailing of the women and then he looked across the Stronghold and in the gray rocks he made out the distant huddled figure of Tesalbestinay and he slowly rode down the trail and the last things he heard were the sounds of the horses and the sounds of the men and the dead cries of the Chiricahua women.

Epilogue

Jeffords lived for more than forty years after the death of Cochise.

Upon the demise of the Chiricahua leader he attempted to resign his post as Chiricahua Agent but he was needed more than ever as the only white man the younger leaders would obey. Reluctantly he continued in his job and on his right hand now sat Tahzay instead of Cochise.

Two years after Cochise died the government ordered the Chiricahua Indians removed from their reservation to the San Carlos Reservation, where a great many other Indians, many of them hostile to the Chiricahuas, already were established. Tahzay attempted to bring the entire tribe to the San Carlos reserve, but many younger leaders now proclaimed the government had broken its word. Half the tribe followed Tahzay and the rest, including Nachise, fled to Mexico where many of the warriors joined Geronimo and began a new bloody war that lasted for another dozen years.

Upon this move of the government, which he regarded as simple double-crossing, Jeffords resigned. He visited the San Carlos reserve frequently, in an unofficial capacity, until, a few years later, Tahzay was taken to Washington on one of the innumerable Indian junkets so fashionable at that time, and died there suddenly of pneumonia.

Nachise, ever jealous of his older brother, had by then become associated with Geronimo, lending him, as a son of Cochise, a prestige Geronimo never had before. Nachise was later captured at the same time Geronimo surrendered for the last time.

Jeffords became an Indian scout again on the many campaigns against Geronimo, and then settled to civilian life, being, from time to time, a rancher, miner and private citizen, living in Owls Head, near Tucson. He lived to see many changes. Less than a dozen years after the death of Cochise, once the most hated Indian in Arizona, Cochise County was named for him, the only county in the territory to be named after an individual Indian, all other counties being named after tribes.

Jeffords did not live long enough to witness the final irony —the establishment, a quarter century after his death, of

452

Cochise Memorial Park, in the middle of the Stronghold where Cochise died. He never saw placed, not far from where Cochise had his wickiups, a bronze plaque which stated:

"In this, his favorite Stronghold, Cochise died in 1874. Greatest of Apache warriors, interred secretly by his followers, the exact place of his burial is unknown."

Jeffords carried the secret of the grave to his death. He died at Owls Head on February 19, 1914. Upon his death former Governor Hughes pronounced an epitaph which must have caused Jeffords—and Cochise, if he found him again—to laugh.

"He was absolutely without fear," said Hughes, "and his word was never broken. He was like an Indian in this respect and when he gave his word it was law."

It had come to pass in Arizona that the word of honor of an Indian was used as a standard.

Jeffords died quite suddenly and very quietly. He was seen in Tucson one day and the next day he lay down and closed his eyes and embarked on the final journey to discover at last whether he would meet his old friend "up there, beyond that hill."

THE END

ABOUT THE AUTHOR

ELLIOTT ARNOLD, journalist and novelist, was born in New York City in 1912. He began working as a newspaperman at the age of eighteen, and published his first novel at twenty. Since then he has published over half a dozen books.

His first big success, *Blood Brother*, was made into the film *Broken Arrow* and later serialized on television. Among his other works are *The Time of the Gringo*, an historical novel dealing with the conquest of Mexico, *Flight from Ashiya*, which was also made into a movie, and *Rescue*. Mr. Arnold now lives in California.